A Glimpse of Glory

In the Gothic Cathedrals of France

by

The Venerable Brian Lucas CB

Archdeacon Emeritus of the Royal Air Force
Canon Emeritus of Lincoln Cathedral

Published by Adastral Books

Published by Adastral Books
'Pen-y-coed'
6 Arnhem Drive
Caythorpe
Grantham
Lincolnshire
NG32 3DQ

brian.lucas@savageclub.com

2 4 6 8 10 9 7 5 3 1

First published 2014

© Brian H Lucas

The moral right of the author has been asserted.

All rights reserved. No part of this publication may be reproduced or transmitted in any form or by any means, electronic or mechanical, including photocopying, recording or any information storage and retrieval system, without permission in writing from the copyright holder.

Unless otherwise stated, all the photographs are from the author's own collection. Every effort has been made to trace the copyright sources of the material used. The publisher would be pleased to hear of any outstanding copyright permission in order that due acknowledgment might be made in any future edition.

ISBN 978-0-9567588-1-1

Printed in the United Kingdom by
CPI Group (UK) Ltd, Croydon, CR0 4YY

I dedicate this book to the Glory of God and to the vision, skill, leadership and faith of the Architects, Masons, Carpenters and Woodcarvers, Artists, Glaziers and Metalworkers who realised the dreams of the clergy and benefactors to such a degree that we can only marvel at their achievement.

ACKNOWLEDGEMENTS

About ten years ago, when I began to think seriously about writing this book, I discussed the concept with the architect Bernard Kaukas, who had been instrumental in saving the façade of St Pancras Station from destruction. He is passionate about the Gothic style and at once encouraged me to write it; indeed, he read some of my early drafts and was enormously helpful in his comment on them. I remember one occasion in the Savage Club when he explained to me the architectural technique known as 'tas-de-charge', and drew a diagram on the back of an old menu card. I am most grateful to him for his continued interest and enthusiasm for this project.

As I became more immersed in the architecture of the Gothic cathedrals of France it seemed natural for me to invite a friend from my time in the Royal Air Force to write a Foreword. Bishop Michel Dubost had been my colleague when he was the catholic bishop to the French armed forces, but he is now Bishop of Evry, to the south of Paris, with the only 20th century purpose-built cathedral in France. He has written a thought-provoking Foreword in blank verse, and I am extremely grateful to him for making time in his busy life to accept my invitation.

Two friends were rash enough to join me in my excursions in France. A life-long friend, Canon Richard Hanford, came on a two-week tour of the northern cathedrals in June 2002. In the Cathedral of St Cyr and St Juliette at Nevers, one of France's double-apsed cathedrals, he looked at the modern glass in the windows and, recalling his time in the Royal Navy, muttered, "Looks like the latest pattern of curtains for Officers' Married Quarters." Both as a medieval historian and as a Latin scholar, Richard has been an invaluable help, and I am grateful to him. The Reverend Brian McAvoy joined me for a week in June 2012 as I checked my notes at Amiens, Laon, Beauvais and Rouen. Having someone to write down my alterations as I called them out meant that we made great progress, and had some fun in the process. Brian is good company and also began to catch my enthusiasm for the architecture.

For my initial visits to the cathedrals in France I used a Dictaphone to describe the architecture and ornaments as I moved about inspecting the aisles and chapels. On my return I handed the tapes to a good friend, Bridget Hankinson, who transcribed them onto my computer. I owe her a great deal of thanks for using her secretarial skill to turn my dictation into coherent text.

Robin Mackervoy is a fellow member of the Savage Club in London, and is a fine artist. I asked him to design a menu card for a Club Dinner when I was the Chairman. I am grateful to him for his permission to include it in the Introduction to this book, and if you look closely you will see the book on the table in the cartoon sketch.

A dear friend, Madame Huguette Rouillard, has not only made the guest suite of her apartment near Troyes available to me on countless occasions, but has also been a skilful translator from French into English. In one city, when we were told that the cathedral was locked because they could find no curator, she persuaded the lady in the Office de Tourisme to hand over the keys so that "this important English Archdeacon" could visit the splendid cathedral. I felt that the responsibility weighed as heavily as the keys as we walked through the streets to the building. I am greatly in Huguette's debt for her friendship and assistance.

A great debt of gratitude is due to my younger son, Simon Lucas, for making time in his busy life to edit this book, and for his skill in preparing it for printing. I also thank Robin Elliott, the former Prepress Analyst at CPI Antony Rowe, for all his sage advice, and for designing the cover.

Finally, a huge 'Thank You' to my wife, Joy, for permitting me to dash off to France several times each year to check my notes, and it comes with my apologies for the innumerable hours I have spent in my study researching and writing this book. I am also in her debt for using her skill in cartography to draw the cathedral plans, and for the time she spent reading carefully every chapter and offering invaluable advice on style and grammar. Any errors that remain are entirely my own.

Brian H Lucas.

LIST OF COLOUR PLATES

Front Cover: Notre Dame, Paris.
Back Cover: Detail from the Passion Window, Bourges.

Section A

Sens, apse clerestory window, centre quatrefoil
Sens, the Choir Screen
Sens, God banishes Adam & Eve, detail from the Good Samaritan window
Sens, the martyrdom of St Thomas Becket
Sens, Paradise, detail from the North Rose
Sens, Christ before Pilate, detail from the Good Samaritan window
Sens, the Good Samaritan takes the injured man to a hostel
Laon, West Towers from the East
Laon, West Rose
Laon, East Rose, detail
Laon, the mockery and scourging of Christ, east chapel window
Laon, Philosophy surrounded by the Liberal Arts, detail from the North Rose
Rouen, the West Façade
Rouen, Passion sequence, Chapel of St Sever, lower window
Rouen, St Etienne Chapel east wall
Rouen, Panegyric of St Romain, window east of south transept door
Rouen, Axial Chapel of Our Lady

Section B

Paris, west facade of Notre Dame
Paris, South Transept rose
Paris, High Altar Pieta
Paris, Vault boss over the crossing
Paris, St Peter curing sick - detail, south transept, west wall
Paris, Christ on the Road to Emmaus, South Choir Screen
Bourges, from the southeast
Bourges, Christ harrowing hell, The Passion window
Bourges, Dives feasting, The Lazarus window
Bourges, Dives cries out in torment, The Lazarus window
Bourges, The Judgement Window
Bourges, The Crucifixion, New Alliance window
Bourges, Christ washes the disciples' feet, Passion window
Bourges, Micah, Jonah & Obadiah, north choir clerestory
Troyes, the window of the Mystic Wine-press, detail

Section C

Troyes, Crucifixion of Christ, eastern window of the clerestory
Troyes, St Catherine, north transept
Troyes, central four Prophets, triforium beneath south rose
Troyes, Crucifixion of St Andrew, Chapel of St Joseph
Troyes, St Peter converts the Centurion Cornelius, Chapel of St Loup
Troyes, the South Rose
Troyes, the Nativity
Auxerre, South Transept Window
Auxerre, David plays the lyre before Saul - detail from the David window
Auxerre, St Mary of Egypt buys bread - detail from the Bishop's Chapel window
Auxerre, Joseph (right) receives his brothers as they beg for food, North Transept lancets
Auxerre, the West Rose
Auxerre, Theophilus befriends the devil, detail from the Axial Chapel window
Reims, centre of the south rose
Reims, the West Façade
Reims, the West Rose
Reims, the West Rose lancets
Amiens, The central portal illuminated, west façade

Section D

Amiens, West Facade
Amiens, the Martyrdom of St Firmin
Amiens, the North Rose
Amiens, Lady Chapel Altar
Amiens, Chapel of Notre Dame du Pilier Rouge
Beauvais, Martyrdom of St Vincent, St Vincent Chapel
Beauvais, Marissel Reredos, Chapel of St Leonard
Beauvais, The Visitation, 13th century south centre lancet, Axial Chapel
Beauvais, The Crucifixion, Chapel of the Virgin
Beauvais, The Fountain of Life Window
Albi Cathedral from the south-west
Albi, Last Judgement (detail)
Albi, Nave Vault Boss
Albi, Nave Vault (detail)
Albi, Rood Screen with St Cecilia
Albi, the Annunciation, south ambulatory
Albi, the decoration above the canons' stalls
Albi, the catafalque of St Cecilia, the Chapel of St Margaret

CONTENTS

FOREWORD viii
INTRODUCTION 1
SENS 9
LAON 33
ROUEN 63
PARIS 105
BOURGES 137
TROYES 175
AUXERRE 195
REIMS 223
AMIENS 251
BEAUVAIS 283
ALBI 307
GLOSSARY 327
ABOUT THE AUTHOR 335
INDEX 336

FOREWORD

by

Monsignor Michel Dubost, Bishop of Évry-Corbeil-Essonnes, France.

Brian Lucas est un ami.
Un de mes amis. Mais aussi votre ami.
Il vous propose – avec toute sa compétence, il est archidiacre
– une visite de cathédrales.
Suivez-le ! Vous serez étonnés.
Certes, on peut voir dans une cathédrale bien des merveilles,
Une cathédrale interroge sur l'essentiel !

Reprenons.
Les premiers chrétiens se sont réunis dans les catacombes.
Leur rassemblement se faisait autour d'un autel-tombeau d'un martyr
Cet autel s'appelait « confession ». il signifiait la foi de nos ancêtres :
Donner sa vie, même jusqu'à la mort, ouvre à la vraie vie, grâce au Christ.
Depuis toute église est une hymne à la vie.

Quand il fut permis d'être chrétien, ceux-ci se rassemblèrent dans des basiliques
Chez les grecs et les romains, chez les juifs, le Peuple n'accédait pas au cœur du Temple
La basilique est en rupture avec le passé : elle est ouverte à tous.
Depuis toute église est signe de l'égalité des hommes devant Dieu :
Chacun est appelé par le Christ à entrer dans l'intimité du créateur.

Vint le temps des premières cathédrales.
A une époque où il n'y avait pas d'imprimerie. L'université naissait
Ce furent les premiers médias de masse.
Ils étaient comme l'expression de toute la culture du temps :
Archives des connaissances architecturales du monde antique,
Représentation symbolique des connaissances de l'époque,

Manifestation du pouvoir politique :
Les cathédrales étaient le meilleur de l'homme offert à Dieu.

Le temps a passé.
Certes, les chrétiens ont continué a construire des cathédrales…
Mais ce n'était plus le même monde :
L'universalité de la connaissance s'est exprimée dans les livres,
Le pouvoir dans l'économie,
Et le chant à la grandeur de l'homme dans un art profane.
Bien plus, l'homme est devenu comme extérieur à son milieu,
Il n'est plus, à ses yeux, intégré dans la nature, intégré à sa société,
Il les juge, il les jauge, il s'en sent quelquefois exclu.

Alors ceux qui se tournent vers Dieu,
Rêvent des temps anciens, recopient, s'enivrent des archives
Essaient brutalement de manifester leur refus du monde actuel,
Ou alors, posent de nouvelles cathédrales comme une question au cœur de la cité:
Toi, l'homme moderne, entends-tu l'appel de Dieu ?
Il n'est pas jaloux de ta grandeur.
Lui est au-delà. Simple. Un.

Brian Lucas est un ami.
Il vous propose , simplement, ce chemin vers Celui qui est Un.

† Monsignor Michel Dubost,
Bishop of Évry-Corbeil-Essonnes,
France.

A Translation of the Foreword

Brian Lucas is a friend.
One of my friends.
But he is also your friend. As an Archdeacon he is highly competent, and in this book he is inviting you to join him on a tour of cathedrals.
Follow him! You will be astonished!
There are marvels to be discovered in a cathedral.
A cathedral will question you on the essential things in your life.

Let us look at the past.
The first Christians used to gather together in the catacombs.
They assembled around an altar, usually the tomb of a martyr.
The name given to such an altar was "Confession" for it represented the faith of our ancestors:
To offer one's life even to death, is, thanks to Christ, the gate to true life.
Since that time, every church has been a hymn to life.

When Christians were permitted to express their life free of persecution, their place of worship became the Basilica.
In the Greek, Roman and Jewish world ordinary people had no access to the heart of the Temple.
The Basilica is a break with the past: it is open to everyone.
Since then every church has been a sign of man's equality before God.
Everyone is called by Christ to enter the intimacy of his Creator.

Then came the age of the first cathedrals.
In the age when printing did not exist and the university was just born,
The cathedrals were the first mass media;
The means of expressing the whole of the culture of that age:
Archives of the architectural knowledge of the ancient world;
Symbolic representations of the knowledge of the age;
The manifestation of political power.
The cathedrals were the essence of the best in man in his offering to God.

Time has passed.
Christian folk went on building cathedrals ….
But it was no longer the same world.
The universality of knowledge found its expression in books;
Power found its expression in economics,
and praise of man's greatness was expressed in profane art.
Moreover, man found himself outside his own environment.

In his own eyes he is no longer a part of nature, a part of his society.
He is, instead, judging, weighing them, and by so doing feels excluded.

So, those who turn to God
Dream of yesteryear; they steep themselves in the environment of times past
Outrageously, they express their refusal of this present world.
Now, the building of new cathedrals poses a question in the heart of a city:
You, the men and women of today, do you hear God's call?
He is not jealous of your greatness.
He is beyond that. He is straightforward: He is the One.

Brian Lucas is a friend.
He just wishes to lead you in the path of He who is One.

† Monsignor Michel Dubost, Bishop of Evry-Corbeil-Essonnes, France.

Cathédrale de la Résurrection, Évry

LOCATION MAP OF THE CATHEDRALS

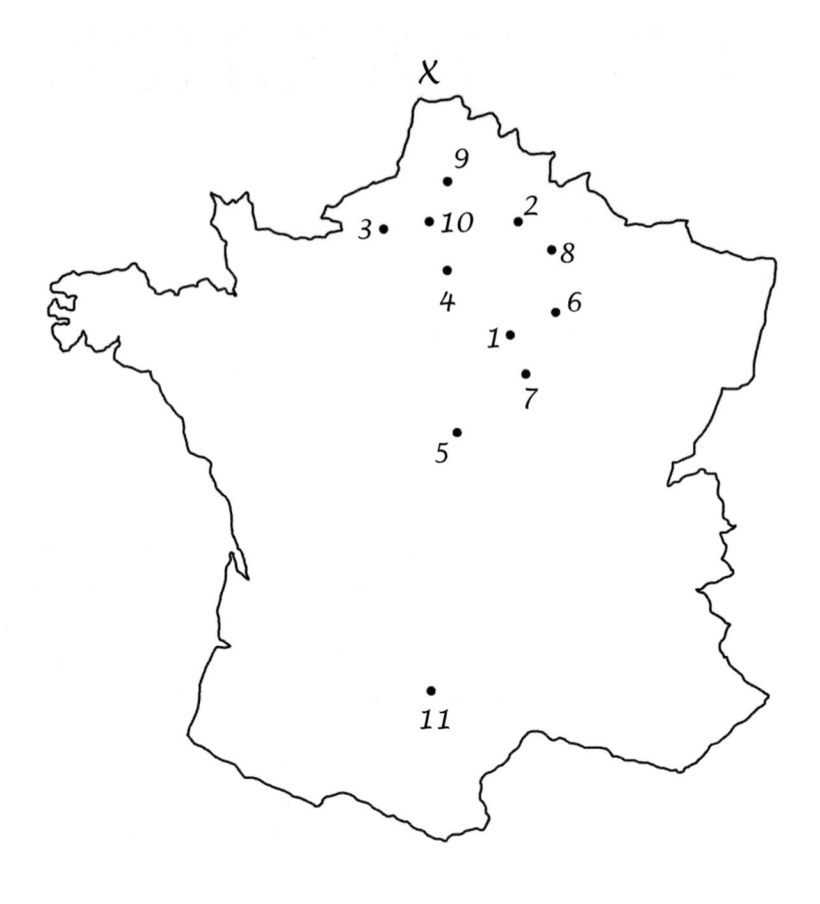

1 ....SENS	7 ....AUXERRE
2 ....LAON	8 ....REIMS
3 ....ROUEN	9 ....AMIENS
4 ....PARIS	10 ....BEAUVAIS
5 ....BOURGES	11 ....ALBI
6 ....TROYES	X............Port of Calais

INTRODUCTION

"Describe to them the temple and its fittings, its exits and entrances, all the details and particulars of its elevation and plan."
[Ezekiel, 43, verse 11]

In all my travels down the years—my wanderings through the countries bordering the eastern Mediterranean; my sojourns in Cyprus, Malta and Germany; my delight in the marvels of Syria, Greece and Italy; explorations in the former Soviet territories, Singapore, Hong Kong and in Africa—France was largely unknown to me. However, I had in my library two books, collected in my youth, which had slumbered unread on the top shelf of a bookcase. One is "The Cathedrals of France" by Helen Henderson, (Methuen, 1929), and the other, "Cathedrals of Normandy" by Canon Jocelyn Perkins, (Methuen, 1935). Jocelyn Perkins CVO, DCL, MA, described as "unkempt but with courtly manners", was Minor Canon and Sacrist of Westminster Abbey from 1901-1958, having already been Minor Canon at Ely for five years. He died in 1962.

Thirteen years ago I noticed these two volumes on the shelf and began to browse through them, and at once I became impatient to see the great buildings described with such enthusiasm. I visited Rouen first, with Perkins' book in my hand, and discovered that so much had been destroyed in the Second World War; and the Second Vatican Council had changed so much in the liturgical arrangement of the building since the book's publication, that it required a revision.

Thus began my present endeavour. Helen Henderson led me beyond the boundary of Normandy into the contrasts of Reims with Rodez, and Paris with Perigeux. I have also discovered jewels of churches, which never sought the status or rank of a cathedral. For example, in an attempt to photograph the east end of Poitiers cathedral I was obliged to enter along a narrow street and so came

A Glimpse Of Glory

across the old church dedicated to St Radegonde, which I found as delightful as the cathedral. Driving from Cahors to Rodez, along the delightful valley of the Lot, I made a small diversion to the ancient pilgrimage church at Conques. It was worth every minute, if only to see the tympanum over the west door. Even when revisiting a cathedral a year or two later to check my notes, I always feel a thrill on seeing the building again, rather like meeting an old friend in the street.

It could be argued, despite the claim of the folk of Sées that St Latuin brought Christianity to their city in 95 AD, that the establishment of the Christian church in France came about through the martyrdom of Pothinus, Bishop of Lyon, in the year 177. By the year 300 the Church in Gaul had at least 25 bishops. Some became saints of the Church: St Hilary of Poitiers (d. 367) and St Martin of Tours (d. 397). In the 3rd century the Rhineland Franks began incursions into the country and other Franks attacked along the north coast, eventually conquering the Gauls. It was only when the Frankish king, Clovis, brought all the Gallic tribes under his rule and was later baptized at Reims by St Remigius on Christmas Day in the year 496 that the future of the Christian Church in that country could be considered to be safe. Indeed, by the 6th century the country had a hundred bishops.

Canon Roger Greenacre, in his book, "The Catholic Church in France", published in 1996, makes the point that France made a major positive contribution to the mediaeval Church by playing a dominant role in the development of monasticism. The Abbey of Cluny was founded in 909 and the Cistercian Order nearly two centuries later in 1098. Meanwhile, in 1084 St Bruno founded the Carthusian Order in the Chartreuse Massif. It was this Order that came to England with St Hugh (c.1140-1200), who was later to become the Bishop of Lincoln.

In order to understand the mutilation and destruction evident on the statuary and fabric of the buildings one has to know a little about the French Revolution, though not all the vandalism can be laid at its door, for France has had a turbulent religious history and endured much suffering in two world wars. The Revolutionaries confiscated all church properties, and sold many of them as they suppressed the monasteries The Civil Constitution of the Clergy of 1790 reduced the number of dioceses to correspond with the new départements and provided for the election of bishops and priests by all people entitled to vote, without reference to the Papacy. This meant that the clergy became employees of the state, and as few of them could in conscience go along with this, in a few days at the beginning of September 1792 three bishops and over two hundred priests were slaughtered in Paris by the revolutionary mob. In 1799 a coup d'état brought Napoleon Bonaparte to power, and in 1801 Pope Pius Vll and Napoleon l issued the Concordat, which re-stated that there should be only one diocese in each Department. History and tradition were thrown to the winds. Splendid buildings, which for centuries had hosted kings, found themselves degraded to the status of parish churches. Some

Introduction

of the cathedrals of the past no longer possess the rank in the full sense of the word. "Laon and Narbonne, Senlis and Lisieux, where in former days the Divine Office was rendered by thirty or more canons…can claim today only a curé", laments Perkins. Nevertheless, for the purpose of this book I shall restrict the canvas to cover what I consider to be the great cathedrals according to their former glory. One glaring omission is Chartres, for while the work of cleaning the mediaeval glass in the windows is continuing (to the greater glory of God and the illumination of the church), during my visits in 2009 and in 2012 the sanctuary, ambulatories and choir are 'out of bounds' and under scaffold as restoration and excavation is carried out. Moreover, Mr Malcolm Miller's publications in English are readily available in the cathedral bookshop.

The cathedrals you will visit belong to the state, and in the last decade or so the state has spent billions of francs and euros in restoration work. On most of the boards outside a cathedral describing the work in progress you will read that the percentage of the cost of the work borne by l'état is 100%; sometimes the région, département or the commune will also share a small portion of the cost. In the more important cathedrals, employees of the Commune, or city, staff the gift shops, unlike the faithful folk in British cathedrals, so do not expect them all to be knowledgeable about the building.

Many enthusiasts prefer the solid confidence of the Romanesque style of cathedral building. I do myself when in Southwell Cathedral in Nottinghamshire. However, I believe that the great Gothic cathedrals of the 12th and 13th centuries are incomparable in their dedication to the glory of God. There is uncertainty about how this Gothic style evolved. In 1091 a humble family gave their ten-year-old son, Suger, as an oblate at the abbey of St Denis to the north of Paris. He was educated at the monastic school of St Denis-de-l'Estrée at the same time as the future King

A Glimpse Of Glory

of France, Louis Vl (1137-1180). Suger soon showed the gifts of diplomacy and administration, which led to his appointment as Abbot of St Denis in 1122. He began to enlarge the abbey church to accommodate the crowds that came on feast days. His narthex, with its façade of three portals flanked by twenty statues of royalty, was consecrated on 9th June 1140. In her book, "Early Gothic St Denis", published by the University of California Press, 1992, Pamela Blum described the church of St Denis as,"the cradle of Gothic Art." So it was, for within ten years of the narthex of St Denis being consecrated, people were marvelling at the Royal Doorway (Portail Royal) at Chartres.

I once asked an university expert on this period of architecture about the birth of the Gothic style at St Denis, hoping that she would explain its sudden arrival on the scene in the mid-12th century; she answered, "It was in the air". My researches have led me to conclude that she was as accurate as anyone can be on the subject. Abbot Suger would have brought his workforce from the countries he had visited. He would have gathered masons and carpenters, artists to paint the glass, metalworkers, and all of them would have set up their workshops on site. This is the "cradle" of which Pamela Blum wrote: "In such an international gathering, the work of each master and his assistants would have reflected the training and aesthetic preferences of their own region. But their exposure to the work of others must have catalysed the experimentation and interchange of ideas visible in the sculpture of the central portal." In other words, it was indeed 'in the air'.

It is fairly certain that such was the enthusiasm of the age that master builders responded to one another's innovative ideas, often freely borrowing specific designs and using them in new ways to accomplish aesthetic results in their own construction. This "intensity of interaction", as Radding & Clark described it in their book, "Mediaeval Architecture, Mediaeval Learning" published by Yale, 1992, shows us the extent to which the builders were receptive to learning from each other. The patrons, bishops and chapters, still made the decisions about the features they considered essential in the building—whether chapels were required, and if so where and how many. They dictated whether transepts were required, and the size and location of liturgical areas. "But the translation of the requirements, the shaping of space around liturgy to the satisfaction of the clergy was the exclusive sphere of the master builders."

During the last twelve years I have travelled all over France tracing the development of the Gothic style of building and recording the local interpretation of that idiom. This book is not a synthesis of what I have found; instead it is a series of monographs, each of which examines one cathedral. On many occasions I have met British folk sitting outside or inside a cathedral wondering what they were looking at in the stained glass or in the sculpture. This is not an academic work; it is an attempt to explain to you what you are viewing, to give some idea of why it

Introduction

is there, and, at the end of each chapter, to highlight things you must not miss if you are on a brief visit. I hope also to share with you the excitement and happiness which I have enjoyed among these glories of France.

My aim is to introduce you to my "friends" in the hope and confidence that you, too, we find them amiable company and enjoy the experience of knowing them better as they reveal to you something of their past and of their life today. And, wonder of wonders, occasionally "craftsman's art and music's measure for thy pleasure all combine", and with a touch of pious shuddering you have a glimpse of the glory of God. It might be in a window or in the symmetry of a nave arcade, a piece of organ music, or even a shaft of light scattering coloured fragments across an aisle: but you know that something intangible has touched you, and it is good. Such an encounter is a Glimpse of Glory.

At each location we will begin with the exterior of the building, at the west front, and then walk in an anti-clockwise direction around the outside the building. We will first examine the sculpture and architecture of the west façade, then move along the south side of the building, and have a look at the east end before returning along the north side to the west door. On entering the building we will examine the west end of the nave (which is sometimes a narthex), the nave itself, and then, beginning at the south west corner (the right hand corner as you enter the west door), we will examine the interior of the cathedral in an anti-clockwise direction, ending up on the north west corner. It is not always possible to walk around the entire outside of the cathedral, because buildings have sometimes encroached right up to the exterior wall, but we shall do our best.

Do not be alarmed if you become disorientated inside a cathedral, especially if there is no sunshine to help you determine which is south. It is very easy to assume that you are looking at the north side of the nave when in fact it is the opposite. In the descriptions of the cathedrals, I have used the cardinal points of the compass rather than left or right, but if I do use left or right it is assumed that I am facing the object described. I have always assumed that the main High Altar is in the east. There are a few cathedrals, such as Albi and Nevers, with an altar at each end of the nave: in such places the title 'High Altar' is particularly important.

A note about my reference throughout this book to learned works. As this is a guide book, modesty forbids me to assume that you will read through it from cover to cover. Each cathedral stands alone in its chapter, and so I shall give the full reference to title, publisher and date of publication each time I introduce a source in a particular chapter. I hope the reader will find this preferable to footnotes, bearing in mind what Noel Coward said of footnotes, that "they are like someone knocking at the front door while you are busy upstairs", or words to that effect.

A Glimpse Of Glory

There are many and various reasons for touring through the French countryside. You may choose to take an intelligent interest in the wines or cheeses of the region as you journey through it, and by so doing endear yourself to the local inhabitants. Or you may delight in visiting the fabulous chateaux of the French nobility. But we have chosen, you and I, to discover glimpses of glory and surprises in cathedrals. I hope you enjoy travelling with me, and that you are encouraged to go off the beaten track in order to discover some hidden gem. So let us go to it!

Brian Lucas,

Michaelmas, 2013.

A BIBLE FOR THE POOR

Medieval religious art was a sacred writing, governed by its own alphabet and rules, full of symbolism and arbitrary signs which were as fixed and unalterable as the devices in heraldry. The artist's knowledge of these forms had to be exact. He was not allowed to ignore the traditional type of person he was trying to represent, nor to deviate from it. You might find the following clues helpful.

The Nimbus: The circular nimbus placed upright behind a head is the attribute of a saint, while the nimbus stamped with a cross indicates divinity. In medieval art the crossed nimbus was never absent from representations of God the Father, Jesus Christ, or the Holy Ghost.

The Aureole: The aureole - a light emanating from the whole person - belongs not only to the persons of the Trinity but also to the Virgin and the saints and expresses eternal blessedness.

Bare Feet: It was customary to represent God, the angels, Jesus, and the apostles with bare feet, while the Virgin and the saints wear shoes.

Expressions of the Invisible: The invisible, that is to say something which was beyond the domain of art, was expressed by means of several symbols. A hand coming out of the clouds and making a gesture of benediction, with the first three fingers raised and the other two folded, the whole surrounded by the crossed nimbus, was the sign of divine intervention - the emblem of Providence.

Another abstract idea, that of eternal rest, is signified by little sexless, nude figures ranged side by side in the folds of Abraham's cloak. This group is seen on almost all cathedrals as part of the Last Judgment scene.

Several concentric curves: These represent the sky.

Waved, parallel lines: These represent water.

A tree, expressed by a stalk: A tree drawn as if breaking into two or three leaves, shows that the scene happens on land.

A tower with a door: This denotes a city, and if an angel is on guard between the turrets, the city is Jerusalem.

Saint Peter has a short, thick beard, and his hair is short and curled tight to his head, showing the tonsure of the priest and has carried the keys from the beginning, in recognition of the power given him to lock and unlock the gates of Paradise.

Saint Paul is bald, with a long beard. From the first century the type of these two

A Glimpse Of Glory

saints has not varied. The others are known by the attributes which they carry, but these attributes were added in the course of the centuries.

Saint John the youngest of the apostles is beardless to the end of his days. The mediaeval book, The Golden Legend, gives this graphic portrait of Saint Bartholomew: "His face is white, his eyes are big, his nose is straight and regular, his beard abundant and mixed with several white hairs, he is clothed with a purple robe and covered in a white mantle decorated with precious stones…." The people were so well instructed in these matters that any deviation from the tradition in type or costume would have thrown them into confusion. They were accustomed to see the Virgin with her veil upon her hair as a symbol of her virginity, and to recognize the Jews by their conical bonnets, the shape affected by them doubtless in the Middle Ages.

CHAPTER 1

SENS

Entering Sens from the A19 to the north, along the D606, I always park my car under the trees between the eastward and westward carriageways of the Boulevard des Garibaldi. It is then only a three minute walk south along the Rue de la Republique to the cathedral. The name of the town came from the tribe of the Senones, who were for a long time one of the most powerful tribes in Gaul. In 390 BC, under Brennus, they invaded Italy and captured Rome itself. When the Romans ruled Gaul, Sens was made the capital of a province of the Lyonnais. While Pope Alexander III resided in Sens in 1163–64, the city became the temporary capitol of Christianity. It is now the principal city in the Department of the Yonne, which takes its name from that beautiful river that meanders south through Auxerre.

Some of the mediaeval houses still cluster around the cathedral, leaving room only for a small market place outside the west front.

THE CATHEDRAL CHURCH OF ST STEPHEN (ST ÉTIENNE)

Construction of the cathedral began in the mid-12th century by Archbishop Henri Sanglier, but most of the work took place between 1140 and 1168. It is said to be the earliest Gothic cathedral in France, coeval with the choir of Abbot Suger's basilica at St. Denis in Paris. In his book, "Gothic Architecture", published by Yale University Press, 1962 (revised 2000), Paul Frankl writes (page 69), *"It is probable that preparations for the building [of Sens cathedral] were made before 1137. For reasons of statics the choir aisles and ambulatories were always built first, and these were designed as part of the first campaign, begun a little before the choir of St Denis. The rib-vaults here rise from corbels which have been squeezed in over the capitals of round transverse arches, confirming that groin and not rib-vaults were originally planned."* Many other buildings have borrowed largely from the design. The architect, Guillaume (William) of Sens, who worked on the completion of St Étienne, used this cathedral

A Glimpse Of Glory

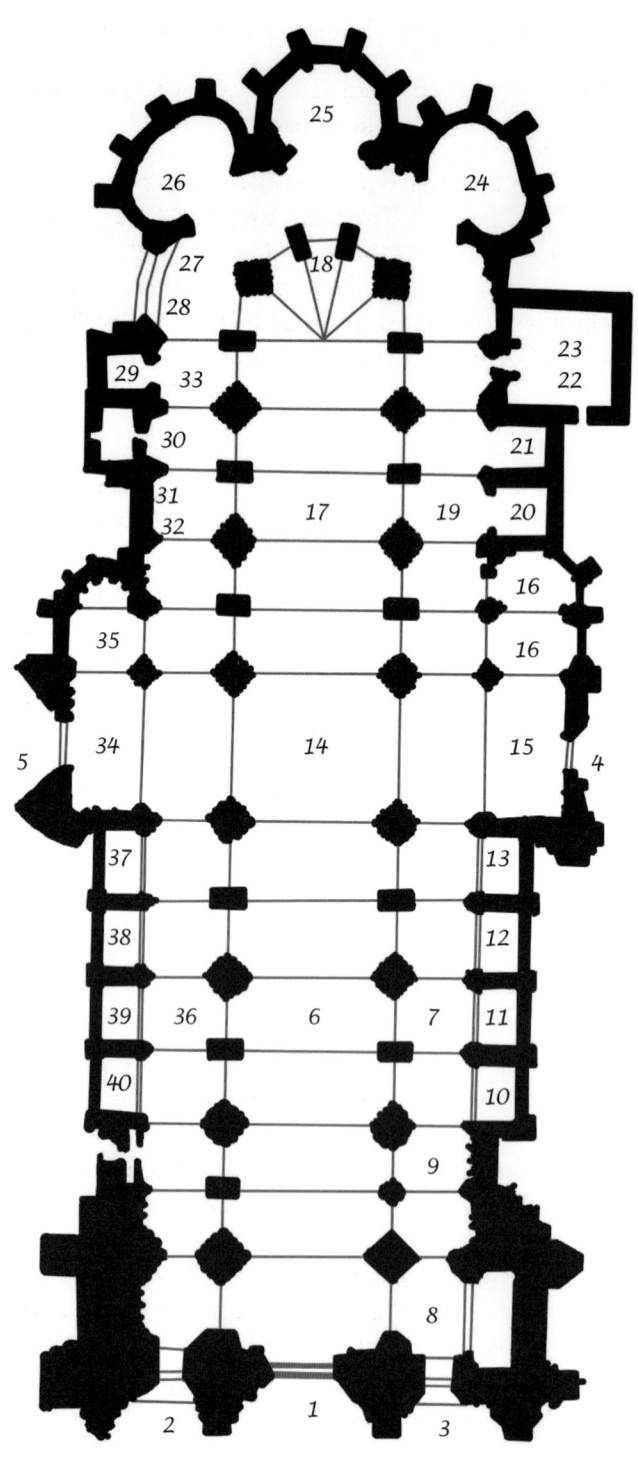

SENS—KEY

1 Central West Portal
2 North west Portal
3 South West Portal
4 The South Façade
5 The North Façade
6 The Nave
7 The South Aisle
8 Bay 1
9 Bay 3
10 Chapel of St Anna
11 Chapel of St Anthropius
12 Chapel of St Margaritta
13 Chapel of St James the Less
14 The Crossing
15 The South Transept
16 The Chapel of the Virgin Mary
17 The Choir
18 The High Altar
19 The South Ambulatory
20 Chapel of St Apolline
21 Chapel of St Martial
22 The Treasury (upper)
23 The Sacristy (lower)
24 Chapel of Sacre Cœur
25 Axial Chapel of St Savinien
26 Chapel of St Colombe
27 Window of the Good Samaritan
28 Window of the Prodigal Son
29 Retable of Becket
30 Window of St Eustace
31 Statue of St Thomas Becket
32 Window of St Thomas Becket
33 The North Ambulatory
34 The North Transept
35 Chapel of St John / Baptistry
36 The North Aisle
37 Chapel of St Sulpice
38 Chapel of St Alban
39 Chapel of St Loup
40 Chapel of St Fiacre

as his model when rebuilding Canterbury Cathedral after a disastrous fire in 1175.

In the late 13th century the clerestory was enlarged and the vaulting was altered to the sexpartite style. It was not until c.1500 that the transepts were added.

Until 1622, the year in which Paris was elevated to the rank of an archbishopric, Sens had pre-eminence over the bishoprics of Chartres, Auxerre, Meaux, Paris, Orleans, Nevers and Troyes; the initials forming the word: Campont. The church council that condemned Abelard was also held at Sens, and the marriage of St Louis and Marguerite of Provence was celebrated in the cathedral in 1234. With the elevation of Paris, the diocese of Sens lost the bishoprics of Meaux, Chartres and Orleans, and when Auxerre was suppressed the Archbishop of Sens also took the title Bishop of Auxerre.

This cathedral church of Saint Stephen is one of the numerous churches restored by Viollet-le-Duc early in the 19th century. Not content with putting things right after the devastation of the Revolution, he was inspired to suppress the rood-screen because it was of a later epoch than the original design, and to tear down the large lateral chapels that had been added to the primitive structure at the end of the thirteenth century, replacing them by low chapels in the spirit of the earlier model. There was a three million Franc restoration in progress when I first visited the cathedral in 2001, of which the state was paying 100%.

The massive columns and wide aisles combine to give the impression of a solid, confident cathedral. The stained glass throughout the church is worthy of special note.

THE EXTERIOR

THE WEST FAÇADE

Like Auxerre and Troyes, Sens has the sense of incompleteness due to its solitary western tower. The northern tower was crowned by a wooden belfry capped with lead and was destroyed by fire in the middle of the 19th century. The west front is divided into three sections, corresponding to the interior nave and aisles, by substantial buttresses. I cannot but wonder whether the façade would have looked more harmonious if the two great Gothic windows above the central and southern portals had not been so abruptly inserted into the older masonry. Both windows have only a hint of any moulding and they do not reflect the full flowering of Gothic enterprise. They dominate and jar with the remainder of the early decoration. The rich sculpture of the three portals was either removed or severely mutilated in 1793 by revolutionaries.

A Glimpse Of Glory

The West Façade

The central section of the façade, between the buttresses, and above the portal contains a very large window divided into six lancets which support three multifoils in the tracery. A passage with a balustrade comprising an arcade of collonettes stretches across between the buttresses, and in the wall above is a blind stone rose, with blind lancets either side. The top section contains three modern colossal statues of a muscular Christ seated in majesty flanked by two angels; they are sculpted in three cusped niches with crocketed gables above. This central section of the façade is crowned with a pierced parapet.

The North Tower is known as the 'Tour de Plomb' because it used to be surmounted by a timbered belfry covered in lead, which was destroyed in 1845. The wall above the stringcourse over the portal is decorated with an arcade of blind cusped lancets, which is capped by a stringcourse slightly higher than that over the central portal arch. Above that stringcourse is a large central lancet flanked each side by a blind lancet. A richly decorated stringcourse above the lancets encompasses the buttress either side and supports a delicate arcade of blind lancets, which are divided by twin collonettes.

Above this arcade the passage continues from the central section of the façade at roughly the same level, but here it is behind an arcade of five tall lancet openings with almost round heads. These, too, extend across the buttresses where they are blind. The top level repeats the motif of five tall lancets which carry over to the buttress either side, but these are all blind and have sharply pointed heads.

At this level there is a single statue on the western face of the buttress each side. Yet, all the other blind lancets at the various levels of this section of the façade have the traces of mounting irons for the missing sculptures. It must have been a glorious array of Gothic art. The tower is crowned by a wall, the base which once supported the belfry.

Detail of the Tympanum, Northwest Portal

The Northwest Portal

The archivolt has three orders to it which rest on three columns either side, which rise from carved heads: a bust in the middle flanked by a grotesque. The tympanum of this 12th century doorway recalls the life of St John the Baptist. On the left hand side is carved the image of the baptism of Christ, the beheading of the Baptist is on the right, and in the centre his head on a dish is being offered at Herod's banquet. At the top Christ sits in Majesty. The wooden doors have fine decorative hinges. A bas relief multifoil decorates the base each side.

Central Portal

A beautiful statue of St Stephen, in the robes of a deacon and carrying the Gospel book, fortunately spared during the Revolution, stands on the trumeau of the main doorway. This work, dating from the end of the 12th century,

St Stephen on the Trumeau of the Central West Portal

A Glimpse Of Glory

is a splendid example of the beginning of Gothic sculpture. The sculptures on the engaged piers framing the doorway represent the Foolish Virgins on the right and the Wise Virgins on the left. The statues of the Apostles, which used to occupy the 12 niches in the splay of the doorway, were removed during the Revolution.

The original tympanum, which supposedly portrayed the Last Judgement, was remade in the 13C: it is devoted to scenes from the Life of St Stephen, who can be seen kneeling (right of centre in the bottom level) as he is stoned to death. Statuettes of angels in the inner order and saints decorate the remaining orders of the archivolt over the portal. In the spandrels a roundel is carved either side which contains a now-empty niche. A decorated stringcourse runs across the top of the portal.

The Wise Virgins Depicted on the Left Jamb, West Central Portal

The bas-relief sculptures about the base of the splay either side of the portal mirror vices with virtues, science with the liberal arts, together with the work of the seasons of the year and a variety of beasts including an elephant bearing a tower, a griffon, an ostrich, a camel and a man riding a fish.

THE SOUTHWEST PORTAL

The portal dates from the 14th century and has twenty-two statuettes of prophets to the north and south of the doorway, and, in the tympanum, the Death, Burial, Assumption, and Coronation of the Virgin. There are two orders of angels carved in the archivolt, all badly damaged. The statuettes, representing the prophets, have been decapitated.

The South Tower or "Tour de Pierre", or "Stone Tower", collapsed at the end of the 13th century and the present structure is mainly of the 14th century but completed only in 1535.

Above a decorated stringcourse over the portal, a section of blank wall leads to another stringcourse at the same height as that below the great west window in the central section. Above is another sharply-pointed window, with four lancets

Bas-relief on the Left Base of the West Central Portal

divided by mullions and with two trefoils and a multifoil in the tracery. The stringcourse over it is the same height as that in the central section, but here there are five tall lancet openings, with a pierced balustrade of three little cusped lancets between each mullion of the tall openings. At the next level there are five lancets similar to those on the northwest tower, but here they contain statues representing the notable archbishops of Sens, which were added in the 19th century.

Peter's Tower is topped by an elegant belfry complete with cupola, and is 78m/256ft high. It houses two bells named Savinienne in A flat weighing 16 tons and Potentienne in F sharp weighing 14 tons (bells take the feminine gender in French). Founded in 1560, they escaped meltdown for ammunition during the Revolution, and are named after two early Christian missionaries to the Senones. Savinien can be seen robed as a bishop on the Salazar reredos in the north aisle.

THE SOUTH FAÇADE

The architect mason Martin Chambiges was called to Sens by Archbishop Tristan de Salazar to make the lateral façades of the cathedral, beginning with the south rose in 1494. His façades at Beauvais and Troyes had made him the most sought-after man amongst architects, and so in the famous south façade of Sens may be seen something very similar to that of Beauvais. Chambiges and eight

A Glimpse Of Glory

workmen are said to have built it, and it is, if anything, more perfect and even more outstanding than the great façade of its prototype.

There is a high arch over the portal, with empty niches in the splay and a denuded tympanum above it. However, some statuary remains in the archivolt. The portal is flanked each side by two blind lancets with tracery, and a gallery of blind lancets frames the arch over the portal, above which rises a crocketed gable terminating in a finial, bearing the modern statue of Christ blessing the city.

A flamboyant balustrade stretches between the buttresses above the arch of the portal, crossing behind the gable without interruption, and behind and above it are ten lancets of varying height which act as a base for the exquisite rose window.

The South Façade

It is an immense window, and as it is a perfect circle, it has small multifoils filling the top of the arch above it. There is more decoration in the spandrels, and at this level there are empty canopied niches on the buttresses either side. There is another pierced balustrade above the rose from which rises the crocketed gable which crowns the façade

As at Beauvais, there are the same parallel lines running vertically up the face of its gable, which is pierced by a decorated roundel having in the centre a quatrefoil. The buttresses either side are topped with decorated finials which are as delicate as filigree, and stop just lower than the gable itself. This portal has been called the Portal of Moses because of the statue of the prophet which surmounts the gable.

THE NORTH FAÇADE

Return past the west façade of the cathedral and continue north; look out for a notice on the wall at the entrance to a passage advertising the 14th century St Denis doorway and the Maison de l'Œuvre, the 16th century chapter library. It is worth entering the yard to see the doorway and these areas of the old cathedral estate. Return to the street, turn right and walk around the corner to the Impasse Abraham to admire the magnificent Flamboyant north façade built by Martin Chambiges and his son.

It is similar to the south façade, but here the portal fills the space between the buttresses, which have niches but are devoid of statuary. There is no room for blind lancets either side. The tympanum has the same vertical row of niches, all empty, and this portal has a trumeau dividing the doors, but, alas, it has been robbed of its statue. There is a remnant of small statues in the orders of the archivolt.

A gable rises from the arch of the portal ending in a decorated finial at the foot of the rose, and there is a similar pierced balustrade behind the gable. There are six lancets supporting the rose, but they are substantially shorter than those on

St Denis' Portal Passage

the south façade as the north portal is a much larger affair. The rose window is again a magnificent sight, and an exact copy of its southern twin. Similarly, the balustrade above the rose and the gable which crowns the façade echoes the south façade, except that there is an attractive little screen of open lancets and finials stretched between the pinnacles of the buttresses either side of the crowning gable. The statue of Abraham, surmounting the gable, is modern.

It is time to return to the west door and enter the cathedral.

THE INTERIOR

THE NAVE

Standing inside the west door one can see at once that this is a confident cathedral. The wide aisles and the solid piers give a sense of the building being well founded.

A Glimpse Of Glory

The Nave from the West

The sexpartite vaulting of this wide 12th century nave is supported by piers clustered around thick columns, which rise to the height of the clerestory stringcourse. Apart from the western bay, the remaining three bays are subdivided by pairs of coupled columns, standing one behind the other, forming a nave arcade of seven bays. These columns have individual capitals but are joined under a common abacus. From this projecting abacus an extremely slender shaft rises through the triforium, which is also subdivided, to the clerestory stringcourse where it supports the ribs of the sexpartite roof vault. Sens has an almost unique feature in these coupled columns of the alternate bays of the nave, choir and apse. It is similar to the choir of Coutances, but the arrangement is not quite the same, and Sens makes more of it. The English visitor will also note the resemblance to the choir at Canterbury, which was built a little later than Sens following a disastrous fire.

Stand with your back to the west door and marvel at the tall arches marching away towards the east end giving the whole area a loftiness which lifts the spirit. It is 113m long, 29m wide but only 24m high. The windows at the west end of the nave, behind the organ, are quite bland.

The West Door is deeply recessed in a wooden porch with the casing and pipework of the Great Organ above. On the first pier on the north side, about 15 feet above floor level facing southwest, is sculpted a very small head, popularly regarded as a portrait of Jean du Cognot, a 14th century lawyer.

The first bay to the north and south of the west end, forming a kind of narthex, has blind arcading at low level. The south wall has above this arcading a window with two lights of clear diamond quarry glass. The north wall of the bay has a small door in the westernmost arch of the arcade. These two western bays are different from the rest of the nave in that they have pointed arches with Corinthian capitals.

Over each of the **two western bays** to north and south, the triforium is divided under two arches, and each arch covers two openings divided by a central column bearing a decorated capital. Between the two main arches a corbel supports the central rib of the sexpartite vault. Apart from the corbels, this pattern is broadly the same throughout the length of the nave.

Above the triforium the clerestory windows each contain two narrow lancets, with very pale blue glass of geometric design. With the exception of the western bays, where the wall space is decorated by two blind arches, this delicate arrangement of the windows continues eastward down the nave, but the remaining windows are wider and larger. The clerestories in the choir were heightened in the 13th century and in the nave in the 14th century. Originally, the clerestory windows were divided into two sections each with two windows, like the triforium beneath it. The present arrangement replaced it in 1268.

In the middle of the south nave arcade stands a fine wooden pulpit with an open pierced sounding board above it, which is crowned

The North Side of the Nave from the East

A Glimpse Of Glory

The Salazar Reredos

by a triumphant angel blowing a trumpet. The staircase has a return in it, making it a very elegant ascent.

Facing west against a clustered column on the north side of the nave is the 16th century Gothic Salazar Reredos, forming part of the tomb erected by Tristan de Salazar, an archbishop of Sens, to his parents, the Spanish adventurer Jean de Salazar and his wife. Under delicately carved canopies with finials, and separated by empty niches, are the statues of St Savinien, St Mary with the infant Christ and, nearest the nave, St Stephen. The reredos faces the cenotaph bearing a headless effigy of the father, which is held aloft on four tall slender columns.

We move now to the south aisle. T. Francis Bumpus writes in his book, "The Glories of Northern France", published by Dennis and Sons Ltd, London, 1905, on page 142, *"Until the restorations conducted under M. Viollet-Ie-Duc's direction in the mid-19th century, the nave aisles were fringed with Middle Pointed chapels. These, solely from the desire to bring back this part of the cathedral to its primitive state, were removed, new walls built, and pierced by large Romanesque windows, below which small triple arcades admit to a series of low, cavernous-looking chapels. All this work is good of its kind and uninterestingly respectable, but the loss of those chapels, whether regarded historically or picturesquely is to be deplored."* It seems that Francis Bumpus did not approve of Viollet-le-Duc's efforts.

THE SOUTH AISLE (FROM WEST TO EAST)

A deeply recessed pointed arch frames a doorway in the west wall of the aisle, with a blind lancet either side. The wall above is blank under a quadripartite vault, which has an aperture for lowering a bell.

There is a blind arcade along the lower wall of the aisle. In the absence of any official title, I have named the chapels after the subject of their windows.

South aisle **Bay 1** has a window in the south wall, filled with an iron grille, and flanked by blind lancets.

Bay 2 has a door in the middle of two blind arches, with a large painting hanging above of Christ healing the sick that are brought into his presence.

Bay 3 has a window by Jean Cousin (1530) with four lights divided by mullions. In the lower section there are cherubs holding shields; above are four scenes and higher still is one scene across all four lights; the two upper right scenes resemble the miracle of the loaves and fishes and the triumphal entry on Palm Sunday. At the top is a rosette above two smaller rosettes.

The Chapel of St Anna has a plain marble altar bearing a statue of a monk. It is enclosed by a rather fine wrought-iron screen. There are three lights in the south wall: St Anna in the centre, flanked with windows of coloured medallions, the angel with Joachim on the left and with Anna on the right, all by E. Didron, Paris 1872. There is in the aisle one large window with glass of geometric designs. The capitals of the pillars at the entrance to these aisle chapels are well carved.

The Chapel of St Anthropius also has interesting capitals. Again there are three lights to the window: in the centre, St Anthropius, wearing a dalmatic, chasuble and mitre and holding a crozier in the crook of his right arm. He is holding a hatchet in his right hand and a scourge in his left.

The Chapel of St Margaritta has a similar screen, pillars and capitals to Bay 4. The centre window portrays St Margaritta holding a sword in her left hand and a martyr's palm in her right, and the windows either side each have two medallions: those at the top depict her tending sheep (left) and driving out a dragon (right); at the bottom she is seen being beaten (left), and beheaded. A statue of St Rita of Cascia (an Italian said to be the patroness of lost causes) is set on a pedestal on the retable of the marble altar. She is holding a crucifix. The aisle has a large window as before.

The Chapel of St James the Less is exactly the same, except that the arcade is fully glazed, making it sound-proof, for this chapel is used for confession: two chairs flank a table on which is placed a purple stole. The middle window is of St James the Less (dated 1872) and each flanking window has two medallions. A statue of St Joseph holding the child stands above the altar.

THE TRANSEPTS

Archbishop Tristan de Salazar added the transepts in the 15th century to mark the division between the nave and the choir. They have good stained glass of the early 16th century from the workshops of artists of Troyes and Sens, whose names have been recorded. These great windows stand out as remarkable features of the church. From this school of glass painters emerged the celebrated Jean Cousin,

A Glimpse Of Glory

the Father, (1500–1589). He was born at Soucy, four miles to the north east, and educated at Sens amongst the glass-workers here. The great flamboyant roses of the transepts are of the latest Gothic period.

THE SOUTH TRANSEPT

The South Wall has two blind arcades each side of the south door and a statue on a pillar of St Michael wearing a breastplate to the east of it. Blind arcading decorates the wall above it below five windows, each with two lancets, the central mullion of each window dividing at the top to enclose a leaf-shape tracery. These five windows are the work of glaziers from Troyes and depict scenes from the life of St Stephen. These ten lancets are shorter in the middle as they support a glorious rose window which fills the top of the south wall and which has as its subject the Last Judgement. Bumpus describes them as, *"whirlpools of gorgeous, though somewhat coarse, 16th century stained glass, executed by four artists of Troyes."* And he cannot help but add, *"The Flamboyant architect has almost transformed this portion of the cathedral, and it is a wonder that M. Viollet-le-Duc, with his love of uniformity, has not transmuted it into Late Romanesque."*

The east and west walls. In the absence of a triforium, there are windows in the east and west walls of the transept on two levels of four lights each, depicting the Tree of Jesse in the left window, and the Legend of St Nicholas. This superb glass was also made in Troyes (c.1500–02).

The Chapel of the Virgin Mary is to the east of the south transept. It is a delicate chapel and was built in the 14th century, hence the elegance of the columns rising to support the rib vaulting. The eye is drawn at once, however, to the beauty of the 14th century statue of Mary, seated and crowned, and with a hint of a smile, above the altar. The base of the statue is decorated with scenes of the Annunciation by the angel, the Visitation to Elizabeth and the Nativity of Jesus. In the latter, the crib appears to be a basket on a shelf above the Virgin's couch. Candles are usually burning in this chapel for the Blessed Sacrament of Holy Communion is reserved here.

On a column to the north side of the altar rail, stands a statue of St Joseph holding the child Jesus, and on the south wall, also on a column, is a large statue of the Virgin and Child. Behind the altar, the northeast window and the east window have three open lancets. The southeast window has three lancets filled with clear and coloured diamond quarry glass. The south wall has four slender lights with similar quarry glass and with quatrefoils at the top.

The western bay has three lancets in the south wall, two blind and one with grisaille glass. There is blind arcading at the lower level, and the bay is closed by a wrought iron screen.

The Nave Altar

THE CHOIR AND HIGH ALTAR

Four steps rise to the level of the semi-circular pavement, which intrudes into the crossing and on which stands the bronze nave altar together with a bronze lectern and a bronze ambo. Red chairs and stools stand either side of the doors in the screen which encloses the choir. This magnificent screen was made in 1762 on the instructions of Cardinal de Luynes, whose arms are displayed above the centre of the screen surmounted by a large crucifix. Beneath the crucifix, a cardinal's hat sends its tassels tumbling down either side of the coat of arms. It is a superb example of wrought ironwork. The whole screen is painted black with gilt decoration. A wrought iron screen encloses the choir and sanctuary.

Two rows of chapter stalls line each side of the choir allowing a wide central space to draw the eye to the high altar with the windows of the axial chapel behind it, and the glorious clerestory windows above. The high altar and its canopy, or baldachino, date from 1742. The four marble columns supporting the baldachino came from Paris, where they once formed part of the original monument to Louis XIV in the Place des Victoires. The archbishop's throne stands on the north side of the sanctuary.

The solid triforium arcade continues around the east end of the apse with a passageway behind the columns. Above, at clerestory level, the three windows lighting the apse, each of two trefoil-headed compartments with a small traceried circle, glow with valuable 13th century glass. The central one contains, within

A Glimpse Of Glory

medallions, a number of small groups of the Passion of Our Lord, who is represented in the act of blessing. The left hand window depicts events in the life of the Blessed Virgin, while the opposite one is devoted to the history of the church and the cathedral's patron, St. Stephen. The six windows of the choir clerestory on either side are in grisaille, but the circlets above the lights have small figures of our Lord and the Apostles.

THE SOUTH AMBULATORY

The airy, spacious and colourful line of the south aisle is continued through two gates in the wrought iron screen which encloses the choir, and which is extended each side to enclose the ambulatories. The blind arcade around the east end of the ambulatory is a part of the original building. Look carefully at the capitals of the pillars of the ambulatories in the apse; they are full of originality and reward careful scrutiny, especially one in which the motif is a pair of doves, their breasts turned outward, plucking at an ear of wheat. A number of these capitals reproduce the interlaced monsters so common in Roman design, others group real and fantastic animals inspired by Oriental fabrics. Enjoy, too, the splayed feet at the bases of the columns.

A Capital in the Ambulatory

Bays 1 and 2 have on the south side the wrought iron screen enclosing the transeptal chapel of the Virgin.

The Chapel of Saint Apolline (14th century). The chapel has a remarkable altar and reredos in this chapel. The delicately carved scenes by Nicolas Godinet in the reredos, dating from the 16th century, depict the Passion of Christ and are separated by niches sheltering small statues of the twelve apostles.

In the south wall of the chapel is a bust of a bishop wearing a ridiculously tall mitre, but in the west wall there is a funerary bust above a sarcophagus, surmounted by a sculpture of a man at prayer with his cloak falling down about the sarcophagus. It is the huge tomb of Cardinal Bernadou (1898) and sadly dominates the chapel.

There is a large window with four lights and a figure in each of them, somewhat fragmented: St Philip on the left, then St Matthias, St Mary and St James. The chapel is enclosed by a wrought iron screen, which was locked during a visit in 2012.

The Chapel of St Martial has a high wooden reredos with a dark painting behind the altar. There is a carved plaque on the south wall. Again, there is one large window with four lancets each containing a figure (left to right: St Mammés, St Martial, St Appolonia, St Ursilinus), but as they are but fragments of ancient glass the characters are difficult to determine. The chapel is enclosed by a wrought iron screen.

East of this chapel there is a 13th century staircase in the arcading of the south wall of the ambulatory which leads to the Treasury (in winter, go via the museum, as the staircase is often closed). Above the staircase is hung a large painting of the Assumption of Mary into heaven.

The Treasury. Among the many precious items on display are the chasuble and mitre of the martyred Archbishop, Thomas à Becket, worn by him during his sojourn at the monastery of St Colombe, near Sens. Francis Bumpus tells how the chasuble was once mutilated to gratify a collector of souvenirs and how Cardinal Manning even tried it on. The ivories of Sens are famous and include the liturgical comb of Saint Loup, a formidable instrument, which was used in preparing him for consecration. Saint Loup was Bishop of Troyes in the 5th century.

In the next bay in an arcade of five blind arches is a doorway leading to the sacristy, and in the top of the second arch from the west can be seen a 12th century carving of the Lamb of God (Agnus Dei).

The Chapel of the Sacred Heart (Sacre Coeur) was built in the 16th century. It is large with a beautiful coffered ceiling. The altar reredos is of classical design, with two gilt wooden columns framing a painting of Christ pointing to his sacred heart. There are paintings either side of the altar: on the north and on the

The South Ambulatory from the East

A Glimpse Of Glory

southeast walls. There is a war memorial on the south wall. A prayer desk is placed before the altar with a priest's stall either side. It was in this chapel that the marriage of the Saint-King Louis and Marguerite de Provence was solemnized, in 1234.

The window behind the altar has three lights with glass made by Jean Cousin the Father (see under 'Transepts', above). The subject is the Sybil showing the Virgin and Child to the Emperor Augustus while the crowd look on. All the other windows have clear diamond quarry glass, making the chapel light and peaceful. The chapel is enclosed by a high screen decorated with winged birds flanking a badge of arms.

The Axial Chapel of St Savinien has a beautiful eight-ribbed vault and was built at the beginning of the 13th century and has contemporary glass in the windows of the apse. It has blind arcading around the lower walls. The northwest bay is blind; the window to the east of it has clear glass apart from a coloured quatrefoil, and this pattern is reflected on the south side of the chapel. The central window in the apse depicts scenes from the life of St Savinien, while the window on the left of it depicts medallions depicting St John the Evangelist, and on the right St Paul. In 2012 the window had been removed for restoration.

On a base behind the altar stands a monumental, almost grotesque, sculpture of the martyrdom of St Savinien. The background to this statuary is a drapery in stucco which partly conceals the 13th century glass in the east window. I agree with Bumpus that from a distance the stucco resembles "a piece of sail-cloth temporarily suspended to facilitate repairs."

Either side of the altar are gilded reliquaries in glass cases, while before it stands a free-standing altar in marble. This fine chapel is enclosed by a high wrought iron screen similar to that surrounding the choir.

THE NORTH AMBULATORY (FROM EAST TO WEST)

The Chapel St Colombe (to the north of the Chapel of St Savinien) has the tomb of the Dauphin, the father of Louis XVI, who was buried in the choir. It is by the younger Guillaume Coustou (1716–77), and properly removed here during Viollet-le-Duc's restoration of the choir, where it occupied a far too conspicuous position. Coustou's drawings of the figures of Religion, Immortality, Time, and Marital Love were approved by Louis XV.

In the north east wall, below the second window, are carved reliefs from the destroyed tomb of Cardinal Duprat, Archbishop of Sens (1525–35). They represent events in his life—one, his entry into Paris as legate, the other into Sens as archbishop.

The large window in the north wall has five lights; the centre depicts St Mary Magdalene before the crucified Christ. The lancets have clear glass apart from coloured quatrefoils at the top which depict, from the left, St Peter, the Crucified Christ, a crucifix, St Savinien and St Paul. In the west wall there is a statue of a bound and seated Christ, wearing a crown of thorns. The chapel is enclosed by a semi-circular screen.

The 12th century windows of the ambulatory. The oldest glass in the cathedral is in the round-headed windows overlooking the north side of the ambulatory, where you are now standing, and which were executed in the year 1184, after a fire which destroyed the town and the cathedral. These four are of marvellous richness in colour and design and seem to belong to the same school as certain windows of Chartres, Bourges, and Canterbury. From east to west they depict the parable of the Good Samaritan, that of the Prodigal Son, the legend of, St Eustatius (St. Eustace), and the life of St. Thomas à Becket.

Of these the most famous is that which relates in a series of thirteen panels, the history of Thomas à Becket, who found refuge in the monastery of Sainte Colombe near Sens for four years, during the time of his exile from England.

The best of the series of carved capitals on the pillars is in the north ambulatory: in one of them two lions seize each a goat; in another winged dragons with serpents' tails interlaced devour a little creature whose hair stands on end.

Bay 1 has an arcade of five blind arches, above which are two round-headed windows. The eastern window has three triangles superimposed on twelve medallions; it is the famed Good Samaritan window. The story of the parable is told in the diamond panels, starting at the top. The two lower registers of medallions tell of the Passion of Christ; the next two registers deal with Moses and the golden calf; the top two registers depict Adam and Eve and their expulsion from Eden.

North Ambulatory Altar Front Bas Relief (See Bay 2)

A Glimpse Of Glory

The western window has twelve square scenes, all in superb glass, and depicts the parable of the Prodigal Son.

Bay 2 is a chapel enclosed with the familiar screen. The window has four lights, each with a figure (left to right) St Julian bearing armour, St Raphael with a fish on his staff, St Thomas à Becket and St Lazarus. There is a bas relief carving on the altar front, which depicts scenes from the life of Thomas à Becket, above which is a painting. In the north wall stands two busts.

Bay 3 has three arches, two of which are blind while the centre arch contains a doorway. Above this door is a large window with two huge roundels of the most beautiful glass, and superimposed in the middle of them are two diamonds, each having four blades radiating from them, containing scenes of the life of St Eustace as follows.

As Placidus, Eustace was a general in the army of the Roman Emperor Hadrian, and while hunting he confronted a stag bearing a crucifix—bottom left. Christ spoke to him from the stag and told him to go with his family to be baptized and so follow him. In the lower diamond is the baptismal scene, depicting Placidus receiving the name Eustace at his baptism by the Bishop of Rome, watched by his wife Theospis and their sons. He is told that he will face the trials of Job, and soon after his servants are killed, his house laid waste and the family decide to take a ship and flee to Egypt (right and left above the diamond). But the captain lusts after Theospis and Eustace is cast ashore with his sons (left below upper diamond). While crossing a great river a lion attacks one son and a fox the other, and Eustace is left alone (upper diamond). He settles down to the life of a farmer (right below upper diamond) until the Emperor requires him to lead his army against strong enemies, and he is returned to his former rank. His sons, meanwhile, have grown up in neighbouring villages having been rescued from the wild animals by villagers on the day they were seized; they visit an inn where their mother was innkeeper, the captain having died before she was taken by him, and they are reunited as a family and set out for Rome to find Eustace (left above the upper diamond). The sons fight in the Emperor's army and lead it to victory (right above the upper diamond), but the new Emperor, Trajan, leads them in victory to sacrifice to the pagan gods (top left). When they refuse, Eustace is stripped of his rank (top right), and they are forced into a raging fire inside a molten bull, where they perish, and their souls ascend to heaven (top centre).

Bay 4 also has three blind arches and in the centre is a 13th century statue of Thomas of Canterbury. It was discovered in 1897, near the cathedral, in the wall of a house in which Becket was said to have lived in 1164. The window above the statue is the famous Becket window which contains in the glass ten roundels with two more superimposed on them.

This window takes up the life of the archbishop from the time that King Louis VII brought about reconciliation between him and Henry II of England, when he left Sens to return to Canterbury. The story begins in the lower left-hand panel with the scene of reconciliation with the King, and continues back and forth, from left to right, picturing the chief scenes in the saint's life after his sojourn at Sens and ending with his martyrdom, his sepulchre, and finally with Christ receiving his soul in Paradise. Over a glass of wine in the square opposite the cathedral I have wondered whether there was once another window dealing with the saint's early life, but if there was, there is no evidence of it.

12th Century Statue of St Thomas a Becket

Bay 5 is formed by three blind arches with a large painting of the martyrdom of St Thomas à Becket above.

Bay 6 is enclosed by a wrought iron screen bordering the chapel of St John in the transept.

THE NORTH TRANSEPT

The North Transept is almost an exact replica of the south. Here, too, the east and west walls of the clerestory have coloured glass, each bay with eight lancets in two levels, all with scenes in them. The two splendid windows in the east wall show sixteen archbishops of Sens on the right, and the story of Joseph on the left; those in the west wall tell the story of Abraham on the right. There is a robust depiction of the sacrifice of Isaac in a lancet in the lower half of the window; an angel stops the blade of the sword from falling. The patron saints of Sens form the subject of the left window. These stained-glass windows were made between 1516 and 1517 by Jean Hympe and his son, glaziers from Sens.

The north wall has three blind lancets either side of the north door, and above the wall is decorated by twelve blind lancets. Higher still is a gallery of ten lancets with coloured glass beneath the rose window.

A Glimpse Of Glory

The great north rose window is of extraordinary beauty. Dating from the 16th century, the subject is Paradise, with Christ surrounded by angels bearing musical instruments and singing his praises. Below are scenes of the Archangel Gabriel. Against the north wall, to the east of the north door, is a statue of Joan of Arc holding the Oriflamme.

In summer it is possible to leave the cathedral via the north transept to admire the façade.

The Chapel of St John to the east of the north transept is built in the Romanesque style and is the Baptistry. Above the altar is a fine 13th century Calvary: the crucified Christ flanked by the Virgin Mary and a grieving St John. Beneath the semi-domed ceiling a blind arcade runs around the lower wall. A font stands in the middle of the chapel. On the north wall is a smaller statue of the bound and seated Christ (Ecce Homo) wearing a crown of thorns. A carving in stone of a bishop with a small figure lying at his feet is on a plinth against the south wall. The lower walls of the chapel are decorated with a blind arcade with fine capitals; three deeply recessed, round-headed windows pierce the north, east and south walls of the apse. There are four lancets in the north wall of the western bay; the two west lancets are blocked, but the two to the east have geometric designs in the glass.

THE NORTH AISLE (FROM EAST TO WEST)

All the capitals are decorated with carved foliage. The chapels are almost identical to those in the south aisle, and, as in the south aisle, in the absence of any official title, I have named the chapels after the subject of their windows.

The Chapel of St Sulpice has three arches springing from carved capitals. A glass-sided sarcophagus lies in the north wall. There are three lights in the window above: St Sulpice in the centre with two medallions in the flanking lights. There is a statue of St Thérèse of Lisieux above the altar.

There is a large lancet with a coloured border surrounding grisaille glass in the wall of the aisle above the remaining bays.

The Chapel of St Alban also has a window with three lights as before, with Bishop Albinus (Alban) depicted in the centre and two medallions either side depicting scenes of his life. There is a statue of Our Lady of Lourdes at prayer on the north wall, and another of St Bernadette Soubirous behind the altar.

The Chapel of St Loup has a statue of St Antony of Padua against the north wall which obstructs the centre light of the window where St Loup is depicted looking rather severe, and holding a crozier in his left hand, his right hand raised in blessing. The light either side has the usual two medallions. Above the altar is an icon of the Black Madonna of Czestochowa, to the northwest of Krakow in Poland. It is housed there in the large monastery of Jasna Góra, which I visited in 1995, and found the exuberant decoration of the basilica to be palatial bordering on the vulgar. Legend has it that the icon was painted by St Luke, but scholars are fairly certain that it is a Byzantine painting of the 13th or 14th century.

The Chapel of St Fiacre has the same arrangement in the window: St Fiacre in the centre with two medallions in the other two lights. St Fiacre was a 6th century Irish saint from County Kilkenny. His skill with medicinal plants has made him the patron saint of gardeners. In the centre of the north wall is a statue of Our Lady of Fatima. The altar is against the east wall.

Bay 3 has a doorway in a blind arcade and above is a painting which fills the blind lancet.

Bays 1 and 2 continue with the arcade of three blind arches, above which the wall is blank.

This concludes our tour of the Cathedral of St Stephen of Sens, but before you leave, sit in the nave for a while and reflect on the lives of those who constructed this glorious building in times long past, and those who come here today, just to visit or to commune with their God.

West Window of the Nave

A Glimpse Of Glory

DO NOT MISS

1. The statue of St Stephen on the trumeau of the west door.
2. The 14th century St Denis' Portal on the northwest side of the cathedral.
3. The remarkable altar and reredos in the Chapel of Saint Apolline.
4. The 13C stained glass of the clerestory.
5. The 13th century statue of Thomas of Canterbury in the north ambulatory.
6. Time to study the 12th century glass in the windows of the north ambulatory.
7. The 13th century Calvary in the Chapel of St John, north transept.
8. The 16th century Salazar Reredos in the north side of the nave.
9. The Treasury.

CHAPTER 2

LAON

Crowning a rocky acropolis over 100m (328 ft) high, overlooking the plain, this Carolingian town to the northwest of Reims has one of the oldest and loveliest Gothic cathedrals in France. It is a great sadness that so many British and European tourists dashing along the A26 to or from the channel tunnel or car ferries, hardly notice the magnificent structure like a crouching lion dominating the hill to the west of the Autoroute, let alone turn off to visit it.

Laon was fortified by the Romans, who named it Laudunum. Its bishopric was founded in 497 by St Remi (Remigius), Archbishop of Reims, who was born in Laon, and during the Carolingian period (9th–10th centuries) it was the capital of France. In the 13th century, the town was surrounded with new ramparts and at the end of the 16th century, the Citadel was constructed. The fortress endured many sieges during the Hundred Years War, and after Waterloo it was a brief rallying point of the defeated army. On 9th September 1870, a French sapper blew up the powder magazine of the Citadel; hundreds of people were killed or injured.

There are two districts in old Laon: the Cité, around the cathedral, and the Bourg. Between the two, on the south side of the hill, is the depression known as the Cuve Saint-Vincent, which was once covered in vineyards. Near the SNCF railway station in the expanding modern Laon on the plain below, a driver-less mini-metro, the Poma 2000, winds its way up to the old city for €1 single fare (2012).

THE CATHEDRAL CHURCH OF NOTRE DAME

It is thought that this ancient site was once the meeting place of Druids. There is evidence that a small church (50m) dedicated to Our Lady existed on the site in the 5th century, its first bishop being a nephew of St Remi. With the coming of the Carolingian dynasty, Laon grew in importance and a new cathedral, dedicated

A Glimpse Of Glory

LAON—KEY

1 The Central West Portal
2 Portal of the Nativity
3 Portal of the Last Judgement
4 The Cloister
5 The South Transept Façade
6 The North Transept Façade
7 The Narthex
8 The Nave
9 The Pulpit
10 The Gentryman's Stall
11 The South Aisle
12 Chapel of the Fonts
13 Chapel of St Leonard
14 Chapel of St Quentin
15 The Lantern & Nave Altar
16 The South Transept
17 Chapel of the Sepulchre
18 The Tournai stone Font
19 The Choir
20 The Sanctuary
21 The High Altar
22 The South Ambulatory
23 Chapel of Our Lady of Liesse
24 The Southeast Chapel
25 The Central Eastern Chapel
26 The Northeast Chapel
27 Chapel of Our Lady of Succour
28 Chapel of Myrian and Marco
29 Chapel of St Anthony
30 Chapel of Nicaise
31 The North Ambulatory
32 The North Transept
33 Chapel of St Paul
34 The Icon of Christ's Face
35 The North Aisle
36 Chapel of St Barthélemy de Jir
37 Chapel of St Thérèse

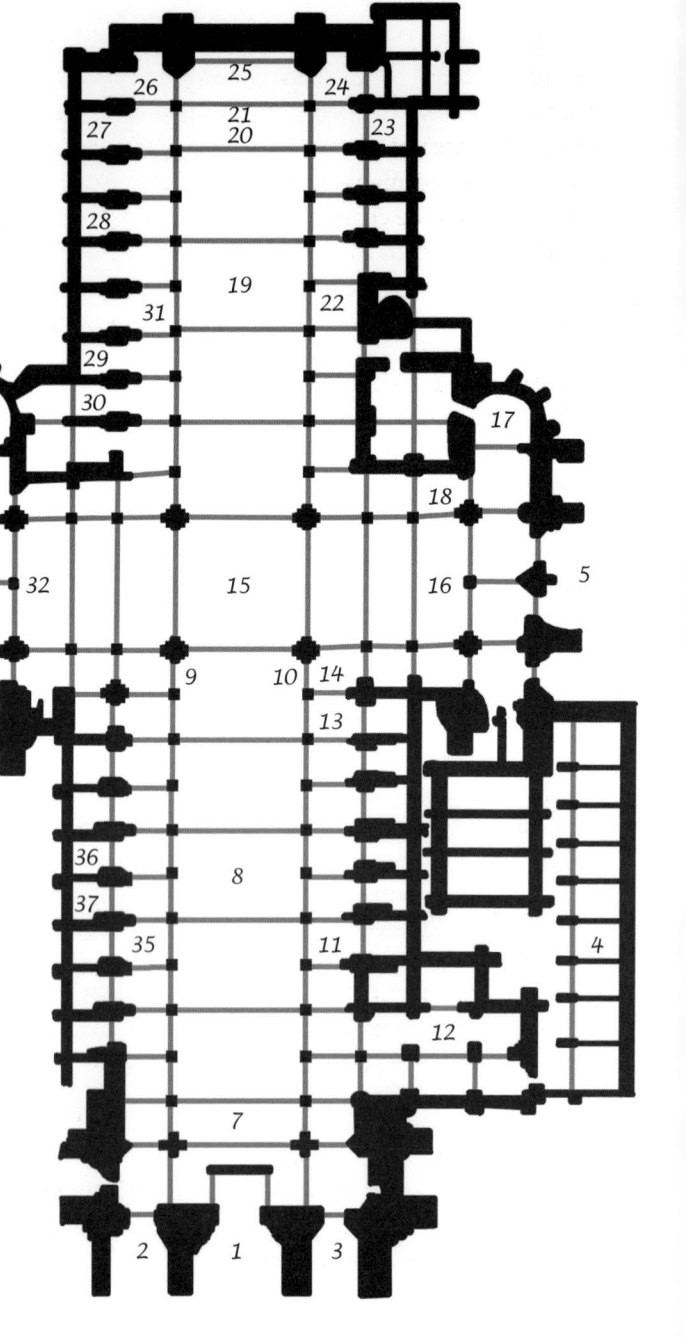

Laon

to St Saviour and St Mary was dedicated in 800 in the presence of Charlemagne. Under the Capetians, a Romanesque church was built on the site, but was gutted by fire in 1112 following an uprising by the citizens against their imperious lord-bishop, Bishop Gaudri, who was beheaded by a serf in his cathedral. It was partly restored with money collected in southern England and northern France:

In his work, 'The Gothic Cathedral', published by Elek Books, London, 1969, the architect and art historian Wim Swann notes, on page 105, that within three months of the fire a group of canons took their most sacred relics and travelled over a wide area of France seeking contributions to the restoration, but while the relics occasioned many miracle cures, the money raised was insubstantial. So the canons crossed the channel to a more prosperous England, where they found many disciples of Anselm, who had been a famous teacher at Laon, holding high office in the church. In seven months they visited Canterbury, Winchester, Salisbury, Exeter, Bristol and Taunton, and returned to Laon with sufficient funds for the repairs.

The present building was begun in 1155 by the new bishop, Gautier de Mortagne (1155–74). He was formerly Dean of the Chapter of Canons here and bequeathed 100 francs to the project, having given 20 francs a year during his lifetime. It was completed in 1225–30. Laon ranks in importance with the cathedrals of Sens and Paris.

The cathedral suffered very badly in the Revolution of 1789. Helen Henderson, in her book, 'The Cathedrals of France', published by Methuen in 1929, records that the Revolutionists' first measure was to close the cathedral and to plant a wheat market in the sacred precincts. Later it became a Temple of Reason, and the alteration of the edifice for philosophic fetes gave the vandals a free hand and they completely ruined the church, breaking the statues, beheading the saints, and violating the ecclesiastical tombs. Finally, the Bishopric of Laon, dating from the 5th century, was abolished in 1790. Degraded from its rank as cathedral it is today a parish church in the diocese of Soissons.

In 1793 the ornaments and furniture of the cathedral were auctioned on the site. Paintings, railings, statues and woodwork were all removed. Dozens of paintings perished in fires. The two Paintings of the Assumption by J.S. Berthélemy (1766 & 1790) escaped destruction, but for the rest, the cathedral was refurnished after the Concordat with items confiscated from former monasteries and abbeys.

During the 1914–18 War the enemy occupied Laon for forty-nine months, and the city was frequently bombarded in 1917–18. Helen Henderson believed that the occupation saved the cathedral, 'Though it had been for a time a stable for six hundred horses, it came through almost unscathed. Its bells, however, were taken down, melted, and used as bullets.'

A Glimpse Of Glory

THE EXTERIOR

THE WEST FRONT

Built about 1200, the façade has a symmetry that is striking and lovely. It is at once both a solid mass of masonry and a soaring statement of faith. The west front with its magnificent, deep-set rose window has been described as one of the most original and beautiful, and perhaps the most powerful of the entire Gothic period. Here the theme of the 'Gateway to Heaven' articulated by Abbot Suger of St Denis finds its first fully successful expression in the three great portals.

The walls dividing the porches of these west doorways absorb the masonry of the two central buttresses, in front of which arise two small open towers crowned with spires. There are shorter versions of them at the outer end of both the north and south façades. Immediately above the porches are three groups of round-headed windows: a group of four above the central porch, interrupted by the pitch of the porch roof, and a group of two above each of the north and south porches. All have clear diamond quarry glass.

Above a foliated stringcourse, the next storey has a deeply recessed window either side of the central rose. In the vousoirs of the arches around these two windows are sculpted depictions of creation and the Liberal Arts. Philosophy, grammar, logic, rhetoric, arithmetic, geometry, astronomy and music are all depicted, and as

West Portals

there was room on the arch, architecture and medicine were added. Mastering the Liberal Arts allowed one to study theology or philosophy, which led to knowledge of God and Creation.

The rose, or wheel window, its 'spokes' radiating outwards from the central oculus, is unusual in that not one of the little columns that form the 'spokes' points to the vertical or horizontal axes of the window. This window, also deeply recessed, had its glass shattered in the subsidence of the façade at the beginning of the 19th century and only five of the medallions are ancient.

The huge window rises above the flanking windows, so the open gallery of blind arcading above it, which echoes the triforium inside, is higher in the central section than the two lateral sections. This central gallery is surmounted with a modern statue of the Virgin Mary holding the Child and flanked by angels.

It is, however, dominated by the two towers which rise either side of her to a height of 170 feet, and which are the glory of Laon. Built on a square base, they become octagonal at this level. The first stage contains the belfry and has two louvered lancets on each face. Above, a tall lancet in each face is open, giving the tower a light and airy appearance. It is divided into two stages by turrets at each corner, which also become octagonal in the top level. In fact, the towers are quite hollow and contain spiral staircases in the turrets.

Where the turrets become octagonal, the famous stone oxen are to be seen. There are sixteen of them, eight on each tower, and they are an acknowledgement that without these beasts to haul the stone up the hill, the cathedral would not have been built. So, full marks to the 13th century workmen for this thoughtful gesture. They are, however, according to Henderson, only half oxen; "they are en façade, they have no hinder parts!" These towers were used as a model for the church at Bamberg in Germany in 1234, so they were complete by that date. At noon the bells chime the hymn tune, "Ave Maria."

THE GREAT WEST PORTALS

To return to the ground, let us examine the great west portals, which some scholars believe were based on the sculptures at Bury St Edmunds. The three west doors are deeply recessed under almost round-headed porches, the central porch being the largest. The spandrels of the porch gables contain intricately carved figures. All the large statues in the portals were so damaged by the Revolutionaries that we now see 19th century replacements.

THE PORTAL OF THE NATIVITY (LEFT DOOR)

This portal pays tribute to the Virgin. The tympanum contains a lovely scene of a solemn Virgin Mary, seated and looking straight ahead, with the infant Christ

A Glimpse Of Glory

on her lap and framed by two columns. To the left are the three Kings, or Magi, offering their gifts, while to the right a bemused looking Joseph is sitting behind a standing angel. With the exception of Mary, all are looking at the Magi. The lintel below features the Annunciation on the left and the shepherds on the right of the central nativity scene with Mary lying on a bed, her covering in delicate folds about her. In the second arch of the archivolt can be seen a contest between vice and virtue and in the third and fourth arches are the prophets and other figures from the Old Testament who foretold the holy birth. Look for the dreaming King Nebuchadnezzar, his cloak wrapped about him in folds. His is the only face left undamaged by the Revolutionists.

There are three large statues either side in the splay of the door. On the left they depict the Visitation, including Zechariah who turns his head away from 'women's talk', and on the right the Presentation of Christ in the Temple, Joseph can be seen on the left with the sacrificial turtledoves in his hand.

The Central Door

The Virgin is also honoured in this portal, where only the tympanum and the archivolt above it are ancient. The lintel was destroyed in the 17th century and the pilasters, both here and in the other two doors, were smashed during the Revolution. They were restored in the 19th century. The tympanum has a splendid carving of a crowned Christ on the right, seated opposite the crowned Virgin Mary who is

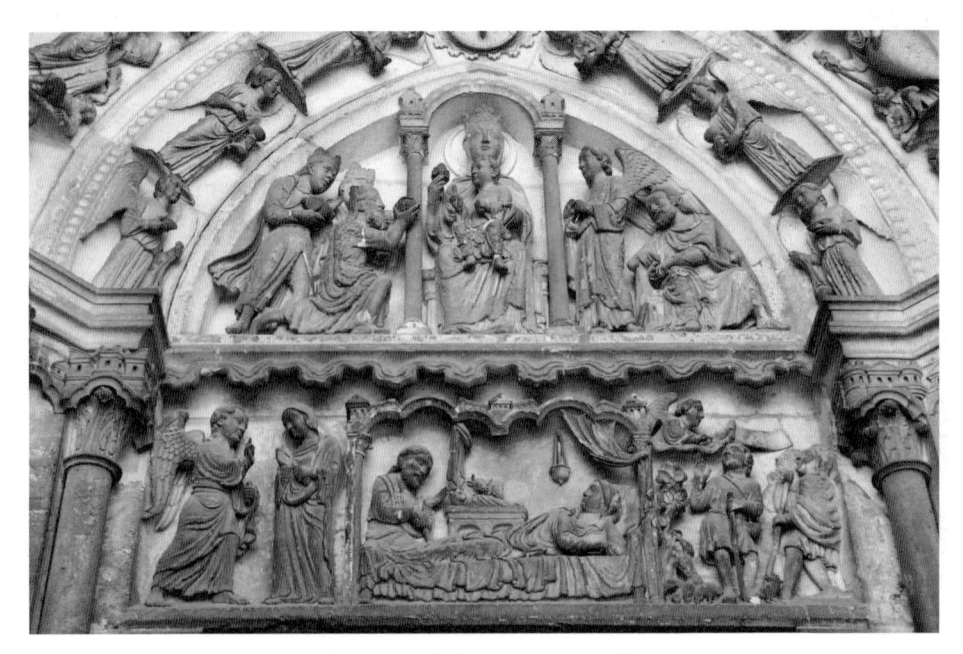

Tympanum of the Nativity, West Façade

holding a sceptre in her right hand. With his right hand he is blessing his Mother as they gaze at each other, his left hand resting on the gospel book. On either side of them are angels bearing censors and torches. The lintel below this scene depicts the death and Assumption of the Blessed Virgin. On the two corbels

Presentation in the Temple, Nativity Portal Right Splay

supporting the lintel are carved: a seated lady in medieval dress (left) and a seated man in similar attire to the right. In the arch mouldings above are angels and in the second and third arches a tree of Jesse, with the prophets who foretold Mary's destiny.

Tympanum, Central Portal, West Façade

A Glimpse Of Glory

Central Portal, West Façade, North Splay

The splay of the door has four large statues either side. On the north (left) side (from left to right) are Abraham with Isaac bound hand and foot standing above a ram with its horns caught in a thicket, the angel of the Lord speaking to him from above (Genesis 22). Next we see a figure standing on a lamb; in his left hand is a staff with a dragon's head, the tail of which is draped about the stem. Then there is a prophet holding a knife with which to kill a sacrificial lamb sitting on a small altar, below which sits a cherub holding a cup with which to catch the blood from the sacrifice. Finally, there is a statue of a crowned figure standing on a lion, a staff in his left hand, holding the three nails of the Crucifixion. The theme appears to be one of sacrifice.

In the splay to the right of the door (from left to right) are four statues of men pointing with the right index finger to symbols of divinity. The first figure has Jesse asleep at his feet; he holds the tree in his left hand like a staff; the infant Christ emerges from the top, his hand raised in blessing. The second statue is in priestly robes holding a nimbus in his left hand; he stands on a bewildered human. Next we see a figure, possibly Simeon, holding the infant Christ. Finally there is a figure of John the Baptist in his hairy robe indicating the Lamb of God, while standing atop a serpent. The trumeau bears a statue of the crowned Virgin and child under a canopy. A serpent bites the hem of her gown in a rather futile gesture.

THE PORTAL OF THE LAST JUDGEMENT (RIGHT DOOR).

The seated Christ in the centre of the tympanum shows his wounds, reminding us that this is a pilgrimage church. Behind him, angels carry the cross, the nails and the crown of thorns. The Blessed Virgin is to the left of him, her hands pressed together in prayer, while the apostles join her in adoration, overflowing onto the first two orders of the archivolt. Beneath all this the dead are rising again from their tombs. The lintel bears the carved scene of the Archangel Michael welcoming the redeemed who advance barefoot, but he is facing the damned: a king, a bishop, an abbot, and a nun, while a miser with his purse about his neck is being seized by the devil at the extreme right. The devil has his hand on the purse and his mouth is open, as if he is saying, "You won't need that any more". In the archivolt you can see angels blowing trumpets, or carrying the souls of children, or giving out crowns and in the outermost order Christ is calling the Wise Virgins to the open door while the Foolish Virgins have the door closed to them.

There are three statues either side in the splay of the portal, a bishop in the centre on the right. The tympanum and possibly the first two orders of the archivolt were made about 1160 and stored until the façade was built. The lintel and the other three orders were carved about 1200.

The archivolts above the recessed windows either side of the central rose are also finely carved. The south window is devoted to the creation. In between two arches of angels, the stages of creation unfold until we come to God resting. The final two sculptures on the right hand side are: a man and angel before God and then a man and woman and a demon!

The west façade is best seen as late as possible in the afternoon, when the sun is in the west. We leave the parvis and walk to the right, to view the south side of the cathedral.

The Procession of the Damned, Tympanum, Judgement Portal

A Glimpse Of Glory

THE SOUTH SIDE

It is extremely difficult to see the south side because of buildings adjacent to the choir and the cloister alongside the nave. However, the south façade is clear, apart from parked cars.

The Cloister

The cloister gallery has seven bays and extends along the south side to form a right-angle junction with the Chapel des Fonts, or Mary Magdalene Chapel at the southwestern end of the nave. The Chapter House stands between the south wall of the church and the cloister and dates to 1225. The hospital is now occupied by the Tourist Information Office at the southwest corner of the cathedral. It was completed in 1177 and is one of the oldest hospital buildings in France. The refectory was demolished in the 14th century and the library was destroyed during the Revolution. In addition, there was once a choir school and altogether, including the canons and their families, a community of over three hundred lived here in mediaeval times.

The Cloister

The South Transept Façade

The façade of the south transept has been treated by the architect as another main façade. Two buttresses divide the building vertically into three, but there are two further buttresses delineating the corners of the façade. The central section has two doorways, matching those on the north side, thus enabling a good flow of pilgrims though the church in the mediaeval period. These doors are framed under three moulded arches with canopies

Laon

South Façade

above each door. In each canopy is a single figure in a niche. The glass in the tympani of the portals has motifs of circles and diamonds. Above the doors is a vast window of six lancets in three groups of two, supporting in the tracery a wheel window. Look carefully and you will see a spectacular mistake in the construction. Painton Cowen informs us in his book, "The Rose Window", published by Thames and Hudson, 2005, [p.260], that the designer had tried to create a seven-fold rose but has made a miscalculation in the spaces between the spokes, and was obliged to insert a triangular fillet at the top to compensate. An open colonnade is above, which is crowned by an open stone railing similar to that on the west front.

The southwestern corner of the transept has a tower called the 'Clock Tower'. As on the north side, two were planned but only one finished. It is also similar to the two western towers, except that the turrets become octagonal in the penultimate level rather than the topmost. Had the two other transept towers been completed, the cathedral would have boasted seven wonderful towers, which is the paradigm of a Gothic cathedral.

We return past the west front to view the north side.

A Glimpse Of Glory

THE NORTH SIDE

As we walk around the northwest corner of the church, notice the door on the north side of the west tower. This replaced the window of the first bay in the nave in 1226. The sculptures depict the martyrdom of St Nicaise when the Vandals destroyed Reims. It was badly mutilated during the Revolution, so it is not easy to pick up the story it portrays.

Solid buttresses support the north wall of the nave and these extend up above the roof of the tribunes to provide a springboard for the flying buttresses supporting the clerestory wall. The north aisle side chapels have buttresses between each window topped with a pinnacled empty niche, which pierces a stone railing running as a parapet from east to west along the top.

THE NORTH TRANSEPT FAÇADE

Again, as on the south side, the façade is divided vertically by four buttresses into three sections. At the base of the central section, a flight of steps built in 1776 leads up to the north doors. These are arranged in two bays under pointed arches, each subdivided into two and separated by a colonnette. The tympani are not decorated. Above the portals is the next stage, which corresponds to the tribune gallery in the nave, and is lit by nine small lancet windows. Above the central five lancets, one of which is partially blind, is the very early (c.1180–90) 'rose' window. It is not strictly speaking a rose window for it is constructed from a central oculus surrounded by eight smaller oculi. Painton Cowen regards it almost as an afterthought, with little relationship with the façade. The central façade is completed by a gallery of blind arches running along the top and continuing into the towers.

It was planned to be crowned by two towers, but the eastern tower was never finished, however, the western tower, known as the St Paul Tower, was

North Façade

44

completed and matches the great towers of the western façade. The eastern chapel in the north transept has a single lancet in each bay in all three storeys.

The Choir

The buttresses extend as piers above the level of the tribunes in order to support the flying buttresses to the clerestory of the choir in exactly the same way as they do for the nave. Similarly, while the side chapels have less robust buttresses than their counterparts in the nave, these have larger empty niches with more pronounced pinnacles, which alone rise above the open parapet. The windows of the side chapels have decorated canopies over them, which rise to the level of the open stone railing, their pinnacles matching in height those of the buttresses. The effect is a pleasing symmetry and far more decorative than the north side of the nave. The four easternmost windows have each two lancets divided by a mullion and supporting a small rose. The remaining windows have three smaller roses above the double lancets. The choir tribune and clerestory each have a single lancet in each bay.

The Chevet

It is only possible to see the east end if you can gain access to the grounds of the former Bishop's Palace. It is now the law courts, so exercise discretion! The rectangular east end has the same solid appearance as the other façades. The now familiar two buttresses divide it into three. Above three lancets in the central section is a beautiful wheel window, nearly nine metres wide. Above it, there is a colonnaded gallery which links two spiral staircases hidden in the buttresses. The gable of the roof juts up above the gallery, surmounted by a little spire. At each end of the gallery there is a short open tower crowned with a spire, similar to those on the porch roofs on the west façade. At either side of the two

The East Façade

A Glimpse Of Glory

buttresses are two storeys with a window in each, one above the other, letting light into the aisles and tribunes of the ambulatory. Two more spires crown the extreme ends of the façade.

THE INTERIOR

The interior is 110m (360 ft) in length, ending in a flat chevet, like Poitiers, 30m (98 ft) wide, and 24m (78 ft) high, built in four storeys. It is a very light and airy church.

THE NARTHEX

The inner porch is supported on four columns. Either side is a narrow blind arch, the northern one containing a British Empire war memorial relating to the Great War. Above the narthex is the organ gallery and above and behind this is the great rose window. Its subject is the Day of Judgement. As I have said above, the window suffered due to subsidence in the 19th century and only five fragments of ancient glass remain: four men rising from their tombs and a medallion of an angel.

The great organ in its five metre tall casing was built in 1697 by a Father Ricard and installed in the north transept. It now rests on the eastern rounded arch of the narthex. At the end of the 19th century it had a radical overhaul by Henri Didier d'Epinal, which converted it to a symphonic instrument with fifty-four stops.

THE NAVE

As you enter the nave, you become aware of its striking width, and the excellent proportion of the nave to the choir. The East Rose Window, supported on its three lancets, is magnificent and draws the eye through the forest of columns and vaulting to its feast of colour at the far end of the church. With the exception of the western bay which has a quadripartite vault, the vaulting is sexpartite (six sections) throughout both the nave and choir, and this, too, draws attention to the sublime unity of the building. This point is well made by George Zarnecki in his book, "Romanesque Lincoln", published by The Honeywell Press, 1988, when he writes of the Lincoln Cathedral vault, "By vaulting two bays under a single pair of diagonal ribs this arrangement has the optical effect of binding the church more effectively together."

Where the nave piers support a lateral rib across the vault, they rest on a substantial square base and have a large square abacus. The intermediate piers stand on an octagonal base and the columns rise from an octagonal abacus.

Laon

The Nave

Above the aisles there are large galleries, or tribunes, each one under a quadripartite vault, with windows set back in line with the south and north aisle walls. The galleries are light and airy, but modern health and safety regulations declare them out of bounds to visitors. In his book, "Gothic Art", published by Thames & Hudson in 1967 (reprinted 1996), Andrew Martindale discussed the use of the tribune chamber in the cathedrals of northern France. Derived from the Romanesque style, the tribune gallery not only added height to the church, but also enclosed the buttresses required to support the height. They can be seen at Lincoln. At Rouen the tribune chamber was included above the nave arcade, but the gallery was never constructed over the aisle; the advance in Gothic architecture had rendered it unnecessary. Except for the western bay, which is blind, there are three open arches per bay in the triforium.

The clerestory above the triforium is simple with one lancet per bay, again excepting the western bay which has a blind lancet. All the windows at the clerestory and tribune levels have glass with a zig-zag pattern, which allows a great deal of light into the building. The four-storey church, with arcade, tribune, triforium and clerestory, was the 12th century style in this part of France, and Laon Cathedral demonstrates the main features of this particular transitional style. Martindale writes on page

A Glimpse Of Glory

20, "[At Laon] the four storeys are clearly in evidence although it is equally clear that the architect was concerned to break up the 'horizontality' of the building by using groups of colonnettes of alternating numbers. These colonnettes are one of Laon's most characteristic features."

The Nave Altar and Choir

The carved wooden pulpit with sounding board is in the second bay from the crossing on the north side. It was brought here from the Carthusian monastery of Val-Saint-Pierre in 1804. The corbel is dated 1681 and the figures depicted on it are three famous monks of the Order. Opposite, on the south side of the nave, is a grand 19th century oak gentryman's stall, backed with a large painting of the crucified Christ, Jerusalem in the background and surrounded by symbols of the Eucharist and the Virgin. The large nave altar is carved like lace and stands on a podium in the centre of the crossing under the lantern tower, which soars above with two lights on each side.

Throughout the nave and ambulatories there are very many memorial slabs in the floor, almost all are now illegible.

THE AISLES

Unlike the nave and choir, the aisles and side chapels have quadripartite vaulting. The elegant Renaissance fronts screening the lateral chapels in both the nave and choir aisles are the last word in stone carving. These façades are almost identical and were erected rapidly, as the dates inscribed on them indicate: 1572, 74, 75, 76 etc. Doric columns stand on a high stone base and support decorated motifs beneath the entablature. Each chapel is entered by a beautifully sculptured oak door. Originally, the whole would have been adorned with gold and colour.

These treasures of the Renaissance period replaced older wooden screens. They give the cathedral an unity and harmony which is breathtaking. Sadly, many of the chapels are used for storage and the doors are locked. Not one has an altar now. The names I have given them are guesses from artefacts found in them, but it might help you to identify them.

Chapel Screen

THE SOUTH AISLE

Bay 1 is really a part of the narthex. It has one clear window, for the south wall has two blind round arches, with a door in the western arch.

Bay 2 is similar except that the door is in the eastern arch.

The Chapel of the Fonts or the Mary Magdalene Chapel, occupies bays 3 and 4. The first of the fine stone screens gives access to the chapel through its central oak door. The chapel extends southward into two bays, each under a quadripartite vault. The window in the west wall has three lancets and in the south wall, to the left of a door giving access to the cloister, there is just one lancet with clear glass above two blind arches.

Bays 5, 6 and 7: These three separate chapels each have on the south wall two blind arches at lower level, above which is a single lancet of glass with geometric zig-zag motifs, except for bay 6 where there are two lancets with a multifoil above. They are not used as chapels, but as storage areas.

The Chapel of St Leonard occupies bay 8. There is a double piscina in the east wall. On the south wall there are two upright indecipherable memorial tablets, one in each of two blind arches. There are carved figures in the spandrels of the arches depicting St Leonard liberating a prisoner. The floor has glazed tiling, which was made in the mediaeval style at Laon in 1996. There is one window with two lancets and a multifoil.

A Glimpse Of Glory

The Chapel of St Quentin (Bay 9). Two blind arches decorate the south wall with carved figures in the spandrels depicting three episodes from the life of St Quentin. Some statues are stored on the floor, including a splendid life-size Virgin and Child. There is one window of two lancets containing geometric zig-zag motifs with multifoil above.

Bay 10: There is a recess in the western blind arch, an excavated rectangle in the floor, and a doorway in the east wall, but with the same window arrangement as in bay 9.

Bay 11: The Chapel was locked in 2012. It contains an altarpiece on the east wall concerning the life of St Elizabeth of Hungary. In the lower section, the Canons who donated it kneel either side of the saint. The upper section is severely damaged, but it is a Calvary flanked by the Virgin and St John. The Chapel has one window with a single lancet of zig-zag pattern motifs.

THE TRANSEPTS AND LANTERN

The vast area of the transepts (54m by 22m), surrounded by huge side aisles, is awesome at first sight. Here, as in the aisles, the vaulting is quadripartite, and also like the aisles, the tribunes run above the transept aisles and across behind the north and south fronts.

The magnificent Lantern Tower over the crossing allows the sun to shine down into the cathedral throughout the day. Above the four enormous lofty arches at the crossing, each side of the square tower is divided into two bays, each with two groups of three open arches. Above each group of three is a single lancet with clear glass. This lantern has eight ribs springing from between the lancets and from the corners, coming together in a forty metre high keystone, to form a lovely early 13th century vault, made lovelier by delicate foliated carving on the ribs.

Lantern Tower Vault

Beneath it, in the centre, is the Nave Altar, made in the

18th century. The motifs on it are of St Roch and his dog, which indicates that it might have been made for some other church or chapel.

The South Transept

The west wall. The southern bay has three arches at ground level, and above is a multifoil window with clear diamond quarry glass. The central bay has two blind arches at ground level, with a statue of the Blessed Virgin Mary of Lourdes in front of the central pillar. There is a window above with one lancet glazed with zig-zag motifs. The northern bay also has two blind arches. Above them, there is a large painting of the Assumption of Our Lady, painted in 1790 by Jean-Simon Berthélemy.

At the tribune level there are three bays each with open arches divided by a central column under a relieving arch. Above them, at triforium level are three arches, in the southern bay it is blind while the other two are open protecting the passage which traverses the triforium. In the clerestory the southern bay is also blind, but the other two each have a single lancet with zig-zag glass.

The south wall forms a kind of solid narthex of two arches beneath the tribune gallery. The arches lead to the two great south doors, which have traceried windows in their tympani. They open onto the south parvis. Above the arches there is a huge window of six lancets grouped in pairs, and in the apex of the window arch is a splendid rose, held in delicate tracery and with glass in the clear latticework pattern.

The east wall also has three bays. At tribune level the central and southern bays each have a single lancet window in the east wall of the tribune chamber; the northern bay is unglazed. At triforium level all three bays conceal a passage, and in the clerestory is a lancet with zig-zag glass.

The Chapel of the Sepulchre projects eastward from the southern bay. Access is through a door in a 15th century wooden screen, which has the inscription, "Sepulcrum Christi, viventis et gloriam vidi resurgentis" over the door; it is a straight quotation from 'Victimae Paschali', the Easter Sequence. The translation is, 'I saw the tomb of the living Christ, and the glory of his resurrection'. This screen has clearly been shortened to fit this bay (in 1840) and it is likely that it was one of many which screened the chapels in the side aisles before the Renaissance stone screens were constructed. The screen continues along the north side of the west bay of this chapel.

The altar is in the eastern apse of this chapel, surrounded by seven blind arches at lower level. The three windows above are blind on north side; the eastern window has modern glass depicting St Génébaud in cope and mitre with crozier in left

A Glimpse Of Glory

hand, his right hand raised in benediction. It was inserted here in 1972. The other three lights all have modern coloured glass. The south west bay of the chapel has three blind arches at the lower level, and above it has one lancet of modern glass. The statue on the altar resembles St Joseph carrying the infant Christ (missing in 2012). There is a low piscina to the south of the altar, on which the Blessed Sacrament is reserved in a tabernacle. There are ancient memorial tablets in the floor.

The Central Bay contains a freestanding Romanesque font in Tournai stone. It dates from the 11th century, but was carved in 15th century. The four faces suggest the Evangelists or the four rivers of Paradise—Tigris, Euphrates, Gihon and Pison. The bird with a snake's tail represents the conflict between vice and virtue. The wall behind it has two blind arches and larger arch above.

The Northern Bay has as wall decoration the two blind arches. The large painting above is the smaller of the two paintings of the Assumption by Berthélemy, which face each other across the transept.

THE CHOIR

The Choir is ten bays long, including the sanctuary, leading to a rectangular east end, with tribune chambers, a triforium with passage, and a clerestory, exactly as in the nave, under an elegant sexpartite vault. In each pair of bays the abacus of the central pier forms a base for three slender clustered columns, which soar upwards to support the ribs of the vault. The columns which support the transverse ribs have additional slender supporting columns.

A superb wrought-iron screen in black and gold, similar to that at Sens, closes the entrance

St Génébaud

Laon

Choir, North Side

to the choir from the crossing. The Rood screen erected in the early 13th century was destroyed in the late 18th century to make way for a new choir screen, which in turn disappeared during the Revolution.

The choir has two long rows of canon's stalls north and south, leaving a grand empty space in the centre. The Choir Organ with its detached console is in the centre of the canon's stalls on the north side.

THE SANCTUARY

The entire area of the sanctuary is enclosed by an 18th century wrought-iron screen, 2.5m (8ft) high, and topped with 126 candle spikes and drip trays, brought from the convent of Villeneuve-St-Germain, near Soissons. During a visit in 2012 I asked an amiable man who was replenishing a stock of candles in the north ambulatory if the spikes were still used. He smiled and explained in French that they date from the era of the great pilgrimages to Santiago de Compestella, when they would have been a source of light and a considerable amount of warmth.

A Glimpse Of Glory

The marble High Altar has a stepped reredos with three candles either side on the steps and a tabernacle on four columns above it in the centre, complete with spire with an angel at each corner carrying the instruments of the Passion. On the front, between marble columns, are carved bas-relief figures of saints on either side of the Virgin and Child. Among them are St Remi, and St Génébaud, whose relics were brought to the new shrine in the choir here in 1220.

THE SOUTH AMBULATORY

Bay 1 consists of a blind arch encompassing the remains of a smaller one, which may have been a doorway.

Bay 2 has two blind arches with decorated capitals at lower level; another above encloses a painting of a vision of the Virgin and Child.

Bay 3 simply a doorway with a grille above

Bay 4 has two blind arches with a window above glazed in zig-zag pattern glass.

Bay 5 and the remainder of the bays have renaissance stone screens similar to those in the south aisle. They stand in front of the pillars with finely carved capitals, and the space behind, once used as chapels, are now used as storage spaces. Each bay has a window of three lights with zig-zag pattern glass, and multifoils and trefoils in the tracery.

Bay 6: there is a Piscina in the east wall with remains of fresco painting, and a memorial tablet to Mgr Claudius Botte dated 1695 on the west wall.

Bay 7: the screen is dated 1620, and here again there is fresco work on the west wall.

Bay 8: The Chapel of Our Lady of Liesse There is an altar against the south wall with a black Madonna and Child (Our Lady of Liesse) above the tabernacle on the altar. In the Middle Ages,

Wrought-iron Grille Enclosing the Choir

the nearby village of Liesse developed a devotion to a Black Madonna presenting Jesus, with his arms open to the world. Tradition relates that this statue was brought back from the Middle East by three crusaders, who had been held prisoners and pressured by the Sultan to reject their Christian faith, but bravely resisted.

There is one window, with three lights containing zig-zag pattern designs in the glass, with a multifoil and trefoil in the tracery. The man with the stock of candles drew my attention to the corbel high in the north east corner supporting a rib of

Corbel, South Ambulatory

the vault which was carved in the form of a Mermaid or Siren. The reader may wish to discover similar corbels in the chapels of this ambulatory.

Bay 9: A half width screen leads to a chapel which continues east beyond the thickness of the wall.

THE EAST END

The original apse, which ended four bays to the west, was demolished in 1205, and was replaced with a rectangular east wall with three chapels, similar to the cathedral at Poitiers.

The Southeast chapel has a statue above the altar of Christ indicating his Sacred Heart. A piscina in the southeast corner is the only interruption to blind arcading on the north, south and east walls. There is a window of one light containing four medallions in the coloured glass. The top medallion shows Christ's betrayal; the next, his crucifixion; then the Last Supper; at the bottom Christ tells the Apostles what lies ahead. The window is dated 1888.

The Eastern Chapel. There is a blind arcade below three tall lancet windows with fine 13th century glass medallions.

The centre window, called the **Easter Window**, has four large medallions arranged vertically, and superimposed on these where they touch are smaller medallions, all describing scenes of the Passion and the Resurrection of Christ. At the bottom, in a half-medallion, is the entry into Jerusalem on Palm Sunday,

A Glimpse Of Glory

and the expulsion of the money changers from the Temple. In the first small medallion is the Last Supper; above is the washing of the disciples feet and the Mount of Olives; then the betrayal by Judas' kiss; then the trial before Caiaphas, the scourging and the Via Dolorosa; then the crucifixion; in the third large medallion is the entombment; then the pious women; above is the arrival of Peter and John; in the top large medallion are the disciples from Emmaus, and finally, in the small medallion at the top, the Ascension.

Polychrome Sculpture of the Crucifixion, Eastern Chapel

The southern (right) window is the **Nativity Window**. It begins with the Annunciation at the bottom. The cavorting creatures in the ninth medallion from the bottom are not in fact Herod's dancing girls, but Daniel dashing the idols to the ground! This southern arch of the arcade, beneath the Nativity Window, is larger than the rest and bears an ancient carving of the Crucifixion.

The northern window is the St Stephen Window. It has six medallions showing the life of St Stephen. He can be seen kneeling as he dies in the third medallion from the bottom to the right. The rest of this lancet is concerned with the story of Theophilus, who sold his soul to the Devil but was redeemed by the Virgin Mary. Beneath this window is an ancient wooden exterior door.

Above these beautiful lancets is the **eastern Rose Window**. In the centre tracery the Virgin Mary sits in a red cloak holding the infant Christ on her lap; above and to left and right are angels, below Isaiah and John the Baptist. The twelve Apostles are sitting around her on a rainbow in the first ring of medallions between the 'spokes'. The quality of the glass is astonishing. It is mediaeval glazing at its finest. There are two buttresses inside dividing the lancets and supporting the gallery beneath the rose window.

The Northeast Chapel has a window of one light with medallions containing scenes from the life of Bishop Génébaud, from baptism to martyrdom. He was the first bishop of Laon. There is a statue of Joan of Arc with the Oriflamme behind the altar and a piscina on the south side of it. The walls have blind arcading.

THE NORTH AMBULATORY

The stone screens are repeated here as in the south ambulatory.

Bay 1: A chapel forms the northeast corner of the cathedral. An east window has two lights of zig-zag pattern glass with a quatrefoil in the tracery, and a larger window on the north side has two lights of similar glass with a multifoil. The altar is against the east wall, but devoid of ornament, even the niche above the altar is empty.

Bay 2: The Chapel of Our Lady of Perpetual Succour. It has one window of two lights with zig-zag pattern glass and a multifoil. There are two blind arches below which contain many votive tablets. The wooden altar is against the east wall and is surmounted by a wooden reredos containing an icon of the Virgin and Child.

The North Ambulatory

Bay 3: The chapel has one window with two lancets and a multifoil above, all in zig-zag pattern glass. This is the arrangement of the windows in all the other bays in the north ambulatory. In addition, they all have two blind arches in the north wall; the eastern blind arch contains the parish war memorial.

Bay 4: The Chapel of Myrian and Marco. The door in the stone screen was locked. Above the altar against the east wall is a statue of the Blessed Virgin standing on a celestial globe with the inscription, "Consolatrice des Affliges PPN" above. There is a memorial to the 1914–18 war on the north wall. An 18th century painting of the Resurrection in poor condition hangs above the altar.

Bay 5: Locked.

Bay 6: The door in the stone screen was locked. In the blind arcade in the north wall are the remains of an ancient fresco painting in each arch. The stone screen, dated 1576, was the gift of Cardinal Louis de Bourbon.

A Glimpse Of Glory

Reredos of Our Lady, Chapel of Myrian and Marco

Bay 7: **The Chapel of St Anthony.** This is a very narrow chapel containing a plinth bearing the statue of St Anthony in a brown Franciscan habit, holding a book on which is seated an infant. A tasselled canopy covers the statue. There is a piscina on the southeast pillar. There is a single window with a trefoil all in zig-zag glass.

Bay 8: **The Chapel of St Nicaise.** The stone screen was locked, but this Chapel has been converted into the Treasury (open on National Heritage Day). The west window is glazed and has a wrought iron grille.

Western Bay: This chapel has no screen, just a doorway. The window has one light of zig-zag patterned glass also with a wrought iron grille.

THE NORTH TRANSEPT

The east wall has three bays each with a quadripartite vault; the southern bay covers the north ambulatory, similar to the south transept. Above the three arches are the tribune chambers, then the triforium, and at the highest storey the clerestory, exactly as the south transept. In the central bay a large wooden statue of the Blessed Virgin Mary stands on a six-foot high wooden plinth. She wears a crown and holds the infant Christ. There is a small window above with zig-zag motifs in the glass.

The wall of the northern bay has two blind arches and a window above of one light filled with zig-zag pattern glass.

The Chapel of St Paul with an eastern apse and enclosed by a wrought iron screen is in the northern bay of the transept. In the apse there are four windows in coloured medallions, three of which relate the life of Christ from his nativity to resurrection. The northern window tells the story of the Black Madonna and was created in 1934 to mark the 800th anniversary of its return from the Crusades. The northern arch of the apse is blind, as are the two southern arches. In the west bay of this chapel there is one window with zig-zag patterned glass in the north wall. There is a blind arcade all around the chapel below the windows. An altar stands in the apse with a red reredos. Before the reredos, there is an icon of the face of Christ. In 2004 it was on temporary loan to the Metropolitan Museum in New York, but in 2011 it had been restored to this chapel. It is older than the cathedral and has a Cyrillic inscription, "Image of the Lord on linen". It came to Laon in 1636. Rescued from severe deterioration in 1988–90, it is now in an airtight case.

The north wall of the North Transept is pierced by two large arches divided by a central column with clustered columns supporting the ribs and vaults of the arches. These support the two quadripartite vaults above the two transept doors, above which is a large tribune chamber. There are four lancets in the huge window above the tribune gallery containing modern glass, which Dr Basil Cottle calls 'Tweed Glass' in his book, "Cathedrals of France", published by the Unicorn Press in 2002. **The 'rose' window** above that has c.1220 glass depicting the liberal arts in its oculi. Philosophy, grammar, logic, rhetoric, arithmetic, geometry, astronomy and music are all depicted. Beneath this tribune are two bays with a door in each forming a narthex.

The west wall has two bays with two blind arches and low down a door in the left hand one, which has a blind arch above.

The North Bay has two arches with a window with a single lancet containing zig-zag pattern glass. In the northwest corner a small door beneath a small window leads to a vestry.

Both the transept and the tribune gallery are covered by a quadripartite vault.

Holy Face of Laon

A Glimpse Of Glory

THE NORTH AISLE

All the bays in this aisle are alike: all with open arches, and a renaissance stone screen. Above the two blind arches in the north wall is a window of two lights of zig-zag pattern glass with tracery of a multifoil and two mouchettes, except in bay one where there is an open arch.

Bay 1: The stone screen was locked. It appeared to be a storeroom.

Bay 2: In the spandrel between the blind arches on the north wall is carved an angel rising from the water.

Bays 3 and 4: were also locked and used for storage.

Bay 5: The Chapel of St Barthélemy de Jir. It has the same stone screen entrance as all the other Bays and two blind arches in the north wall, with foliage carved in the spandrel painted green. To the north is a large black marble sarcophagus, engraved with a bishop in full vestments, a crozier in the crook of his left arm and

North Nave from the East

West Portals

hands joined in prayer. He is Bishop Barthélemy (1158). Other tombstones adorn the walls.

Bay 6: The Chapel of St Therese. There is a statue of St Therese of Lisieux against the east wall.

Bay 7: There are fine carvings of angels rising from the water in the spandrels of the two blind arches in the north wall. There is an expressive carving in the corbel supporting the northeast vault rib.

Bay 8: The chapel contains a massive 13th century square font, about 80cm (3 ft) across the top, on a 19th century stone column. It used to stand in the Chapel des Fonts across the nave, but came originally from the bishop's palace.

In the spandrel between the blind arches there is a carving of a smiling Christ with hands outstretched, and a king and queen either side. There is another interesting corbel supporting a vault rib.

Bay 9: The bay has only one lancet in the window.

Bay 10: There is one large blind arch above the lower arcading.

Bay 11: This forms the north side of the narthex.

This completes our tour of this ancient and venerable cathedral.

A Glimpse Of Glory

DO NOT MISS

1. The sculptures in the western portals.
2. The oxen on the western towers.
3. Look up at the early 13th century vault of the Lantern Tower at the crossing.
4. The 11th century Romanesque font in Tournai stone in the south transept.
5. Time to study the three eastern lancets and rose (use binoculars).
6. The icon of the face of Christ in the north transept.
7. The view across the plain from the ramparts to the north of the cathedral.

CHAPTER 2

ROUEN

Rouen was still ruled by Rome when the first Christian missionaries arrived in Normandy. A young Welshman named Mellon (Mellonius), who was born c.229 AD near Llandaff, Cardiff, journeyed to Rome with the local Tribute money, and became a Christian. He was baptised by Pope Stephen l, who ordained him priest, then consecrated him bishop and sent him to northwest Gaul. He found at Rothomagus (Rouen), in the year 260, a flourishing city with streets and vineyards, art and industry. Mellon began to preach the Gospel, and soon he erected a church dedicated to The Holy Trinity and the Holy Virgin. He died in 314 AD and lies buried in the crypt of the church of St Gervais, Rouen.

In 841 the fair city was pillaged by the Vikings and later by the Normans, who destroyed it under Rollo, who then became the first Duke of Normandy. In 913 he became a Christian and began rebuilding the city, including a new cathedral.

Today Rouen, the capital of Seine-Maritime in Normandy, is a seaport for Paris and a major manufacturing centre. A large part of the town was destroyed by the Second World War, but most of its numerous architectural monuments were restored after 1945. The major buildings include the Gothic Cathedral of Notre-Dame; the Church of Saint-Maclou, and the Church of Saint-Ouen, both good examples of late-Gothic architecture; the Palais de Justice; and the Tour de d'Arc, a tower in which Joan of Arc was imprisoned in 1430. In 1431 Joan was burned at the stake in the city square, where there is today a tourist *Museum of Jeanne d'Arc* (closed for renovation in April 2013) in which the English are not much esteemed.

During a visit in 1998, I sat with my back to this Museum, under a restaurant awning, enjoying my evening meal as the rain teemed down. There were no other diners until I was joined by a Frenchman, who began to converse with me. When he heard my French accent he said, *"Ah! You are English."* Mindful of the ghoulish exhibition in the building behind me I replied, *"Non, monsieur, je suis un Gallois."*

A Glimpse Of Glory

ROUEN—KEY

1 Central West Portal
2 Portal of St John
3 Portal of St Stephen
4 St Romain Tower
5 Butter Tower
6 The Calende Portal (south)
7 The Booksellers Portal (north)
8 The Nave
9 The South Aisle
10 Chapel of St Étienne
11 Chapel of St Eustace
12 Chapel of St Leonard
13 Chapel of St Peter
14 Chapel of St Columbe
15 Chapel of St Catherine
16 The Masons' Door
17 Chapel of St Margaret
18 Chapel of St Romain the Less
19 The Crossing
20 The Nave Altar
21 The South Transept
22 Chapel of St Joseph
23 Chapel of St Joan of Arc
24 The Choir
25 The High Altar
26 The South Ambulatory
27 Tomb of Richard Lionheart
28 Chapel of St Bartholomew
29 Axial Chapel of Our Lady
30 Tomb of Hugh of Amiens
31 Window of Joseph
32 Chapel of S Peter & S Paul
33 Window of St Julian
34 The North Ambulatory
35 Chapel of Holy Sacrament
36 Chapel of Our Lady of Pity
37 The North Transept
38 The North Aisle
39 Chapel of St Anne
40 Chapel of St Nicholas
41 Chapel of the Fonts
42 Chapel of St Eloi
43 Chapel of St Julian
44 Chapel of St Sever
45 Chapel of St John of Nave
46 Chapel of Agatha
47 Chapel of St Mellon
48 The Baptistry

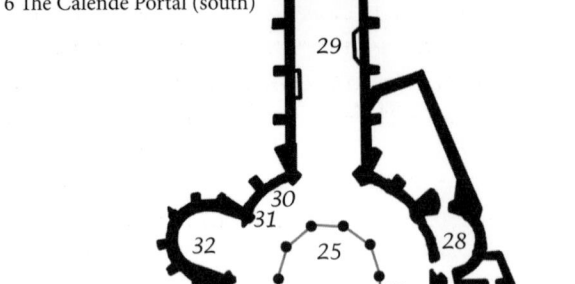

That got him onto Welsh Rugby Football, and the moment passed happily. He introduced me to Livarot cheese, and we enjoyed an hour of great conviviality and conversation.

THE CATHEDRAL CHURCH OF NOTRE DAME

Walking towards the cathedral in 2004, under the ancient l'Horloge, as the city awakened in the narrow streets around, I glimpsed the shadowy west front of the cathedral through an early morning mist, reminding me of the paintings of Claude Monet, and with the sun shining through the skeleton of the Spire it appeared to be balanced delicately atop the solid central tower, and was ethereal in its beauty. During the 3rd century, the first bishops of Rothomagus, the ancient name of Rouen, were Celts: the Welshman Mellon, Nicaise, Ouen and Romain, all of whom were later canonised as saints. When Duke Rollo became a Christian he began to endow the city with a fine cathedral. Both he and his son, William Longsword, were buried in it. Robert the Magnificent became archbishop in 989. During the forty-eight years of his archiepiscopate the building was advanced far enough for it to be dedicated to St Étienne (Stephen) in the presence of William the Conqueror in 1063, although Robert did not survive to see that great day. In 1160 the first stone of the northwest tower was laid, called St Romain Tower since 1477. It was a tragedy that a disastrous fire swept through Rouen, reducing the cathedral to ashes, on Easter Day, 1204. All that remained on this site was the lower stage of the St Romain Tower and the two outer portals of the west façade.

From a canonry in Rouen cathedral, Gautier of Coutances had travelled to England to become a royal chaplain and subsequently Bishop of Lincoln. In 1184 he was translated as Archbishop of Rouen, but was still able to accept the high office of High Chancellor of England. Indeed, when the Lionheart travelled outside his kingdom, Gautier acted as Regent. This is the man who began to rebuild his cathedral church in Rouen. Even when King John lost Normandy, his successor, Philip Augustus, supported the work. Seven years later Gautier died, leaving the remaining work in the hands of successors. The names of the builders become known at this point in history: Enguerrand, who undertook the first work in the early Gothic style evident in the western portal, and Durand, whose name is found high on the last vault of the nave.

It is hard to imagine this serene and lovely building, full of treasure and priceless artefacts donated over the centuries, as the scene of such mindless vandalism as it endured in the horror of the Revolution in 1792. The lead on the roof was sold; the royal throne, the exquisite wrought-iron grilles, and bells were smashed and melted beyond recognition. The nave became a Temple of Reason, with seats fitted like a theatre. The Lady Chapel was let as a granary, which at least preserved the

A Glimpse Of Glory

splendid tombs. Dawson Turner wrote in 1822, "The effects produced by the French revolution upon the religious state of the country, were scarcely less important than upon the political. In both cases, the nation hurried, with the blindest fury, from extreme to extreme; in both, they followed phantoms of ideal perfection through an unexampled series of excesses and sufferings; in both, they rested at length from exhaustion much more than from conviction; and, happily for mankind and for themselves, they finally attained in both nearly the same end, reverting indeed to their original constitutions, but tempering them with a most seasonable mixture of civil and ecclesiastical liberty." It was not until 1802 that religion was restored.

Enough! Let us examine the Cathedral which stands before us.

THE EXTERIOR

THE WEST FAÇADE

The cleaning of the west front had begun when I paid a visit in 2003. By the time of my visit in 2013 it had been completed and is a vast improvement. The west front of Roullant Le Roux and the generations of Norman craftsmen which followed him is one of the great statements of Gothic architecture.

For a moment, try to ignore the two great towers which flank the west front, and concentrate on the centre portion, which is a classic Gothic three-door façade surmounted by four square turrets. Their elaborate finials and pinnacles were added later. Only one is original. Its companions collapsed during a great storm in 1683, and were only replaced towards the close of the nineteenth century.

There is very little remaining to help us to imagine the 13th century appearance of the façade, for it is the 14th century builders who gave to the world the wonderful arcaded screen we see before us, with its graceful gables, and its wealth of statues.

Six almost symmetrical compartments stand there, three on either side of the great rose. The statuary has suffered terribly with the lapse of time. The two side portals are dedicated to St. Stephen (St. Etienne) and St John (St. Jean), and are survivals from the Romanesque Cathedral which was badly damaged by the great fire on Easter Day 1200. It is remarkable that they have emerged unscathed from the successive reconstructions of the façade during the three following centuries.

The Central Portal

By the beginning of the 16th century, when the princely Cardinal Georges d'Amboise was occupying the archiepiscopal throne, the old thirteenth-century porch had begun to threaten speedy collapse. First of all they built two pyramidal

Statues on the West Façade

buttresses on either side of the door to provide additional support to the nave. They covered the entire surface with statues, canopies and pedestals; three tiers in all at the outset, though much of the work has perished. The buttresses rise to support pinnacles, which frame the central gable. Behind which is a deeply recessed rose window.

Between the two pinnacles they created the canopy over the great central portal containing a series of three orders in the archivolt, which are alternately decorated with bands of acanthus leaves, volutes and geometrical designs. A fourth, outer order melts into the wall. In the splay of the central doorway three finely decorated columns stand either side on an elevated plinth, each supporting a bracket, and above each bracket is a decorated canopy which once sheltered a statue. All the statues are missing. These columns correspond to the archivolt. The pedestals for the most part are covered with a mass of sculpture representing events in the Passion. The door jambs are decorated with beautiful bands of foliage. The effect is unusual in northern France, and relates more to a Moorish influence, which was, perhaps, brought here from Sicily by the sons of Tancred. I have seen similar decoration in the cathedral of Monreale, near Palermo.

The huge tympanum over the doorway is covered with a sculpted Tree of Jesse. We see the patriarch lying prone, and from his side grows a tree bearing the images of the family from which Christ was born, the highest place being occupied by the Virgin Mary. Unfortunately some of the figures have lost their heads. There is no

A Glimpse Of Glory

Tree of Jesse Tympanum

trumeau, because during the 18th century the Chapter removed the elaborately carved central pillar to secure additional room for their processions. Certain alterations, which have been made on the lintel of the doorway, also proclaim their decadence only too plainly.

Above the portal, a gallery connects the two pinnacles and in turn supports a gable which rises almost to the top of the rose window, partly obscuring it. The delicate decoration around the arch framing the rose has been described as 'a picot of lace'. The rose is enclosed within a series of arches, the inner of which is crowned by a figure of Our Lady flanked by two angels holding tapers. Above is another openwork gallery making an arcade of eleven arches, crowned alternately with canopies and flowered gables. Just behind appears the great gable of the nave surmounted by an elaborate cross.

Over each of the lateral portals of St Stephen (Étienne) and St John (Jean) is a delicate blind arcade, above which rise three slender arches, each with a crocketed gable, and each topped with a decorated finial. On the south side these three arches are filled with blind lancets in the lower section, above which are two galleries of statues, and crowned with quatrefoils and trefoils in the tracery. Over the north portal the lower level of blind lancets also has a gallery of statues. Massive round arches once surmounted the portals, but now survive only over the two lateral doors.

The Portal of St. John. The sculpture in the tympanum of this northern doorway depicts the violent death of John the Baptist (St Matthew's Gospel, chapter 14, verses 1 to 12). Herod is seen feasting with his

Salome Dancing for the Head of John the Baptist

courtiers; Salome is standing upon her head in the course of her wild dance; a soldier is portrayed in the act of decapitation, while the dish with its hideous contents is being presented to Herodias. In the upper compartment the single scene represents the saint's burial.

The Portal of St. Stephen on the southern side depicts the stoning of St Stephen, the first Christian martyr, but the sculptures of the saints have suffered severely.

The Tower of St Romain (northwest). The Tour St. Romain was originally separated from the Cathedral by an open space of ten or more feet. At a later date, a junction was formed between the two buildings by means of a bridge, decorated with a series of blind arches, and surmounted by an openwork screen. The junction between the façade and the northwest tower has decoration in the stone as fine as lace, for above this screen rises an additional compartment, which with its statuary and traceried open gable adds a very beautiful feature of irregularity to a glorious piece of work. It is crowned by the statue of an angel.

The tower has been described by Canon Jocelyn Perkins, in his book "The Cathedrals of Normandy", published by Methuen in 1935, as the "grand old twelfth-century fortress." That is a fair description of the ground level section, as its foundations were laid possibly as early as 1160. It is a solid, square construction and is divided into five separate stages above the ground story, separated by string-courses. Flat buttresses, sloping as they ascend, support the tower, a pair at each angle, with a third in the centre of each face.

The further the tower rises, the greater is the emphasis laid upon the pairs of windows. As we saw in the lateral portals, the round arch is in evidence below; but the majority of the windows above display a slight suggestion of the lancet. They are considered to be the oldest specimens of the pointed arch extant in Normandy. On the eastern side stands a tower containing the staircase, a replica of the mighty giant which rises above. Perkins regards the Tour St. Romain as "the alpha and omega of gothic architecture."

At low-level is the ancient stonework which was damaged by the fire in the year 1200. The next two levels are decorated with blind arcading, and the 4th and 5th levels form the belfry, all crowned with a solid square tower added in 1468 by the master builder Guillaume Pontifs, and above which is the slated pinnacle with golden sun bursts on it, topped with two iron-work crosses. On 31st May 1944, just days before the Allied landing, the area to the north and west of the cathedral suffered extensive bombing, which set fire to the entire area. A strong wind fanned the flames which set the tower alight, to such a degree that the bells melted in the heat. Further damage to the tower was caused by an incendiary bomb on 1st June 1944. After the war the decision was made to clear the ruined area before the

A Glimpse Of Glory

west façade, thus permitting the front of the cathedral to be viewed in all its glory. Pontifs work was destroyed, but beautifully restored in 1987.

The Butter Tower (southwest). The Tour de Beurre forms the third element in the west front, and contains a fifty-six bell carillon. The first stone was laid in 1485, just over fifteen years after the completion of the Tour St. Romain, and the building work was again entrusted to Guillaume Potifs. Its popular name came from the mediaeval practice of permitting the devout to eat butter and drink milk during the fasting period of Lent on condition that they paid a sum of money towards the construction of the tower.

To harmonise the façade, he adopted the same arrangement as the St Romain Tower; four richly decorated buttresses with niches and statuary, and terminating in elaborate pinnacles, soar upwards at each angle, while all four faces are divided vertically by a similar buttress. The three lower stages are separated by fairly plain string-courses. The lowest stage encloses the Chapel of St. Étienne la Grande Eglise. Its east, west and south faces are fitted with windows containing flamboyant traceries in their heads and divided horizontally by transoms. The second and third stages are similar save for the traceries. The third is crowned by a beautiful openwork balustrade. Statues of patriarchs and prophets abound, and on the central buttress at the third level, at the middle of the west face, your binoculars will reveal statues of Adam and Eve, their hands covering their nudity. The fourth stage is smaller, and each face contains two arcades of narrow but extremely graceful windows, divided horizontally by transoms and surmounted by ogee-shaped arches, the pinnacles of which pass through an extremely beautiful balustrade of openwork.

The final stage is the octagonal lantern, which is supported by eight buttresses terminating in a pinnacle, each connected with the great buttresses of the tower by means of a flying arch. The eight faces of the lantern are filled with windows, while another fine parapet of openwork completes this crown, completed in 1506 by Jacques le Roux and his nephew Roulland.

The South Side of the Nave

The south side of the nave has also been cleaned. There is a buttress separating the bays, each of which has a window of four lancets, with a multifoil in the top of the tracery supported by two quatrefoils. The window has a central mullion, and two slender mullions either side divide the lancets. The arches of the bays are each crowned by a crocketed gable, which rises through the pierced parapet, which is decorated with quatrefoils and which runs along the top of the wall.

Each buttress along the length of the south aisle wall has at the top a small plinth with four slender columns supporting a highly decorated canopy, which in 1935 contained statues of kings, but are now are devoid of sculpture. The buttresses counter the outward thrust from the clerestory by means of a flying buttress which springs over the aisle roof. These flying buttresses abut the wall of the clerestory and are also crowned with a pinnacle, which projects above the parapet running along the top of the clerestory wall. There is a similar arrangement at Bourges.

The clerestory windows are recessed under an archivolt and are divided into four lancets in each bay, which have a hint of the pointed arch, and with two quatrefoils and a multifoil in the tracery. Above the windows is a delicately carved stringcourse decorated with two rows of foliage, forming a cornice, while a sixteenth century balustrade crowns the entire south side. The whole is very delicate and attractive; the great range of windows, gables, flying buttresses and balustrades is indescribably grand.

THE SOUTH TRANSEPT FAÇADE

John Davy was the supervisor of the Booksellers' portal in the north transept, and the Calende portal here in the south transept. Started in 1280, it took fifty years for the façades to be completed. Before the river was confined by quays, the Place de Calende below the transept was formerly known as the Port of Ships and the Port of Our Lady, as the Seine lapped at the walls of the cathedral.

The Calende Portal. The popular name for this south door comes from the Latin word 'calend', which corresponds with the first day of each month in the Roman calendar, and from which our word 'calendar' is derived. The date in Roman times was measured relative to days such as the Calends, Nones and Ides: the first day is called the Calends; six days later is the Nones of March, May, `July and October, but four days later for the remaining months; and the Ides is eight days after that. At the beginning

The South Façade

A Glimpse Of Glory

The Calende Portal

of each month a brotherhood met in this portal, hence its name.

The portal is framed by the symmetrical trunks of two unfinished towers. Three arches with elongated gables form the lower level of the portal itself. Behind the central gable there is a decorated gallery and traceried windows, with the rose, or rather wheel, window above them. The façade terminates in a richly decorated niche which contains the sculpted scene of the Coronation of the Virgin. The two narrower arches of the lower storey continue upward as two ornamented buttresses and end in delicate pinnacles high above the towers which frame the façade. These two towers have a blind arcade at ground level above which is a window divided by mullions into lancets. These windows form the southern ends of the transept aisles. At the second level each tower has another window divided by mullions, but it is unglazed, and a decorated balustrade crowns the entire façade.

The three tiers of the 14th century tympanum above the door contain the Crucifixion at the top; the middle section depicts (from left to right) the arrest of Jesus in the garden, Judas' hanging, the scourging of Christ, carrying his Cross along the Via Doloroso and the entombment. The bottom section depicts Easter morning: the women at the empty tomb; the risen Christ appearing to Mary Magdalene; the descent into Hell as Jesus pulls Adam from the jaws of the Leviathan; the Ascension and finally the Holy Spirit descending on the Apostles in the form of a dove at Pentecost. The three orders of the archivolt have an abundance of angels and other figures. The large figures in the splay of the portal, and which spread across the face of the narrow arches either side, are replica statues of the Apostles. The trumeau bears the statue of a regal, sombre Christ.

However, the most remarkable feature of the portal is the series of bas-relief carved quatrefoil medallions with which the pinnacles and lower portions of the

Bas-relief Panels on the Calende Portal

jambs and buttresses are adorned. Two hundred and seventy of them tell the stories of Job, Jacob, Joseph and Judith in graphic and tender detail, together with the lives of the two Archbishops St Romain (on the buttress) and St Ouen (on the buttress return). They should be read like a book, from left to right and from top to bottom.

THE CENTRAL TOWER AND SPIRE

The central lantern tower is the focus of unity for the building; it stands four-square and locks the nave, transepts and chevet into a single edifice. The lower stage, which squats at the centre of the crossing, has four faces decorated with narrow blind lancets beneath a stringcourse. The level above it has on each face two large windows, each divided by mullions into narrow lancets with tracery. All this is 13th century work, but the upper level and the buttresses at the angles of the tower, which are crowned with lofty pinnacles, are the work of Roulland le Roux. The two western pinnacles were sheathed in scaffolding in 2013.

A Glimpse Of Glory

This tower is sheer elegance and superlative architecture in its own right. If only it wasn't dominated by the structure which it was designed to support, and which, in my view, ruins the grandeur of the building: the wretched spire.

The Spire, rising to a height of a hundred and fifty-one metres above ground level, is the tallest in France and weighs 12,000 tonnes. The lead covered wooden spire over the crossing, nicknamed the needle, caught fire in 1514 during repairs to the lead and was destroyed. Roulland le Roux, master mason of the cathedral, raised the crossing tower by a stage and a Robert Becquet, a carpenter, put up a wooden spire sheathed in gilded lead in 1557. This was destroyed by lightning in 1822–1823 the architect Jean-Antoine Alavoine proposed the cast-iron spire in the Gothic style. The project was completed in 1884. It was again restored from 1975 to 1981 after the ravages of time and war damage, when it was reinforced with steel.

THE CHEVET

There is an angular building jutting out from the South Ambulatory wall, and east of it we see the first of the small radiating chapels. In front of the radiating chapels is another low building with four round windows fitted with iron bars. The pinnacles of the buttresses which support the lancet windows either side of the

Cours des Libraires

Chapel are decorated with tiny blind arches. The very large Lady Chapel projects east from the ambulatory.

To continue our examination of the exterior, it is quicker to retrace our steps to enter the Calende door and cross the cathedral to the north transept door.

THE NORTH TRANSEPT FAÇADE

There is a great similarity in the 13th century north and south transept façades of architect John Davy, for here we see again the solid twin towers framing the portal. However, as their lower levels are obscured by the old Archiepiscopal Palace to the east, and the wall of the library and former cloister to the west, the façade can be viewed only from the passage between them, in which the booksellers' stalls were erected from the 14th century onwards. Dom Pomeraye, writing in the 17th century, described the passage as "bordered on either side by little shops."

The Cour des Libraires, as this delightful court is known, was designed by Pontifs in 1481. The outer portal is a splendid example of flamboyant architecture. Two great bays crowned by ogee-shaped decorated gables close the courtyard from the Rue St Romain. Behind the pinnacle of these gables a mullion rises to support a delicate statue. Above the bays are four windows filled with narrow lancets and elaborate tracery, while higher still is a series of round arches surmounted by gables and linked together by an openwork arcade surmounted by pinnacles.

The Portail des Libraires (the Booksellers Door). John Davy began to build the exquisite Booksellers' Portal in 1278, a little later than the Calende Portal, but it was largely complete by 1300. Ruskin described it as the zenith of French Gothic art. On the pillars in the splay either side are three empty niches set on square pillars, with a trumeau between the two wooden doors. The faces of these pillars are decorated with a hundred and fifty panels and medallions sculpted in bas-relief. The subjects range from the creation and fall of man to animals such as baboons, goats, pigs and the fabulous creatures of centaurs and unicorns.

Bas-relief of a Man fighting a Bear

A Glimpse Of Glory

Upper North Façade

There are three orders of carved angels and saints in the archivolt over the door. The sculpted figures in the tympanum represent the Last Judgement in the middle, and the resurrection in the lower level. The upper section was never completed. A splendid openwork gable rises above the portal, containing a rose of trefoils about a central quatrefoil. The statue of the Father holding a crucified figure within a multifoil, at the lower right of the gable, has been identified by Canon Perkins as the crucified figure of St Peter. The gable terminates in a finial bearing an angel.

Behind the gable can be seen an arcade of narrow lancets forming a gallery, behind which are five windows divided by mullions into ten narrow lancets, which, in turn, support the great rose window. A column of sculpted figures rises each side of this rose, which then forms an archivolt of angels, their wings folded high behind them, all around the top. Crowning the rose is yet another great crocketed gable, full of flamboyant tracery and terminating in a decorated finial.

The buttresses either side of the doorway rise up in decorated levels containing blind arcading, statuary and empty niches, with decorated slender gables, which terminate in elongated finials at the height of the transept roof, and the first bay of the passage on the east side is decorated in a similar manner, in an attempt to disguise the narrowness of the passage and therefore the portal as a whole.

Rouen

We pass through the Cours des Libraires into Rue St Romain and turn left alongside the wall that marks the area known as the Courtyard of Albane. Local archaeologists have been excavating here since 1986 and have discovered the remains of the early 5th century basilica of St Vitrice, and a part of the 8th century Cloister.

THE INTERIOR

THE NAVE

At the west end of the nave, above the big west doors, is the great organ gallery. The organ was first erected here in 1490 by Archbishop Robert de Croixmare. Dr Dennis Keene, the international organ recitalist and conductor, who studied privately in Paris with Marie-Madaleine Duruflé, has written that for centuries, there existed in France a very special musical tradition called 'alternatum'. The Gregorian chant was sung in one end of the church by the choir, a verse at a time, and then the organist at the Grand Orgue at the other end of the church would improvise on that chant. And back and forth it went. If the organist was really special, the liturgy and music created quite a magnificent drama. This tradition in France started in the middle ages and continued down through the centuries until Vatican II. Rouen Cathedral still had a boy choir of note at the end of the 19th century when Monet camped across the street, creating his famous series of paintings of the cathedral's façade. In 1910, a young boy joined the choir by the name of Maurice Duruflé.

Above the organ pipes can be seen the great west rose. The splendour of its intricate, flamboyant traceries is almost indescribable. The early 16th century glass has been destroyed, but Canon Perkins, writing in 1935 described it thus: *"God the Father surrounded by the hosts of heaven. The effect*

Looking West from the High Altar

77

A Glimpse Of Glory

of these innumerable circles of cherubim and seraphim upon a ground of blue or gold is perfectly overwhelming."

To the south of it, in the nave, there are four lancets with three quatrefoils in the tracery. The clerestory glazing on both sides of the nave is temporary following damage in the Second World War. To the north side of the clerestory in Bay 1 there are five trefoils and a quatrefoil. Bay 2 has two quatrefoils and a multifoil at the top, repeated in the easternmost four bays on the north side.

Interior Surface of the West Door

The clutter that filled the recess of the central doorway on my first visit in 1999 has now been cleared away and the great west door can be inspected closely. The door itself is covered with little wooden fleurs-de-lys, and possibly the original metal furniture. This was once the exterior surface of the door, which was turned inside out at the time of the Revolution to hide the little wooden symbols of royalty. The door is painted in a shade of red. During a visit in 2003 I was inspecting the door with my small torch when I heard a tour party nearby being addressed by their French guide in English. I moved to the fringe as she spoke about the grandeur of the nave, and I waited for her to turn and relate the history of the great doors. But no, she led the tourists away into the nave; it appears that the history of the reversal of the doors has been forgotten.

Standing at the west end facing east, the immediate impression is one of great height, due in part to its four levels: arcade, tribune, triforium and clerestory. But in fact it is a modest 28 metres (90 feet). The clear glass in the windows permits ample light, but as the piers of the nave arcade are so massive, little can be seen of the aisles, and this makes the nave, although 11 metres wide, appear rather narrow.

Above the tribune arch is a very low arched triforium with a balustrade and above that the clerestory. The impression of great height is because the five engaged pillars around the nave piers soar to the vault from the capitals of the nave arcades, and the ribs of the vault spring from them. The respond columns

The Nave

each have a capital with an abacus, from which spring the archivolts of the nave arcade.

An unadorned string course runs above the eleven bays of the nave arcade, above which in each bay there is a large open tribune arch. Above the tribune arches there is a frieze of small trefoils, above which is a balustrade pierced by eight small arches in front of the triforium passage. Above the passage is a shallow arch in each bay, which acts as a relieving arch supporting the clerestory. A foliated string course runs below the clerestory windows. In each bay of the clerestory there are four lancets with two large quatrefoils in the tracery and a third above them, the upper half of which is blind. This is repeated throughout the nave.

The nave was, for the most part, reglazed during the second half of the 15th century by Guillaume Barbe, the cathedral's master glazer from 1459 to 1485. He was ordered to fill the windows with white glass adorned with coloured borders and centre-pieces in each panel. Several have since received figures of saints with a tapestried background.

In the northeastern bay of the nave stands the modern wrought iron pulpit. It was made in 1959 by one of the most renowned French metalworkers of the Art Deco period, the master iron worker Raymonde Subes, and is of massive proportions with two staircases leading up to the five foot high base.

A Glimpse Of Glory

THE SOUTH AISLE (FROM WEST TO EAST)

The aisle vault is level with the top of the false tribunes. The chapels in both the south and north aisles are shallow, as they were formed between the buttresses in the 14th century. All are enclosed with a low wrought iron screen, each with a slightly different design, and with the exception of the Chapel of St Stephen under the Butter Tower, all the chapels have a quadripartite vault.

In the 13th century, the interior of the cathedral would have resembled that at Chartres; the side aisles had tall coloured lancets, singly or in pairs, while the lower walls were decorated with blind arcading. There are a few remnants of this former glory, but a great portion of this wealth of art has been destroyed.

During the 14th century the ancient Duchy of Normandy grew in wealth and influence. The number of clergy connected with the cathedral was augmented and various guilds and confraternities demanded special chapels for their own festivals. This led to the side walls being knocked down and most of the glass was lost. What remains is in the north aisle in the Chapel of St Sever. The buttresses were extended and the eighteen chapels of the nave were constructed between them. A quadripartite vault was added at the same height as the aisles. It only remained to add altars and piscinas. The upper section of the external wall of each Chapel was filled with a lofty pointed window with elaborate traceries.

A Bay of the Nave from the South Aisle

The south aisle has many engaged columns surrounding the nave pillars, which each rise to a decorated capital and an abacus which supports the springing of the arches forming the arcade. This abacus extends into the aisle like a sort of platform, as if there was to be a tribune chamber, and supports a semi-circular group of a particularly beautiful cluster of detached shafts, five in each, decorated with anulets rising to a capital which supports the ribs springing across the aisle vault and the tribune arch itself. The sculpture of the capitals is quite superb, in particular the groups of heads on the first, second and fourth pillars from the west in the south aisle. The effect of this long succession of groups is probably unique and is extremely pleasing to the eye.

Equally striking is the 13th century tracery above the western doorways of the aisles which continues at the false tribune stage. It consists of a pair of lancets with richly moulded arches resting upon groups of columns, while the large tympanum above is pierced with a wheel shaped rose. Beneath the arches is a balustrade.

The Chapel of St Étienne la Grande Eglise. The first bay leads through to this small flamboyant gothic chapel which projects along the south side of the wall on the ground floor of the Butter Tower. Before the Revolution this chapel was the parish church for folk who lived in the cathedral precincts, but since the Concordat of 1801, when a parish was assigned to the cathedral, it has been an ordinary chapel.

Against the south wall there is an altar with a fine carved reredos of the Crucifixion enclosed in a round arch with elaborate floriated moulding, below which is a carving of the stoning of Stephen, and the front of the altar bears a carving of the Last Supper. Either side of the altar is a 17th century white marble statue: to the east, facing south, is the kneeling figure of Claude Groullard, former President of the Parliament of Normandy who died in 1607, and to the west the recumbent figure of his spouse Barbe Guiffard, who died in 1599. The tombs were destroyed by the Revolutionaries, but the effigies were returned here in 1864.

The early 16th century glass is different from the other glass in the cathedral, the vivid colouring and the coarseness of the construction indicates a Germanic influence. There are two windows on the east wall, each with four lancets in two levels. The left-hand upper pair depicts creation and St Peter walking on the water. The lower left-hand pair depicts St Peter with keys and St Andrew with his diagonal cross. The right-hand upper pair depicts God in Majesty and the disciples witnessing the Ascension. In this scene the six kneeling figures of the donors point to the period of Louis Xll. The right-hand lower pair depicts St James as a pilgrim on the left and St John the Evangelist with the chalice and serpent on the right. Above the altar are two further lancets with a depiction of St Thomas pointing to Jesus' wounds.

A Glimpse Of Glory

Bay 2 also leads to this chapel but contains the bookshop.

The Chapel of St Eustace in the next bay has an 18th century picture of the Last Supper on the west wall. Above the altar against the east wall stands a late 17th century statue of an abbot, St Herbland, in polychrome wood which has been brought here from the church dedicated to that saint in Rouen which was demolished in 1824. The window has three lancets in temporary glass and without tracery; a 4th lancet is blind.

The Chapel of St Leonard has an 18th century marble statue of St Anthony from the hospital of St Beaucaire in the Departement of Garde in the south of France. The window has four lancets. The glass is by the master glazier Max Ingrand (1956) a gift of the Caisse Nationale de Congres. The subjects are the entry to the Promised Land, the earthly paradise, Joshua stopping the sun and the Flood. There was evidence of fire damage in the southwest corner in 2003 but this has mellowed by 2012.

The Chapel St Peter. A 16th century picture of the Scourging of Christ adorns the west wall; the décor was a gift of the Federation de Batiment Culture group. Above the altar on the east wall is a work by the sculptor Lagriffoul (1955) of the Virgin holding the infant Jesus and welcoming the offer of the restored cathedral, glittering like a jewel, presented by two craftsmen. There are three lancets in the south wall, the glass is by Max Ingrand and dates from 1955 and is dedicated to the building trades. The scenes depict the Ascension; the feast of bricklayers, accompanied by St Joseph, patron saint of carpenters; and St Eloi, the patron of metalworkers. There is a piscina in the south wall. In 2013 a model of the cathedral had been placed on a table in the centre of the chapel.

The Chapel of St Columbe (sometimes called The Holy Innocents chapel). There are four lancets in the window in the south wall, all in modern glass by Max Ingrand, dated 1956, depicting the growing of corn and related parables. The chapel is now consecrated to the aim of obtaining from the farmers of the diocese sufficient corn to bake the bread for the Sacrament.

The pictures have as their subjects the Holy Family and the mystical marriage of St Catharine. They are 17th century works by Terano. Beneath them are two angels carrying bread and hosts in a ciborium, symbolising wheat becoming the life and body of Christ.

The Chapel of St Catherine. Again there are four lancets in the south wall, with modern glass in the lower registers. The glass in the upper registers is 15th century by William Barbe, 1465–1470, and depicts the Virgin Mary with the infant Christ, St Simon presenting a donor, St Nicholas and St Catherine. It was restored in the 19th century and again in 1960.

There are 17th century wooden panels around the south and west walls representing the life of St Brice, a 15th century Bishop of Tours. The coats of arms on the pillars separating the paintings are those of members of the Brice family, several of whom were canons of the cathedral. The painting of the Scourging of Christ on the reredos panel is from the 16th century Italian school. The altar frontal is embroidered in silver and gold and is 17th century.

This is the only Chapel on the south side to survive the bombing of the 19th April 1944. If the flying buttresses at this point had been destroyed the entire nave and transept would have collapsed.

The Masons' Door. Canon Jocelyn Perkins reports that the ancient door which led to the masons' lodgings had long been bricked up and a chapel constructed in the space. Following the destruction of 1944, the Masons' Door has been reinstated. It was also known as the door of St Simeon because of the tympanum depicting the Presentation of Christ to Simeon in the Temple, which is now placed in the north Chapel of St Julian. Today, the tympanum of the door is blank. Two fluted columns in Carrera marble, a remnant of the rood screen built by Courure in 1777, frame the doorway without bearing a pediment.

On the original rood screen six such columns defined three openings, in which the Chapel of St Cecilia was to the left, the entrance to the Choir in the centre, and the Chapel of Our Lady of the Vow on the right. The rood was dismantled in 1884, and the other four columns and a part of the entablature are kept in the Salle De Jubé in the Museum of Fine Arts in Rouen.

There are four lancets in temporary glass with three quatrefoils in the tracery. The doorway often accommodates an exhibition of photographs of the cathedral after the bombardment of 1944. One of them shows how the south side was destroyed apart from two flying buttresses flanking the one surviving Chapel of St Catherine.

The Chapel of St Margaret (also called the Chapel of the Vow). The window depicting the Life of St Veronica and a huge monument to Cardinal Leon Thomas, Archbishop of Rouen from 1883–1894, which once stood in this chapel, were destroyed by the bombing in 1944. Set into the floor is the tomb slab of Cardinal Thomas, all that remains of his monument. There is a piscina in the south wall. The present altar is dedicated to Our Lady of the Vow.

The original altar dated from the early 14th century, when Canon François Le Tourneur presented an alabaster statue of the Virgin Mary, which was set on the rood screen in 1357. A few years he later bestowed an endowment on condition that every Saturday, and on the Eves of great festivals, a beautiful chant known as the *'Inviolata'* would be sung before this altar, which was then on the south side of the rood screen. The name of the altar commemorates a vow made by

A Glimpse Of Glory

The Altar of the Vow

the inhabitants of Rouen to avert the plague. In 1637 the city presented a costly silver lamp to the cathedral; it was to burn day and night before this altar. Sadly, the altar and statue were removed by the 'restorers' and Revolutionaries in the 18th century and were lost.

The local sculptor Lecomte was commissioned to design a new altar in 1778. An entombment in bas relief is carved on the front of the altar. I find it remarkable that when Canon Perkins wrote in 1935, he was able to say, *"The Chapter reverently maintains the customs of their ancestors. A lamp still burns before the Altar of the Vow, and every Saturday afternoon, and on the eves of festivals, immediately after Vespers, Chapter and Choir as of old take their station in front of the Altar, and solemnly chant the beautiful melody of the Inviolata"* [see the words of the "Inviolata" at the end of this chapter]. This lamp was re-established in 1994 as a memorial to the fact that the cathedral had been miraculously saved from total destruction in the 1944 bombing. In 2013 the lamp was a candle burning in a wrought iron stand before the altar.

The picture of the Holy Family on the west wall is late 17th century/early 18th century. The window of four lancets of temporary glass has two trefoils supporting a multifoil in the tracery.

The Chapel of St Romain the Less. The Altar, which was rediscovered during the excavation of the chancel after the war, incorporates a Renaissance bas relief dating to the 16th century. There is a piscina in the south wall. The two 16th century pictures are of scenes from the life of St Romain, Bishop of Rouen, which was the subject of the original 15th century glass in the window lancets. The four lancets are now glazed in temporary glass with three trefoils in the tracery.

Sens, apse clerestory window, centre quatrefoil

Sens, God banishes Adam & Eve, detail from the Good Samaritan window

Sens, the martyrdom of St Thomas Becket

Sens, Paradise, detail from the North Rose

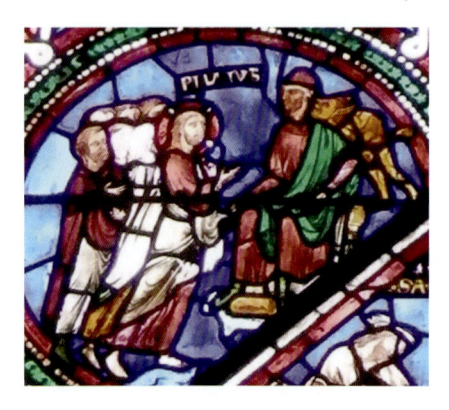

Sens, Christ before Pilate, detail from the Good Samaritan window

Sens, the Good Samaritan takes the injured man to a hostel

Laon, West Towers from the East

Laon, West Rose

Laon, East Rose, detail

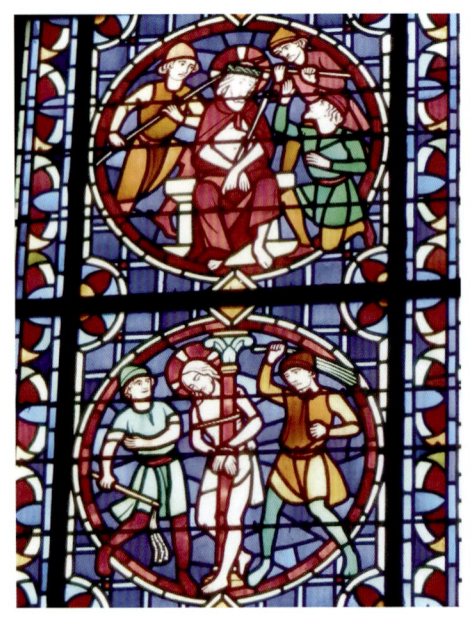

Laon, the mockery and scourging of Christ, east chapel window

Laon, Philosophy surrounded by the Liberal Arts, detail from the North Rose

Rouen, the West Façade

Rouen, Passion sequence, Chapel of St Sever, lower window

Rouen, St Etienne Chapel east wall

Rouen, Panegyric of St Romain, window east of south transept door

Rouen, Axial Chapel of Our Lady

This is the final bay of the south aisle which turns here to form the west aisle of the south transept.

THE CROSSING

The mediaeval rood screen was destroyed during the religious wars and eventually replaced in 1777 by a classical gallery borne on six fluted columns of the Ionic order. These columns defined three openings, in which the Chapel of St Cecilia was to the left, the entrance to the Choir in the centre, and the Chapel of Our Lady of the Vow on the right. Two of the columns now frame the Mason's Door (as we have seen). I have a picture of this rood with a large crucifix standing in the middle of the loft, the arms of the cross as high as the triforium. The rood was dismantled in 1884, and the other four columns and a part of the entablature are kept in the *Salle De Jubé* in the Museum of Fine Arts in Rouen.

The open space in the centre of the crossing is not quite square due to the fact that the entrance to the choir is wider than the nave. But one's attention is immediately seized by the dozens of slender columns which cluster around the four massive piers, and which rise without a break to the lofty capitals. In each corner is a single shaft which soars upwards to support four of the ribs of the octopartite vault of the Lantern Tower, fifty-one metres above the ground. The other four ribs spring from engaged columns which each rest on a corbel carved in the image of a head.

The stage above the four great arches is a fine blind triforium. Above a moulded stringcourse, underscored by a frieze of little pierced trefoils, there are three large pillars each with three engaged columns, and that in the centre supports a pointed arch, thus creating an arcade of four arches each side of the tower. Each arch is subdivided into two trefoil-headed arches by a slender shaft decorated by a large anulet. The second stage is even more beautiful, perhaps because it is well lit. Above a row of quatrefoils is a delightful parapet, which supports an arcade of four pointed arches, decorated with rich mouldings and resting on groups of clustered collonettes. Behind a passage are four great 15th century windows, each subdivided by a mullion, and the tracery in some take the form of a fleurs-de-lys. The lantern really is a most glorious gem of 13th century architecture, which the builders of the 15th century worked to enhance.

The nave altar below the tower appears to be a cube of stone and is raised on a platform. The altar is covered in a cloth of gold made from the cope worn at the Coronation of Charles X in 1824. A communion rail encloses the area to the north, west and south. The Lectern in wrought iron is 14th century. The Clergy seats around the Altar were made by Raymond Subes in 1956. Against the massive column in the southeast corner of the crossing is a throne, behind which is a tapestry.

A Glimpse Of Glory

The Nave Altar and South Choir

THE TRANSEPTS

Each transept consists of three bays of unequal size with side aisles to east and west. A large chapel of two bays with a three-sided apse lighted by tall lancets opens eastwards from each of the central bays. The inner bay on either side links the nave aisle with the ambulatory. Unlike the nave, there are no false tribunes in the transepts, and this gives a striking impression of great height. This impression is enhanced by the fact that the shafts supporting the high vault of the transepts soar from the floor unbroken until a capital is reached about half the height of the clerestory. Above the piers with their richly moulded arches runs a row of trefoils, surmounted by the triforium of pointed arches, the number varying with the breadth of each bay. The clerestory reveals evidence of 15th century remodelling, for alongside the 13th century big lancets with their plain oculi are windows with quatrefoils and multifoils of the later Flamboyant gothic period. As in the nave, all the clerestory windows contain temporary glass.

The South Transept

The wall of the west aisle is divided into two bays which have a charming arcade of pointed arches resting upon single columns with foliated capitals adorning the greater part of the dado. There are two arches above the stringcourse and two lancet windows above those, one in each bay. The bays are divided by a pillar with five engaged columns, as in the nave.

Above the string course, the wall of the north bay is blind, but to the south of a delicate column which supports the vault, is a single lancet containing 14th century panels brought here in 1956 from the Chapel of St Jeanne d'Arc (called the chapel of the Holy Spirit prior to1914).

In the south bay of the west aisle there is a single lancet in the west wall containing two late 16th century panels depicting the life of John the Baptist, which were brought here from the church of St Laurence in Rouen.

In the south wall of the aisle, above the blind arcade, are two lancets, both in mid-15th century coloured glass depicting the Massacre of the Infants by Herod, the Virgin and Child and the Flight into Egypt.

The west wall of the transept has an arcade of three high arches. The northern one is narrow, covering the south aisle. The centre arch is wider, supported on piers which have engaged columns which soar through the triforium and half-way up the clerestory to capitals from which spring the ribs of the quadripartite vault of the transept. Above the three high arches there is a blind arcade protecting a passage giving access to the triforium of the nave. Above this arcade are the four lights over the North Bay with quatrefoil tracery, and above the other two arches are two windows with an oriole in the spandrel. All have temporary glazing. Below the blind arcading is a fine row of tiny pierced trefoils.

The south wall of the transept has two blind arches either side, each with a quatrefoil head. The right hand arch on the west (right) side has a doorway. Above these blind arches are four sculpted statues, two each side, with the inner pair lacking their heads, above them are four glorious crocketed gables with quatrefoil tracery. Between the gables are five carved statues beneath a richly moulded canopy.

A band of foliage separates the lower stage from the splendid openwork triforium. There are six clear lancet windows, each subdivided by a slender mullion, all in temporary glass so that the decorated gable over the portal can be seen through them. Above and below these lancets runs a gallery of open-work quatrefoils.

Above the triforium is the rose window dating from c.1280. It is really a wheel window, for it uses the double-lancet window with a quatrefoil tracery as a building block, and inverts this motif alternately as they radiate like spokes of a wheel from a central multifoil. The concept can be seen to greater effect in the north rose (c.1270) at Sées Cathedral, and it signals the end of the Rayonnant period of

A Glimpse Of Glory

French glass. Sadly, the ancient glass of this window has been lost and has been replaced with temporary glazing.

Flanking the South Door to the east (left) is a three lancet window in beautiful colour and tracery depicting, in seven scenes, the cardinal and theological virtues exhibited in the life of St Romain. Note how with Fortitude he casts out demons, and how he resists with Temperance the temptation of a woman acting at the behest of a demon.

The East Wall of the transept is a mirror of the west wall; the north arch is over the entrance to the south ambulatory, the central one has a wider span.

The east wall of the east aisle.

The Chapel of St Joseph is in the southeast corner of the transept. Above the blind arcade on the south wall, there is a three lancet window and tracery which depict the miracles in the life of St Romain (Romanus).

The Miracle of the holy oil of Chrism (Sainte Ampoule) can be seen: the legend relates how Romanus was preparing to consecrate some baptismal fonts but found he had forgotten the holy chrism. The deacon he sent to look for it was in such a rush to return that he dropped and broke the vase containing the chrism, which leaked out onto the earth. Praying all the while, Romanus gathered up the pieces of the vase, which then put itself and its contents back together. Other miracles depicted are his destruction of the pagan temple, and his miraculous intervention when the Seine threatened to inundate Rouen. The most dramatic is the Miracle of the Dragon (or Gargoyle). On the left bank of the Seine were wild swamps through which rampaged a huge serpent or dragon that "devoured and destroyed people and beasts of the field". Romanus decided to rid the people of this menace, but could only find one man to help him, a man condemned to death. They arrived in the serpent's land and Romanus drew the sign of the cross on the beast. It then lay down at his feet and let Romanus put his stole on him as a leash, in which manner he led it into the town to be burned on the parvis of the cathedral. This legend was the most likely origin for the bishops' privilege (lasting

The Bound Christ

until 1790) to pardon one prisoner condemned to death each year, by giving the pardoned man or woman the reliquary holding Romanus's relics in a procession.

Below the east window is a modern Altar with a statue of St Joseph and an elaborate piscina with two arches rising to about 5 feet to the right of the Altar.

On the south wall in the blind arcading is the statue of a seated and bound Christ (Ecce Homo) on a plinth and column.

The Chapel of St Joan of Arc is to the east of the central bay of the transept. A statue of her tied to the stake as the flames curl upwards, by Saupiqué dated 1956, stands on the Altar. Her motto together with a cross and a sword were fashioned by the master ironworker Raymond Subes in 1956 and decorates the front of the Altar. There is blind arcading around the lower walls of this Chapel, except for the south side when the arches are open and contain two tombs. One is an effigy of Monsignor Fuzet, Archbishop of Rouen 1899–1915, by Gauquie, 1918. Above these are two modern glazed windows and the east window is also modern. The windows depict the life of St Joan and are another work of Max Ingrand, 1956, the gift of the city of Rouen. To the south of the Altar above the piscina is another modern window with dramatic scenes. Above the blind arcading on the north side of the Chapel are arches giving light from the choir.

The chapel is enclosed by a fine gilded wrought-iron screen.

The Chapel of St Joan of Arc

A Glimpse Of Glory

THE CHOIR

There is a very heavy feel to the choir due in part to the massive unencumbered columns, with their simply decorated capitals, and arches springing east and west from the abacus. But then the slender columns ascend from the abacus through the triforium and straight up past the Clerestory windows into the high quadripartite vault. The choir is enclosed by a 4 foot-high wrought iron screen. The Archbishop's throne was constructed by Raymond Subes in 1956, and had an Aubusson tapestry depicting Aaron the High Priest (missing in 2012 and 2013).

There is an inscription at the foot of the sanctuary steps recording the fact that Charles V, King of France and Duke of Normandy, left his heart to be preserved in this cathedral when he died in 1380. His mausoleum was removed from the choir in 1736. The lead box containing his heart is kept in the crypt.

The Organ of Albert Dupré was given by his son, the organist and composer Marcel Dupré, 1886 to 1971. The Canons' stalls of 1457–1470 are by Philippot Viart, and Flemish Carvers. The misericords are carved to represent biblical subjects, fables, craftsmen, scenes of daily life and grotesques.

THE APSE

The crucifix behind the altar is echoed in the east window high in the clerestory above. The glass is circa 1470 by Etienne Guiot and Guillaume de Gronville, from a design by Lionet de Montigny, but the windows either side of it depicting the Virgin Mary and St John are in 19th century glass. The remainder of the clerestory windows contain temporary glazing. Below them is the blind arcading and passage of the triforium below which is a foliated string course, which, in turn, is borne by the fine pointed arcade. The capital of each arch of the arcade has on it a carved face.

THE HIGH ALTAR

The altar has a top of green Aosta marble, resting on four columns bearing the symbols of the four Evangelists in gilded lead by Bizette-Lindet. Each side is a

High Altar

sculpted angel in bronze by the sculptor Caffierei. They came from the church of St Vincent in Rouen when it was destroyed. The huge 18 foot crucifix is by the sculptor Clodion, and was placed on the choir screen in 1788. It is flanked by six candles. Either side of the steps descending to the choir are two large bronze incense burners.

THE SOUTH AMBULATORY

In the blind arcading around the wall of the Ambulatory are placed casts of the statues on the west façade of the cathedral.

The 1st and 2nd Bays are formed by the open arches screening The Chapel of Joan of Arc.

The first tomb in the ambulatory is that of Rollo, first Duke of Normandy, whose inscription can be translated: "at the heart of this temple reposes Rollo, who died enfeebled by toil, at over 80, in the year 933." The late 13th century effigy of him, which used to be in the Chapel of Petite St Romain, was destroyed in 1944. It has been replaced by this 19th century copy of the effigy of Henry le Jeune, 1867. The other tomb of note is the late 13th century tomb containing the heart of Richard the Lionheart, Duke of Normandy, King of England, who died 1199, and is buried

The South Ambulatory

A Glimpse Of Glory

at Fontevrault. The lead box which contains his heart is kept in the cathedral treasury.

The 3rd Bay contains a large painting above the blind arcading. It depicts Christ at the well with the Samaritan woman.

The 4th Bay has two arches giving light to a balcony and a chamber beyond it. There is a round window below the balcony with clear glazing.

The Chapel of St Bartholomew (Southeast Radiating Chapel) is empty. It is enclosed by a fine stone screen decorated with blind tracery at the lower level and with four slender lancets above, with trefoils and quatrefoils in the tracery. The four sections are separated by slender fluted columns and to the west of them is a fine decorated doorway.

There is blind arcading on the west and south walls of the chapel, and a doorway in the east wall. There are blind lancets in the east and west walls above the arcading but the three windows on the south wall contained fragments of coloured glass, a lovely blue colour in the southeast lancet.

The 6th and 7th Bays have lancet windows above the blind arcading. Each has 3 blind arches in the lower arcading and above is a single lancet in coloured glass.

The Axial Chapel of Our Lady The present Chapel was built in 1302 in the Rayonnant Gothic style, but the Baroque altar and reredos, carved in gilded wood by Jean Racine in 1643, which rises to the tracery in the east window and hides the window itself, dominates and overpowers the elegance of this Chapel. The painting of 'The Adoration of the Shepherds' on the reredos is by Philippe de Champaigne (1629). The East wall of the Chapel has glass dated 1470 from the Church of St Vincent de Rouen, which was destroyed in 1944. In the north and south windows early 14th century glass depicts the Saint Bishops of Rouen set in a grisaille background. There are two lancets in each of the three bays, with quatrefoils and multifoils in the tracery and with coloured glass in two panels.

On the south side of the Chapel is the tomb of George I d'Amboise, who died in 1510, and his nephew George II d'Amboise, who died in 1550. They were sculpted in marble (1516–1525) under the direction of Roulande le Roux and Pierre des Aubeau. George l was a friend of the Duke of Guordin—the future King Louis Xll—and was governor of Normandy amongst other titles. He was the most prestigious of the Archbishops of Rouen.

The two Cardinals can be seen on their knees, *"supported by their virtues and the prayers of their mourners (below), strengthened by a the intercessions of all their patron saints (on the slab behind), an assertion that they have kept intact the faith as announced by the Prophets, proclaimed by the Apostles, and proven by the Martyrs at a cost of their lives (in the baldachino), like Jesus before Pilate they go humbly to submit to the judgment of God (at the Apex)"*, as described by Jean de Bailly, 1959.

On the north side of the chapel is the tomb of Cardinal Prince de Croy, Archbishop 1824–1844, by the sculptor Fulconis (1856). The tomb of Louis de Brèzé, (died 1531), the grandson of Pierre de Brèzé (see below), but erected by his widow Diana de Poitier, is probably the work of Jean Goujon in the mid-16th century. Across the cadaver of the deceased is inscribed, "Diana pleads with the Virgin". On the upper stage there are four caryatids representing victory, faith, prudence and glory, forming the frame of the equestrian statue. In a niche at the apex is a female figure symbolising the four Cardinal virtues—strength, justice, temperance and prudence.

In the walls of the chapel are plaques commemorating the Archbishops of Rouen. There is a tomb niche of Pierre De Brézè, died 1465, and his wife Jeanne de Bec-Crespin, and a kneeling effigy of Cardinal de Bonnechose, who died in 1883, sculpted by Chapu in 1891. The west bay of the chapel has four blind lancets to the north and south. The chapel is closed by a head height wrought iron screen which is painted in black and gold.

THE NORTH AMBULATORY

The blind arcading continues all along the ambulatory at the lower level. In each bay there are three arches with a single coloured lancet window above.

Bays 1 and 2 are divided vertically by a slender column supporting a vault rib. To the right there is a tomb behind the arches with a line of 'weepers' at the base, which are very badly damaged. It is the tomb of Bishop Hugh of Amiens, a 12th century Bishop

Tomb of St Hugh of Amiens

A Glimpse Of Glory

of Rouen. He is carved wearing a mitre, and with angels in the archivolt above. This tomb is older than the present building, having been transferred from the earlier Romanesque cathedral.

In the lancet above, set in quatrefoils alternating with circles, are scenes from the life of the patriarch Joseph. He can be seen in prison in Egypt at the top. An inscription can be seen in the glass announcing that it was made by Clement, a glazier from Chartres (1228–1230). The window reads from top-to-bottom, unlike the St Julian window. To the left, in the lancet above the three blind arches the story continues with the scenes from the life of Joseph, with his explanation of Pharaoh's dreams and his recognition of his father, Jacob, in seven medallions. The window was a gift of the tailors and drapers; they can be seen with their scissors and other tools.

On the floor at the base of the ambulatory pier is an inscription to the memory of Jehan Titelonze, father of organ music in France, and organist of the cathedral from 1588 to 1633. There is also an inscription marking the burial of John, Duke of Bedford, who died in Rouen in 1435. He was Regent of France and Governor of Rouen at the time of the trial of Joan of Arc.

The Chapel of St Peter and St Paul has a semicircle of seven bays. The east and west walls are blind, but a piscina is set in the east wall. The three western bays have blind arcading at the lower level, as in the first bay, with plain capitals and an octagonal abacus. In each bay a slender column rises to support the vault. The north and northeastern windows have temporary glass. The east window has modern coloured glass which contains fragments of glass from 1200 depicting the Twelve Sleepers of Ephesus. These seven martyrs were walled up in a cave in the 3rd century AD, and lay asleep miraculously for two centuries. The northwestern and western windows are filled with grisaille glass.

Beneath the "sleepers" window is an inscription commemorating the transfer of the bones of the Empress Matilda, rediscovered at the Abbey of Bec in 1846, and placed here in 1871. Matilda or Maud was the daughter of Henry I, King of England and Duke of Normandy, the wife of the Emperor Henry V of Germany, and the mother of Henry II, King of England, Duke of Normandy and father of Richard the Lionheart. The inscription can be translated thus: "Great by birth, greater by marriage, still greater by her children, here lies the mother of the Henrys: Matilda."

The Altar is missing, but there is a fine carved wooden altarpiece. The reredos is a painting of Simon of Cyrene, which is flanked by ornately carved columns.

Bay 4. The window of St Julian Hospitaller. The window above the doorway to the west of the above chapel is the window of St Julian the Hospitaller, who is said to have killed his parents accidentally and spent the rest of his life in penance, helping travellers and the sick. "The Legend of Saint Julian the Hospitalier", which Flaubert published in 1877 in the volume Trois Contes, describes how Saint Julian went hunting in a forest when a deer sprang out of the thicket and a badger crawled out of its hole, a stag appeared in the road, and a peacock spread its fan-shaped tail. He is later troubled by the spirits of all of the animals. That story was inspired by the window now before you. The window is a mosaic of predominantly red and blue colours, and should be read like a cartoon strip in a modern newspaper, except that it is read from the bottom to the top. So we begin to read it at the bottom left-hand side, where the lower three pictures show the Fishmongers of Rouen at work; they were the donors' of the window.

There follow scenes from the life of St Julian, but during restoration work the 3rd scene from the bottom on the left-hand side has been interchanged with the 6th scene from the bottom on the left-hand side.

So above the bottom three scenes of fishmongers, numbers 4, 5 and 6, depict Julian's childhood, when he was told that he would kill his father and mother.

The next scene is the 6th up on the left where he leaves his house to avoid his wicked destiny and joins his master, and then we come back to the middle and right scenes in the third register, which tell of him waiting on his master at table and taking care of him in his ill-health.

The 4th register up shows Julian assisting at his master's death, his marriage to the master's widow, and going off to war.

At the 5th level Julian is asleep in his tent, his parents search for him, and Julian's wife welcomes them to his house allowing them to sleep in her bed.

At the 6th level we have to return first to the 3rd scene from the bottom on the left-hand side, where we see Julian returning home by night, then, returning to the centre of the 6th level, Julian believes his wife is committing adultery in their bed and mistakenly kills his parents, in the right hand panel his wife tells him the truth.

In the 7th level Julian and his wife leave the house to do penance, in the centre he founds a hospital by the river, and on the right he becomes a ferryman. At the 8th level he is summoned at night to the other side of the river, first by Christ and then by the devil, who tries to make them break their vow of continence. He and his wife resist the devil's advances and die a holy death.

At the very top of the window can be seen Angels taking their souls to Christ who sits in Majesty. It is a very fine window. Saint Julian is patron of hunters and shepherds.

A Glimpse Of Glory

On the inner wall of the North Ambulatory, opposite the St Julian window is the 13th century tomb of Henry le Jeune, or Count Martel, the eldest son of King Henry II, and brother of Richard the Lionheart, who was crowned to ensure the succession to the throne of England, but who died before his father in 1183. His body was seized on the way to Rouen by the men of Le Mans, and was rediscovered in 1866.

Bay 5. The lower level blind arcading continues with a door in the middle arch; above are two blind arches rising to the vault.

Bay 6. Above the lower blind arcading are two open lancet arches. The 14th century tomb of William Longsword is on the inner side of the ambulatory here. William Longsword was the second Duke of Normandy, who died in 942. He was the son of Rollo, and established the frontiers of Normandy. He died a victim of treason. Until 1942 this tomb was in the North Aisle in the Chapel of St Anne, opposite the effigy of Rollo which stood in the south Chapel of St Petite Romain.

The east wall forms the chapel of the North Transept.

Bay 7. There is a wide open lancet above the blind arcading giving light to the chapel beyond.

THE NORTH TRANSEPT

The North Transept is similar to the South Transept in that it has aisles to the east and west, thus making it a broad area. In the south bay of the east wall is the small chapel of the Holy Sacrament.

The Chapel of the Holy Sacrament (originally named the Chapel of St John the Baptist by the Fonts, when it was the Baptistry). The blind arcading below the dado accommodates a 13th century piscina and, on the north side, two tomb recesses. One has an inscription to the memory of Cardinal de Bois, (Archbishop of Rouen 1916–1920), and the other to the memory of Mgr Andre Peiller, (Archbishop of Rouen 1968–81). The glass in the north windows was given by Azon le Tort, 1266, and the fragments recomposed by Max Ingrand in 1959. To the left, in the first window from the north, can be seen a female donor, then the baptism of Christ. And in the second window we see Saint John the evangelist writing the Apocalypse, with the seven cities of Asia in the background. The third window (on the right) depicts the Virgin and Child and the donor with his wife and members of the le Tort family presenting the window. In the east window are the symbols of the passion by Max Ingrand, 1959. The south wall is open to the north Ambulatory. The stone altar has a bas-relief of the last supper in its centre and on the reredos angels sculpted in white marble bear the tabernacle.

Rouen

The Chapel of Notre Dame de Pitié in the northeast corner of the transept has a stone altar with a 13th century double piscina to the south of it. A fine Pietà (1590) by Etienne Desplancher is carved as a reredos and has a pediment above. Above the Altar there are two open arches divided by a slender pillar and enclosing a passage which traverses the east end of the cathedral above the blind arcades. Behind the

Pietà, Chapel of Notre Dame de Pity

two open arches are two lancets with temporary glazing. Both bays of the transept are covered by a quadripartite vault.

The north wall of the transept mirrors the south wall of the south transept, with the exception of two lancets in temporary glazing above the doorway, as it has four crocketted canopies, the two centre doors, and, in niches above the two blind arches either side, are two carved statues. The westernmost arch has a doorway. Above the crocketted gables are ten small lancet windows behind a passage protected by a parapet. The temporary glazing permits the exterior gable to be seen clearly.

Above these lancets is a most wonderful rose window, the work of Guillaume Nouel at the end of the 14th century. In the centre of the window, which is actually a wheel window, in a medallion superimposed on six small roundels, each containing a fleurs-de-lys, is the image of the enthroned Christ. The mullions radiate like spokes from this central multifoil, and between them is a cusped lancet, sixteen in all, each containing a medallion; in the medallions of the lower segments are the symbols of the four evangelists, while in others are apostles, bishops, kings, martyrs, St Peter and St Paul and the coronation of the Virgin. These images spill over into the outer ring of thirty-two lancets, two to each lancet of the inner circle. Each pair of lancets terminates in a quatrefoil. It is an almost perfect ensemble;

A Glimpse Of Glory

The Bookseller's Staircase

a masterpiece of grisaille glazing.

The west and east walls of the transept also mirror those in the south transept.

The west aisle has a sublime stairway in the north corner, which gives access to the Library. It is regarded with awe all over the world. It is one of the legacies of the genius Guillaume Pontifs (1479). The two upper flights are, however, an 18th century addition, and lack the delicacy and grace of the earlier work.

A catalogue of books written in the 12th century shows its early existence. By the 15th century the collection had so increased that a building was built on the north side to accommodate it, and this staircase to give access to it. The first library was destroyed by the Huguenots and the second by the Revolutionaries. Only a few ancient volumes survive.

The northern bay of the west aisle has a partially bricked up and temporary glazed window, and one blind arch above the door which leads to the sacristy. The blind arcading continues across the remaining two bays of the west wall of this aisle. Above the arcading, in the central bay, is a single lancet with medallions in red and blue. In the next bay there is a painting of an allegorical scene titled, *"The Vow of Maria Leczinska, the wife of Louis XV, presenting the Dauphin, Louis, to the Virgin Mary."* It is from Natoire, 1700–1777. Here, again, there is a blind lancet above blind arcading as in the south transept.

THE NORTH AISLE

The architectural arrangements of the north aisle chapels reflect faithfully those in the south aisle.

Rouen

The Chapel of St Anne. There are four very tall lancets, with quatrefoils and trefoils in the tracery, with glass by Guillaume Barbe, 1465–1470. The lancets depict (left to right) St Clare, then a bishop accompanied by a donor, St Mary Magdalene, and finally St Ann teaching the Virgin. There is no altar but a statue of Christ exposing his Sacred Heart stands on a plinth. In the north wall is a double piscina carved in a niche with a trefoil in the gable. There is a painting on the west wall.

The Chapel of St Nicholas. The wrought-iron gate with gilded details—leaves, anchors and harpoons—was given by the Guild of Watermen in the 18th century and is thought to be the finest wrought-iron work in the cathedral. A large moulded arch fills the north wall, with the double piscina below decorated with trefoils in the tympanum. The four lancets in the window depict St Margaret, St Mary Magdalene holding her jar of ointment, St Nicholas, and the Virgin and Child. The glass is by Barbe, dated 1465–1470.

The chapel contains the Altar of St Cecilia with the seal of the saint's burial. The front of the altar is in white marble carved in bas relief. There is also a painting above the altar depicting the death of St Cecilia. A statue by Clodion (1777) was formerly in the left side of the choir screen, which was destroyed in 1884. The 17th century picture of the Virgin and Child on the west wall is from the Provençal School. In the west wall is an epitaph in 10th or 11th century lettering to Adolphus.

The Chapel of the Fonts. In this bay there is a doorway leading to the Sacristy, but on the east wall is an overpowering baroque altarpiece. The retable is in the Spanish style with 17th century gilded wood. It was given in 1937 from a disused church in Evaela in the north of Spain (compare with the domineering 17th century retable in the Axial Chapel). There are four lancets in temporary glass.

The Chapel of St Eloi. The glass in the window is by Barbe: there are four lancets with trefoils in the tracery above and they depict from the left, St Eloi, St Lawrence, St John the Baptist, and St Nicholas who is attached to St Romain and the monster which he tamed. The altar has been removed from the east end. The chapel has a 17th century picture, from the French 17th school, of "St Paul before Agrippa with his sister Berenice" (*Acts of the Apostles, chapter 25, verse 23*), and an 18th century copy of a work by a Ter Brugghen, 1588 to 1629, of St Irene releasing the dead St Sebastien. There is a double piscina in the north wall in a niche which has a trefoil in its gable. This chapel, and the remainder of the chapels in the north aisle, are enclosed by low wrought-iron screens.

The Chapel of St Julian. There are four lancets in the window, with two quatrefoils and a multifoil in the tracery. The glass is by Barbe, and depicts St Michael on the left then St Julian, St William and St Genevieve. The tympanum from the former

A Glimpse Of Glory

door of the masons, also known as St Simeon's door is displayed in this chapel. The damaged 13th century carving depicts the Presentation of Christ in the Temple (St Luke, chapter 2, verse 25). There is a picture of the Crucifixion on the east wall by Michael de Joncquoy (1588).

Beneath an 18th century painting of the Annunciation, a confessional occupies a recess in the east wall. This is found in all the chapels in this aisle.

The Chapel of St Sever. The glass in the four tall lancets, which consist of medallions in the richest reds and blues, is from the former aisle windows, re-used and supplemented by 1275 in the windows of the aisle chapels, thereafter known as the **Belle Verrieres**, and completed by the atelier of Guillaume Barbe in 1468–69. On the left are depicted the legends of St Nicholas 1200 to 1210 and 1220 to 1230, then St Sever Bishop of Ravenna, St Sever Bishop of Avranches, and St Catharine 1220–30. In the borders there are flowers and towns of Castile, a reference to St Louis and his mother Blanche de Castile. In the lower register there are four scenes of the passion and a lovely floral display in the most realistic manner, 1468–69.

In 1724 this chapel was decorated in honour of the Association of the Sacred Heart. Queen Marie Leczinska, consort of Louis XV, became a member and masses were offered here for her happy delivery of a son. Her prayers were answered and she commemorated the event by a generous bequest to the cathedral.

In the north wall is the usual twin piscina with a trefoil in the gable. There is no altar; instead there is a model of the cathedral and parts of the arches and vaulting in wood for the visually impaired. There are two paintings in the Chapel: on the west wall Christ with the little children, and on the east wall the Holy Family.

The Chapel of John of the Nave (also known as the Chapel of Our Lady of Lourdes). The four lancets are in my view the very best examples of the "Belle Verrieres", depicting from the left the life of St John the Baptist, 1200–10; Legends of St Catharine, St Nicholas and St Stephen, 1220–30; a female donor presenting the window, 1270, with vignettes representing the corporations which gave the windows: groups of late 15th century carpenters, church builders, and tanners at work. In the lower supplementary register can be seen the beheading of John the Baptist, the women at the tomb, the meal at the House of Simon, and the "Noli me tangere", "Do not cling to me", (*St John, chapter 20, verse 17*) by Guillaume Barbe, 1468–69. There is the usual double piscina in the north wall, which was used for candle storage in 2012. The statue on the altar is of the Virgin Mary with her hands in the attitude of prayer. The statue of Notre-Dame de Lourdes by the sculptor Gauquié was given by Monsignor Fuzet, 1900.

The Chapel of St Agatha. The glass in the four lancets is by Barbe, and depicts, on the left, St Victor, the Virgin and Child, St Agatha and then St Sebastian. The lancet depicting St Agatha is brutal in showing her hands tied above her head while her captor grips her right breast in a pincers. The martyrdom of St Sebastian on the right is just as brutal, with arrows piercing him.

On a bracket above the altar, on the east wall, there is a late 16th century statue of St Nicaise, which is the only remnant of the Church of St Herbland in Rouen, always visited by the Archbishops of Rouen on the way to their enthronement. The church was demolished in 1824. St Nicaise was appointed to evangelize the region and was martyred on the road to Rouen. There is the usual twin piscina with a gable.

The Chapel of St Mellon. Dedicated to the first Bishop of Rouen, it is no longer used as a chapel, but as a small office (accueil). The four lancets have temporary glazing with three trefoils in the tracery. There is a large crucifix on the east wall.

The Baptistry. The last bay in the North Aisle leads to a chapel, beyond which is the lower room in the tower of St Romain. The wrought-iron door is beneath a cusped tympanum above which is a large open arch giving some light to the Baptistry. The closed wrought-iron screen is by the master iron worker Ferdinand Marrou (1900). Inside, on the west wall, are 14th century statues of Adam and Eve, removed in 1911 from the west wall of the nave, where they were hidden by organ pipes. On the right is a statue of the Virgin and Child from the hospital at Beaucaire in Garde in the south of France. The black marble and bronze plaque

The Baptistry

A Glimpse Of Glory

by Alphonse Cailoux commemorates the great explorer De La Salle, 1643–87, a native of Rouen. The glass in the narrow windows consists of re-used fragments assembled by the master glazier Gaudin in 1960. The stone font was manufactured by Ferdinand Marrou in 1913.

THE CRYPT

Although it is not always possible to visit the crypt, I was fortunate to secure the assistance of Mme Marie Noelle, a member of the cathedral staff (ask at the bookshop). It is the sole remaining feature of the Romanesque cathedral, and as it was built only partly underground, in order to accommodate its ribbed vault the floor of the Romanesque cathedral was raised by fifteen steps throughout the choir and sanctuary during the 11th century.

When the Gothic cathedral was built, the ancient crypt was levelled, filled in and forgotten. Excavations in the early 1930s revealed a horse-shoe shaped building with three radiating chapels and an ambulatory. Of great interest was the discovery of a clear-water well that might have been used by the builders of the cathedral. A lead-lined chest in a wall niche contained the heart of Charles V, king of France. The renovations which took place after the Second World War revealed another, more recent, rectangular crypt.

In the Chapel of Joan of Arc, Mme Noelle led me down a flight of steps, which descends in a curve behind the altar, and unlocked an iron gate. Disappearing in darkness to the left is the passage of the original exit for pilgrims; the entrance would have been a corresponding passage on the north side of the choir. We went ahead through a roughly-hewn tunnel made in the excavation of the 1930s, and which broke through into the southeast radiating chapel of the ancient crypt. All that can be seen today is the axial chapel in the ambulatory of the Romanesque crypt, with the well, and, in a niche in the west wall, the lead-lined chest. Alas, Mme Noelle assured me that it was empty when it was opened in 1945.

The Crypt Chapel

Rouen

Reliquary of Charles V and Well

IN CONCLUSION

As you prepare to leave this venerable edifice, reflect, too, on its historical context. Through those great west doors have entered a procession of noted figures of European history: St Louis (the only canonized King of France) with Blanche of Castile, Charles V (Holy Roman Emperor), Richard (Duke of York), King Louis XI, Napoleon and many others whose aims and prayers were often dissimilar. For in the disputed territory of Normandy the scenes were sometimes quite bizarre.

In 1419 the city of Rouen had fallen to the English and their Norman king. In her book, "The Cathedrals and Cloisters of the Isle de France", published by G.P. Putnam's Sons in 1910, Elise Whitlock Rose wrote, *"After the siege, Rouen was a mass of ruined houses and churches, in every street corpses were lying, hundreds of people were crying out for bread, and for many days such large numbers died that there was scarcely time to bury them. Through this ghastly, mournful city, the victorious King Henry V of England passed to the cathedral. The chronicler of the day writes that Henry rode upon a great horse and wore a doublet of black damask. A golden cross glittered on his breast, his cloak swept the earth, and he was followed by a great procession of bishops, princes and lords in resplendent armour. Having dismounted before Notre Dame, he entered its portal to the sound of trumpets."*

A Glimpse Of Glory

Thirty years later King Louis XI returned to his own, his horse caparisoned with blue velvet and gold fleurs-de-lys, and was received at the city gate by the Archbishop and crowds of acclaiming people as he made his way to this cathedral where he knelt, and gave solemn thanks to "the God who protects France." We are not told whether he thought of the young girl who had made his triumphant entry possible. She had never stood by his side here as she had at Reims, but between Henry Plantagenet's triumphal visit and his own, Joan had been imprisoned in Rouen Castle, been declared a renegade by French bishops (no doubt prompted by the English), and led into the square in the centre of the city where the stake had been erected and the faggots had been laid. I think it unlikely that he gave Joan of Arc a thought, for he had come to meet Queen Margaret, who held Calais: he had matters of aggrandisement on his mind.

DO NOT MISS

1. The statues on the West Façade.
2. Salome dancing, depicted on the tympanum of the Portal of St John.
3. The little wooden fleurs-de-lys on the inside of the great west door.
4. The simple candle burning to honour the Vow in the Chapel of St Margaret.
5. The window of St Julian Hospitaller.
6. The 15th century stairway in the North Transept.
7. The Cours des Libraires (via the North Transept).
8. A visit to the Crypt.

THE WORDS OF THE INVIOLATA

Inviolata, integra, et casta es Maria, quae es effecta fulgida caeli porta.	*O Mary Who wast made the radiant gate of the King.*
O Mater alma Christi carissima, suscipe pia laudum praeconia.	*Holy mother of Christ most dear, receive our devout hymn and praise.*
Te nunc flagitant devota corda et ora, nostra ut pura pectora sint et corpora.	*Our hearts and tongues now ask of thee that our souls and bodies may be pure.*
Tu per precata dulcisona, nobis concedas veniam per saecula.	*By thy sweet sounding prayers obtain for us forgiveness forever.*
O benigna! O Regina! O Maria, quae sola inviolata permansisti.	*O gracious queen, O Mary, who alone among women art inviolate.*

CHAPTER 4

PARIS

Even in winter, when the leaves of the trees have long since sailed down the Seine, Notre-Dame de Paris still looks regal and serene, confident on its island in the river. Instantly recognizable, it is one of the major landmarks of Europe. This is the cathedral where King Henry VI of England was crowned King of France in 1431; where the rehabilitation of Joan of Arc began in 1455; where Mademoiselle Maillard was crowned Goddess of Reason during the horror of the Revolution; where Napoleon crowned himself Emperor and then crowned Josephine as she knelt before him on 2nd December 1794. What pomp, ceremony and sacrilege these stones have witnessed!

When the weather is inclement, exit the Metro either by the stairway signed, "Hotel Dieu", or that signed, "Notre-Dame Parvis", for they will decant you on the square before the west end of the cathedral, and this is the closest you can get to the cathedral while under cover, apart from taking a taxi.

If I have light luggage I take a hotel near the Gare du Nord; the Hotel Ibis in rue La Fayette or the Hotel Art in rue d'Hauteville are cheerful three-star hotels and they are both just off the Place Franz Liszt, only a seven minute walk from the railway station. They will permit you to store luggage on your departure day, so that you are free to go about the city until it is time to return and walk back to the station. The Metro station at Gare de Nord is ideal for visiting Notre Dame; take the RER line B, towards Robinson or St Remi, for it is only two stops.

If, on the other hand, I have a heavy suitcase, and intend taking a taxi from Gare de Nord, I prefer the Hotel Trianon Rive Gauche just off the Boulevard St Michel in the quiet rue de Vaugirard. The hotel is only a five minute walk from Notre Dame. It is also only a five minute stroll from the restaurants of the Latin Quarter.

A Glimpse Of Glory

PARIS—KEY

1 The Central West Portal
2 The Portal of the Virgin
3 The Portal of St Anne
4 The Portal of St Stephen
5 The Porte Rouge
6 The North Transept Portal
7 The Narthex
8 The Nave
9 The Pulpit
10 The South Aisle
11 Chapel of St Eloi
12 Chapel of S Francis Xavier
13 Chapel of St Geneviève
14 Chapel of St Joseph
15 Chapel of St Peter
16 Chapel of St Anne
17 Chapel of the Sacred Heart
18 The Crossing
19 The Nave Altar
20 The Chancel
21 The Sanctuary
22 The South Transept
23 The South Ambulatory
24 Entrance to the Sacristy
25 Chapel of St Denis
26 The Treasury
27 Chapel of St Mary Magdalene
28 Chapel of St Guillaume
29 Chapel of St George
30 The Axial Chapel of Our Lady
31 The North Ambulatory
32 Chapel of St Marcel
33 Chapel of St Louis
34 Chapel of St Germain
35 Chapel of St Ferdinand
36 The North Transept
37 The North Aisle
38 Chapel of St Clotilde
39 Chapel of St Landry
40 Chapel of Our Lady of Guadeloupe
41 Chapel of St Vincent de Paul
42 Chapel of St Enfance
43 Chapel of St Charles
44 The Baptistry

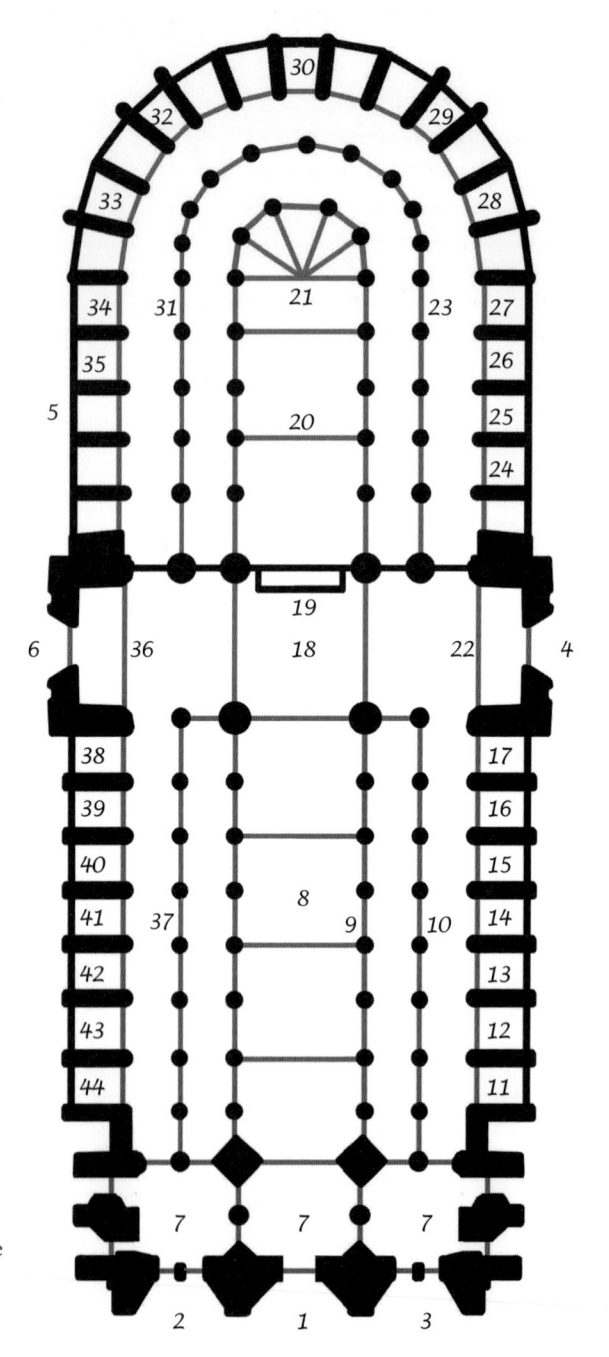

Paris

THE CATHEDRAL CHURCH OF OUR LADY

"Notre-Dame is to France what the choir of Canterbury is to England, her vastest and most noble example of the Transition—a structure in which the great principles of Pointed architecture stand prominently forward, even before the Pointed arch had fully assumed its sway", wrote Francis Bumpus in his book, "The Glories of Northern France", published by Dennis & Sons, 1905.

With the establishment of Christianity in Paris, probably about AD 365, under the Roman Emperor Valentinian l, a Christian who certainly visited Paris, a church was founded at the eastern extremity of the city in honour of St Stephen, always a favourite dedication in France. This early Church was situated to the south of the present building, hence the statue of the first martyr on the trumeau of the south transept door. But the rich, populous city, ever greedy of novelty, deemed the basilica inadequate when Clovis raised Paris to the dignity of capital of a Christian kingdom. So, about 555, Clovis' successor, Childebert l, caused a second cathedral, which he dedicated to the Blessed Virgin, to be constructed a little to the north of the church of St Stephen.

At the beginning of the 10th century the two churches were in a very dilapidated condition, but the care of the bishops was chiefly concentrated on Notre-Dame. It was restored in 907 and in 1123 the roof was repaired, and the Abbé Suger enriched it with stained glass. However, in spite of his works, the old church neither met the requirements of the increasing population of Paris nor kept pace with those great works of Christian art which were making such strides during the second half of the 12th century, not only in France but also in England, Germany, Italy, and Spain.

In an attempt put things right Maurice de Sully, the 62nd Bishop of Paris, decided to amalgamate the two structures into one new cathedral designed on a scale not previously attempted in France. In 1163 he saw the first stone of the existing structure laid by Pope Alexander lll. The High Altar was consecrated on the Wednesday after Whitsun in 1182, and Maurice de Sully was arranging the final touches to the choir when he died in 1196. By this time, the work in the transepts and nave was far advanced, hence their unity of design. Note how the great cylindrical piers of the former, with their capitals carved in a bold development from Corinthian lines, are identical in design with those in the choir.

In all essentials Notre-Dame was complete in 1208. It is fairly certain that spires were intended to crown the towers, but I am not sure whether such an addition, however authentic, would have improved the façade. Violet le Duc's spire at the crossing is characterised by a much greater exuberance than the medieval one destroyed in the 18th century.

A Glimpse Of Glory

"Thus by the middle of the 14th century the Cathedral of Paris had assumed a shape we see today. We find no trace of 15th century work, nothing being left for future ages to accomplish, at least externally, the spires excepted." [Bumpus]

THE EXTERIOR

We begin our tour with the west façade, and to view it as a whole we are obliged to walk some way west across the parvis, or square, in front of the cathedral. This open area is a godsend to photographers; the only way to obtain a photograph of the west façade without tourists is to arrive before they wake up, a mission in which I have not yet been successful. Binoculars will be an asset as we examine the façade.

THE WEST FAÇADE

Although the west front is not symmetrical, for the northern tower is broader than that in the south (note the extra statue in the gallery of the kings above the northern portal), it has been called 'a majestic statement of Gothic grandeur. Victor Hugo drew attention to its *"three ogival doorways carved as it were out of a flat wall."* I am not so certain of this grandeur, for compared with many other great Gothic cathedrals I consider the west façade of Notre-Dame de Paris to be rather a straightforward structure. It was surely the work of one architect, but his name is not known. However, in August 1793 the Revolution came close to destroying it. An act of the Commune gave eight days notice for the statues in the gallery of the kings to be thrown down and destroyed, together with the religious effigies, prior to the destruction of the basilica. It was saved by Citizen Chaumette's successful claim that the building was a monument to art and philosophy, but not before a great deal of damage had been carried out.

There are three portals under high recessed arches, separated by pilaster buttresses, on which we see a statue of St Stephen to the extreme left; a statue depicting 'the Church', her eyes fixed on Christ as she holds up a cross and a chalice, between the north door and the central door, and another depicting 'the Synagogue', her eyes bandaged and downcast, between the central and south door. St Denis, the Patron Saint of Paris, is at the extreme right.

The row of sculpted Kings above the doorways is beneath a pierced parapet, and represents the twenty-eight Kings of Judea, mentioned at the very beginning of St Matthew's Gospel, as the ancestors of the Virgin. This is a feature of many cathedrals dedicated to Notre Dame, and can be compared with the gallery of kings at Amiens, Chartres or Poitiers. David has been identified as the king standing on a lion, another holding a cross and a ring as Solomon. The statues, which are often mistakenly described as kings of France, have been extensively restored by Viollet-le-Duc.

Three hundred carved fragments of stone sculptures were discovered in 1977 and are now displayed in the Musée du Moyen Age (or Musée de Cluny). They have, to a large degree, confirmed the accuracy of the 19th century restorers. When they were broken off the west façade in 1793, they were purchased from the revolutionaries by M. Bertrande, a builder, who in turn sold them to an architect who used them in 1796 as foundation stones for a mansion he was building for a M. Jean-Baptiste Lakanal-Dupuget. This building was developed as the headquarters of the Banque Française du Commerce Exterieur (now the Banque Natexis) in 1977, when the sculptures were discovered and donated to the museum by the bank. [*See: Musée de Cluny, in the end section of this chapter, "Do not miss"*]

The next level has a fine rose window filling the centre panel which is flanked by the buttresses rising upwards. Twelve slender colonnettes radiate from the central medallion, with an outer ring of twenty-four colonnettes, all contained in a decorated round-headed arch.

Above the rose there is a delicate row of tall pointed arches extending across the whole façade, above which is another open parapet. The north and south towers continue upwards, with two tall lancets in each side.

Look closer, and you will notice that the towers are decorated all over with crockets; the arches of the central section are in fact two distinct rows, one behind the other, and protect a passage which runs behind them from north to south. In the centre of the parapet above the gallery of the kings there are the figures of the Virgin Mary, flanked by angels, while statues of Adam and Eve stand on the parapet to north

West Rose

A Glimpse Of Glory

and south. Each door has a trumeau and statues on the splayed jambs either side, and delightful decoration in the archivolts.

We shall begin a closer examination on the north (left) side of the façade, where the queue forms to ascend the tower.

The North Doorway or The Portal of the Virgin

Viollet-le-Duc described this door, destroyed by the Revolutionaries, as "a poem in stone". The 15th century statue of the Virgin Mary with the infant Jesus on the trumeau was brought here from another church, for the original statue was sent to the abbey of St Denis. Above her canopy is the shelter for the Arc of the Covenant, which divides the lowest level of the tympanum. To the left of it are seated three prophets who foretold the coming of the Messiah, their heads covered with veils, and to the right, three crowned kings, ancestors of Mary. The reflective attitude of the faces and the folding of the robes make these six statues outstanding examples of their time.

Above them, the next level of the tympanum depicts the death, or Dormition, of Mary, and portrays her body being laid in a decorated sarcophagus by two angels surrounded by Apostles. The Apostle at either end holds his head in his hand and thus accommodates the curve of the arch! At the top of the tympanum Mary is seated and crowned, Christ sharing her throne. They are flanked by angels, each holding a candle. The four orders of the archivolt above are filled with little sculptures of angels, patriarchs, kings and prophets.

Either side of the door are four statues: to the left, Constantine and, between two angels, the martyr St Denis carrying his decapitated head; to the right are John the Baptist, St Stephen, St Geneviève and St Sylvestre. Either side of the trumeau are carved symbols of the seasons and the ages of man, while on the door jambs can be seen signs of the zodiac and work to be done in the seasons of the year. Don't miss the exquisite carving, beneath the statue of the Virgin on the trumeau, of the fall from grace in the Garden of Eden.

The Central Portal or The Judgement Door

This is the largest door and its theme is the struggle of good over evil, a contest known to all of us, culminating in the coming of Christ at the end of time—known as the Second Coming. It has six statues of Apostles in the splay either side and six orders in the archivolt above. If you have visited the cathedral at Amiens you will recognize the statue of Christ on the trumeau, for Viollet-le-Duc's ablest sculptor, Geoffrey Dèchaume, modelled the statue on the Beau Dieu of the trumeau of the centre door at Amiens. It was necessary not because of the vandalism of the Revolutionaries but due to the vandalism of the Bishop and his clergy. For in

West Façade Central Portal, Tympanum

1732 the cathedral clerics instructed the architect Soufflot to remove the pillar and the lintel of the tympanum to make room for the canopy used to cover the Holy Sacrament during grand processions. The 13th century doors went at the same time. It is almost unbelievable wanton destruction by men who should have known better. Fragments of the original lintel can be seen in the Musée de Cluny.

Either end of the restored 19th century lintel angels can be seen sounding the last trumpet to signal the resurrection to new life. In the tympanum above is the mediaeval sculpture depicting the day of judgement, St Michael is seen in the centre weighing souls, the devil trying to tip the balance in his favour, with the redeemed to the left, being led by angels to Heaven, and the devil roping in the damned to the right. At the top Christ is enthroned, with the earth as his footstool, showing his wounded hands and flanked by angels holding a spear and a cross, with the Virgin and St John kneeling at either side. This has been considered one of the most important works of the 13th century. It has been said that this tympanum glows with the warmth of the effaced decoration.

The six orders in the archivolt represent the heavenly court, where Abraham receives the righteous on the left and the damned are condemned on the right. At the bottom of the second order on the right can be seen a blindfolded knight riding to certain death in combat without a thought for his friend (of whom only a left leg remains). The archivolt is crammed with angels, patriarchs, saints, martyrs holding palms, and devils, and it retains to this day the power to stop the tourist in

A Glimpse Of Glory

his tracks as little groups of people stare up at the sculptures as they try to work out the meaning – not only of the sculptor, but also, perhaps, of their own life.

On the jamb supporting the lintel either side of the doorway are small, modern statues. They represent the Wise virgins on the left, with the doors to Paradise wide open above, and the foolish virgins on the right, with the doors firmly shut.

THE SOUTH (RIGHT) DOORWAY, OR THE PORTAL OF ST ANNE

This door was originally dedicated to the Virgin when it was created by Bishop Sully as the central door in an earlier design for the façade, which turned out to be too small. It was therefore torn down and the façade reconstructed on a larger scale, but this doorway was considered by the architect too good to put on one side, and so it was re-used, and in the 13th century it became known as St Anne's Doorway. It therefore dates from the1150s, and is a Romanesque door made Gothic by clever alterations. It was too low to balance the Virgin's door on the north side, so an extra level of sculpture was introduced to raise the tympanum. The round arch was changed to Gothic by simply building up to a point, with the addition of extra sculptures in the archivolt to fill the enlarged bay.

The sculpture on the trumeau represents St Marcel, the 9th Bishop of Paris, and is a modern copy of the original, which is now in the Cluny Museum together with fragments of the statues of St Peter, St Marcel and St Paul. With their elongated

West Façade, St Anne's Door, Tympanum

figures, sharp folds of drapery and clear low-relief decoration on the hems of their clothing, these sculptures belong to the birth of Gothic art. On either side of the doorway are four more statues: to the left can be seen St Peter, King Solomon, the Queen of Sheba and an ancestral King, and to the right are St Paul, King David, Bathsheba and another ancestral King.

The 12th century lintel has scenes from the life of the Virgin Mary, below which, carved on the inserted panel, are scenes from the life of her parents, St Anne and St Joachim. In the upper levels of the tympanum is the cathedral's oldest carving, which deals with the life of the Virgin Mary. The Annunciation, the adoration of the shepherds, the Presentation in the Temple can all be seen. The crowned Virgin with the infant Christ at the top is typical of Romanesque work. Mary stares straight ahead, as does the Child she holds before her. She is flanked by two angels and the cathedral patrons, a bearded Bishop Maurice of Sully, standing on the left, and Louis the VII, kneeling. The archivolt of four orders is filled with little sculptures of angels in the inner order, succeeded in each order by Prophets, Kings and figures from the Apocalypse.

Before moving on, examine the door furniture – the hinges, locks and superb metal decoration. As you admire the blacksmith's skill remember that the work on this door is original 13th century; the restorers of the other doors modelled them on this exceptional example of mediaeval achievement.

It is time to leave the West Front and move towards the river and turn to the left to examine the south side of the cathedral.

THE SOUTH SIDE

It is not possible to walk along the exterior of the south side of the nave because of a private building which accommodates the Archpriest, the architects' department and the cathedral administration office.

Nevertheless, as we walk through the little park between this building and the river, we can see that buttresses rise between each bay along the south side of the cathedral, and continue, free-standing, to mid-clerestory level where they provide support for flying buttresses which spring from them at two levels to support the tribune and the upper clerestory wall. Between each buttress is a window filled with four lancets, each with a large quatrefoil over two smaller quatrefoils in the tracery, which give light to the chapels of the south aisle. Each window is covered by a crocketted gable, above which can be seen the multifoil of the tribune gallery, and, higher still, the double lancet and multifoil of the clerestory. Look at the ridge of the nave roof: it is crowned with a decoration of foliage in what appears to be wrought iron.

A Glimpse Of Glory

The South Transept Façade

The Portal once opened to the Episcopal Palace, before it was totally destroyed by the mob, and the Archbishop's library thrown into the Seine, in the July Revolution of 1830. It is dedicated to St Stephen the first martyr, which was the dedication of the earliest church on this site. It can be seen only from the park as it is not open to the public. Although dating to a time just after 1258, already sculptural style and technique has moved on. The sculpture in the tympanum is well-developed, and is less of a frieze and more of a moving, dynamic group of statues. The lintel depicts scenes from the life of St Stephen and has a cross-legged figure of a judge on the right, who is observing with equanimity the martyr being led away to his cruel death by stoning. This lapidation is depicted in the middle level, the figure of Saul squatting on the left offering to hold cloaks. To the right can be seen the martyr's burial, while an apostle is reading from the scriptures. A figure of Christ with an angry expression and flanked by angels is carved at the top of the tympanum. The doorway is divided by a trumeau bearing a statue of St Stephen and it supports the carved lintel and the tympanum. There are three orders to the archivolt over the tympanum; the inner one has carved angels. A large crocketted gable rises above the portal containing a large open multifoil beneath a small quatrefoil in the apex. Either side of the portal there is a group of three carved statues, each under a smaller gable, with a carving of St Martin and the beggar in the small tympanum above the right hand group.

South Façade, St Stephen's Portal, Tympanum

The façade rises above the gable and is filled with a row of sixteen narrow, glazed lancets, either side of which is a statue in a niche, and above them is the delicate south rose window. This, too, is flanked by a statue: to the west is John the Baptist with bare feet and holding a motif of the Agnus Dei, and to the east is St Peter holding the keys to the Kingdom. The façade terminates in another fine gable decorated with a smaller imitation of the great rose window. Two little turrets flank this rose and atop the gable Christ looks out across the Seine, with a bishop (Sully?) to the left and a saint (Stephen?) to the right. The sacristies built by Viollet le Duc extend out to the south east of the transept.

THE CHEVET

To the east of the South Façade, the flying buttresses appear to be more like thin veils of masonry suspended between the clerestory windows. At ground level, the great mass of glass in the windows of the radiating chapels make the lower wall of the chevet appear like a mere screen.

The first three chapels on either side of the choir were constructed at the order of Bishop Regnault de Corbeil. The 12th century buttresses did not project far enough from the walls of the ambulatories to give them sufficient depth to construct chapels between them, as in the nave. The present chapels date from the first half of the 14th century.

The great pinnacles placed at the base of the flying buttresses around the choir were constructed at this time, as were the small flying buttresses placed between the two greater ones, and serving as a support for the chevet of the tribune. Therefore, far more slender buttresses now rise between the chapels and are crowned with delicate turrets that serve to give sufficient downward pressure to redirect the outward thrust of the flying buttresses to the ground. The decoration above the clerestory windows is imaginative and splendid; three courses of stone each project out above the one below in a kind of inverted crenellation. Above it, and immediately beneath the roof parapet, is a frieze of stiff-leaf decoration. Viewed through binoculars it can be seen that the detail is exquisite. The bay to the south of the axial chapel has lost its share of the fine parapet which crowns the lower wall. On the north side of the chevet there is a series of metre-square bas-relief carvings beneath the chapel windows. They were carved around 1320, and depict episodes from the legend of the Virgin Mary and St Theophilus (see the North Doorway below).

THE PORTE ROUGE

Do not miss the delightful little north east door, the Red Door, so called because of its colour. Constructed in 1270, it has a sculpture of the Coronation of the Virgin

A Glimpse Of Glory

Mary in the tympanum, and around the door are carved sculptures of the life of St Marcel. We see him baptizing, celebrating Mass, preaching, casting out demons and healing the sick. This door was built at the direction of Regnault de Corbeil. The architect was Pierre de Montreuil, whom St Louis had commissioned to build Sainte Chapelle in 1248.

The North Transept Façade

This portal once led into the cloister and it is similar to the South façade. It was constructed in 1270 and the sculptor was Jean de Chelles. The trumeau of the doorway has a statue of the Virgin Mary. She has a most maternal face, tilted up to gaze at her Child. But the infant Christ was broken off and stolen in 1820.

The tympanum above it has three levels: at the bottom left is a nativity scene (note that the crib is tucked under Mary's couch); then the Presentation in the Temple; the Slaughter of the Innocents; and the Flight into Egypt on the right. (Look for Joseph's 'flowerpot' hat!) The middle level relates the story of Theophilus, who sold his soul to the Devil in order to take the place of his bishop. From the left, we see him with a demon, humiliating his bishop, repenting and praying to Mary, and her intervention as she threatens the Devil with the Cross of Christ. At the top Theophilus makes his peace with his bishop, who is holding a model of the cathedral. There are three orders in the archivolt and, as before, the inner one contains sculpted angels. The empty niches either side of the door are thought by some to have accommodated statues of the Magi, or Wise Men. Two heads of such kings were found in 1977 and are deposited in the Cluny Museum.

A crocketted gable with a blind multifoil in the tympanum surmounts the portal and a small gable either side rise above three empty niches. Above the portal a row of eighteen small lancets supports the north rose window, which fills the width of the transept. A large multifoil and two smaller quatrefoils decorate the crocketted gable which rises above the transept façade. At

North Transept Portal

the pinnacle a statue of a bishop holding a crosier gives his blessing to the city, and is flanked either side by an angel in a niche blowing a trumpet. Sadly, the angel to the east (left) has lost its instrument, apart from the mouthpiece.

THE NORTH SIDE

There is a great mass of solid buttresses dividing the bays of the nave, each crowned with an open turret, where the flying buttresses spring across to the clerestory wall. Each bay has a window of four lancets and three multifoils in the tracery.

We return to the square, or parvis, at the conclusion of our tour of the exterior of Notre-Dame.

The Bells

With the sole exception of the Bourdon, or Great Bell, named Emmanuel, which is housed in the south tower, the famous ancient bells of Notre Dame, including the Bourdon Marie (cast in 1378), were taken down and melted during the Revolution. Emmanuel is rung on the great Christian festivals and on important occasions, such as the election or death of the pope. Weighing thirteen tons, it was cast in 1685. Since 1856, four bells have rung in the belfry of the north tower to call the faithful to worship, but they were ill-matched and out of tune.

A new era dawned on Saturday, 23rd March 2013, when nine newly cast bells weighing twenty-three tons in total, and named after saints and prominent Catholics, were commissioned to mark the 850th anniversary of the Cathedral's founding in 1163. They had been blessed on the 2nd February 2013 by the Cardinal Archbishop of Paris, His Eminence André Vingt-Trois. The new bells joined with Emmanuel as they rang out over the city on the eve of Palm Sunday. The cathedral, and the whole area of the parvis and along the banks of the Seine, was crowded with Parisians and others from all over Europe, to hear again ten bells ringing out as it used to be from the Middle Ages up until the French Revolution. Eight of the nine new bells were cast in a foundry in the Normandy town of Villedieu-les-Poeles. The ninth, a Bourdon named Marie in honour of the Virgin Mary and in memory of the mediaeval Bourdon by that name, was cast in the Netherlands.

Marie is tuned to G#; next in weight comes Gabriel (A#) in honour of the archangel; Anne-Geneviève (B) in honour of St Anne, the mother of the Blessed Virgin, and St Geneviève the Patron Saint of Paris; Denis (C#) in honour of St Denis the first Bishop of Paris; Marcel (D#) in honour of St Marcel, a 5th century Bishop of Paris revered for his care of the sick and poor; Étienne (F) in memory of the earlier cathedral here which was dedicated to St Étienne (Stephen); Benoit-Joseph (F#) to commemorate the fact that the cathedral's 850th year began in the

A Glimpse Of Glory

Pontificate of Pope Benedict XVI; Maurice (G#) in memory of Bishop Maurice de Sully who laid the foundation stone of this cathedral in 1163; and Jean-Marie (A#) in honour of Cardinal Jean-Marie Lustiger, Archbishop of Paris until 2005.

It is time to enter the great building through the St Anne's door in the west façade. Admire once again the work of the 13th century blacksmith on the doors.

THE INTERIOR

Entering the cathedral from the bright sunlight demands care and some time for the eye to adjust to the dark interior. Meanwhile, sit down near the back and look at the eastern clerestory windows through binoculars; they appear to be shimmering in the distance, such is the delicacy of the modern glass. Apart from the three great rose windows, all the 12th century glass in the cathedral was taken out by the Canons during the 18th century age of Enlightenment, and lost. No trace of it remains. Clerical vandalism on such a scale leaves me breathless.

THE NARTHEX

As you stand inside the west door, turn to examine the west wall. It is plain either side of the wooden porch, which has a statue of an angel blowing a trumpet in the centre on top, and which is framed by a broad arch. Above is a narrow sexpartite vault. To left and right is another wooden porch. The north wall has two single lancets with geometric designs in the glass, which are separated by a pilaster with three engaged columns. The south wall has the same arrangement. There is one further bay of the narthex, to the east of the narrow vault, in which is the great organ gallery, which almost obscures the great 9.7 metre diameter of the rose window in the West Façade.

From the time of Pérotin, the first organist and Master of the Music in 1188, as Maurice de Sully was completing the construction of the cathedral, Notre Dame has been famous for its musical tradition. As early as the 14th century a children's choir was established and the cathedral became a centre of early polyphony. The children's choir still exists as a primary school, and together with young adults, the children sing Vespers daily and at the Solemn Mass on Sundays. The organ has always been a vital part of the architecture of the cathedral. There are two organs in Notre Dame; the Great Organ here in the narthex, with 113 stops and 8,000 pipes, making it the most powerful instrument in France, and the modern Choir Organ with 30 stops and 2,000 pipes, built in 1966.

While the Great Organ still uses some mediaeval pipes, the instrument was completely re-built by Aistide Cavaille-Coll in 1863. In 1900 Louis Vierne was appointed organist; the Kyrie from his *Messe Solennelle*, op 16, still moves me to tears. He brought international attention to the music of Notre Dame, and died during a recital at his beloved instrument in 1937.

In 1989 the Ministry of Culture decided to carry out a complete overhaul of the organ and to computerise it. This was a fundamental innovation which has enabled organists to obtain note and stop change requests at the rate of 16,000 per second. Another computer controls the amount of wind sent to the pipes: no chance of the organ 'blowing out' when it is played at full power. The organ was returned to cathedral use in December 1992, when the choir sang the Messe Solennelle by Louis Vierne. Twenty years have passed since that day, a period of great advance in computer technology, and so the French Government has completed yet another overhaul in time for the 850th anniversary celebrations.

The window, like the cathedral, is dedicated to the Virgin Mary. She sits in a medallion of modern glass at its centre surrounded in the upper half by mankind's struggle to conquer vice with virtue, and in the lower half by the work of the seasons and the signs of the zodiac, a popular theme with the mediaeval artist. The cathedral's oldest surviving window, it was erected before 1220, but has suffered extensive restoration in the 16th century as well as in the 18th and 19th centuries.

The aisles to north and south do not begin for yet one more bay, so there is quite a large area or either side of the western bay of the nave which allows for tourist movement to and from the west doors. Once the eyes are accustomed to the light it is time to move into the main part of the church.

THE NAVE

The early Gothic nave rises in three levels: the main arcade, the tribune chambers, and the clerestory. Bishop de Sully was determined that his cathedral for Paris should be unequalled in splendour, so he designed a ground plan with double aisles throughout the nave. The lofty arcade of Bourges and Reims had not then been imagined, so he constructed a spacious tribune, already a feature in the architecture of northern France, above his aisles. Over this he built a third storey as a kind of triforium, containing large traceried roses, which had a clerestory of single lancet windows above. Bumpus is unsure that the elevation would have been a pleasing sight. Overhead is a lofty sexpartite vault.

Sitting at the west end and looking towards the altar, the eye is focussed on the solid mass of masonry at ground level, a sure sign of its early date. There are eight bays in the arcade and the easternmost is slightly narrower. The drum piers supporting the arcade to north and south are solid, round, unencumbered, and culminate in capitals decorated with finely carved foliage, a common feature of Romanesque churches.

A Glimpse Of Glory

The Nave Vault

The arches spring from the abacus which also supports the three slender respond columns which rise without interruption through the tribune level to support the springing of the vault from smaller capitals halfway up the clerestory. The last two western piers either side have enclosed columns. To be precise, the penultimate pier has one enclosed column facing into the nave, whereas the westernmost has four, one on each face, which cut through the decoration of the capital and end in minor capitals of their own.

It is thought that these short drum piers were chosen by the unknown architect of Notre Dame because they were used in the choir of St Denis, Abbot Suger's definitive Gothic abbey. He was most likely unaware that Suger used them only out of a desire to match the 8th century nave arcade of the earlier Abbey Church.

The clerestory, north and south, has two lancets and a rose in each bay, except for the last bay before the crossing, which has an open rose beneath a short wide single lancet in grisaille, and the westernmost bay, which has only a short lancet in grisaille high up, but with no roundel beneath it. We can only guess how the clerestory might have looked in de Sully's day from these exceptions, for they have been 'restored' like this by Viollet le Duc in the 18th century. It seems that the clerestory was lighted by large pointed windows placed under the ribs of the great vault. They were without tracery. The tribune gallery was covered on the outside with a lean-to roof which reached the base of the clerestory windows, and lit inside by large traceried circles. Between 1230 and 1240 the upper level disappeared due to the lengthening of the clerestory windows, which were brought down to the stringcourse above the tribune galleries.

In spite of the disgraceful behaviour of the 18th century clergy in removing and then losing the mediaeval glass, the modern programme of glazing is at least pleasing to the eye. The nave clerestory windows are filled with coloured fragmented shapes, and are beautifully designed.

The tribune gallery above the arcade is framed by a large arch in each bay which is subdivided into three open lancets by two slender columns. The exterior wall of the galleries contains lancets and roses filled with the fine stained-glass used in the clerestory.

In the fifth bay on the south side stands the Pulpit. East of the pulpit, to north and south, the chairs of the nave spill into the inner aisles and this arrangement gives the church an impression of great width. The chairs in the last bays before the crossing are turned to face the nave altar.

Let us turn our attention to the side aisles.

THE AISLES

Either side of the nave there are double aisles, which give the cathedral great width and space and a sense of grandeur. The columns dividing these double aisles alternate between unencumbered round columns, smaller versions of those in the nave, with fine capitals decorated with carved foliage, and clustered columns. There are three such clustered columns each side, and from the abacus of these columns spring the arcade ribs, and the lateral and cross ribs of the quadripartite vault above the aisles. Their capitals are decorated with acanthus leaves, but are not as elaborate as those on the unencumbered pillars, of which there are four each side.

Sometime between 1240 and 1290 the 12th century outer aisle walls were removed to make way for a series of Chapels, which were formed between the huge buttresses of the nave. It is these chapels which gives the nave its impression of width. Each chapel is lighted by a large traceried window, and all the chapels in the north and south aisles have low wrought iron screens.

From 1449, the Silver and Goldsmiths of Paris offered to the Blessed Virgin Mary a green tree as a gift on the 1st May, the month devoted to Mary, hence in England it was known as the 'Mary month of May'. In 1481 it became a gift in gold instead of the tree. From 1630, they offered instead of the tree a painting of a New Testament subject by famous artists, all of the same dimensions. They were known as the 'Mays' of Notre-Dame, and the fourteen now displayed, out of seventy-six presented, date from the 17th and 18th century. They were formerly hung on the

A Glimpse Of Glory

columns of the nave, but are now in the chapels of the north and south aisles and transepts.

We shall continue our tour of the interior on the south (right) side, beginning at the west end.

THE SOUTH AISLE

All the chapels in this aisle, with the exception of the St Anne Chapel, have four lancet windows with geometric designs in the glass and with a large multifoil above two smaller multifoils in the tracery.

Bay one. A large crucifix stands on a marble column against an otherwise bare south wall.

The Chapel of St Eloi (St Eligius) (formerly the Chapel of St Anne) but still known as the 'Goldsmith's Chapel'. Against the east wall there is a modern gilded altar by Philippe Kaeppelin, with a bas relief carving of a goldsmith and a builder on the front. He also made the crucifix above, which matches the metal of the altar, as does the statue of St Eligius (Eloi), near the piscina in the south wall. Eligius was born in Limoges in the 7th century, and is the Patron Saint of Metalworkers. On the west wall is a large painting: it is the May of 'the Stoning of St Stephen'. The south wall is filled with four lancets in geometric designs, and a tracery of three trefoils.

The Chapel of St Francis Xavier (formerly the Chapel of St Bartholomew and St Vincent). The chapel is glazed across the front and has a roof of glass below the window level, as it is in use as a confessional Chapel. The May of 1647, depicting "the Martyrdom of St Andrew", was hanging in this chapel during my early visits, but has since been removed. There is a small free-standing statue of St Francis Xavier baptizing a convert, who is wearing earrings and a necklace of shark's teeth. It is not surprising, as this 16th century founder member of the Society of Jesus (the Jesuits) was a missionary in the East Indies; his shrine is in Goa.

The Chapel of St Geneviève (formerly the Chapel of St Philip and St James). This chapel is also glazed for use as a counselling area. There are again four lancets in the window but the tracery has a multifoil at the top supported by two quatrefoils. There is a bare stone altar against the east wall with a statue above of a lady wearing a pendant, which might represent St Geneviève the 5th century Patroness of Paris. Two paintings above the altar flank the statue, and there is a 'May' on the west wall, of the Crucifixion of St Peter. There is a piscina in the south wall.

The Chapel of St Joseph (formerly St Anthony and St Michael). Again the same four-lancet window, but the tracery contains a large quatrefoil and two smaller ones. A bare altar stands on two square pillars, with a statue of St Joseph holding the hands of the infant Christ on a bracket above the altar. The piscina is in the south wall. The 'May' on the west wall is of St Peter at Jerusalem.

The Chapel of St Peter (formerly St Thomas of Canterbury). St Peter, Paul and the Apostles were the witnesses of Christ's ministry and resurrection. The 16th century wood carvings around the walls depict the Saints and Apostles. There is a statue of an Apostle on a bracket above the bare altar, which stands on four decorated pillars. The Piscina is in the south wall as usual. The 'May' on the west wall is a painting of 'the Centurion Cornelius at the feet of St Paul'. The tracery in the window contains a multifoil, supported by two quatrefoils.

Conversion of St Paul (detail)

The Chapel of St Anne (formerly St Augustine). In the tracery of the window, in the central diamond, there is a quatrefoil which depicts St Anne, the mother of the Virgin Mary, with her infant daughter, supported by two smaller quatrefoils. Five medallions depicting kings and prophets in each lancet are intertwined in the branches emanating from a sleeping Jesse at the bottom. The window is signed, "Didron, Paris, 1864." The 'May' of 1637 on the west wall is a large painting depicting 'the Conversion of St Paul'. The Piscina is in the south wall, and the bare altar stands against the east wall; above it is a painting of the Holy Family.

The Chapel of the Sacred Heart (formerly Mary Magdalene). The altar against the east wall has a statue of Christ on a bracket above it. The chapel is glazed as a counselling area, like the chapels of St Francis Xavier and St Geneviève above.

We have now reached the crossing, but first turn right into the south transept.

THE SOUTH TRANSEPT

As you walk towards the South Door, you will notice that the south transept is quite shallow having only one bay under a quadripartite vault to the south of the

A Glimpse Of Glory

double aisle. There is a good reason for this shallow vault. Bishop de Sully's transept façades had terminated in line with his double aisles, but the construction of the aisle chapels required the removal and reconstruction of the transept façades. This shallow bay, matching the depth of the chapels, was added to both transepts, and they were given their present façades, each with a rose and a series of small lancet windows below. To the north of it is a sexpartite vault covering the double aisle, before the huge quadripartite vault of the central crossing. This pattern is repeated in the north transept.

The south wall is decorated with three large crocketted, blind arches, divided east and west into four blind lancets with tracery. The gables over them are also crocketted with empty niches under pinnacles rising between the three gables. There is a wooden porch over the South Door which fills the central arch. To the left (east) of it, on a pedestal, stands a statue of St Thérèse, and to the right (west) is a statue of St Joan of Arc. Running across the south wall above the gables is the row of sixteen small lancets each with a figure of a prophet in the glass. They are the work of M. Alfred Gerente, who also carried out the 19th century restoration of the rose windows. In the centre four lancets can be seen Isaiah, Jeremiah, Ezekiel and Daniel bearing on their shoulders the evangelists Matthew, Mark, Luke and John, a device copied from Chartres. A passage in front of them is protected by a row of open arches. Above is the superb rose window.

The work of the Parisian master glass painters of Sainte Chapelle have been detected in the two transept rose windows. In the book he co-authored with Catherine Brisac, "Gothic Stained Glass 1200–1300", published by Thames & Hudson, 1985, page 109, Louis Grodecki has identified some of the hands in the north rose as being identical to the work in that Royal Chapel. The south rose is later than that in the north transept. Work began in 1258 and was modelled on the north rose, but it was substantially restored in the 18th century and again in the 19th century under Viollet le Duc. The subject is the Glorification of Christ, and he is depicted reigning in Heaven with the symbols of the book Revelation, surrounded by apostles, saints, martyrs, angels carrying the symbols of the Passion, and knights. The portrayal of the wise and foolish virgins indicates the theme of judgement. Unlike the cold blues of the north rose, here are warm reds which blaze when lit by the noonday sun, flooding across the floor of the transept in a sea of coloured hues.

The west wall is decorated with four blind lancets and tracery under a crocketted gable, above which are two levels of six blind lancets. The bay above the south aisle is divided by a pilaster, with two slender engaged columns rising up to the vault to form the arch over the slightly pointed windows, which have geometric designs in the clerestory, one above each of the two south aisles. There is an open rose in each bay below the two windows. At the tribune level there is the same arrangement as in the nave, except that here there is a round window in each tympanum. The two bays are identical.

The eastern wall of the transept has also two identical bays. There is a large picture of St Thomas Aquinas (1225–74) teaching at the University of Paris, by Antoine Nicholas, 1648, and above it there are two levels of six blind lancets as on the south wall. Crocketted gables surmounted with a finial crown each of the arches. The tribune gallery above has an arch, subdivided into two in each bay, and as far as can be seen from the ground, each tribune chamber has a quadripartite vault. Above the tribune is a rose and a coloured window in each bay. Each window contains two figures: to the north a king and a bishop, and to the south two bishops.

THE CROSSING

The central Crossing has a large quadripartite vault with a stunning boss at its centre, which depicts the Virgin and Child: Mary is standing on a crescent surrounded by twenty-one stars against a blue background.

The platform of five steps rising to the nave altar intrudes half way into the bay of the crossing, the altar itself is positioned on a dais of a further three steps just forward of the chancel arch, and is the work of Paul Touret (1989).

Looking East from the Crossing

A Glimpse Of Glory

Against the south east pillar, on a pedestal, is a fine 14th century statue of the crowned Virgin and Child, known as "Notre Dame de Paris", purchased during the restorations of the 19th century by Viollet le Duc. A statue of the 3rd century martyr St Denis stands against the north east pillar. The mediaeval Rood Screen once closed the chancel between these two pillars, linking with the sculpted stone screen in the ambulatories.

THE CHANCEL

I have never been able to gain access to the chancel and have only observed it from the ambulatory and nave. Yet, it never ceases to shock me by its dramatic shift of style from Gothic to 18th century French Baroque. The chancel was enclosed by a decorated stone screen in the mediaeval period, much like the screen present today in Albi Cathedral in the Tarn Region. The side walls are largely extant here in Paris, and are described when we each the south ambulatory, but together with the western portion of the Rood Screen, the Gothic canons' stalls were swept away as a part of Louis XlV's re-ordering of the chancel and sanctuary, and were replaced by the work of Robert de Cotte. The mediaeval stalls had hanging above them, presumably attached to the back of the remnants of the mediaeval stone screen, tapestries which were woven in 1657, and which related the life of the Virgin Mary. As the new stalls were higher than the old, there was now no room for the tapestries, and they were sold in 1739 to the Chapter of Strasbourg Cathedral. The high backs of the present restored stalls contain nine carved panels each side, approximately three stalls to a panel, which depict scenes from the Virgin's life.

THE SANCTUARY

It was King Louis Xlll who made a famous vow to rebuild the Sanctuary and High Altar as he dedicated his kingdom to the Blessed Virgin as a thank-offering for the safe birth of his heir. Alas, he died before he could carry out the vow, but in 1699 the vow was renewed on his behalf by his son, Louis XlV.

Ancient manuscripts told of the magnificence of the mediaeval altar, but the King tore it all out, and replaced it. Today we see a marble altar decorated across the front by seven cusped arches containing gilded trefoils and gilded carved foliage at the bottom. Towering above it is the white marble Pietà, now overshadowed by the modern gold cross of Marc Couturier, which appears somewhat bland in its baroque context, for either side are the kneeling statues of the two kings offering their crowns to the Blessed Virgin. The Pietà was done by Nicolas Coustou in 1714–15, the statue of Louis Xlll by his brother Guillaume Coustou, and Louis XlV by the sculptor Coysevox. In order for the faithful to see the statues of the vow, portions of the ancient stone screen were replaced by the present wrought-iron screens. Bronze angels either side carry instruments of Christ's Passion.

THE SOUTH AMBULATORY

Following the pattern of the Aisles, there is a double ambulatory, and the columns dividing the double aisles are cylindrical.

The inner wall of both south and north Ambulatory, forming the back of the chancel stalls, is one of the treasures of the cathedral. Above a decorated blind arcade is a series of sculptured scenes all in polychrome. This southern section was created by Jehan Ravy, 1328–51. The scenes from the life of Christ begin in the North Ambulatory, but here in the South Ambulatory it starts with the resurrection appearance of Jesus to Mary Magdalene and the disciples on the first Easter Day. As we move along the ambulatory we follow Christ on the road to Emmaus and see him breaking bread with the two disciples inside a little house. We see St Thomas the doubter touching the wound of Jesus, an incident not actually mentioned in the Gospels, Christ on the seashore with his disciples, and his farewell to them before his Ascension. It is a remarkable piece of mediaeval sculpture. These two stone screens are remnants of the medieval Rood. The missing central part, which stretched across the entrance to the chancel, contained sculptures depicting the Passion of Christ. The Descent into Hell can be seen in the Louvre museum, and a statue of Adam is preserved in the Musée de Cluny.

At the eastern end of the screen is a pair of ornate wrought-iron gates, which, when unlocked, allow access to the chancel and sanctuary. The wrought-iron screen continues around the apse on top of a stone wall.

As we walk along the ambulatories look across at the pairs of clerestory window lancets on the opposite side of the chancel and sanctuary. The 19th century glass from the workshop of M. Maréchal, with its images of saints, kings and prophets, imitates the mediaeval glass at Bourges and Strasbourg. I shall identify them, in each case naming first the image on the left.

Christ on the Shore

A Glimpse Of Glory

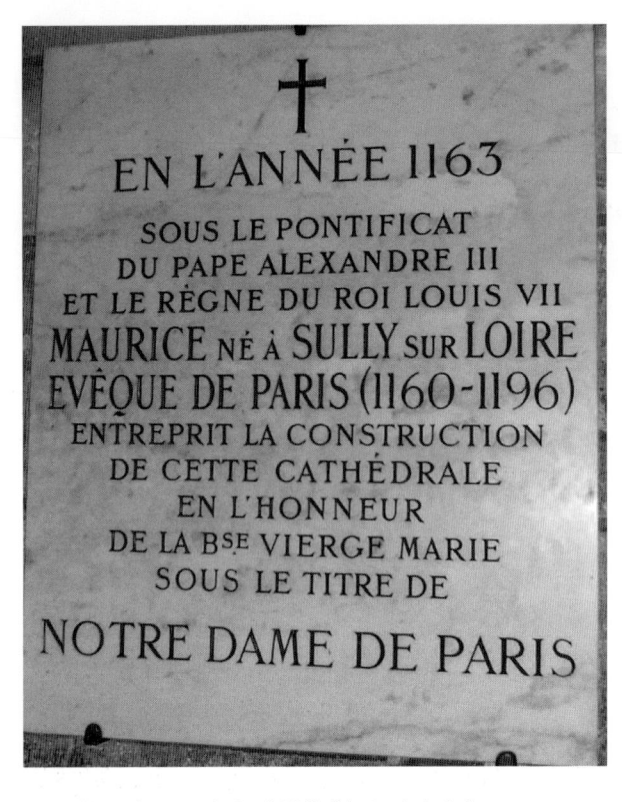

Plaque on the South Wall of the South Ambulatory

The east window depicts the Coronation of the Virgin by Christ. In the bay to the north (left) of it is an Angel and the Virgin Mary (the Annunciation), followed by Dionysius and Maurice de Sully; then Ambrose and Gregory; above the wrought-iron gates on the north side are the evangelists Matthew and Mark; to the left of them are Isaiah and Ezekiel; then Melchizidek and Aaron; Laurence and Stephen; Louis and Gregory Vll; Remi and Martin. The figures spill around the corner into the clerestory windows in the east wall of the transepts. I shall identify the windows on the south side when we reach the North Ambulatory.

Bay 1. This bay is partly blocked with stone, with a doorway on the right which gives access to a spiral staircase. A plaque on the wall tells how in 1163, in the pontificate of Alexander the third, in the reign of King Louis Vll, Maurice Sully, Bishop of Paris 1160–1196, began the construction of this cathedral in honour of The Blessed Virgin Mary under the title Notre-Dame de Paris. A wooden screen hides the remainder of this bay, but the south window can be seen to contain four lancets in geometric designs with a large multifoil and two trefoils in the tracery, similar to the chapels of the aisle. It has a quadripartite vault painted blue with little gold stars and a gilded boss.

Bay 2. The window has three lancets with geometric designs and a large trefoil in the tracery. The bay is filled with a wooden doorway, which leads, via a long corridor, to the Sacristy used for the mass.

The Chapel of St Denis. There is a stone altar resting on two columns against the east wall, and behind and above the altar is a fresco painting depicting the life and martyrdom of St Denys in the 3rd century. His remains were transferred to the Abbey of St Denis in the 7th century. He has also been confused with Dionysius the

Areopagite, converted by St Paul at Athens (Acts of the Apostles, 17, verse 4), and with the 6th century Dionysius the Pseudo-Areopagite who combined Christianity with Platonic philosophy. On the front of the altar and on the retable there is a decoration of floral patterns, and a crucifix and two candles on the retable. In the piscina stands an icon of St Dionysius the Areopagite, the first Bishop of Athens in the second century, confirming the confusion referred to above. A monument in marble with a large marble backing plate on the west wall is in honour of Monsignor Affre, Archbishop of Paris 1840–1848. He was mortally wounded as he tried to mediate in the riots of 1848.

Bay five. This bay is the entrance to the Canons' Sacristy and houses **the Treasury**. It is worth the €2.5 entrance fee to see the small chapter house with little doors giving access to the stalls, and the great chapter room containing superb figures in the glass and a fine model of the cathedral. On the north wall of the entrance to this sacristy there is a 14th century mural painting removed from the apse.

The Chapel of St Mary Magdalene (formerly St Giraud). The window has three lancets with geometric designs and a multifoil tracery above. On the east wall above the altar is a fresco of Mary Magdalene washing Christ's feet. The bare altar rests on four of fluted columns with a crucifix on the retable. A piscina is in the south wall, and facing east on a plinth against the west wall is a large white marble statue of a nobleman at prayer.

We now come to the point where the ambulatory begins the turn into the apse. These radial chapels were constructed between 1235 and 1250.

The Chapel of St Guillaume (St William) (formerly St Remi), the chapel of the Ursins. This Chapel occupies two bays and each bay has a

Choir, North Side

A Glimpse Of Glory

window of four lancets with multifoil and quatrefoils in the tracery, and each has a quadripartite vault painted blue with gold stars. There is a very large painting filling the west wall of the chapel, and in the western (right) bay, facing east beneath the window, are the kneeling painted statues of Jean Juvenal des Ursins, the merchants' Provost, and his wife Michele de Vitry. The eastern wall is painted with gold "H"s, and forms the background to the large marble sculpture by Pigalle, which is the 18th century mausoleum of Count Claude-Henri d'Harcourt. The remainder of the chapel is used as a storage area.

Notice the skill of the architect in his arrangement of the columns and vaulting. There are five arches in the choir arcade, but they are doubled in the arcade dividing the two aisles of the ambulatory. He has placed a column in the ambulatory opposite the centre of each arch in the choir arcade. Look up and see that the vault is constructed of almost equal triangles, and because it is quite high there is a fine sense of great space in the turn of the Apse.

The Chapel of St George (formerly St James, SS Crispin & Crispinian, and St Stephen). This chapel occupies three bays. Each of the three bays has a quadripartite vault painted blue with little gold stars.

In the west bay the window has four lancets, each having six medallions with scenes, and the tracery above of a large multifoil and two quatrefoils. In the centre of the large multifoil is a scene depicting the Israelites worshipping the Golden Calf while Moses was receiving the Ten Commandments. On the west wall is a large painting of a hilltop castle and a horseman in the centre. Against the dado, marble plaques flank a marble statue of a priest.

The centre bay has a bare wooden altar with a crucifix and six candles on the retable, and the four lancets in the south wall above the altar have four scenes in each of them, and again a multifoil and two quatrefoils in the tracery. In the centre of the multifoil a seated St Stephen is depicted, his hand raised in blessing. To the west of the south wall is a piscina.

The eastern bay has a window as before—four scenes in each lancet. A buttress intrudes into the east wall, before which on a plinth, is a statue of Joan of Arc, facing west, her sword raised above her head. In the centre of the multifoil in the tracery can be seen a French king on horseback.

The Axial Chapel—The Chapel of Notre-Dame of the Seven Sorrows (formerly St Nicaise, St Louis, and St Rigobert) the chapel of the Gondi family. This Chapel, too, has three bays, each with a quadripartite vault painted blue with gold stars. The window in each bay contains four lancets each with four scenes, and each with a multifoil and two quatrefoils in the tracery. The glass is dated 1884 except for the centre windows which are dated 1855.

The south bay (on the right) has a large statue of a kneeling figure against the east wall facing north. It is a statue of Pierre, Cardinal de Gondi, Archbishop of Paris 1568–1598. On the south wall there was a large fresco painting of the seated Virgin Mary flanked by kneeling figures beneath a crocketted canopy.

In the centre bay there is an altar against the east wall with a tabernacle in the retable. The reredos above has a sculpture of the Deposition from the Cross in the centre, the burial of Christ in the tomb on the left, and on the right the women at the tomb being met by the angel. The statue above the retable of Our Lady holding a crown of thorns, the greatest of her Sorrows, is from the Second Empire (1852–1870).

In the North Bay there are frescoes dated 1887 filling the wall with scenes of Christ's Passion along the lower level. Facing south against the East wall is a large statue of Albert de Gondi, 1522–1602, Duke of Retz, and Marshal of France, at prayer. All the tombs in the chapels of the ambulatories were removed in 1790 and returned to the cathedral only in 1955.

Against the inner wall of the ambulatory, behind the High Altar, is a marble effigy of a bishop closed by a wrought iron screen. Coloured stones decorate the mitre, collar and gloves.

THE NORTH AMBULATORY

The Chapel of St Marcel (formerly St John the Baptist). The windows in the three bays have the same arrangement as the radial chapels in the south ambulatory, but all in grisaille, which makes the chapels rather dark. The three vaults are all quadripartite. In the right bay there was a huge monumental sculpture. At the time of my last visit the chapel is used largely for storage, which is a disgrace in the Cathedral of the capital city.

The Chapel of St Louis (formerly St Martin, St Anne, St Michael or the Chapel of Nuailles). Louis IX was crowned the King of France at Reims in 1234. He was a just ruler and his devotion led him to acquire the Crown of Thorns from the Emperor in 1239. He took the Cross as a Crusader and died of dysentery in Tunis on his second crusading journey in 1270. He was canonized as St Louis in 1297 by Pope Boniface Vlll.

This chapel extends over two bays with both windows in 18th century grisaille, except for the centre of the multifoil windows in the tracery where can be seen the arms of Jean le Vier. An altar in marble is decorated with a floral design on the retable and ten small painted arches flank a larger central arch which is above the tabernacle. Around both bays of this chapel the dado is painted with gold fleurs-

A Glimpse Of Glory

de-lys on blue horizontal bands interspersed with gold crowns on yellow bands, after Viollet le Duc. On the east wall above the altar there is a fresco painting of four figures. The decoration is repeated in the north bay, but there are two marble plaques with the bands either side in place of the altar on the north wall. Like the east wall of the other bay, there is a fresco painting of four figures on the north wall.

Above both frescoes, which are in four blind lancets in each bay, is a tracery of a multifoil with two quatrefoils. The very slender vertical mullions of these blind lancets support in each case three corbels decorated with heads, on which rest three short columns bearing statues. Each bay has a quadripartite vault painted in blue with small gold stars.

The Chapel of St Germain (formerly St Ferrioi and St Ferrutien). A native of Autun, Germanus became Bishop of Paris in 555. The Chapel has a quadripartite vault, and the windows are as in the other chapels: grisaille dated 1864. A bare marble altar stands against the east wall. The south wall has a poor fresco which is dark and damaged. There is a piscina in the north wall, and a monument against the west wall to Monsignor Le Clerc de Juigne, Archbishop of Paris 1781–1801. Having witnessed the desecration of the cathedral he died one year before Catholic worship was restored. This chapel, too, is used as a storage area.

At this point in the inner aisle of the North Ambulatory a large candelabra has been lowered to the ground. It measures about four metres across and I counted 32 candles around the circle and 21 candles at low-level in groups of three.

This is a good place to pause and observe the south clerestory windows across the sanctuary and chancel. The bay to the south (right) of the east window depicts Elizabeth and Mary (the Visitation, matching the Annunciation to the north). To the right are the former Bishops of Paris Eudes de Sully and Marcel; then Augustine and Jerome; above the wrought-iron gates are the evangelists Luke and John; then Daniel and Jeremiah; David and Abraham; George and Martin; Charlemagne and Leo lll; Hilary and Irenaeus.

It is with some relief that we can now lower our eyes and return to our examination of the ambulatory.

The Chapel of St Ferdinand (formerly St John the Baptist and St Magdalene). The window has grisaille glazing. Against the east wall there is a marble monument to J B de Budes, Marshal of France, 1643. There is also a statue of a kneeling figure on a plinth, and the name Bec Grespin is mentioned, but it is not possible to determine which name goes with which monument. There is a marble wall plaque on the west wall.

North Choir Screen, the Nativity

At this point on the inner ambulatory wall, above the blind arcade of the dado, the sequence of superb mediaeval carved scenes of Christ's life, which forms the back of the chancel stalls, begins at the eastern end with the Visitation of Mary to her cousin Elizabeth. Such a sequence usually begins with the Annunciation by the angel, so one must conclude that this section has been removed to make way for the wrought iron gate to the chancel. There follows the Nativity of Christ, the visit by Shepherds and the Magi (or Kings), Herod's anger resulting in the slaughter of the children, the flight of the Holy Family into Egypt, the Presentation of Christ in the Temple, his Baptism, the wedding at Cana, the triumphal entry into Jerusalem on the first Palm Sunday, the Last Supper, Christ washing the feet of the disciples, and concluding on this side of the cathedral with Christ praying in the Garden of Gethsemane while the disciples sleep.

The next bay. There is a window in the north wall as before, and blind arcading on the east and west walls. A wooden screen closes this bay because inside there are rows of staff lockers.

The final two bays are also screened from the ambulatory, and so we turn right into the north transept.

THE NORTH TRANSEPT

As we noted in the south transept, the north façade was enlarged around 1250, slightly earlier than the south. It also comprises one shallow bay under a narrow

A Glimpse Of Glory

quadripartite vault, and, as in the south transept, the north wall has a central porch flanked by four tall, blind lancets with three roundels in the tracery. A statue stands to the right of the porch. Above is a row of M. Gerente's coloured lancets protected by a gallery, over which soars the great north rose window.

The great **rose window** was inserted in the north wall in 1252. Sixteen 'spokes' ending in cusped trefoil arches radiate from a central medallion on which can be seen the Virgin and Child, and are succeeded by an outer ring of thirty-two smaller spokes that also end in a trefoil. Each of the trefoils terminates in a medallion and the whole is surrounded by a further ring of individual trefoils bearing a medallion. So there are eighty medallions on which the theme is presented: an inner ring of Old Testament prophets, who prepared the way for the coming of Christ, surrounded in the outer ring by the Judges and Kings of Israel. More Kings and Priests appear in the ring of trefoils. It really is a glorious window largely glazed in blue. Legend has it that the young Viollet-le-Duc, taken to Notre Dame by his father, cried out that the rose was turning on its central medallion, so delicately is it balanced. The eighteen Kings of Judah in the gallery below the rose are by the 19th century restorer. The north rose itself has endured hardly any significant restoration and is almost entirely in its original form.

The east wall is plain and bears a large 17th century May painting of "The Triumph of Job". There are three blind lancets at the level of the rose window.

The west wall is similar, with a May painting by Laurent de la Hyre, dated 1635 depicting St Peter curing the sick with his shadow.

THE NORTH AISLE

With the exception of the Chapel of St Enfance and the Baptistry, all the windows in the chapels have four lancets with a multifoil and two quatrefoils in the tracery, all in 18th century grisaille glass. There is quadripartite vaulting throughout.

The Chapel of St Clotilde (formerly St Nicholas). Clotilde was an early 6th century Burgundian princess who became the Queen of Clovis, King of the Franks, and converted him to Catholic Christianity. He was baptized by Remigius, at Reims in 496. After his death in 511 she retired to the abbey of St Martin at Tours, where she died in 545.

A statue of Our Lady stands above the altar. There is a piscina in the north wall, beside which is an ancient bas relief carved stone, which is the funerary tablet of Canon Yver (died 1468). A buttress intrudes into the west wall.

The Chapel of St Landry (formerly St Catherine). Against the north wall there is a statue on a plinth of a mitred Bishop his right hand raised in blessing.

There is a large painting by Matthew Elias of 'The Sons of Sceva beaten by the Devil', the May offered on 1st May 1702. In 2011 a plaque by the chapel entrance mentioned the 'Martyrdom of Catharine' depicted in a painting on the east wall, but it had been replaced. The bare altar rests on two pillars.

The Chapel of Our Lady of Guadeloupe (formerly St Julian Le Pauvre and St Mary the Egyptian). The 1687 May painting on the west wall of this chapel is by the artist Louis Cheron, and depicts 'The Prophet Agabus foretells the Suffering of St Paul'. The altar is similar to that in the last chapel, but it has bouquets of flowers all over it.

The Chapel of St Vincent de Paul (formerly the Chapel of St Laurence). Vincent de Paul was ordained priest in 1600 and from 1613–25 was Tutor in the house of the Count de Gondi in Paris. He later founded the Sisters of Charity in 1633. He was canonized in 1737.

On the west wall is a large painting by Gabriel Blanchard with the interesting title, 'St Andrew thrills with joy at the prospect of his torture', the May of 1670. There is a Piscina on the north wall. There is a bare altar with a statue of St Vincent de Paul on a short plinth on the retable. A monument against the north wall is in memory of Cardinal Amette, 1850–1920, Cardinal Archbishop of Paris from 1908.

The Chapel of St Enfance (formerly the Chapel of St Geneviève). There is a bare altar as before with a statue on a bracket above it of the seated Christ with two children. The Piscina is in the north wall against which there is a statue on a plinth of a mother teaching her daughter to spin (perhaps St Anne teaching the Virgin Mary). The large painting by Louis Testelin on the west wall is the May of 1655 and its title is, 'The Flagellation of St Paul and St Silas'. There is just one large multifoil in the tracery of the window.

The Chapel of St Charles (formerly in Chapel of St George and St Blaise). Below the window is a statue on a plinth. There is a bare altar as before with a fine painting of a Pietà on east wall above the altar. It is by Baugin, 1610–83. The large painting by Nicholas Loir on the west wall is the May for 1650, and depicts 'St Paul making the false prophet Bar Jesus blind and thus converting the proconsul Sergius'. There is a Piscina to the east of the north wall.

The Baptistry (formerly the Chapel of St Leonard). There is a painting on east wall of 'the Nativity' by Jerome Franck. On the west wall is a painting by Jacques Blanchard of 'The Descent of the Holy Spirit', the May of 1634. There is a 19th century font in this Chapel, which appears to be bronze and is after Violet le Duc. The window contains two wide lancets with a roundel above all in grisaille.

The final bay has a blank north wall under a quadripartite vault.

A Glimpse Of Glory

We have returned to the west end of the church and now concluded our visit. If you have the stamina for it, you might wish to join the queue for the ascent of the northwest tower. On the other hand, you might wish to cross the road for a well-deserved pastis.

The Nativity, Baptistry

DO NOT MISS

1. The portals of the west façade.
2. The carving beneath the statue of the Virgin on the trumeau of the north door of the west façade.
3. The Red Door (Porte Rouge).
4. The polychrome mediaeval stone screen in the ambulatories.
5. The Treasury.
6. The Rose Windows.
7. The Baroque sanctuary.
8. The Chevet from across the river.
9. The Cluny Museum—to find the museum cross the bridge to the south bank of the Seine into the Latin Quarter, turn right along the river and take the next left into Boulevard St Michel; the museum is about a three-minute walk and it is on the left.

CHAPTER 5

BOURGES

First mentioned in 52 BC as a part of Caesar's domain, Bourges is situated on the site of Avaricum, an important Roman settlement and the place where Leocardius, a Prefect of Rome and Governor of Aquitania, had his palace. The story relates that Saint Ursin came here to preach Christianity, bringing with him from Rome the relics of the first martyr, St Stephen. Leocardius was converted to the faith and offered his palace as a sanctuary for the relics.

After the battle of Vouillé, in which Clovis conquered the Visigoths, Bourges submitted to Clovis and was united to the kingdom of the Franks under Clotaire II in the 7th century. Philippe l took possession of Bourges in 1102 and the city was attached to the royal domain. Louis VII was crowned here on Christmas Day 1137, and it was the birthplace of Louis XI, who became king of France in 1423. Later it became the capital of the ancient province of Berry, and when the provinces were split into départements it became the chief city of the Department of Cher.

It is almost in the centre of France, but off the usual tourist trail. I first travelled to Bourges from Chartres and approached the city across rolling pastures. Soon, I saw the cathedral on the horizon, looking like a huge beached whale. It soon disappeared from view behind landscape features, and then I was driving downhill into the lower city, with only occasional glimpses of the great building. When visiting Bourges I always stay in the Ibis Hotel in Rue Vladimir Jankélévitch, which has a convenient car park to the rear of the hotel. This means that I have to stroll through some delightful narrow streets to the upper city, where the cathedral sits on the crown of the hill.

THE CATHEDRAL CHURCH OF ST STEPHEN (ST ÉTIENNE)

Surprisingly, the name of the architect of the present cathedral is unknown; as is the date of commencement, but it is believed to be in the time of Archbishop Saint

A Glimpse Of Glory

BOURGES—KEY

1 The West Central Portal
2 Portal of St Guillaume
3 Portal of the Blessed Virgin
4 Portal of St Stephen
5 Portal of St Ursula
6 The Huge Supporting Butress
7 The South Façade
8 The North Façade
9 The West End of the Nave
10 The Nave
11 The Meridian Gnomon
12 The South Inner Aisle
13 The North Inner Aisle
14 The South Outer Aisle
15 The Sacristy
16 The Copin Chapel
17 The Le Roy Chapel
18 Chapel of the Sacred Heart
19 The Pulpit
20 The South Door
21 The Nave Altar
22 The Choir
23 The High Altar
24 The Sanctuary
25 The South Inner AmbulaTory
25a The South Outer Ambulatory
26 The Tullier Chapel
27 The Aligret Chapel
28 The Boisratier Chapel
29 The Joseph Window
30 Chapel of St Francis de Sales
31 St Thomas in India Window
32 The Apocalypse Window
33 Chapel of All Saints
34 The Passion Window
35 The Judgement Window
36 The Axial Chapel of Our Lady
37 The New Alliance Window
38 The North Inner Ambulatory
38a The North Outer Ambulatory
39 The Prodigal Son Window
40 Chapel of Our Lady of Lourdes
41 The Good Samaritan Window
42 The St Stephen Window
43 Chapel of the Holy Cross
44 The Dives & Lazarus Window
45 The Jacques Cœur Chapel
46 The Trousseau Chapel
47 The Chapter House
48 The Dr Breuil Chapel
49 The North Outer Aisle
50 The De Bar Chapel
51 Entrance to the Crypt
52 The North Door
53 The Beaucaire Chapel
54 The Fradet Chapel
55 The Baptistry
56 Entrance to the North Tower

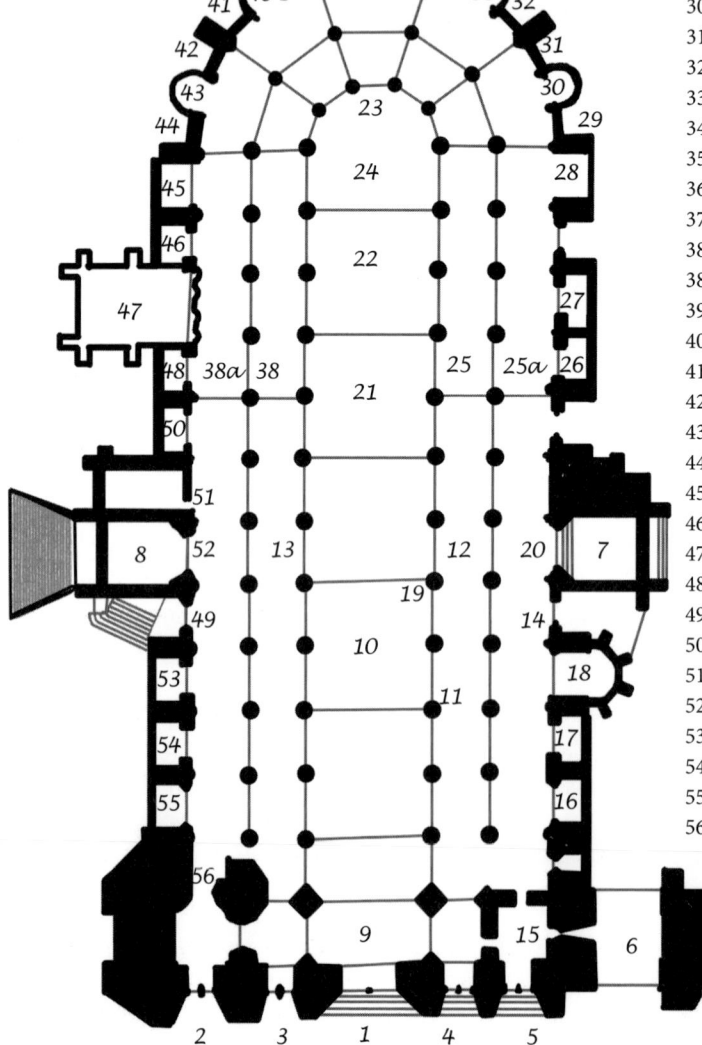

Guillaume (William). In 1195, Archbishop Henri de Sully, William's successor, donated a large sum of money for the repair of the collapsing cathedral at Bourges. The fact that he was the brother of Eudes de Sully, Archbishop of Paris, might explain why it is Paris, rather than Chartres, which influenced the architect of Bourges. As in Notre-Dame, it has two aisles on each side of the nave, and a double ambulatory. Like Mantes, Sens and Vienne, there are no transepts. Christopher Wilson, in his work, "The Gothic Cathedral" (published by Thames & Hudson, 1990), suggests that the sense of hugeness at Bourges is due to the "exceptionally long" bays of sexpartite vaulting, which is a breath of freedom after the heavily-stressed vaults of Chartres, and which also allow greater visibility of the aisles, which, Wilson affirms, "are more impressive than any other gothic church" [p.107]. Wilson notes that Cluny had five vessels with high arcades, and that the uncle of Henri de Sully had been Abbot there in the 1170s.

The eastern chapels resemble small blisters in the wall of the apse. Work began in the eastern end, and by 1214 the choir (that is the turning bays and the first two double bays immediately following it) was complete. Radding & Clark, in their book, "Medieval Architecture, Medieval Learning", published by Yale, 1992, report that, "An inspection of Bourges Cathedral in 1214, proves that the main part of the ambulatory was serving as a place of worship, and it can be deduced that the windows in this part of the building were in place."

The interior, however, gives an immediate impression of the giant arcade reminiscent of Romanesque churches. The architect of Bourges developed this style and brought it up to date. He made no provision for a tribune gallery; but instead used the whole of the vertical space for the arcade, leaving a relatively small triforium and clerestory high up in the curve of the vault. The result is superb.

Helen Henderson, in her book, "Cathedrals of France", published by Methuen, 1929, gives us this cautionary tale, "It is not until the year 1209 that we begin to have definite news of the building and then only indirectly. An old manuscript relates that in that year, when Guillaume was about to set forth upon a crusade against the Albigeois (Albigensians), he preached a farewell sermon to his flock in the cathedral, but since the place where he stood was ' open to the four winds' he was taken with a severe chill, followed by a violent fever, which carried him off shortly afterwards. Now the archbishop's place would have been the pulpit at the side of the nave of the old cathedral, and for it to be thus exposed the construction of the choir must have been well under way."

Christopher Wilson has a more academic deduction, "The choir was completed only around 1214, so it would have been possible at many points to modify the design without impairing its homogeneity or leaving telltale traces like those in

A Glimpse Of Glory

the presbytery at Canterbury. How far the design actually was modified is a matter of dispute."

In any event, on the 5th May, 1324, Archbishop Guillaume de Brosse consecrated the church, so that the cathedral of Bourges was built in a little over a hundred years.

THE EXTERIOR

THE WEST FAÇADE

My first glimpse of the astonishing west front of the cathedral as I emerged from Rue Porte Jaune stopped me in my tracks. With five western portals, instead of the usual three, and soaring buttresses and towers, it hits you like a tidal wave. It is a while before one can take in the immense scale of the building. The twin towers disguise the triangular plan of the structure, even though the five porches indicate the five aisles behind them.

In "Medieval Architecture, Medieval Learning", Radding & Clark are clearly impressed, as we read on page 134: *"At thirty-six metres, Bourges was the tallest*

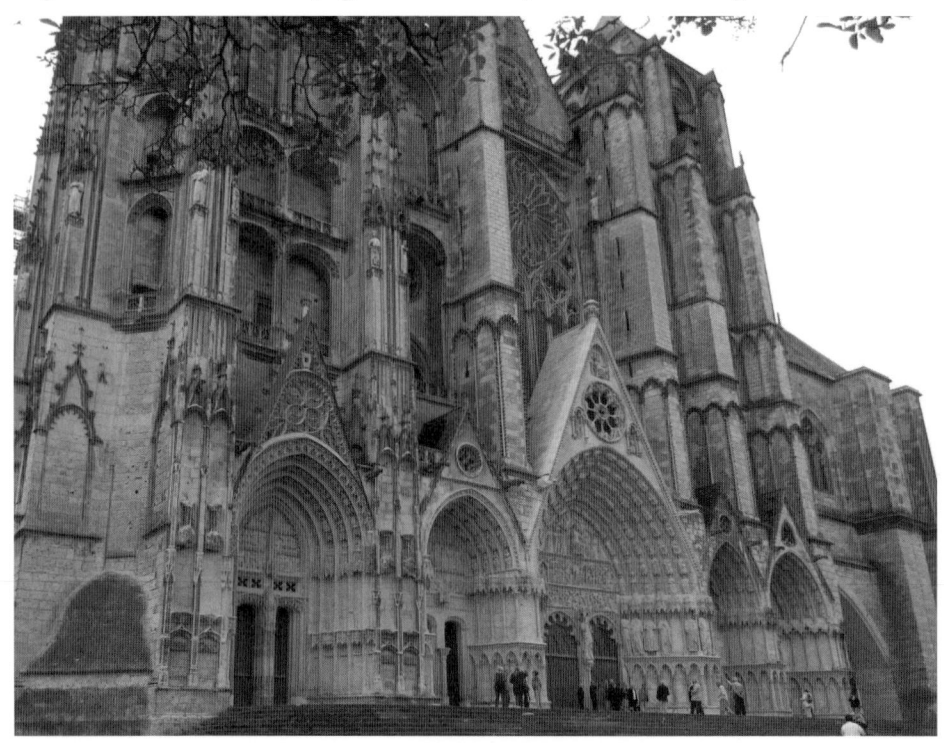

West Façade 2013

building of the twelfth century. What the builder designed was a building nearly as wide as it is tall and almost triangular in cross section because the inner aisle is dramatically higher than the outer aisle... yet the height of the inner side aisle permits the viewer to see through to the windows of the exterior wall despite the building's great width."

The west façade gives an immediate impression of massive stonework; the buttresses between the aisles project forward from the west wall and rise, with relatively simple adornment, to the height of the roof. The canopies of the portals rise between them, but the ornate and delicate sculptures and decoration seem to sap the strength of the massive stonework at ground level. Framed by the buttresses above the central portal is the central façade known as the 'grand hosteau': six lancets with quatrefoil tracery support the great rose window made by Guy de Dammartin at the end of the 14th century. Here again the architect has acted with innovative courage, for the rose is not round, but takes the shape of a lozenge in order to fill as much of the wall as possible. Spaces in the spandrels are decorated with blind trefoils above and glazed quatrefoils below. A pierced parapet surmounts the rose and above it, under the canopy, is a blind rose formed of cusped trefoils. The 'grand hosteau' was so admired that it was copied at Le Mans and Tours.

The twin west towers were completed to the height of the great vaults by 1250, but within ten years the south tower began to settle, causing concern about the adjacent vaults. Any thought of building the towers higher was abandoned together with any provision of bells. Even so, the south tower showed signs of leaning, and it was probably in 1313 that the canons had a huge supporting buttress built at the southwest corner to prevent the tower collapsing. The inclusion of the five portals, causing the bases to be narrower, had indeed sapped the strength of the buttresses, for in 1506 the north tower collapsed. It was rebuilt by 1530, and became known as "the butter tower" when folk who wished to avoid fasting in Lent could continue to eat butter on payment of a sum of money towards the rebuilding. Without regard for symmetry, at 65 metres it is higher than its former twin, the "tour sourde", the 'deaf tower'.

Let us now examine the great 14th century west portals or doorways. They are not as cavernous as those at Amiens or Reims but deep enough to contain archivolts filled with a multitude of exquisitely carved figures. The walls on either side are lined with canopied niches, which the hammers of the protestant Huguenots under Gabriel de Lorges, Count of Montgomery, have almost entirely denuded of their statues in May 1562. They threw ropes around the statues and hauled them to the ground, causing severe injury to the profaners in the process. These canopied niches are returned across the face of each great buttress, and so continue across the entire 55-metre width of the façade, unifying the structure. The spandrels formed

A Glimpse Of Glory

by the arches of these arcades bear the remains of a continuous series of carved episodes taken from the book Genesis, from Creation to the Covenant with Noah.

We begin with the left (northern) door.

The Northern or St Guillaume (William) Portal. The two deeply recessed doors are divided by a trumeau bearing the badly mutilated figure of the former Archbishop of Bourges. The top of the doors are round and decorated with carved trefoils and with foliage in the moulding and in the spandrels. Resting on the arches either side of the trumeau is a panel pierced by two quatrefoils. So deep is the recess that it permits five orders of carved figures under canopies in the archivolt, and five empty niches with canopies either side on the walls of the splay. There are small carved panels under these canopies. The sculptures in the tympanum represent the miraculous works and the founding of the church here by Saint William.

The North Inner or Blessed Virgin Portal. At first glance this portal appears bland as the two doorways are crowned with round, unadorned arches and divided by an empty trumeau. On closer inspection, however, the trumeau and its empty bracket are delicately sculpted, and beneath the tympanum is a delightful frieze which is filled with intricate scroll-work under a band of stiff-leaf decoration. There are three arches, and one on the return, each side of the splay of the porch. Under their canopies is sculpted a shell, but the statues they once sheltered are missing. Even the sculpted scenes in the spandrels have been badly mutilated. Above the arcade slender columns continue the division of the wall into three sections, each of which has a richly decorated canopy. From above these canopies spring the delicate sculptures which decorate the four orders of the archivolt. The tympanum depicts scenes from the life of the Blessed Virgin Mary.

These two northern portals were severely damaged when the north tower collapsed, and were rebuilt in the 16th century, only to be mutilated later by the protestant Huguenots and the Revolutionaries.

Central West Portal Trumeau

Bourges

The Great Centre Portal. This is an enormous cavern of a portal, with two wide doors, each covered with a cusped arch, and divided by a finely decorated trumeau bearing a statue of Christ with his right hand raised in blessing and holding the book of the Gospels in his left. An arcade of five large arches with sculpted spandrels and canopies forms each side of the splay of the porch. These two arcades support a series of columns which in turn rise to five richly decorated canopies each side; sadly, apart from some mutilated figures in the upper level on the right, they are all devoid of statuary. However, springing from these canopies are the six orders of statues of the archivolt. The innermost two orders contain angels, and the remainder have statues of Biblical figures all seated under canopies.

The tympanum of the central door of Gothic cathedrals was traditionally filled with sculpted scenes of the Last judgement, and Bourges is no exception. For its moving pathos alone, it is one of the most celebrated pieces of mediaeval religious sculpture.

The tympanum is divided into three registers: in the lower section we see the resurrection of the dead as they push aside their tomb covers; an abbot can be seen

Central West Portal Tympanum

143

A Glimpse Of Glory

second from the left, while third to his right is a king still wearing his crown as he clasps his hands in prayer.

In the middle register the souls are being weighed by Archangel Michael, who stands between the clothed redeemed, who look to Abraham carrying souls in his bosom on the extreme left, and the naked damned, who look thoughtfully as they are prodded by grotesque creatures to the right where two devils with bellows are heating a great cauldron. Two figures are already in the cauldron, and a toad bites the tongue of the man while another bites the breast of the woman. According to Jean-Yves Ribault, in his current guide to the cathedral (published by Editions Ouest-France), the monk in a Franciscan habit seen leading the procession of the redeemed bears a stigmata on the back of his hand, and is thought to represent St Francis of Assisi, who died in 1226 and was canonised in 1228, making this almost a contemporary statue.

In the top register, an austere Christ, the marks of the nails visible in his hands, sits on his throne as the divine Judge, with angels either side bearing the instruments of his passion.

The South Inner or St Étienne (Stephen) Portal. The recent cleaning of the west façade serves to emphasise the lack of decoration in this portal. The two doors culminate in a lintel which bears two trefoil windows above it. They are separated by the column of the trumeau, bearing a statue of St Stephen vested as a deacon, carrying a palm branch over his right shoulder. From its origin in the ancient Middle East, the palm branch has signified victory, and in the Christian church the martyr enduring death for his faith is such a victory. The canopied niches at two levels continue either side of the splay of the doors, and, again, all are empty of statuary. But in the spandrel between the outer arches on the left can be seen Noah's Ark, with little figures peeping out. The patron of the cathedral is the subject for the sculptures in the three registers of the tympanum (1230 AD). In the centre of the middle register, Stephen can be seen kneeling in prayer as his assailants prepare to stone him to death for blasphemy. At the extreme left Saul (later St Paul) can be seen receiving the cloak of an attacker (Acts of the Apostles, chapter 7, verse 58).

The Southern or St Ursin Portal. The empty canopied niches continue in the splay of the door as before, but don't miss the spandrel in the arch on the front of the buttress which divides this portal from St Stephen's Portal: Noah can be seen holding his hand out to see if the rain has stopped; then trees can be seen on dry land as the water level dropped. On the left of the splay within this portal a spandrel depicts the grounded Ark as a floating mansion. The two doors, which are each covered with a cusped window under a pointed arch, are divided by a trumeau with a simple slender column bearing a statue of St Ursin in Mass vestments and mitre, his hand raised in blessing as he stands on the body of a

Noah, St Ursin Portal

demon. The archivolt contains three orders of seated figures under canopies, and an inner order of standing angels. In the tympanum (1230 AD) we see episodes in the life of St Ursin: his commission from St Peter to evangelise Gaul with his companion, St Just (lower right); burying St Just who died on the way; walking on alone carrying the relics of St Stephen; preaching to the people of Bourges; he consecrates the first church here, dedicated to St Stephen (middle section); St Ursin converts and baptises the Roman Prefect, Leocardius, and his son (top). All are stories recorded in the mediaeval work, "The Golden Legend" by Voragine (translated by Ryan and published by Princeton, 1993).

THE SOUTH SIDE

We turn now to the right and passing under the enormous arch of the emergency buttress inserted in 1313, we move into the former Archbishop's formal garden to the south of the cathedral, with its flower beds, parterre and avenue of lime trees. There is a sense in which I agree with Francis Bumpus, when he suggests in his book, "The Glories of Northern France", published by Dennis, London, in 1905, that the proportions of the west façade tend to overpower the building so that only at the side can the beauty of the cathedral be appreciated. I think he overstates the case, but the view from the garden is one of majesty and great beauty.

A Glimpse Of Glory

The piers between the aisles rise through the roof of the inner aisle, while the buttresses between each bay of the outer aisle are even more visible, as at Chartres, and form a stone palisade around the exterior of the cathedral. The former serve as a support, like the pier of a bridge, between the first arch of each double-tier flying buttress, which carries the thrust down from the main roof vault, and the second one, which passes it down to the outside piers. The arrangement is even more evident from the top of the northwest tower, which is open to the public. Radding & Clark, again, comment thus, "*In effect, the forces from the main vaults and roof* [are] *stepped successively down to the vaults of the inner and outer aisles, with the steep arches of the flying buttresses helping to convey the forces directly to the ground.*"

North Roof from the Northwest Tower

This is clearly seen from the former Archbishops' garden. A rectangular buttress strengthens the clerestory wall between each bay where the flying buttresses receive the force from the roof. These rectangular buttresses rise above the level of the main roof and terminate in little spires decorated with crockets, forming a final statement of grandeur. These delicate spires rise behind a balustrade pierced by quatrefoils which runs around the entire building at the level of the high roof.

THE SOUTH FAÇADE

The north and south portals were intended for the west façade of the earlier Romanesque cathedral, and so they were already sixty years old when they were incorporated into the present building around 1225 AD.

This south portal is dedicated to the theme of Christ in Majesty. Framed by two simple buttresses, a slender column divides the portal into two arches with cusped decoration at the top. A multifoil opening above the central column appears to be slightly out of alignment with the simple arch which encloses the top of the portal. A pierced balustrade links the tops of the two buttresses.

In the tympanum of the doorway a stylized Christ sits in a vesica surrounded by symbols of the four Evangelists, Matthew, Mark, Luke and John. The twelve Apostles are seated in round-headed arcades in the architrave below. Three saints in niches supported by short carved columns line the door jambs. In two orders of the archivolt in the semi-circular arch over the door are little seated figures, while the other two are moulded. A statue of Christ stands on the trumeau.

South Door, West Columns

The doors are superb examples of Late Gothic wood-carving. The upper panels have crocketted ogee-shaped arches with the following request for prayers for the repose of Reginaldus Boicelli: *"Orate pro defunctis et benefactoribus ecclesiæ. Reginaldus Boiselli."* (*Pray for the departed and the benefactors of the church*). The way his name is at the end obviously means that the primary 'objects' of prayer are, of course, the 'benefactores', but by adding the general word 'defuncti' as well, he cleverly includes himself in the request. He was the executor of the donors of this doorway, Jaques Cœur and his son Jean, Archbishop of Bourges, in whose memory the letters I (for Jean) and RB are carved in the panels of the doors.

THE CHEVET

Like the chevet at Le Mans, this aspect of Bourges reminds me of the bows of a great ship rearing up above my head when viewed from the garden of the former palace of the archbishop. The buttress supporting the last bay before the turn of the chevet on the south side of the choir is much larger, higher, and terminates in a spire, because it houses the staircase to a gangway on the slope of the flying buttress, which leads to a door in the choir clerestory permitting access to the high vault.

A Glimpse Of Glory

The Tympanum, North Façade Portal

THE NORTH FAÇADE

There is a declivity in the ground from south to north, for whereas on the south side there are no steps up to the south portal, here there is a flight of twenty-four steps to reach the north door. The portal is identical to the south doorway, except that above the arch, a gabled window of two round-headed lancets and a round oculus above them gives light to a room above the porch. The portal is dedicated to the Blessed Virgin Mary, and in the tympanum can be seen the Annunciation and the Visitation on the right, and the Adoration of the Magi, albeit somewhat mutilated, on the left. In the centre are the Virgin and Child. Here, only one saint in a niche supported by a short carved column stands either side of the door. The top of the right hand columns are particularly delicately carved.

THE INTERIOR

From the first moment I entered Bourges Cathedral I have been enchanted by it. I think it is because of the space and the light, and the coolness on a hot day, in which the enormous width of the aisles on each side is a major factor. The nave really is vast, and the inner aisles soar to the level of the triforium of the nave, with their own triforium and clerestory so that they mirror the arrangement of the nave. *"Thus, from the outer wall on one side it is possible to see all three levels of the main elevation, as well as all three levels of the outer wall of the inner aisle,*

Paris, west facade of Notre Dame

Paris, South Transept rose

Paris, Vault boss over the crossing

Paris, High Altar Pieta

Paris, St Peter curing sick—detail, south transept, west wall

Paris, Christ on the Road to Emmaus, South Choir Screen

Bourges, from the southeast

Bourges, Christ harrowing hell, The Passion window

Bourges, Dives feasting, The Lazarus window

Bourges, Dives cries out in torment, The Lazarus window

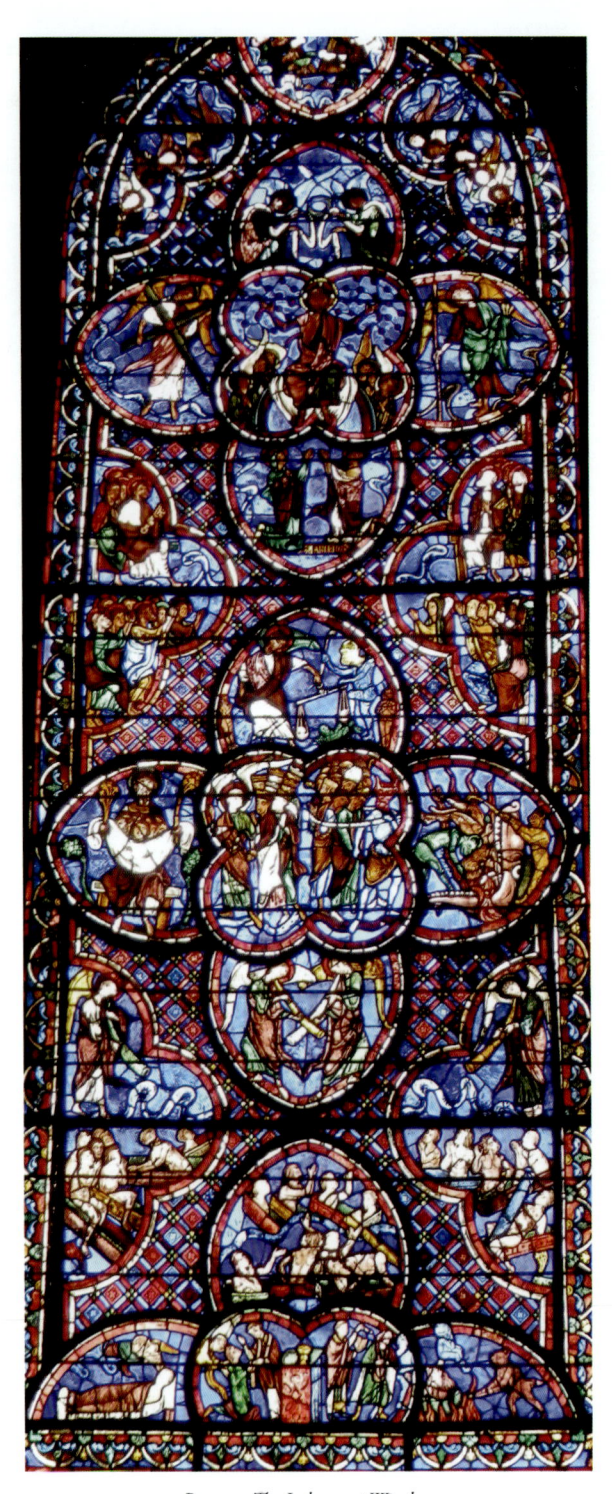

Bourges, The Judgement Window

Bourges, The Crucifixion, New Alliance window

Bourges, Christ washes the disciples' feet, Passion window

Bourges, Micah, Jonah & Obadiah, north choir clerestory

Troyes, the window of the Mystic Wine-press, detail

and, at the lowest level, the windows of the outer aisle, giving the visual impression of five stories with three levels of windows and two wall-passages, an audacious visual scheme." Radding and Clark p.134.

The great height of the main arcade, together with the sexpartite vaulting, makes it impossible for the nave to dominate the interior. In "The Gothic Cathedral", Christopher Wilson offers the view that *"the most remarkable thing about Bourges is that the spatial effect which its five parallel vessels create is not diffuse but unified and concentrated. The concern to give these qualities their full value is probably sufficient explanation for the omission of transepts."* It is because the central aisle is unbroken by a crossing, one has the impression of a very long cathedral, although, at 405 feet in length, it is among the shortest.

THE WEST END

The west end has a large, flattened arch over the western doors, above which is the wooden organ loft and pipework casing. Over the organ, divided into two arches of three lancets in each, are six lancet windows, each containing a figure in the central registers beneath a decorated canopy, and above that, in the top of the two major arches, there are two trefoils supporting a larger quatrefoil. All this supports the beautiful big lozenge-shaped rose above it, which fills the wall right up to the vaulted ceiling.

The Nave

A Glimpse Of Glory

THE NAVE

As there is no transept, the sweep of wall along the nave and around the chevet turns the church into a single, vast space in which all of the bay divisions are subsumed into the whole. The nave has huge columns soaring up to the height of the inner aisle clerestory vaulting. However, their massive bulk is made elegant by slender enclosed shafts equally spaced around the column, all soaring up to a very small decorated capital with an abacus, except that the engaged shafts pierce the decorated moulding of the capital and the abacus. The arches of the bays spring east and west from the abacus, but the engaged slender shafts rise through the triforium up to the stringcourse of the clerestory, where some spring around the arch of the clerestory and others reach out as ribs across the roof vaulting. It is beautifully done. There is an impression of immense height because of these uncluttered engaged shafts rising right up to the roof, and also because of the aisles behind them. It's vast. Furthermore, it is my view that this is the finest example of sexpartite vaulting in the Gothic world. Paul Frankl in his book, "Gothic Architecture", published by Yale, 2000, takes a similar view:

> "There is at Bourges a new solution to the demand for combining uniform piers with sexpartite vaults. Around each of the round piers, which are so surprisingly high because the double aisles on either side of the nave force the triforium upwards, there are eight shafts at equal intervals. Above the abaci, the shafts supporting the ribs can therefore go up between those supporting the transverse arches and those supporting the wall-arches. This is certainly more intelligent than any other similar attempt to solve the problem."

THE SOUTH SIDE OF THE NAVE

The 1st bay of the nave at the west has a massive pillar because it supports the south tower. It is truly a huge pillar with many engaged shafts rising to the height of the nave

North Nave Arcade

Bourges

arcade arches, but the central cluster rises to the bottom of the clerestory, where the columns support the ribs which spring across the vault of the nave. The huge pointed arch spanning the nave in this bay has a central boss bearing a shield with a rampant lion surmounted by a Cross of Lorraine. The triorium has four arches in the middle and a single arch each side with a blank rosette above, all giving way to a blind wall behind the passage (which continues around the church). Above that are three blind arches with three pierced and decorated rosettes in the bottom of them and a large blind rose at the top of the three blind arches. This arrangement is repeated on the north side of the nave.

The 2nd bay has a round column with evenly spaced engaged columns rising to the capital from which spring the arches along the nave. An extra intervening column continues to the clerestory, and from it the vault ribs spring from a decorated capital. In between the two huge columns in the west and the first of the regular ones to the east of them, there is a string course at triforium level and above that the four arches, with a smaller one each side making six arches in all, and a rosette above under a moulding and then a clerestory of three lancets with an oculus above. The glass in the lancets has geometric designs with little coloured triangles, but the little oculus has quite a lovely colour. This is the pattern for all the other bays in the nave. The exceptions are:

The 4th Bay has a little doorway in the triforium. In the floor near the base of the column is a brass strip aligned north to south, which crosses the cathedral from the 3rd Bay on the north side; it is a part of the Meridian Gnomon. This is an instrument for calculating the exact time based on the position of the sun. Two viewfinders have been inserted in windows above the inner aisle of this bay, one in the lancet and one above the elbow of a figure in the rose above it. Every day at noon (GMT) a ray of light coming through one of the viewfinders strikes the ground at a point along the brass strip. If the sun is obstructed by buttresses, or is too low, a second instrument located in the 8th Bay is used: a rope is lit at noon through a viewfinder inserted in a grisaille window.

The 6th Bay has a huge pulpit with two staircases, one each side, leading up to it.

Nave, The Meridian Gnomon

A Glimpse Of Glory

The 7th Bay gives access to the south door. The north door is opposite.

The nave continues with two more even bays, forming a nave of nine bays, although, the nave altar intrudes into the nave east of Bay 9.

THE NORTH SIDE OF THE NAVE

The North Side of the nave is identical to the south side: the clerestory windows in grisaille with the coloured oculi above. The only difference is that the 2nd and 3rd clerestory windows from the west have clear diamond quarry glass in the lancets, except for the central registers which have little coloured coats of arms, and in the centre of each oculus in these two bays there are little figures in gold outline.

THE AISLES

The wall dividing the double aisle has an arcade of bays, with a blind triforium above. This triforium has four arches over the three centre bays and three quatrefoils above filling the wide arch which spans the bay. Then above that level there are two lancet windows with an oculus in the tracery above. The much lower outer aisle gives access to the chapels lining the nave. The aisles have quadripartite vaulting.

THE SOUTH INNER AISLE (FROM THE WEST TO EAST)

In the west wall of the south aisle, there are two doors with trefoils above. Higher still, there is a rounded arch which looks modern. The triforium also has an arch, but divided in two with a quatrefoil above, and with a passage behind it. Above are two lancets in grisaille, with a scene in the oculus. This latter arrangement continues throughout the clerestory of this aisle, beginning in the

South Inner Aisle

second bay east of the west doors.

In the western bay of the south arcade, the triforium has two blind lancets and an oculus, and this is repeated in the north aisle.

The 1st Bay has just one lancet and a half of the oculus above, the arrangement starting in its entirety in bay 3.

Oculus in Bay 8, South Inner Aisle

The 2nd Bay frames the astronomical clock facing into the nave. Built in 1424 by Canon Jean Fusoris, it is the oldest in France to be preserved in its original state. Thanks to a scientific grant in 1994, it chimes again the first four notes of Salve Regina. A king holding a sceptre can be seen in the half oculus window in the clerestory.

Bays 3—8 the clerestory lancets all have grisaille glass or geometric patterns in them with little scenes in the round oculi above, as follows:

Bay 3—two noblemen facing each other in debate.
Bay 4—a saint threatened with a gridiron, perhaps St Lawrence.
Bay 5—an artisan building an organ.
Bay 6—two royal figures with an idol.
Bay 7—similar figures with musical instruments.
Bay 8—David (left) soothing Saul with the harp?

The 9th Bay, as on the north side, changes to two lancets glazed in diamond quarries.

Here the aisle becomes the ambulatory.

THE NORTH INNER AISLE (FROM THE WEST TO EAST)

The Western Bay has only half a lancet because the tower encroaches into it.

The 3rd Bay there are the two arches with an oculus above; the first has diamond quarries with a coat of arms in the central registers of each lancet; that in the left hand lancet seems to be the arms of a cardinal, with another coat of arms in the oculus above.

A Glimpse Of Glory

From bay 4 the clerestory windows have grisaille or diamond quarry glass with scenes in the round oculi as follows:

Bay 4—two crowned figures, the left playing a harp and the right holding a staff.

Bay 5—two crowned and seated figures, the left playing a harp the right appears to have dark skin.

Bay 6—two seated and crowned figures, the left one holding a staff and the right playing a harp.

Bay 7—two seated figures, the king to the left is playing a clarinet or a recorder, while the other is holding what appears to be a closed accordion.

Bay 8—two seated figures, the left is a demure crowned lady with long hair and on the right a figure with equally long hair holding a staff but wearing a mitre.

The 9th Bay from the west is where the arrangement changes. Here the aisle becomes the ambulatory.

THE SOUTH OUTER AISLE (FROM THE WEST TO EAST)

The 1st Bay is enclosed as a Sacristy, so the aisle begins in bay 2 as the inner aisle opens up to the outer aisle.

The 2nd Bay has a door in the west wall giving access to the Sacristy, above which is a single deeply recessed window in a rounded arch. In the south wall there is a single lancet with a trefoil above, all in diamond quarries, giving a view through to another window beyond. On the lower wall is a framed altar frontal embroidered with a Maltese cross.

The Copin Chapel has one window divided by mullions into four lancets with Rayonnant tracery above. It depicts two scenes: in the upper registers is the stoning of the deacon St Stephen (recorded in Acts of the Apostles, chapter

South Outer Aisle

7), and in the lower registers the story of St Laurence, who was a deacon in Rome. He was commanded by the Prefect of the city to hand over the treasures of the church so he gathered before the Prefect the poor of the city to whom he had already given the treasure. For this he was martyred by being roasted on a gridiron in the year 258. The gridiron can be seen in the lower right panel of the window. In the tracery above are symbols of Christ's passion and crucifixion, even a cockerel. Beneath the window stands a marble altar.

On the west wall is a statue of a nun holding crosses under an ornate canopy, and above that on a bracket is a small figure of an angel blowing a trumpet. On the east side is a statue of Christ on a bracket with a canopy, and above it another statue of an angel blowing a trumpet. A delightful vaulted ceiling has a fine boss coloured in dark blue, with two angels bearing instruments of Christ's crucifixion, such as a pincers and a ladder. There is a statue of St Anthony of Padua on a plinth. All around the entrance arch of this chapel are little grotesque figures.

All the chapels are enclosed by low wrought iron grilles.

The Le Roy Chapel, (1473) dedicated to the Apostles, has a window of four lights with Rayonnant tracery above. Each lancet has a little group of three apostles in the glass. The altar is fairly plain marble, decorated with quatrefoils below and with a tabernacle in the centre. On the east wall is a statue of Our Lady crowned and holding the infant Christ, and on the west wall is a painting of the Nativity.

The Sacred Heart Chapel has an apse in the south wall. This was formerly the d'Étampes Chapel. Robinet d'Étampes was a friend of the Duke de Berry. There is a large tapestry on the east wall of St Peter proclaiming the deceit of Ananias and his wife Sapphira [Acts of the Apostles 5.1f], and another on the west wall of St Peter with St John healing the cripple near the Beautiful Gate in Jerusalem [Acts of the Apostles 3.6]. These tapestries are by Gobelin after the cartoons of Raphael and were destined for the Sistine Chapel. The cartoons are preserved in the V & A Museum in London. The tapestry on the west wall took sixteen years to make while that on the east wall took thirteen years. These tapestries were discovered in the museum of the Vatican and were given to the state by Cardinal Dupont in 1845. When I visited the cathedral in May 2012 the tapestries had been removed for renovation, but I was pleased to see them back in place in June 2013.

The window on the south wall has three lights, each of two lancets. The middle light depicts, in the left lancet, Christ praying in the garden of Gethsemane, while the right hand lancet depicts the sleeping disciples, while an angel bearing a cup of sacrifice hovers over them. There are stars in the Rayonnant tracery above. In the lancets to east and west of it are kneeling angels in the bottom registers holding a shield filled with fleurs-de-lys—the arms of the Duke of Berry (early 15th century,

A Glimpse Of Glory

View from the South Aisle

but installed here in the 19th century). There are canopies behind them and above is a pediment with a canopy. In the tracery are scrolls with the sacred heart pierced with a sword.

The altar is supported on two barleytwist columns and has a bas-relief carving on its base of two angels censing a monstrance, and a painted reredos of Christ sitting in judgement. The lower walls are panelled in wood. A small freestanding pulpit with a fine carved wooden staircase is against the south wall of the aisle.

The 6th Bay is behind the nave pulpit and has one tall lancet window with modern geometric designs, except in the third register from the bottom where there are two coloured squares making an interesting little scene.

The South Door is framed in wood with two large doors which swing on little wheels although access is often through a little door to the west of the main portal.

The 7th Bay has a wooden doorway under a round arch of three unadorned moulded ribs, and a small window in the centre of the arch beneath a crucifix. Below the little window is a large painting of St Stephen at the point of death.

The 8th Bay also has a doorway, above which is a single lancet window in geometric design with figures in the second register.

Two steps lead up to the south ambulatory.

THE CHOIR

The choir is to the east of the 9th bay in the nave and is enclosed by a wrought iron screen mounted on a five foot high stone wall. The Nave Altar stands on a platform in the centre of Bay 9 of the nave to the west of the Choir.

There are two rows of chapter stalls, with a throne on the west end of the south side. In the centre of the north side is the choir organ with a freestanding console in front of the chapter stalls. There is a bronze baptismal font to the eastern end of the chapter stalls with a Paschal Candle alongside it. Three steps lead up to the pavement on which stands the unadorned and plain high altar with a cross and six candles on the retable. On the north side is what was once the Bishop's Throne, or cathedra, but all that remains is a wooden canopy.

THE TRIFORIUM

Each bay of the choir triforium has six narrow lancets framed by a single, larger one. The four central lancets are slightly higher than the two outside ones. In

The Crossing Vault

the axial bay of the apse, instead of there being four large arches and two smaller ones in the triforium there are only four arches of equal height.

THE CHOIR CLERESTORY WINDOWS

Each bay has three coloured glass lancets, except that once the choir turns into the apse they reduce to two lancets with a rose above as before. The subjects follow a definite order. Those in the central portion, above the high altar, contain on the north side the series of the prophets who announced the coming of Christ, from Moses to John the Baptist. These are colossal in size and possess a savage grandeur. For example, study the 4th bay from east in north clerestory: Amos is in the centre, with Sophonias to his left and Nahum to his right. In the centre lancet is the Virgin holding the Infant in her arms. She is followed, on the south side, by the apostles who were sent to preach the Gospel to all nations. John the Baptist stands on her right, while St Stephen, the patron of this cathedral, stands on her left hand, followed by Peter, Paul, Andrew, John, James the Great, Philip, Thomas, Bartholomew, Matthew, Simon, James the Less, Barnabas, Thaddeus, Mark, Luke, and finally, to finish the series, three disciples of the apostles.

Grodecki and Brisac, in their book, "Gothic Stained Glass 1200–1300" (published by Thames & Hudson, 1985), trace a development in the glazing and consider the windows to be of local origin: "It is likely that the workshop of the "Master of the Relics of Saint Stephen"—probably local in origin—continued to work on the upper windows and on those in the inner ambulatory and transformed its style as the general trend changed. The large figures of prophets and apostles in part of the choir can probably be traced to this workshop."

THE INNER AMBULATORY AISLES

The double ambulatory continues in an apse, resembling Notre-Dame in Paris.

In the north and south, while there are still four arches in the triforium, there are now two narrow lancets and a small, quatrefoil in the clerestory.

The Inner Ambulatory Clerestory Windows

On the south side, the lancets and quatrefoil are in diamond quarry glass. This continues up to and including the turn of the southeast ambulatory. Only two lancets are coloured south of the axial clerestory window. The obviously later style clerestory windows of the inner ambulatory, again surrounding the choir, continue the theme of the choir clerestory by representing the canonized bishops of Berry, with wide eyes, straight nose and pursed lips, the two erect fingers of the right hand held in blessing. There are gaps in the series, where eighteen windows were taken out in 1760 by the clergy on the appalling grounds that they obstructed the light. Unfortunately, of the eight that remain, only three have been identified with certainty: two are on the left side and represent Saint Ursin and Saint Sulpice-Sévère, while one on the right pictures Saint Guillaume (William), who was responsible for building the cathedral, and as he is shown with a halo, these windows must date after his canonization in 1218. The two western bays of the north side have clear diamond quarry glass.

THE SOUTH OUTER AMBULATORY AISLE (from the west to east)

The Tullier Chapel was presented to the Virgin Mary by the Tullier family c.1530. It has one large Renaissance window in four lights in the south wall with quatrefoils and trefoils in the tracery above. In the lancet to the left is a Virgin and Child seated under a canopy and in the lancet to the right of her is St Peter holding the keys gesturing to her with two kneeling figures in front. To the right of that are the members of the Tullier family in white robes, with a standing figure holding a martyr's palm (St Stephen?) pointing to them but looking at Peter, who in turn is looking back at them. The right hand lancet has more members of the family in white kneeling with their hands together and another figure looking at them, and in the background is a canopied walkway with the city in the distance. In the tracery above are angels playing harps and viols and other instruments. In amongst all this are two armorial shields: one with three fleurs-de-lys and one with a lion on the right and a fleurs-de-lys on the left. This detailed window is the work of the master of French Renaissance glass making, Jean Lécuyer (1532), and is said to be his finest work.

Against the east wall is a plain stone altar with above a sculpted St Anne with a small crowned Mary as a young girl. There is a piscina in the south wall. A quadripartite vault graces the ceiling.

The Aligret Chapel was given by the family of Simon Aligret, Chancellor of the church and doctor to Duke Jean de Berry [15th century]. It has the same arrangement of one window divided into four lancets with tracery above. Each lancet has a figure in the glass; that on the left appears to depict an early saint holding a spear, with three kneeling youngsters and beneath it is a shield with the device of three geese. In the lancet to the right of it is St Catherine wearing a Virgin's crown and holding a wheel; in the next lancet there is a bishop with his crozier and right hand raised in blessing, and the right hand lancet has a priest holding a sword with three nuns and an abbess holding a palm in the lower register. All are under canopies. Above there are again angels playing instruments in the tracery. A marble altar stands against the east wall with a tabernacle and behind is a statue of St Joseph and the infant Christ. The south wall has a fine piscina in a niche with a decorated canopy. The Chapel was closed for renovation in 2013.

The next bay has a single lancet window in the wall, glazed with medallions and a decorated border. There are some fragments of a window dedicated to St Cecilia and other incomplete subjects including a 'signature' of the weavers.

The Boisratier Chapel was founded by Gillaume Boisratier, Chancellor to Duke Jean de Berry and Archbishop of Bourges [15th century]. It has one light with three lancets divided by mullions, each containing a scene, and with tracery of three quatrefoils above. On the left is a bishop facing west holding a crozier pointing backward. Below it, kneeling at a prayer desk, is a smaller bishop also with a crozier but which points forward. I was taught by my first bishop that only the Bishop having the cure of souls in a diocese allows the crook of his crozier to point forward towards his people and that his assistants or visiting bishops reverse their crozier in his diocese. There are two angels in mid-air holding a coat of arms with the Cross of Lorraine above it and a Gothic canopy in the upper register. In the middle light is a standing figure holding a martyr's palm branch and a sword in the right hand and with a book in the left; looking up from the left is a little lamb and to the right of it there is a bishop kneeling at a prayer desk with his crozier pointing forward. Again there are angels above holding a coat of arms with a cross above it and the letters N M under a canopy in the upper registers. In the right hand light is a standing figure holding a blue staff with a nimbus about the head. Below and to the right is another kneeling bishop with the crozier pointing forward, angels above holding a coat of arms with a Cross of Lorraine and three crosses on the shield and again all under a canopy in the upper registers. In two of the quatrefoils an angel bears in each a coat of arms consisting of three fleurs-de-lys, while in the top quatrefoil the angels hold a shield with six legs radiating from the centre, like the emblem of the Isle of

A Glimpse Of Glory

Man gone mad. It could even be a sunburst. Above it are crossed keys. Medallions of angels surround the arch itself. It is a fine window.

The dado is panelled in wood. On the west wall is a large wall-painting of the crucifixion and on the east wall another large wall-painting of the Virgin Mary kneeling with sheep about her feet. The quadripartite vault is decorated with gold stars on a blue ground and with the ribs picked out in gold culminating in a fine boss, bearing a shield with four fleurs-de-lys. The marble altar supported on two pillars stands against the east wall and covers a reliquary. The reredos has a wooden carving of Gothic designs around a tabernacle, and a fine sculpted niche in the south wall contains a piscina.

The Apse begins at this point as the ambulatory turns to the northeast; note how the vaulting accommodates the turn. The inner ambulatory has vaulting ribs similar to those in the crypt beneath, while in the outer ambulatory the large bays have a triangular cell cut off from each side of the vault, leaving a trapezium that tapers outwards. It is thought that this complicated solution was caused by the late addition, while work was already in progress, of five chapels, each attached to a section of the ambulatory, and taking up the central third of the periphery of each curving bay. But in "Medieval Architecture, Medieval Learning", Paul Frankl considers that these chapels were intended and built from the start. In each chapel the inner wall both side (nearest the ambulatory) is blind, and the outer wall contains three single lancets.

The 13th century Windows

All five bays of the apse contain a single lancet window either side of the chapel. Here, the glass is much older. The windows were made early in the 13th century and should be 'read' upwards from bottom to top, and from left to right. In many of these windows the mark of the guilds that donated it can be seen.

Grodecki and Brisac, in their major work, "Gothic Stained Glass 1200–1300", page 81f, believe that the programme of the glazing in these windows might have been devised by Saint William, Archbishop of Bourges from 1200 to 1209. In the Axial, or Lady Chapel, there was probably a series of windows depicting the Childhood of Christ and a Jesse Tree (windows lost since the 16th century). They argue that either side of this series were theological comparisons between the Old and the New Testaments, and between moral lessons drawn from the lives of prophets and saints and the parables of Christ. They suggest that The New Alliance, or New Covenant, corresponds to the Last Judgment; the Passion scenes correspond to the visions of the Apocalypse; the Parable of the Prodigal Son parallels the moral lesson of the Relics of Saint Stephen. The Parable of the Good Samaritan corresponds to the story of Dives and Lazarus; the life of the Apostle

Thomas parallels the story of the Patriarch Joseph, both considered lessons in salvation. This theory makes good theological sense and is certainly in accord with mediaeval teaching and learning.

Grodecki and Brisac identify two other great artists working here at that time, although they are referred to simply as 'the Master' of their best window. It was not the practice before the Renaissance to exalt art or artists, so their names are unknown. One is referred to as the "Master of the Good Samaritan" as he was responsible for the Good Samaritan window, the Passion and the Apocalypse windows in the ambulatory and for the Saint Nicholas, Saint Mary Magdalene, Saint Mary of Egypt and the Martyrdom of Saint Stephen windows in the radiating chapels of the apse. Only a few authentic panels from the last window survive. His style was almost aggressive; some of the scenes conveyed through gesture, the fall of folds and the fierce expressions of wild eyes and of violently drawn locks of hair. As none of this is found in the clerestory windows of the cathedral, and certainly not in the choir, it can be assumed that the Master and his workshop had left Bourges around 1215.

The principal master has been named the "Master of the Relics of Saint Stephen". His masterpiece, the Relics of Saint Stephen window, was fairly extensively restored in the 19th century. His Dives and Lazarus window is striking in the vigour of its blue and red mosaic grounds. The same workshop "master" was responsible for the Prodigal Son window. Its picturesque account of this parable is charming, but the outlines of the figures are difficult to characterize because of their great variety. Only the heads, too large for the thin bodies, with their sad expressions due to the large eyes, the long noses and the receding chins, can be distinguished from the style of the other two artists who worked in the ambulatory.

The 1st Bay of the apse has first a lovely single lancet with diamond medallions up the centre and medallions in between. The scenes tell the Old Testament story of the life of the Patriarch Joseph. The Joseph window is the only one with a subject taken from the Old Testament (Genesis chapter 37). There is a magnificent panel representing Joseph's dream. It is a square set on its angle: across the centre Joseph lies sleeping, above him are the bundles of wheat, the stars, the sun, and the moon. The whole story follows in detail. The window is striking because of its rich blue glass. It was donated by the coopers, carpenters and cartwrights.

The Chapel of St Francois de Sales is a little semi-circular bay. The east and west walls are blind, while the apse has three lights. The three single lancets contain coloured medallions depicting the lives of St John the Evangelist, John the Baptist and St James the Great. On the altar is a reliquary of St Ursin, the first Bishop of Bourges. The columns framing this chapel are beautifully coloured in dark green and designs in gold, the outer column in red and gold, and the walls painted and

A Glimpse Of Glory

decorated below the dado level. It is a splendid chapel and was given by the baker's guild.

To the left of the chapel is a single lancet with largely blue medallions depicting the legendary ministry of the apostle St Thomas in India Window. The King of India seeks an architect and Christ appears to Thomas telling him to accept the appointment. In the lower left scene in the centre medallion Thomas is presented to the king and above it he receives his orders to construct a palace. To the right of that the king shows Thomas the treasure that will pay for it. At the lower left of the top medallion Thomas can be seen giving the treasure to the poor. To the right of that, not unexpectedly, Thomas is cast into prison. In the top left panel Thomas converts a rich lady to Christianity, and, to the right, she frees Thomas. However, in the top of the window Thomas is martyred for refusing to worship an idol. The window was donated by the guild of stonecutters and sculptors, who can be seen at work in the bottom centre scene.

The 2nd Bay begins with the single lancet, containing medallions largely in red, which is known as the "Apocalypse Window." In the lower quatrefoil, which is superimposed on the medallions, is a figure of the Christ of the Transfiguration bearing a sword in his mouth (Rev. 19, verse 15.) The lower left medallion depicts six apostles with the Virgin, and to the right is the baptism of St Paul. The central section has at its centre the Christ of Pentecost: six apostles each side receive the Holy Spirit, while above them are six patriarchs each side. Then, in the top section, is the Christ of the End of Time. The centre medallion depicts the return of Christ in glory in a mandoria held by angels. Above him to the left can be seen the Agnus Dei (Lamb of God), the symbol of Christ as the sacrificial lamb.

The Chapel of All Saints should have been called the chapel of the three martyred deacons, for that is the subject of the three superb lancet windows. The right hand one has scenes from the life of St Vincent: in the left hand bottom cartouche St Vincent receives the chalice from Bishop Valerius of Saragossa at his ordination, to the right St Vincent preaches to the people, while in the upper part of the cartouche Vincent and his Bishop are being led bound before the Governor; to the right the Governor is pointing to the little statue of his God, which Vincent is refusing to venerate. For his refusal he is believed to have been martyred on a gridiron like St Laurence.

The centre window is mostly in a beautiful red and contains scenes from the life of the first martyr, St Stephen, (Acts of the Apostles, chapter 7, verses 54f) who was stoned to death for witnessing to the risen Christ.

The left window has five large medallions each with four scenes in them of the life of St Laurence, who was martyred on a red-hot gridiron. The second one up in the third register has St Lawrence washing the feet of the poor (whom he regarded as 'the treasure of the church') and to the right of that medallion is his healing of the blind Crescentius (Crescens). There are marble funerary tablets on the two blind walls and a single piscina in the west wall. The statue on the retable is of the crowned Virgin Mary.

The bay is completed by the single lancet with scenes of Christ's agony and passion (St Matthew, chapter 27, verses 27–54) in the "Passion Window". The second medallion up on the left hand side is the triumphal entry to Jerusalem, and to the right is part of the same scene. The third up depicts on the left the last supper, and to the right is the foot-washing. In the fourth medallion, on the left, is Christ's betrayal by a kiss; on the right, the preparation for the crucifixion. The reading of the glass reverses order at this point, so above on the right is seen the piercing with a lance, and to left is the deposition from the cross. Above, to the left, is the Resurrection of Jesus with the guards sleeping, and to the right, the redemption as people are being dragged from the jaws of a leviathan. This fine window was donated by the furrier's guild, which can be seen about its business in the bottom medallions.

The 3rd and Axial Bay begins with the usual single lancet. It is the wonderful 'Judgement Window'. In the bottom register on the left the redeemed are depicted, illustrated by angels carrying away the soul of a dead person, and on the right the damned are being pushed into a boiling pot. In the centre at the bottom left a soul rises from the grave and is commended, while on the right the book records that he's not that good. It symbolises the Church's authority, derived from Christ's instruction to St Peter to bind or loose sins. Above, in the next register, people are rising with their hands together in supplication – those on the left being told they are redeemed and on the right they are still hoping for the best. Above that two angels are sounding the trumpets announcing the day of judgement. In the right of the central medallion a devil with red hair holds a loop of rope around some bishops and even kings as they are led away to be fed into the jaws of a leviathan. On the left, souls are in a blanket in Abraham's bosom. Above that can be seen St Michael the archangel with scales; underneath the right hand scale is a little devil trying to change the balance in his favour, and in the higher quatrefoil is Christ in majesty with angels above him, and angels either side, and below are the supplicants. Beneath the right hand supplicant are the words Maria and St John. Either side of them in the corners are St Peter and St Paul. In the top of the arch are angels all looking down on what is happening beneath. In the very top can be seen the Holy Spirit in the form of a dove. It is a very bright beautiful window and was donated by the Confrérie de la Bonne Mort [the Brotherhood of the Good Death].

The Lady Chapel has three lancets each depicting a scene. The original glass was lost in the 16th century. There is a statue of the Virgin and Child above the stone

A Glimpse Of Glory

altar. Another altar stands to the west of it so that this small chapel contains two altars. On the north side is a statue of St Joseph on a tall plinth and on the south side is a statue of St John holding a chalice from which a viper escapes and alongside and to the east of each of these plinths are little niches, which might contain a piscina. The columns framing the chapel are painted, as is the roof of the vault. To the north and south of the entrance to this chapel are statues of kneeling figures in period dress at prayer desks; they are the Duke and his second wife Jeanne de Boulogne and date from the 15th century. Their heads were knocked off during the Revolution and have been remodelled form Holbein's drawings of them.

Completing the 3rd bay (to the north of this chapel) is another splendid lancet: the 'New Alliance Window', with two big medallions and a little one in the middle. In the centre of the lower medallion Christ is carrying the cross while Simeon comes to his aid; in the bottom left Abraham is about to sacrifice Isaac, and to the right Abraham turns at the request of an angel to see a ram caught in a thicket. In the top left hand register of that medallion Elijah meets the widow of Sarepta and her son and resides with her. On the right hand side the Jews keep the Passover in Egypt and sacrifice a lamb. In the centre little medallion depicts Christ on the cross. The upper large medallion has the Resurrection of Jesus in the centre, and in the upper left scene Elijah raises to life the son of the widow of Sarepta (1 Kings, chapter 17, verse 9). At the top, the patriarch Jacob gives his blessing to his son, Joseph. This window was donated by the butcher's guild, and they are depicted in the bottom scenes.

THE NORTH OUTER AMBULATORY AISLE (FROM EAST TO WEST)

The 4th bay to the north of the axial bay has the usual single lancet which is the "Prodigal Son Window", with two big quatrefoil medallions with fine scenes depicting the Parable of the Prodigal Son (St Luke, chapter 15, verses 11–32). At the bottom of the lower medallion the son asks for his inheritance, and to the left his father gives it to him. In the centre his brother works on the farm while to the right the prodigal leaves the family home, until, in the top segment, he is accosted by a seductive woman. In the little roundel above he is crowned king of the feast and dance. In the upper large medallion we see him down on his luck and penniless. In the centre he is given a job minding the herd, and on the right he is disconsolate and aware of his big mistake. In the top segment of the medallion he returns to his father, who sends to kill the fatted calf in the top left-hand semicircle. In the roundel at the top there is a welcome home feast, but in the semicircle on the right his brother refuses to join in. But at the very top the father is united with both his sons. The tiny roundels each contain the head of a king. It was donated by the tanners, who can be seen along the bottom of the glass.

Bourges

The Chapel of Our Lady of Lourdes has, in the window, scenes from the lives of St Martin, St Peter and St Paul, and St Denis (Dionysius) in the window medallions. Scholars have discerned three very different styles in the windows. It is thought that the Master of the 'New Alliance' and the 'Judgment' windows also worked on the poorly preserved windows in this chapel, which are modern in parts: the Saint Dionysius (Denis) window, the Saint Peter and Saint Paul window and the Saint Martin window. The marble altar has a tabernacle with a low stone shelf behind it. There is a statue of Our Lady of Lourdes.

The single window, which completes this bay, is the 'Good Samaritan Window' (St Luke, chapter 10, verses 29–37.) This window is the exception to the rule, for the parable has to be read from the top down and is told in the roundels. At the top, the man leaves Jerusalem for Jericho, and in the next roundel he is attacked by robbers and stripped of his robes. In the next he is beaten and left for dead by the side of the road. In the second from the bottom a Priest and a Levite pass by on the other side, and in the bottom half-roundel the Samaritan puts the man on his horse and takes him to an inn. The subject of the semicircles at either side of the upper three roundels is 'Creation and Fall' of man. To the left below the third medallion from the top Adam and Eve are sent from the garden after falling for the temptation, and to the right an angel shuts the door to Paradise behind them. The semicircles surrounding the fifth roundel deal with loyalty and idolatry: the Hebrews can be seen worshipping the golden calf in the lower right semicircle. At the bottom left Christ is scourged and on the right he is seen on the cross. The window was donated by the weaver's guild and they can be seen plying their trade in the centre at the bottom.

The 5th Bay. The single lancet is the 'St Stephen Window' and has three large round medallions relating the finding of the relics of St Stephen. The tale is told in full in 'The Golden Legend', and the Venerable Bede includes it in his chronicle, too. The first thing to note is that two segments of the window have been transposed during restoration. The 'story' begins in the lower segment of the middle medallion, which should change places with the lower segment of the bottom medallion. Assuming that has been done, the tale starts with Gamaliel instructing the priest Lucian to search for the relics of the first martyr, Stephen, for the bottom left segment depicts the martyred body abandoned to wild animals. The sepulchre is discovered in the right hand segment, and in the upper part of the first medallion Lucian repeats Gamaliel's vision of the relics to Bishop John of Jerusalem. The relics are discovered (bottom segment of the window) and in the left segment of the middle medallion they are installed in the church with due ceremony. In the upper segment, a rich lady named Julienne claims the body and in the semicircle to the upper left of this medallion she brings it to Constantinople. The top medallion takes up the story in the left hand segment where she undergoes

A Glimpse Of Glory

various tribulations until, in the right hand segment, she comes before the Emperor with the relics, but in the upper segment we see that the horse pulling the carriage has had enough and refuses to continue. It is believed that the top three semicircles depict the translation of the relics to Rome. The window was donated by the suppliers of water, an essential trade in the middle ages.

The Chapel of the Holy Cross has three lovely windows, which depict the lives of St Mary Magdalene, Saint Nicholas and St Mary of Egypt. The latter subject (in the left lancet) is one of the most poignant of the stories narrated in 'The Golden Legend'; it concerns Saint Mary the Egyptian, a courtesan of Alexandria who, having heard of the Cross which was being exhibited in Jerusalem, made up her mind to go there to see what this curiosity might be. She made an 'easy bargain' with the boatmen who conveyed her across (2nd register), and soon found her way to the place where the faithful were gathered in adoration of the relic (3rd register). She was one of those who came to scoff, but remained to pray (4th register). She was then sent into the desert to repent of her sins. She did so, for forty years, by which time she had no clothes but was covered by her long hair (7th register, right panel). A saintly Abbot came to see her and found a strange figure burned black by the sun. He gave her his cloak and promised to return with the sacrament (8th register). The end of the tale is tragic, for when he returned a year later he found her lying there dead (9th register). He noticed written in the sand beside her head a message which can be translated as, 'Bury Mary's little body, return her dust to the earth and pray for me to the Lord.' At the very top she can be seen held safely in Abraham's bosom.

The altar is plain and so is the unadorned niche on the south side containing a piscina.

Completing the 5th bay, and the apse, is the single lancet known as the "Bad Rich Man Window", which I prefer to call The Dives and Lazarus Window. It has six medallions with scenes and further scenes in semicircles either side of them, depicting the poor man Lazarus and the wealthy man Dives (St Luke, chapter 16, verses 19–31). The window was donated by the masons, and they can be seen at work along the bottom of the window and in the first register, where the rich man has given them a commission to build a castle for him. Reading from left to right, the story develops the life of the rich family, until, in the third medallion from the bottom we see the rich man's feast, with poor Lazarus at his gate to the right. Then the order changes, for the story of Lazarus continues up the right hand semicircles with his death, his ascent to heaven by an angel and, in the top medallion, Lazarus is held in the 'bosom of Abraham'. Meanwhile, the rich man also dies in the fourth medallion and in the fifth medallion he is cast into the inferno of hell. In the semicircle on the left he begs Lazarus to save him, to no avail. The parable can be found in St Luke's Gospel, chapter 16, verses 19–31.

Bourges

The Jacques Coeur Chapel fills the next bay. Jacques Coeur was the Treasurer to Charles Vll, and built this chapel in 1450, with the window dated 1451. He had great influence both at court and in the church. His palace in the centre of Bourges is worth a visit. In 1450 he persuaded the Pope to appoint his 16 year old son John as Archbishop of Bourges and attended his enthronement in the cathedral! However, as this window was being installed in the chapel he was facing corruption charges. He had made many enemies in the nobility by buying their land cheaply as surety for lending them money. In 1453, under torture, he confessed to the crimes of which he was accused and found guilty of high treason and condemned to life imprisonment. He escaped from Poitiers Castle and joined the papal fleet on crusade. He died of illness on the island of Chios in 1456 and so, in 1552, the chapel was acquired by Claude de l'Aubespin, Baron of Chateauneuf.

The unvested and unadorned altar is against the east wall with coloured wooden panelling rising to the vault. In the centre of this reredos is a painting.

The window has four lights, all forming one scene of the Annunciation: a kneeling angel wearing a cope faces the left where the Virgin Mary reads a book, and to the east of her stands another figure, bearing a palm and a sword in her hands, and on the extreme left is a saint in purple cassock and cotta reading from a book, with a vaulted apse in the background. Above, in the tracery, are coats of arms, with God the Almighty at the very top and a descending dove (the Holy Spirit) below him. The roof has a fine vault with a pendant ending in a boss in the form of an angel with golden wings.

On the west side of the chapel are three kneeling figures: they are Guillaume de l'Aubespine, a member of the Council of State who died in 1629, in the centre his wife Marie de la Châtre, and their son Charles, Lord Chancellor, who died in 1653. Above these statues on the west wall are two carvings of ladies in sorrow and above that a large painting. The chapel has a fine vaulted ceiling with gilded pendants, and the ribs of the arch framing this chapel have crockets picked out in gold. Below the window in the north wall, half the dado is panelled and half is recessed under a canopy, which looks like a little monastic cell, with a writing desk, a kneeling desk and two small lancet windows with a knot-work design in colour, and a little blind arcade either side of it.

The Trousseau Chapel was donated c.1410 by Pierre Trousseau, Archdeacon of Bourges. There is an altar against the east wall bearing a large reliquary, which was missing during my visit in 2012 and was still absent in June 2013. There is above the altar a painting of a lady robed like an abbess, with a child holding her hand. To the south of the altar is a niche for a piscina and a carved bracket on the wall above holding a statue of the Madonna and Child.

A Glimpse Of Glory

The window of four lights again contains four scenes depicting the presentation of the family of Pierre Trousseau to the Virgin: in the left hand lancet there are three kneeling figures, a lady in the middle, and a crowned lady holding a palm standing behind them; to the right is a standing figure with his hand on the shoulder of a kneeling figure before him; to the right of that is an old man standing with two kneeling figures wearing coats of arms in front of him; and on the extreme right is Our Lady with the Child and two ladies behind, the right hand figure has a mitre and crozier.

There is fine, unadorned vaulting in the ceiling. On the west wall is a bronze bas-relief plaque of St Jehan (1462–1505), Joan the Queen of France and Duchess of Berry. She is holding a little chapel in her hand.

The 5th Bay has a beautiful canopied doorway leading to the chapter house and sacristy. The door has a flat moulding with a slight ogee arch in it at the top, above which there is a very flamboyant arch with pinnacles either side rising above the arch to a window, which has flour little lancet windows containing diamond quarries, above which there is tracery with a pediment above. There is a coat of arms either side with another in the centre of the crocketted pinnacle, which rises in the centre of the arch up to the lancets above.

The Du Breuil Chapel (also called 'John the Baptist Chapel', which is somewhat confusing) is square with a window of four lights, each containing a figure, with tracery above. They depict the Adoration of the Magi with John the Baptist on the left ushering the two canons Jean and Martin du Breuil. The east wall has a wall painting of the Resurrection appearance of Christ to Mary Magdalene on the first Easter morning. A niche to the south of the plain altar contains a piscina. The west wall is painted with a crucifixion scene. The whole of the vaulting and the columns framing the chapel are painted in red with decoration. This chapel marks the end of the north ambulatory.

Two steps lead down to the north aisles.

THE NORTH OUTER AISLE (FROM EAST TO WEST)

The De Bar Chapel has a glorious window (1520) of four lights each with four scenes – sixteen scenes from the life of St Denis, and with angels in the tracery above. It is remarkable that, in all the agonies he suffers and the extremities of life he endures in the scenes, he manages to keep his mitre firmly on his head! On the east wall there is a statue above the stone altar, which could be Joan of Arc. To the south of the altar is a piscina in the classical style. On the west wall is a figure in black robes with a nimbus, but to the left are the keys of Peter and the Papal crown and at the bottom, on the frame, are the words: "A gift of the Emperor".

Torture of St Denis, De Bar Chapel

The 2nd Bay has two doorways; the right hand one is plain with four steps leading up to it, in the centre is a little grille enclosing an enormous cross in wrought iron, and on the left of that is the entrance to the Crypt.

This door, too, has a lovely ornate canopy with an ogee arch rising to a decorated finial, which pierces a frieze decorated with foliage carving. The spandrels are decorated with lozenges and circles, and there is a seated carving of Our Lady and Child in the tympanum, a statue of a bishop to the right, and to the left is St Stephen with a martyr's palm in his right hand, both standing on foliage brackets, which also act as a stop for the moulding above the door.

The 3rd Bay forms the North Door and again has a carved wooden frame with little clear glass panes in it.

The 4th Bay has a single lancet window filled with clear diamond quarry glass.

The Beaucaire Chapel has a fine vaulted ceiling and the usual arrangement in the window, that of four lancets, each with a figure depicting the Doctors of the Church, St Ambrose, St Augustine, St Gregory and St Jerome, and dated c.1467. In the east wall is a stone altar, hollowed underneath, and above is a statue of a bishop with his crozier pointing behind him surmounted by an ornate canopy. On the west wall is a painting of the Nativity. A model of the cathedral stands on a table in the centre of the chapel.

The Fradet Chapel was built in 1460. It is not enclosed; the wrought iron screen has been removed to one side. There is a single window in the north wall with the usual four lancets, each of which has a figure of an Evangelist: St Mark, St Matthew, St Luke and St John, each carrying a scroll. The glass dates to about 1465. On the east wall is an unvested and unadorned wooden altar surrounded by panelling. Above it is the painting of a monk writing on a scroll, a mitre and a crozier on the floor in front of him, with two people whispering together behind his chair and a lady to the right, her hands clasped in prayer. In a niche to the south of the altar is a piscine, above which is a delicate little (c.10ins x 16ins) blind arcade. On the west wall is a lovely ornate bracket bearing a bust of a very self-satisfied looking person. In the corbels of the vaulting are little carved statues of angels holding crests.

In 2013 access to The Baptistry Chapel was closed by the siting of the bookshop in front of it. This chapel has the usual arrangement of four lights but it is all one scene in two registers with tracery above. It is the Assumption Window. The lower registers depict two kneeling people, the donors Marshall de Montigny and his wife. Above, one can see an open grave with the date 1619 on the side of it. In the upper registers, the apostles are around the empty grave with flowers and the discarded robe, for in the upper tracery Mary is depicted as the Queen of Heaven surrounded by angels. On the east wall there is a large painting of the Baptism of Christ, beneath which is a marble font. At the west wall is another marble statue of the Duke de Berry kneeling at a prayer desk. The vault has two fine bosses, one of which has a shield of three lambs in a circlet, from which are suspended the letters "LB".

The 8th Bay is interrupted on the nave side, between the two aisles, by the enormous column of the tower, which has some fine decoration on the lower part of it where it juts into the inner north aisle and with quite flamboyant blind tracery reaching up to the level of the triforium. But in the outer aisle there is a cash desk beside a door in the north wall, beneath Rayonnant tracery. This door leads to the northwest tower, and at the desk one may buy a ticket for admission to the tower and the crypt.

The final bay has in the west wall two doors, with a narrow light above under a round arch. A stone shaft interrupts the vaulting.

THE CRYPT

It is not actually a crypt, but rather a basement, as the structure is not underground. When it was decided to build the choir of the new cathedral further

Bourges

east than that of the older building, it had to be built over the town ramparts, and it therefore became necessary to build a substructure, with a double ambulatory, over the six metre deep ditch beyond the Gallo-Roman walls.

The entrance and exit corridors are at the eastern ends of the outer aisles, but only that in the north aisle is in use today. The young lady who sold me the entrance ticket told me that it also

Crypt, Ambulatory

allowed me to climb the northwest tower. When I replied that it was "too hot today", she laughed and said, "Non! It's good sport."

A vaulted corridor slopes downhill to the crypt. The first corbel on the right has a face with both ears being pecked by birds.

The corridor opens into the outer ambulatory of the crypt, and on the paving stones is engraved a full-size drawing of the west rose window; a template from the days when the masons used this basement as a workshop. This outer ambulatory is divided into triangular bays, while the inner ambulatory consists of trapezoid

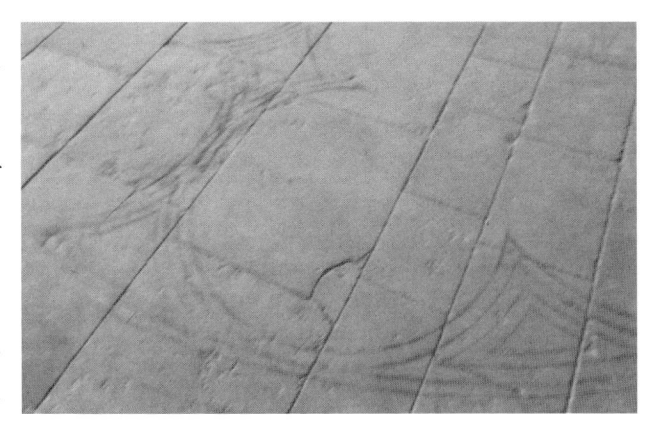

Crypt, Mason's Templates

bays. It has been said that it required all the experience of masons, accumulated since the time of the Romanesque, to make their construction possible, and their execution at Bourges is the performance of a past master.

A Glimpse Of Glory

Several fragments of the mediaeval Jubé (Rood Screen) are on display. The screen was discovered at the end of the 19th century. A model of the screen shows it to be free-standing across the entire width of the nave , with a staircase at each end of it. The arched remains are well presented, as are the panels of the Passion of Christ which adorned the pediment above the Jubé. I was fascinated by the panel depicting Adam and Eve, released from death, crushing a devil or two under their feet; Eve with her hand placed modestly. And the unhappy faces of the damned peering over the top of the boiling pot.

Crypt, the Sepulchre

In the eastern bay of the inner ambulatory is the original tomb of John, Duke of Berry (1340–1416) by the sculptor Jean de Cambrai. The Duke is dressed in an ermine cloak, his feet on a chained bear; a copy is in the Jacques Cœur Palace. He is also seen with his first wife, Joanna of Armagnac kneeling in prayer.

West of the tomb is the entrance to the Rotunda, the site of a tower in the ancient city wall, and the location of the tombstones of the Archbishops of Bourges since the Revolution. At the west end is a splendid Holy Sepulchre, a polychrome stone construction (donated in 1520). The only statue not in colour is that of the donor, Canon Jacques Dubreuil, kneeling next to St James the Great, his patron saint. Nicodemus and Joseph of Arimathea are at either end of the body of Christ. St John supports the Blessed Virgin.

To the side of the Sepulchre, steps lead into the crypt of the old Romanesque cathedral. During the life of that cathedral the relics of St Stephen were displayed here for pilgrims in the choir above to venerate through an oculus drilled through the vault of this ancient crypt.

This concludes our tour of Bourges Cathedral. If you feel like some 'sport', you might be tempted to climb the 400-plus stairs of the northwest tower—the view is certainly reward enough.

Bourges

IN CONCLUSION

It is a fine cathedral; light and airy. I shall always look forward to a visit with excitement; I shall never tire of it. The chandeliers, which line both sides of the nave and during the day interfere with the architectural vista, come into their own at night, and when lighted appear like little Christmas Trees along the nave and are quite enchanting.

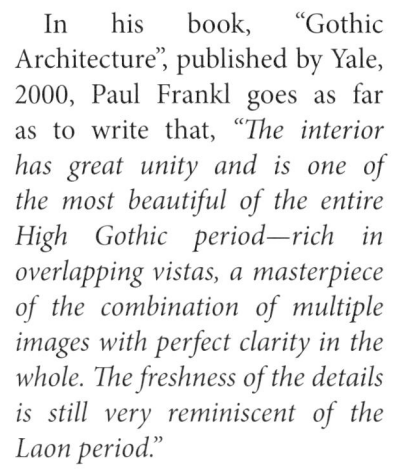

In his book, "Gothic Architecture", published by Yale, 2000, Paul Frankl goes as far as to write that, *"The interior has great unity and is one of the most beautiful of the entire High Gothic period—rich in overlapping vistas, a masterpiece of the combination of multiple images with perfect clarity in the whole. The freshness of the details is still very reminiscent of the Laon period."*

High praise indeed. Grodecki and Brisac, in their work, "Gothic Stained Glass 1200–1300", published by Thames & Hudson, 1985, consider that, *"the exceptional quality of the windows in the ambulatory and the radiating chapels at Bourges and the monumental*

Crypt, a Romanesque Chamber

The Western Bay of the Nave

A Glimpse Of Glory

development in the upper windows must be counted among the greatest achievements in stained glass in the first third of the thirteenth century."

Bourges was not widely imitated in France, perhaps because of its great width and height, which would commit any imitators to build an immense church at huge expense. So, as Andrew Martindale concludes in his book, "Gothic Art", published by Thames & Hudson in 1967, page 31, *"Bourges remained an isolated phenomenon; a fine aesthetic conception and a most impressive use of the lately devised flying buttress."*

Take time to sit quietly, and, whatever your faith, add your prayers to the millions who have been moved by what they have experienced here, to give glory to God, and resolve to imitate the holy men and women of the past in their attempts to draw close to him. And if you profess no faith, ponder on what you have seen and try to discern the purpose of your life.

DO NOT MISS . . .

1. The West Façade.
2. The sculpted spandrels of scenes from Genesis on the west façade.
3. The vista from the west end of the nave.
4. The Choir Clerestory windows.
5. The 13th century lancets in the ambulatory.
6. The Crypt.
7. The view from the top of the Northwest (Butter) Tower.
8. The south side of the cathedral from the gardens of the former Archbishop's Palace.

West Rose

CHAPTER 6

TROYES

Located on the upper reaches of the River Seine on the border of Burgundy with Champagne, Troyes was born, like Paris, on an island in the Seine. The city was a major commercial centre long before the arrival of the railway. From medieval times two annual trade fairs were held here, which set their own standards of weights and measures, such as the Troy weight, which became the recognized standard and is still in use. The city was an ancient Celtic capital and a Roman stronghold; once the capital of Champagne it is now the capital of the Department of Aube. Appropriately, the outline of the ancient city on a map resembles the shape of a champagne cork.

St Loup was among the first bishops of Troyes. He is renowned locally for averting an attack by Attila in the 5th century. Troyes was sacked by the Normans in 890 and again in 905, meanwhile, Louis II was crowned king here by Pope John VIII in 877. Troyes fell into the hands of the Burgundians and the English and it was here the Treaty of 1420 was signed, acknowledging England's Henry V as Regent of France. The Treaty also provided for Henry's marriage with Catherine of France (or Valois), which was solemnized here in the Church St John. The latter part of Shakespeare's "Henry V" is set in the palace of Troyes. In 1429 the city was taken by Joan of Arc at the head of an army, and her protégé, the Dauphin, became Charles VII.

The city has many historical buildings; in addition to the Cathedral of Saint Peter and St Paul and the Church of St John (St Jean), there is the church of La Madeleine with its outstanding Gothic rood screen, the Church of St Pantaléon containing a vast quantity of fine sculptures, and the Church of Saint Urbain, which contains the relics of Pope Urban IV, who was born the son of a shoe-maker in Troyes.

THE CATHEDRAL CHURCH OF ST PETER AND ST PAUL

In his book, "The Gothic Cathedral", published by Thames & Hudson, 1990 (Revised 2000), Dr Christopher Wilson writes on page 123f, *"No opportunities*

A Glimpse Of Glory

TROYES—KEY

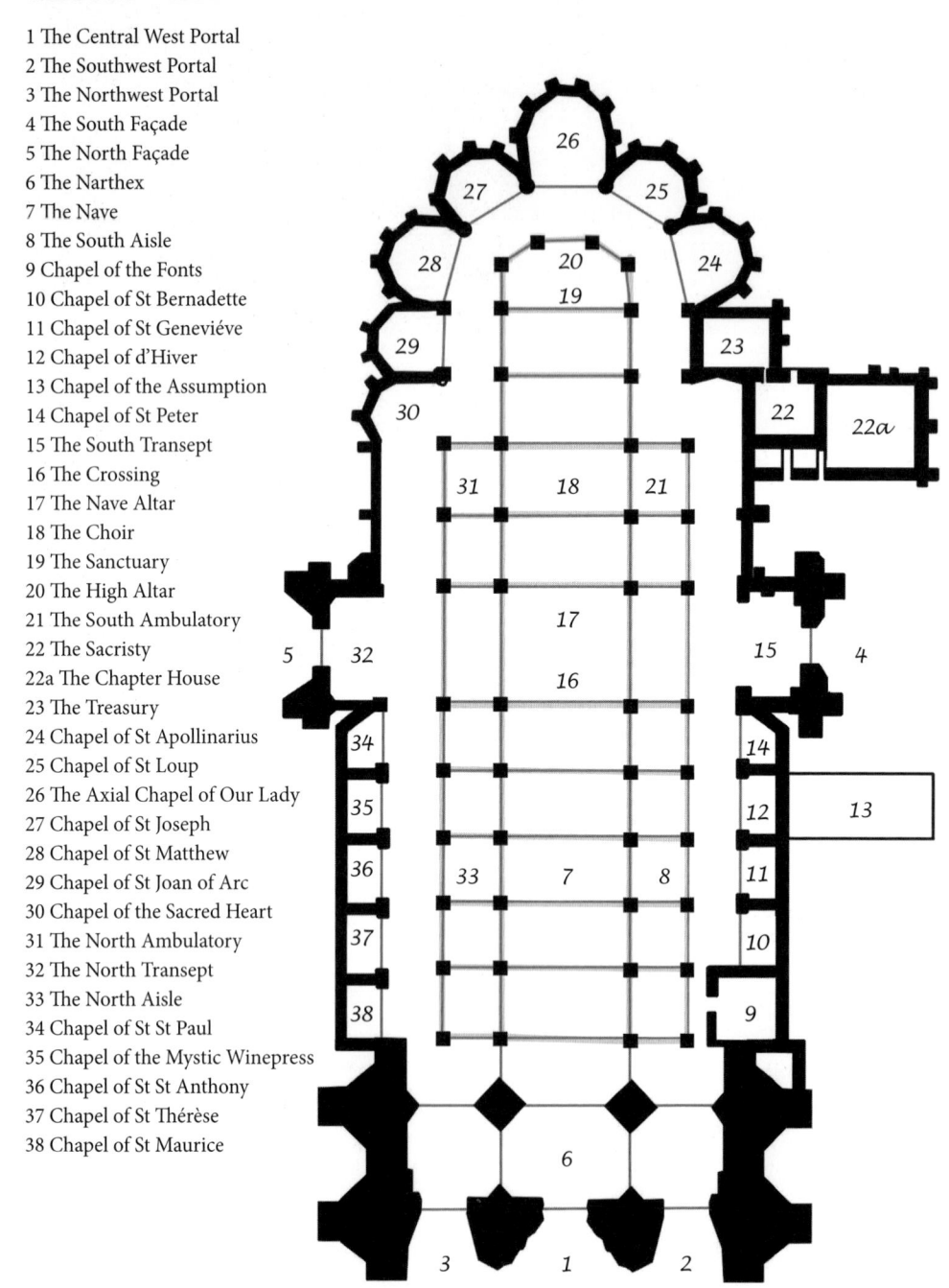

1 The Central West Portal
2 The Southwest Portal
3 The Northwest Portal
4 The South Façade
5 The North Façade
6 The Narthex
7 The Nave
8 The South Aisle
9 Chapel of the Fonts
10 Chapel of St Bernadette
11 Chapel of St Geneviéve
12 Chapel of d'Hiver
13 Chapel of the Assumption
14 Chapel of St Peter
15 The South Transept
16 The Crossing
17 The Nave Altar
18 The Choir
19 The Sanctuary
20 The High Altar
21 The South Ambulatory
22 The Sacristy
22a The Chapter House
23 The Treasury
24 Chapel of St Apollinarius
25 Chapel of St Loup
26 The Axial Chapel of Our Lady
27 Chapel of St Joseph
28 Chapel of St Matthew
29 Chapel of St Joan of Arc
30 Chapel of the Sacred Heart
31 The North Ambulatory
32 The North Transept
33 The North Aisle
34 Chapel of St St Paul
35 Chapel of the Mystic Winepress
36 Chapel of St St Anthony
37 Chapel of St Thérèse
38 Chapel of St Maurice

Troyes

to implement the whole St Denis system arose in the Ile-de-France during the later 13th century, but several incomplete High Gothic cathedral choirs were crowned with upper storeys which converted their main vessels into approximations of the Rayonnant manner. The most important instances are Tours (begun 1241), Beauvais and Troyes, the last an almost literal copy of St-Denis and presumably begun very soon after its model."

The previous cathedral was destroyed, together with a large area of the city, in a great fire in 1188. Much of Europe was still involved in the Holy Wars and so twenty years elapsed before anything was done about rebuilding. Bishop Hervé planned the building and laid the corner-stone in 1208, but the choir and the piers supporting the crossing of the transept and the nave were not completed until the end of that century, while the transept and the nave were only built between 1350 and 1380. The work dragged on through four centuries, and even then it was left without a south-west tower.

The West Façade

The Hundred Years War meant that work was abandoned for a long period, and recommenced in the reign of Charles Vll. Martin Chambiges of Paris planned the west façade in 1507. The canons of Troyes called Chambiges "Supremus Artifex", for he was famous for his façades at Beauvais, Sens and Senlis, as well as for his work at the Hotel de Dieu in Paris.

His son and son-in-law continued with his work on the façade. The cathedral has suffered other natural disasters: part of the choir was destroyed in a hurricane in 1228, and the roof was set alight by lightning in 1389. A steeple, with a height of 110 metres, once stood over the crossing, but it was ruined by a tornado in

A Glimpse Of Glory

1365, and struck by lightning in 1700, after which it was not rebuilt. The cathedral escaped destruction during the French Revolution, but was turned into a Temple of Abundance for several years. Later, the rood screen was removed by 'modernizers' and the architect Viollet le Duc rebuilt the choir and south façade. The rood was significant for another reason. In "Great Gothic Sculpture", by Jean René Gaborit, published by Reynal & Company, 1978, we read, *"In France the first definite mention of a clay model, probably life-size, was of a rood screen for the cathedral of Troyes in 1381."*

THE EXTERIOR

Mediaeval streets and houses surround the Cathedral. From the Rue de l'Évêché, a draughty lane leading to the southwest corner of the cathedral, one is confronted by a huge niche rising up to the base of the missing southwest tower. It is a polygonal bay, carved out of the wall, complete with crocketted arch and extending into an ogee arch and a canopy. It rises high to the top of the balustrade that surmounts the lower level, and then ends suddenly. The polygonal shape is taken up again to the top of what was to have been the southwest tower, but ends two levels higher.

I imagine that these niches would have been utilised as late mediaeval dwellings when it was the practice to have shops and stalls clustered around the cathedral.

THE WEST FAÇADE

This is the work of the architect/mason Martin Chambiges and his son, Pierre. The single tower, named St Peter, with little turrets on the west side of it above the level of the bell chamber, rises to 220 feet, yet it looks rather lost. The absence of the southwest tower, St Paul, gives the façade an imbalance. It is also somewhat grimy, although when I last visited the building in 2012 a programme of cleaning was under way, and the cleaned areas were splendid. To see the west front at its best on a sunny day one should wait until the late afternoon. The three west doorways are divided by substantial buttresses, each one highly decorated.

The Central Portal has two wooden doors, each with three horizontal panels, and it is covered by a round-headed arch. The trumeau is devoid of sculpture, and above it is the large blank tympanum with two carved animals in the spandrels. There was once carved figures on the tympanum representing the Passion of Christ; all we see now are the remains of securing hooks, but the figures themselves did not survive the Revolution. There is moulding around each doorway and three rows of empty niches fill the archivolt, interspersed with crockets.

Either side of the centre portal are the substantial buttresses rising to the top of the building, with four niches under delicate decorated canopies at each level, all empty of the statues which once filled them. The top two levels have five empty niches because they are smaller. A balustrade, decorated with cartouches containing sculpted fleurs-de-lys, links the buttresses above the high pointed arch of the central portal. Above this arch a crocketted gable cuts through the balustrade and rises to the centre of the rose window, which is set back behind the balustrade and surrounded by decorative moulding. On the front of the gable, which rises thus, is a seated figure under a canopy in the centre with either side some weathered carving in the spandrels. Above the seated figure (missing in 2013) is some intricate decoration which is evidence of high Gothic art.

The Southwest Portal arch is similar to the central door except that it is much smaller and the archivolt has only one row of empty niches with a crocketted rib either side of it. In the splay of the door and on the buttresses either side the niches are devoid of sculpture. The tympanum was once adorned with a relief of the life of St Paul. The balustrade decorated with fleurs-de-lys links the central section to the lateral buttress, but at the lower height of this door arch. Again it is bisected by a crocketted gable which rises above the top of the arch over the central portal. Above the balustrade are three niches, each with a bracket and decorated canopy which once contained a statue. The little canopies terminate in a riot of decoration. The top of the façade is crowned by a pierced parapet.

The Northwest Portal resembles the south. They both have two doorways in wood like the central door, the trumeau on each has an empty niche and on all three doors this niche has no canopy. The tympanum of the north door once had a relief of the life of St Peter. The major difference is that above the north-west portal there is a clock and bell tower that rises above the façade of the northwest side. The north and south sections are alike up to the level of the pierced parapet, but on the north side the buttresses, above the parapet, are decorated with a blind arcade: groups of three lancets each under a round-headed arch, and

The West Portals in 2007

A Glimpse Of Glory

surmounted by a gable. The surface above the portal is filled with a clock face. The top level houses the belfry, and was built in the 17th century in the Classical style, complete with barley-twist columns and twin cupolas crowning the western face.

Basil Cottle, in his work, "Cathedrals of France", published in 2002 by the Unicorn Press, writes on page 224, *"This gorgeous Flamboyant façade deserves a better crown than this severe upper north tower and the truncated south tower… [but] despite the Revolutionary vandalism of the portals, the porch gables and the rosace are among the most felicitous Gothic in France."*

THE SOUTH FAÇADE

Years of neglect became evident on the south façade and it had to be rebuilt in the 19th century. The first time I saw it I was struck by the modern look of its clean lines and lack of Gothic ornament. A low curtilage wall adds to the appearance of an English parish church, were it not for the very grand rose window. A cluster of slender columns either side support the arch over the doorway with a single column against a pillar dividing the two wooden doors. The tympanum is decorated with two blind cusps and a multifoil. Above the arch there is a rectangular hood-mould, which extends either side at the height of the doors. Above this moulding either side a single blind lancet rises to just below the triforium, and is the only relief on an otherwise blank wall.

The triforium has six lancet windows, each subdivided into two by a slender column, and with a quatrefoil in the tracery; a trefoil is squeezed into the spandrels between each of the six lancets. The buttress either side has an empty niche, and a stringcourse runs above the lancets, both features offering some

The South Façade

ornamental relief. Above the stringcourse is the rose window, occupying a third of the mass of this façade, and set in a square. It is a glorious construction: a multifoil at the centre from which radiate an inner circle of little lancets, but the mullions continue outwards to form an outer ring of larger lancets, with a profusion of traceried motifs at the extremity. A multifoil and two roundels occupy each corner of the window.

The buttresses terminate at the top of the window, and above the rose is another decorative stringcourse above which is a balustrade pierced by a row of quatrefoils. The façade is crowned by a crocketted gable in which there is a window of two cusped lancets with a quatrefoil in the tracery. Either side, the lateral buttresses are crowned with a crocketted spirelet which rises almost to the height of the gable.

THE NORTH FAÇADE

As I usually park my car on rough ground off Rue Simart, I approach the cathedral along Rue Mitantier, where the north side towers ahead over the houses. But my increasing excitement at the huge scale of the north side is dissipated as I come up to the north façade and observe the vandalism of the Revolutionaries. The two light-coloured wooden doors seem to emphasise the dereliction of the scene. The splay of the portal is simply decorated each side with three columns interspersed with slender columns. This reflects the arrangement of the unadorned archivolt. The trumeau and the tympanum are blank, although there is some evidence of attachments for statuary in the latter. In stark contrast with the crocketted gable which rises in an ogee arch over the portal, with some decoration in the spandrel, and with the columns either side, while containing empty niches, rising to decorated finials, the doorway is disappointing.

The North Façade

A Glimpse Of Glory

In the triforium, which peers from behind the portal's gable and the two decorated finials, there are six lancets, each subdivided by a slender column. A balustrade runs above the triforium and is decorated with fleurs-de-lys alternating with what appears to be crossed keys, but that might be my fanciful imagination. Above the balustrade is the north rose window. It is an echo of the southern rose, but is strengthened by a stone mullion, which rises to the height of the gable above. Another pierced balustrade runs above the rose, behind which is a row of blind round-headed lancets at the base of the façade's gable.

The gable is decorated with a series of blind cusp-headed lancets, some of which have empty brackets. In another echo of the south façade, the lateral buttresses terminate in crocketted spirelets, while the gable itself has large crockets and is crowned by a large finial in the shape of a cross.

THE INTERIOR

THE NARTHEX

The west doors give access to the Narthex, which is a full bay deep. There is a semi-circular vault with a small barrel vault above at both the north and south ends

The Nave

of the bay. At each corner there is a niche in the wall, again with a semicircular top, but all four are empty. In front of the two western niches there are statues of St Peter (holding the keys to the Kingdom) and St Paul (holding a sword). They stand on high bases facing east. The two central doors are each surmounted by a blind arch containing tracery and flanked by finials. The central finial rises to the top of the portal's arch.

The south side has a double door crowned with tracery in two pointed arches and divided by an empty trumeau. The ceiling bears a quadripartite vault with a circular trap door to enable a bell to be raised or lowered. The columns bearing the weight of the tower are absolutely enormous.

In 1808 a huge neo-classical organ case was built over the Narthex. It houses the great organ of Clairvaux Abbey, built by Jacques Cochu in 1737, and was bought for the cathedral when the fixtures and fittings of that famous Abbey were sold at auction following its seizure by the Revolutionaries. The great pipes rise up before the 16th century West Rose window by Jean Soudain, largely obliterating it from view.

THE NAVE

The cathedral has a very fine nave. It has an appearance of great width, which might be explained in part by the vista of the five great clerestory windows in the apse and in part by the double aisles to north and south. Certainly the whole vessel seems to have great space and elegance; it is, in fact, 374 feet long, 166 feet wide, and 93 feet high. Five engaged columns soar right up from the bases of the very solid pillars, through the triforium level and on to reach half way up the clerestory, before springing out in support of the quadripartite ribs of the

The North Side of the Nave

A Glimpse Of Glory

ceiling vault. The uninterrupted simplicity of these slender columns not only lifts the eye to heaven but also lifts the soul. The pillars have other engaged columns, each of which are crowned with a plain abacus resting on a capital decorated with carved acanthus foliage, and which support the springing of the arches along the length of the nave. In each bay, where the diagonal vault ribs meet at the ridge, there is a splendid boss. The western bay is narrower, with three lancets in the triforium and clerestory glazed in diamond quarry glass with small rosettes.

The glory of the nave is, for me, the gallery of 16th century windows, each with six slender lancets, which fill the length of the clerestory on the south and north sides. They begin high above the Chapel of the Fonts on the south side with the story of Daniel with the lions on the right, then Belshazzar's Feast, Susanna, and on the left Daniel again. In the next bay we can see the story of Joseph (which continues in the triforium beneath); in bay 3 the story of the Prodigal Son is illustrated; in bay 4 there is Lyévin's Tree of Jesse (1498) with Christ and the Virgin Mary at the top. In bay 5 the lancets depict local saints.

Crossing to the north side we see, high above the chapel of St Paul in bay 5, the legend of St Peter. In bay 4 there is the story of Tobias; in bay 3, scenes from the life of Job; in bay 2, the story of St Sebastien, and in bay 1, the legend of Heraclius, the Cross, and Jacob's Dream.

There is, however, a cautionary note to be added here. 'Modernizers' and restorers of the 19th century paid great attention to the glazing programme throughout the cathedral, to such effect that Professor Lillich in her book, "The Armor of Light: Stained Glass in Western France 1250-1325", published by the University of California Press, 1994, wrote on page 323, "Nineteenth century restorations at Troyes are insensitive and ubiquitous." Not all the panels in some of the older lancets are original.

Fine quadripartite vaults cover all four aisles, and beyond the outer aisles are small chapels to north and south.

THE SOUTH AISLE CHAPELS

The wall of the first bay is blind, but it has two ancient tombstones against it.

The Chapel of the Fonts is enclosed by a fine Renaissance stone screen, the work of Jean Bailly (1551). The lower half acts as a base to support the upper section which is divided into five arches by fluted columns, which rise to bear a lintel on which stands a decorated pediment. Each arch frames a miniature façade of four columns bearing a lintel on which stands a pediment supported by three small arches. Above the central wooden door, there is a classical pediment.

Troyes

Within the chapel there is a stone altar on the east side with a 16th century painting of the Last Supper above it. There is a large piscina in the south wall beneath a decorated ogee arch. There is a small free-standing font. Against the west wall is a splendid polychrome sculptured group in stone (1549) of the baptism of Saint Augustine by St Ambrose at the Easter Vigil in Milan in AD 387. His power of oratory had brought the young Augustine from Carthage to Milan, where the Imperial Court was in residence, and where Ambrose was Archbishop.

The Baptism of Saint Augustine by St Ambrose

There is a window of six lancets: the second, third and fourth (from the east) depict in the centre registers a scene of the Virgin of the Apocalypse, a crescent moon beneath her feet and surrounded by a choir of angels. The Rayonnant tracery above contains shields, while Christ is seated on the throne of judgement at the top.

The Chapel of St Bernadette also has a window of six lancets, each with diamond quarry glass in a decorated border. In the tracery above there is fleurs-de-lys in gold on a blue background. On the altar retable stands a statue of St Bernadette with her hands clasped together. There is a piscina in the south wall above which is a painting of four Doctors of the Church with a lion between them at their feet; from left to right they are St Augustine, St Jerome, St Gregory and St Ambrose. On the west wall are two more paintings. The walls are decorated with blind arcading.

The Chapel of St Genevieve again has a window with six lancets. The central four depict four figures in the lower register and four more in the upper registers. The faces of two figures have been restored, or even brought in from somewhere else. Above is quatrefoil and trefoil tracery with seraphim and pieces of old glass. There is a stone altar against the east wall on which can be seen an ancient wall fresco. There are two carved tablets in the retable either side of the tabernacle and behind the altar is a statue of a devout woman, possibly St Genevieve. On the south wall is there is the tombstone of Catherine de la Marche and her daughter dated 1361. On the south and west walls there is again evidence on the lower level of fresco painting. There is blind arcading around the walls.

A Glimpse Of Glory

The Chapel d'Hiver has a window with the usual six lancets. The lower three registers are glazed with diamond quarry glass and the two registers above depict scenes, while above them is the tracery of quatrefoils and trefoils. Blind arcading adorns the walls either side. There are two paintings on both the west and east walls. There is a double piscina on the south wall to the left of the doorway where the south wall was breached in the 19th century to permit access to the Chapel of the Assumption. This is a modern chapel and is the place where the Blessed Sacrament is reserved and so it is used for private prayer. There is a window in the south wall containing 17th century glass by Linard Gontier depicting the Blessed Virgin Mary surrounded by the virtues attributed to her in the Book Revelation. As you leave the chapel you are faced with the back of the pulpit in a bay in the inner aisle.

The Chapel of St Peter has an angled east wall with an altar against it behind which stands a crucifix. A large painting forms the reredos and is framed by two fluted columns bearing a classical pediment behind which is some blind arcading. Either side of the retable, on the plinth of the columns, is a carving of crossed keys. There is blind arcading on the west and south walls and the latter also has a single piscina. There is a window of three lancets, the lower three registers of which are glazed with clear quarry glass while the three upper registers each depict a figure beneath a canopy. Above that the tracery has three quatrefoils.

We have reached the end of the south aisle, and turning right, we enter the south transept.

THE SOUTH TRANSEPT

At ground level there is a stone bench running around the wall. All three walls have blind arcading decorating the lower level, above which is further blind arcading up to the triforium.

In the triforium above the south door there are twelve lancets, each with a figure which represents an Old Testament prophet: Habakkuk, Nahum, Micah and Jonah forming the central four. Each pair has a quatrefoil above them, and above is a string course below the great South Rose. This masterpiece by Chambiges is filled with 19th century glass, and is set in a square frame with glass in the corner spandrels. The figure of Christ in Majesty in the centre (missing in 2012) is surrounded by twenty-four figures, which are surrounded in turn by scattered trefoils in an attempt to mirror the north rose.

On the west side of the transept the triforium continues over both south aisle arches to the huge columns springing up from the end of the nave to carry the high transept roof. Thus there are three bays at both the triforium level and the clerestory level. In the triforium there are three arches in each bay, each subdivided into two lancets by a single column, and beyond the walkway can be seen the glass of the triforium windows. The southern bay has coloured glass; the centre bay has clear diamond quarries, except for medallions in the centre of each register, and a clear quatrefoil above. That is repeated in the innermost aisle. The clerestory in the southern bay has three tall lancets, each having the same kind of decoration as the inner triforium window: clear quarry glass with little circles at each register. Above these lancets there are two multifoils and a trefoil. In the next bay the clerestory has three lancets with the same decoration, except the central lancet has a figure in it and above there are three quatrefoils. The clerestory of the inner bay has again the three lancets, repeating the arrangement in the middle bay, but the tracery in the top repeats the outer bay.

The east side of the transept also has three bays at triforium level, and the southern bay is a mirror of its counterpart in the west wall. Above, at clerestory level are six lancets the northern four of which have grisaille glass, the southern two and the tracery, which is Rayonnant, have clear diamond quarry glass. The middle bay has the same arrangement, but the centre four clerestory lancets have figures in the middle registers, and the two end figures have each a coat of arms beneath them. The Rayonnant tracery has some colouring in the upper area. The northern bay has exactly the same arrangement except for the absence of coats of arms.

THE CHOIR AND SANCTUARY

We move now to the central crossing, once closed by a stone Rood Screen, and examine the choir and sanctuary. The simple nave altar on its stone platform intrudes into the crossing between the transepts, thus providing a large area for liturgical worship at the head of the nave. To the north are three seats, the middle one for the bishop when he presides, and to the south are three other seats, the middle for the priest when he presides at the Eucharist. The nave altar is new (2012), and consists of a slab of rough stone supported by a sheet of metal underneath which rests on a stone upright at each end. Lying on the top of the rough stone surface is a sheet of clear tough glass. A priest allowed me to stand behind the altar in the position of a celebrant, and I felt that it had an excellent liturgical 'feel' to it.

The three western bays of the choir contain eighty-two 18th century canons stalls brought from Clairvaux Abbey and arranged in two rows. A huge lectern stands in the centre, and the console of the choir organ fills the second bay on the north side.

The seven bays encircling the apse enclose a vast area totally devoid of furniture, apart from the Bishop's Throne on the north side. A crucifix and six candlesticks surmount the fairly plain high altar at the east end. On the pillars about the

A Glimpse Of Glory

The Choir

sanctuary are eight modern statues of St Hervé, St Camelian, St Savinien, St Peter, St Paul, St Loup, St Bernard and St Urban lV.

While I deplore the removal of the rood screen, its absence and a general lack of clutter in the choir and sanctuary allow the eye to be drawn easily to the frieze of brilliantly coloured 13th century glass in the clerestory windows. If you have brought binoculars you will be able to follow the subjects which now surround you.

South: (from the west) Bay 1- Legend of St Theophilus; Bay 2- Relics of Constantinople; Bay 3- The parable of the Wise and Foolish Virgins (Matthew, 25, 1-13); Bay 4- Saints and Martyrs of Troyes; North (from west) Bay 1- Legend of St Helen; Bay 2- Legend of St Savinien; Bay 3- Bishop Hervée and the great men of the age; Bay 4- Legend of St Nicolas.

Returning to the south we turn left into the south ambulatory.

THE SOUTH AMBULATORY

The first two bays have the double aisle carried over from the nave, so it is very spacious at this point. Blind arcading continues along the south wall. The back of the choir is enclosed by a stone screen decorated with six arches and three cinquefoils above the arches.

The first bay has a window of four lancets with clear quarries and the tracery above has three multifoils in clear quarry glass.

The blind arcading in the south wall has a large niche in it in the second bay; it seems to descend to a lower level and could be a light shaft for a crypt. Again the window has four lancets with similar tracery, except that the two eastern lancets are bricked up at the lower registers. There is a doorway beneath the window, and nearby is a bronze statue of St Anne teaching her daughter, the young Virgin Mary, to read.

The ambulatory begins to turn towards the axial chapel as the next bay in the outer aisle comes to an end in a small hemisphere where the windows have been bricked up at some stage. There is also an arch bricked in on the south side. Below the arch is a wooden door which leads to the sacristy and chapter room. On the northern side of the ambulatory at this point is a wrought-iron screen which encloses the sanctuary.

The next bay has a fine stone staircase, with a cusped and decorated balustrade, rising in a blind arch with a multifoil high up in it and which is glazed in clear quarry glass giving light to the Treasury in an upper room. In June 2013 I went to Troyes in an attempt to visit the Treasury, but it was closed for restoration. Underneath the stairway is a wooden doorway.

The South Ambulatory

St Anne & Mary the Virgin, South Ambulatory

A Glimpse Of Glory

The Chapel of St Pius and St Apollinarius has seven bays with blind arcading around the walls at the lower level with a bench below it. Above are two blind arches north and south, and five lancet windows in the southernmost walls. In the south wall there is a wooden altar in poor repair with a wooden canopy above as if a statue once stood there. The floor has some memorial tablets and around the walls more are placed in the blind arcade. The two outermost windows east and west, have geometric patterns in them, but the central window has scenes from the life of St Apollinarius, the first Bishop of Ravenna, while the lancets either side depict scenes from the life of St Francis of Assisi; they were made in 1897.

The Chapel of St Loup has a stone altar in the east wall with three carved arches on its front and a pillar behind bearing the statue of a bishop, probably St Loup. He was one of the earliest bishops of Troyes, and he averted an attack on the city by Attila in the 5th century. The lower walls have blind arcading all around above a bench. The south-east wall has a double piscina. This chapel also has seven bays, the north and south walls are blind, and the remaining five possess windows. The centre three are coloured depicting the life of St Loup in the centre lancet and of St Peter in the lancets either side. In the bottom medallion in the left lancet St Peter converts the Centurion Cornelius (Acts of the Apostles 10), and at the top of the right lancet a medallion depicts Peter's inverted crucifixion. The north window has grisaille glass and the southern one has clear quarry glass.

The Axial Chapel of Our Lady has nine bays as it's a slightly larger chapel. The north and south bays are blind, leaving seven windows. The left and right windows are filled with 18th century grisaille glass but in between there are five windows with superb glass. The central lancet (19th century) depicts the nativity and infancy of Christ; that to the left depicts Joachim and Anne, the parents of Mary, and her birth; the lancet on the right deals again with the infancy of Jesus and is thought to have replaced the Jesse window. The east end of the chapel has a delightful altar, carried on six columns: two at each end and two in the centre framing an ancient carved marble front. A 19th century white marble statue by Charles Simart of the Virgin Mary holding her child stands above the altar reredos.

We continue our anti-clockwise journey into the north ambulatory.

THE NORTH AMBULATORY

The Chapel of St Joseph has a similar pattern to that of the Chapel of St Loup. It has seven bays with blind arcading all around the lower level. A stone altar stands against the east wall with three arches carved in it, and a plinth on the retable bearing a man with a child, probably St Joseph. Above the string course there are five central windows, the north and south bays are blind. The southwest window has 18th century grisaille glass; the north-west window has clear quarry glass. The central window has three medallions with scenes depicting the martyrdom of St Andrew. The window to the right has eight medallions depicting the miracles of St Andrew, and that to the left has six medallions relating the legend of St Nicholas.

The Chapel of St Matthew is similar to the previous chapels as far as the number of bays and blind arcading is concerned; the outer bays are blind. In the east stands a wooden altar with a statue above it of the young Virgin Mary. The two outer windows have grisaille glazing and the three eastern ones are glazed beautifully. The centre window has four diamond medallions in the centre with semi-circular scenes either side depicting the legend of St Matthew. The lancet to the right has seven round medallions with foliage enclosing them which depict the life of Christ and the Virgin. The northern window has three medallions which depict Mary at the crucifixion, her Assumption and her coronation in heaven. The semicircles in between depict Old Testament scenes – Abraham's sacrifice of Isaac, Moses, Judith and Esther.

The Chapel of St Joan of Arc retains the seven-bay arrangement with blind arcading at the lower level. The first two bays to the north and the last bay to the south are all blind. The plain wooden altar has a statue of St Joan holding the Oriflamme standing behind it on a plinth. There are statues to left and right of the altar: St Mary the Virgin standing on a serpent to the left, and Archangel Michael to the right. There is a statue of Brother Jean de Gaud holding a rosary in the south-eastern corner. The lancet containing the Tree of Jesse is very beautiful; the lower two lozenges and the top two date from the early 13th century. The subjects are descendants of Jesse (recorded in Matthew 1, 6-17): David playing an instrument, Solomon writing on a tablet, Jehoshaphat, Josiah, the Virgin Mary holding a palm in her right hand and, at the top, Christ with his hand raised in benediction.

The Chapel of the Sacred Heart occupies the next three bays. The eastern bay is enclosed by a wrought-iron screen, and has an apsidal vault, with the usual blind arcading continuing behind the altar and along the three-bay north wall. The east wall has two blind arches rising from the arcade to the vault. The two lancets in the north wall of this little apse are glazed with diamond quarries set in broad coloured borders; they date from c.1200 and are therefore older than the cathedral. Behind the altar, on a column, there is a statue of Christ revealing his sacred heart.

The next bay is open to the ambulatory and has a window of four lancets surmounted by two multifoils filled with diamond quarry glass in the north wall. On a bracket on the south pillar there is a statue of Christ wearing a crown of thorns (Ecce Homo).

A Glimpse Of Glory

In the final bay of this chapel the north wall has two lancets with a multifoil in diamond quarry glass and two blind lancets. A 14th century stone statue of the Virgin and Child is mounted on a bracket on the south pillar.

THE NORTH TRANSEPT

Turning right into the north transept we can see the three quadripartite vaults which cover the transept.

East Wall: in the north bay the lower level has a blind arcade and is similar to the west wall, except that the north lancet is glazed in diamond quarries but has only half a quatrefoil in the tracery, and a slender lancet south of it. The triforium continues over all three bays, but is blind behind the gallery in the northern bay, whereas it has six small lancets in coloured glass in the remaining two bays. The clerestory in the two southern bays has coloured glass, except for the last lancet to the south, which has clear diamond quarries.

Sacred Heart Chapel, 14th century Virgin and Child

North Wall: the blind arcading continues at the lower level, above which two blind lancets decorate the wall either side of the north door. The triforium gallery continues above the stringcourse with twelve small lancets. Above them, the north rose fills the wall to the height of the vault. The North Rose is almost a copy of that in the south transept, for Chambiges kept to much the same template for the ease of the glaziers. The glass is 15th century and was constructed in the Rayonnant style of St Denis and Notre Dame de Paris. This style was quickly copied because it was so elegant and at the cutting edge of architectural achievement. I have seen exquisite examples in Tours and as far south as Carcassonne. In his book, "The Rose Window", published by Thames and Hudson in 2005, Painton Cowen expresses surprise on page 104 that Troyes was still following this pattern as late as the 15th century.

The thinness which made the pattern so attractive also brought with it structural problems, hence the strengthening mullion rising from the stringcourse through its centre. Depicted In the centre of the four corner multifoils are St John (top left), St Matthew (top right), St Luke (bottom left) and St Mark (bottom right).

West Wall: in the north bay the blind arcading continues at lower level and above are two blind lancets with quatrefoil tracery, and one slim lancet without tracery. The triforium continues along all three bays, each with three arches subdivided into six small lancets. In the clerestory are three lancets with tracery in each bay, as in the south transept. The central lancet in the centre bay alone contains a figure, that of St Catherine in a blue gown, wearing a martyr's crown and holding a small wheel, the symbol of her martyrdom.

THE NORTH AISLE

The Chapel of St Paul is the easternmost chapel in the north aisle and the east wall is angled (similar to the chapel of St Peter in the south aisle). There is a large painting above the altar, which is framed by a classical pediment supported on two fluted columns. There is a double piscina in the north wall, where the mullions which divide the lancet windows descend to the ground. The glazing is by Edouard Didron (1874), and the subjects depicted in the left lancet are: the Annunciation, the Visitation and St John the Evangelist. In the right lancet we see: the Adoration of Magi (2 panels) and St Michael. In the little roses above are St. Peter, St Paul and Christ in Majesty. The west wall is decorated with two blind lancets. The chapel is enclosed by a wrought-iron grille.

The Chapel of the Mystic Wine-Press is so named for the remarkable window by Linard Gontier in 1625. The east and west walls are both decorated with two blind lancets. An altar stands against the east wall with a large statue on the retable. The 16th century statue is of St Roch. He is holding his cloak about his shoulders with his right hand, and a child stands at his right holding his robe open to expose his right leg; a dog stands up to take a bite out of a loaf of bread held in the saint's left hand. There is a double piscina in the north wall, where the mullions dividing the lancets descend to the ground.

The window has six lancets, the outer one to left and right is glazed in diamond quarries, but the central four lancets contain this intriguing picture of the wine-press. Christ lies under the press at the bottom of the middle two lancets,

St Roch, Chapel of the Mystic Winepress

his blood flowing into a chalice beneath him. To the left of him a donor, Canon Jean Bareton, with his patron saint, St John the Baptist; to the right of the press kneels another donor, Chevalier of Malta François Vinot, with his patron St Francis of Assisi. From Christ's chest grows a vine, which bears in its branches the twelve Apostles. The phrase, "TORCULAR CALCAVI SOLUS" is inscribed below it; it is a quotation from Isaiah 63.3: "I have trodden the wine-press alone." This chapel is not enclosed by a grille.

The Chapel of St Anthony has the same decoration as previous chapels: the east and west walls with blind lancets and the mullions dividing the lancets in the window in the north wall descending to the ground, with a double piscina in the north wall. The window of six lancets, restored by Didron in 1876, depicts on two levels the twelve Apostles, each in a canopied niche. An altar stands against the east wall with a statue above it. The 16th century statue is of St Anthony holding a book in his right hand, and in his left a stick, a rope and a bell. A small dog stands at his feet.

The Chapel of St Thérèse and the Infant Christ has a wooden altar against the east wall, which is decorated with two blind lancets but without a central mullion. The reredos above the altar is an ancient painting on wood of the Crucifixion of Christ, flanked by the Annunciation by the angel, and the Presentation of the infant Christ in the Temple. A statue of St Thérèse of Lisieux stands on a bracket to the north of the altar. There is a single piscina. The six lancets in the north wall are filled with diamond quarry glass, but the mullions descend to the floor as in the other chapels. The west wall is entirely without ornament.

The Chapel of St Maurice is dominated by a lofty classical pediment supported by two ribbed pilasters above the altar against the east wall. A neatly pleated curtain is suspended from the pediment, and forms a background to a statue of a Roman soldier holding a cross in his right hand. The base is round, indicating to me that it once stood on a column; it would certainly be more at home in a baronial hall than in a cathedral. The window of six lancets is filled with clear diamond quarry glass, except for small roundels containing heraldic arms. Below this window in the north wall is a French War Memorial. The blank west wall forms the western end of the north aisle chapels.

DO NOT MISS

1. Time to study the clerestory windows in the nave
2. The sculpture of the baptism of Saint Augustine, south aisle
3. Statue of St Anne teaching the young Virgin Mary to read, south ambulatory
4. The 13th century clerestory windows in the choir
5. The 14th century statue of the Virgin and Child, north ambulatory
6. The Treasury

CHAPTER 7

AUXERRE

Rising on a gentle slope above the River Yonne, the city of Auxerre gives an impression of lazy gentility. From the east bank of the river the cathedral dominates the skyline; only the abbey of St Germain to the north competes with it. Yet, it is a busy centre of commerce and its suburbs are full of bustle and traffic.

I always stay at the Hotel Normandie on the inner ring road, with its secure car park at the rear, and which requires only a short stroll downhill to the quays with the river craft, or uphill to the city centre, with its shops, restaurants and the cathedral of St Stephen. In the mediaeval period the eastern part of the city was under the jurisdiction of the bishop, and the remainder under the authority of the counts of Auxerre. The cathedral formed a major part of the bishop's domain. The capital of Lower Burgundy, Auxerre is surrounded by vineyards such as those of nearby Chablis.

CATHEDRAL CHURCH OF ST STEPHEN (ST ÉTIENNE)

The present church is on the site chosen by St Amator (c.386–418) for his cathedral. It was certainly completed by 418, for in that year St Germain was elected Bishop here on the death of St Amator. Like so many of the ancient cathedrals of Europe, it was destroyed by fire in 887, as was its successor built by Bishop Herifried in the fire of 950. Again the cathedral was rebuilt only to perish in the fire of 1023.

This was followed by yet another cathedral during the episcopate of Hughes de Chalon in the first half of the 11th century. All that remains of that fine Romanesque church is the crypt, which now forms the foundation of the choir. The present choir was begun in 1215 by the young Bishop William (Guillaume) of Segnelay, appointed as the fifty-eighth bishop of Auxerre in 1207. The new Gothic style of cathedral building was sweeping across France from the north and William was

A Glimpse Of Glory

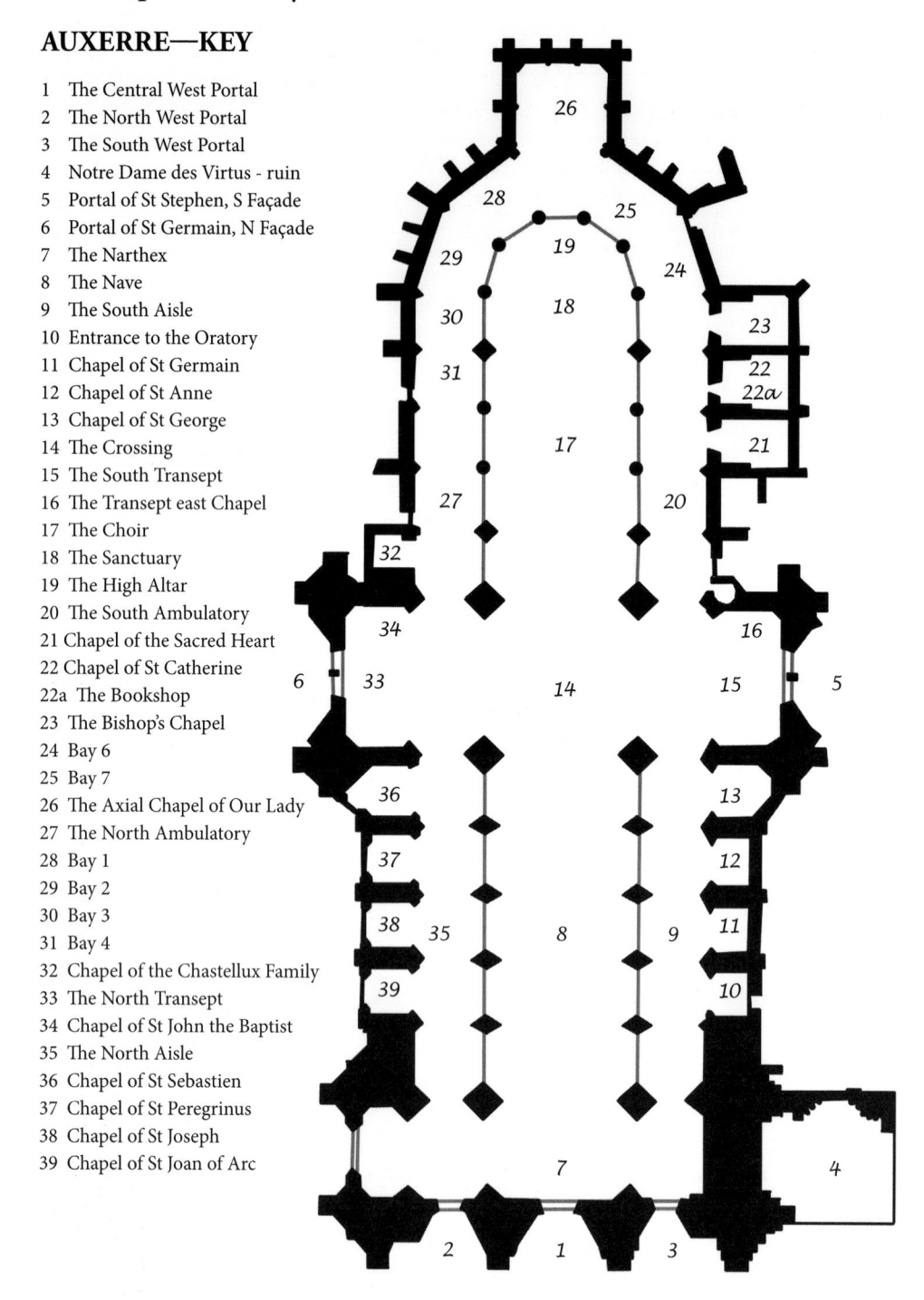

AUXERRE—KEY

1. The Central West Portal
2. The North West Portal
3. The South West Portal
4. Notre Dame des Virtus - ruin
5. Portal of St Stephen, S Façade
6. Portal of St Germain, N Façade
7. The Narthex
8. The Nave
9. The South Aisle
10. Entrance to the Oratory
11. Chapel of St Germain
12. Chapel of St Anne
13. Chapel of St George
14. The Crossing
15. The South Transept
16. The Transept east Chapel
17. The Choir
18. The Sanctuary
19. The High Altar
20. The South Ambulatory
21. Chapel of the Sacred Heart
22. Chapel of St Catherine
22a. The Bookshop
23. The Bishop's Chapel
24. Bay 6
25. Bay 7
26. The Axial Chapel of Our Lady
27. The North Ambulatory
28. Bay 1
29. Bay 2
30. Bay 3
31. Bay 4
32. Chapel of the Chastellux Family
33. The North Transept
34. Chapel of St John the Baptist
35. The North Aisle
36. Chapel of St Sebastien
37. Chapel of St Peregrinus
38. Chapel of St Joseph
39. Chapel of St Joan of Arc

Auxerre

enthused by this artistic renewal. The choir of Auxerre is contemporary with those of Tours, Chartres, Soissons, Rouen, Troyes, Angers, Reims, Beauvais and many others. It was a great era for French architecture.

Auxerre is glorious, and although it is a co-cathedral with Sens, it is to be regretted deeply that it no longer holds episcopal rank in its own right, for it is one of the many sees suppressed at the redistribution of dioceses after the Revolution.

EXTERIOR

THE WEST FAÇADE

Viewed from the parvis, it appears to be incomplete with only one tower to the northwest, but it has a modest grandeur. There are three portals in the west front, and a rose window partially obscured by the gable over the central portal, yet it has a quietly pleasing aspect. Either side there is a doorway with a canopied arch. The inside of all three west porches were very dirty on my previous visits, but in 2008 the west façade had been cleaned and now it gleams in the sunshine. It is also easier now to interpret the bas-relief panels which adorn the base level of the door splays, with delightful scenes from the Old Testament illustrating a continuous story from north to south.

The central door is surmounted by a large canopied arch supporting an exquisite gable. The canopy of the central door is highly decorated with lancets on which is superimposed a small traceried rose. Behind the gable lancet windows supporting the West Rose can be seen. A fillet is inserted above the rose to fill the arch which covers

The West Façade

A Glimpse Of Glory

it. This entire arch has stepped decorated brackets in blind lancets with canopies, but no statuary. It has the appearance of a fringe of lace above the arch. A pierced parapet runs the width of the bay above the arch, behind which is a gallery of blind lancets. This is crowned by the gable end of the nave, which is decorated with a splendid blind rose. The gable is framed by a decorated frieze which resembles the parapet.

In the first storey on the north side there are three blind lancets surmounted by shallow gables which terminate in decorated finials. In the second storey there is a central arch containing a small window and three empty, pinnacled niches with brackets on either side, all sadly devoid of statuary. The third storey has a row of extremely tall blind lancets which return on the south side of the north buttress. They are divided into two levels by empty brackets, and are all delightfully canopied such that the decoration looks like a lace curtain from a distance. This lacework is continued on the west face of the north-central buttress. Above is a pierced parapet, which runs along the top of this storey and continues southwards until it comes to an abrupt halt at the finial of the central gable of the west façade. Above the parapet is the bell chamber with louvered windows. Finally, crowning the tower, there are two little walls decorated with blind arches; they are, in fact, the tops of the buttresses which support the whole tower. There is a buttress springing from the north tower across to the roof of the central pinnacle in which there is a blind rose window.

On the south side, the first storey mirrors the north side, but in the second storey there are only three brackets and pinnacles adjacent to the central section shaft, and above them, in the third storey, only two of the tall lancets were started on the buttress rising to support the south tower which was never built. They abut a white triangle which is the west wall of the nave.

The Northwest (left) Door

The theme here is creation. The Old Testament bas-relief panels begin at the base of the buttress to the left of the left splay with the story of creation. In the splay, in the top left panel we see the creation of Adam, then Eve, and at the right God forbids them to eat the fruit of the Tree of Good and Evil. The story is continued in the top of the panels in the right splay of the door, with Eve giving in to temptation, then they are called to account, and on the right they are driven out of the garden.

Back in the left splay, the story continues at the bottom with Cain and Abel offering produce to God, Cain killing his brother Abel, and God cursing him for ever. This is continued in the right splay, with God resolving to save Noah from the destruction of a depraved world, and in two panels Noah with his family afloat in a first-class cabin in the ark, while the animals are like sardines in steerage.

The canopied niches above the base panels are all empty, as is the large arch of the tympanum. The lintel, however, bears a delightful sculpture of the coronation of the Virgin by her Son, attended by angels. The three orders of little sculptures decorating the archivolt tell the story of the Virgin Mary, but they are badly mutilated.

bas-relief of Noah, north-west portal, left splay

The Central Door

The theme of this portal is the Last Judgement. The bas-relief panels in the left splay depict the life of Joseph; in the two panels in the top centre, that on the right shows him being lowered into a well by his brothers, and the next to it to the left depicts him being pulled out for sale into slavery to travellers from Egypt. To the left of that panel, and in lower panels, he interprets dreams for Pharaoh.

In the splay to the right of the door the panels are said to represent the Parable of the prodigal Son, but they are so badly damaged that I cannot discern any particular scene, except in the top panel furthest from the door, where in the top left the prodigal can be seen feasting in bad company, and to the right he is sharing a bath with an immoral women. In the centre a woman is suckling animals (representing 'lust') and below to the right the prodigal is seen feasting with his father on his return home. The niches above the panels contain statues of two unknown men talking together, although one niche is empty on the right hand side.

The tympanum has a sculpture of Christ enthroned, his feet resting on a globe, the Virgin and St John kneeling either side of him. The lintel above the doors depict the Last Judgement: St Michael weighs the souls of the dead in the centre, and to the left the enormous gaping mouth of the Leviathan is ready to receive the damned, while the redeemed are led to the right by angels. In the moulding above the lintel, angels gather more souls in large cloths. The lintel itself is supported by corbels held in place by sculpted angels. The six orders of vousoirs in the archivolt are most delicately carved with small fascinating scenes of the early church.

The large niches each side of the door would have once been filled with statues; the central portal usually depicted the apostles. The door jambs are carved with (right) the foolish virgins, while the wise virgins are to the left. The doors are studded with the royal fleurs-de-lys.

A Glimpse Of Glory

THE SOUTHWEST (RIGHT) DOOR

The theme of this portal is the forerunners of Christ. The bas-relief panels at the base of the splays depict King David who, though chosen by God, and although he was the ancestor of Christ (who was 'of the house of David), was nevertheless a sinner. He is depicted in the right splay observing Bathsheba bathing (left and centre), then he sends her husband, Uriah, to fight in battle. In the left splay we see Uriah killed in battle (left), and so David then marries Bathsheba (centre and right).

The tympanum depicts scenes from the life of John the Baptist. At the bottom we see the Visitation of the Virgin to Elizabeth to the left; in the centre Elizabeth gives birth to John; on the right the scene depicts John's circumcision. In the central register is the baptism of Christ in the River Jordan by John. At the top of the tympanum we see Herod's feast; to the left Salome dances for the guests, and to the right she brings to the table John's head on a dish.

To the south (right) of the west façade is the Parochial Office, and from the car park inside the gate can be seen the remnant of the Chapel of Notre Dame des Vertus, which was completed in 1561. It was severely damaged by the Huguenots and later fell into ruin. All we can see now is the Renaissance pediment under a delightful arch decorated with splendid tiles, and the tops the niches either side decorated with carved shells, above which is a small intricately carved frieze. The statue which has been venerated here since the mid-1300s is now to be found in the Lady Chapel at the east end of the cathedral.

That concludes our examination of the west façade, and now we walk along rue Caylus to the south, before turning left into rue Ph. Roux in order to circumnavigate the Parochial Offices, and turning left again to arrive at the south façade.

THE SOUTH FAÇADE

Constructed at the beginning of the 14th century, in 2013 this façade still had some of the grime I first encountered on the west façade.

The St Stephen Portal. The splays of the portal are decorated with cusped blind arches, with a trefoil above the cusp. Above these arches are canopied niches which are devoid of statues, but rising from the canopies are three orders of sculptures decorating the vousoirs of the archivolt with images of prophets and angels gathered around the first Christian martyr. The trumeau dividing the two doors has a bracket and a canopy, but the statue of the patron saint, St Stephen, is missing. Little carved angels crouch in the corners of the doorway.

The decorated canopy of the trumeau divides the lintel into two sections, each carved with four statues of Old Testament figures. The tympanum rises above to fill the arch and has three registers of sculpture. The bottom register depicts the ceremony where Stephen was made a Deacon in the church. Although the heads of the statues have been smashed, to the left we see the Apostles laying their hands on him in confirmation of his appointment; in the centre we see him preaching in Jerusalem; to the right he is arrested for preaching. In the middle register he is kneeling in the centre while either side are scenes of lapidation [Acts of the Apostles, 7, verses 54–60]. To the extreme left can be seen the young Saul of Tarsus holding the cloaks; he is to become St Paul after his Damascus breakdown. An open gable rises above the portal with a rosette filled with trefoils in and around it, and the buttresses either side terminate in a delicate crocketted pinnacle.

Behind the gable there four tall lights, each with two lancets and the outer lights have a quatrefoil in the tracery. Above them the façade is filled by the large south rose window, with a small fillet above it to complete the arch. In order to square the façade, the corners are filled with blind trefoils.

A pierced parapet above the rose links the two substantial buttresses which flank the façade, and forms the base for the gable which is decorated with blind trefoils and lozenge shapes, and which is further decorated by a repeat of the parapet motif up the slope of the roof to the finial which crowns the façade. The buttress either side is crowned with a splendid pinnacle, carved with niches, canopies and crockets. It is indeed High Gothic at its best.

We are obliged to retrace our steps past the west façade to arrive at the north façade.

THE NORTH ELEVATION OF THE NAVE

The massive buttresses which divide the chapels of the north aisle rise like sentinels in a row along the north side. They receive the balustraded double flying-buttresses which support the clerestory wall, and are crowned with a decorated ridge roof. The western window has the mere hint of a pointed arch and simple cusps in the oculi of the tracery over the three lancets. Similar tracery can be seen over the two lancets in the window of the eastern bay which forms the junction of the nave with the transept. The two central bays are slightly lower than their neighbours, and have definite pointed arches containing flamboyant tracery over four lancets.

The clerestory windows contain quatrefoils in the tracery over the lancets, with blind trefoils in the spandrels. The upper flying buttress in each bay is crowned at roof level by a decorated pinnacle. A parapet which graces the top of the wall is pierced with open quatrefoils.

A Glimpse Of Glory

THE NORTH FAÇADE

This façade was completed towards the third quarter of the 14th century. Clean and fresh from renovation, the Portal gives entrance to the North Transept. Apart from the flight of steps leading up to the portal, the façade has distinct similarities to the south façade, in that two slender buttresses rise either side of the portal, and terminate in delicate pinnacles, while more substantial buttresses flank the central section of the façade and rise to the height of the roof gable.

The St Germain (or Germanius) Portal. There are three cusped blind arches either side of the splays at low level; above them are empty niches, each with a bracket and canopy for a statue. From the canopies three orders of sculptured scenes decorate the vousoirs in the archivolt of the porch. The scenes depict the lives of St Amator and St Peregrinus, the predecessors of St Germain. The trumeau has an empty bracket and a canopy where once a statue of St Germain once stood.

North Façade from the north

The lintel is carved with depictions of the sun at the left and the moon at the right with plant life in between them. Above it the tympanum depicts the life of St Germain in three registers of statuary. In the bottom register we see the nobleman Germain hunting; in the centre he is ordained priest by Bishop Amator, and to the right he himself is consecrated bishop. In the middle register, to the left he raises a friend from the dead, and to the right we see him victorious over the Picts and Saxons in Britain in his mission to drive out Pelagianism. At the top, Germain's body is returned to Auxerre on a hearse. A pointed crocketted arch surmounts the porch, decorated with flamboyant tracery and crockets.

Behind the arch eight lancets fill the width of the façade, each with cusps at the top. The outer two lancets either side rise higher having fine flamboyant tracery above them. These lancets support the North Rose. In the spandrels formed by the arch over the rose and the pierced balustrade above it, which runs between the buttresses, the wall is decorated with small blind lancets.

Auxerre

The North Rose

The gable at the top of the façade is decorated with a large blind rose of eight cusped 'petals'; in the corners at the bottom is a trefoil each side, and a quatrefoil at the apex. The pierced parapet frames the pitch of the gable and terminates in a delicate finial, which is slightly lower than the pinnacles of the flanking buttresses.

Note an ancient painted notice on the buttress to the west of the north portal, quite high up, which reads in rough translation: "You are liable to be arrested by the police on pain of prison if you deposit any ordure or throw anything on this wall of the church."

THE INTERIOR

THE WEST END

Above the west door is a really glorious rose window (1550) given by Bishop François II de Dinteville, depicting God the Father in the centre of a heavenly concert of ten seraphim, surrounded by twenty angels playing instruments. The row of lancets underneath(1573), the two outer taller than the four inner, each depict the patron saint of the donor canons: (left to right) St James the Great, St Christopher, St Charlemagne, St Sebastien, St Nicholas, St Claude, St Roch and St Eugénie. In 2013 the lower registers had temporary glazing while restoration takes

A Glimpse Of Glory

place. In the centre of the west wall, below the rose, there is a central recessed arch framing the great doors, and either side are two blind arches each with a cusped head. There is blind arcading filling the triforium and the clerestory on the south and north walls of this western bay.

The west end of both the south and north aisles has a doorway in a deeply recessed arch with no ornamentation at all.

THE NAVE

There is a descent of five steps from the entrance into the western bay, or narthex, where the quadripartite vault and the clustered columns which support it, are much larger than in the other bays of the nave as they were built to provide a sure foundation to the western towers. Begun in 1309, the narthex is followed by five bays which direct the eye towards the east end, 98 metres away, and the magnificent sight of Christ crucified and in majesty in the clerestory windows of the apse.

The arch mouldings spring from slender attached shafts. Above the arches of the nave is a rather solid triforium consisting of a pierced parapet with arches above it concealing a passage, which runs the length of the nave. This is surmounted by the

The Nave

Auxerre

lofty clerestory, where all five bays each have a window of four lancets with three quatrefoils in the tracery. The clerestory windows were partly destroyed in 1567. What remains is mostly 15th and 16th century glazing. The nave is covered by a quadripartite vault with a fine coloured boss in each bay. The colour is also applied to a small portion of the ribs which radiate from the bosses.

THE SOUTH NAVE CLERESTORY WINDOWS (FROM WEST TO EAST)

Bay 1 has an arch about a metre lower than the others, although the stringcourse is about the same height along the south side. In the clerestory the lower four panels have geometric designs in otherwise clear glass; the fifth panel has a pinnacle over the lower panels and above that is a scene across all four lancets of Mary interceding and suckling her Son. The donor is portrayed as a monk in this early 16th century window.

Bay 2 has an identical early 16th century window, except that the scene extends one panel lower. In the extreme western lancet Saint Stephen steers a ship representing the church, carrying a palm in his left hand and a book in his left; demons attempt to destroy the masts

Bay 3 is similar except that the early 15th century central five panels are covered with scenes of Mary's family: St Anne; the second lancet from the left is of the Virgin and Child; then Mary Salome with her children and, finally, Mary Cleophas with her sons James and John. This window had temporary glass in 2013 while restoration is carried out.

Bay 4 has only two quatrefoils because the top of the tracery has a rosette. The late 14th century eastern lancet has a large figure, which is St Peter holding keys, and three kneeling donors appear in the other three lancets.

Bay 5 has geometric designs in the lower three and the top two panels, with a figure in the middle four panels of each lancet. The figure in the left (eastern) lancet is St Charlemagne carrying a sword and looking very solemn, then comes St Catherine, St Louis and St James the Great.

The following note is from Canon W R Hanford: Charlemagne was canonized in 1165 at the instigation of Frederick Barbarossa as part of a political folie de grandeur on his part. The trouble was that he had Charlemagne canonized by his Antipope Victor IV. The 'real' pope was the formidable Alexander III, who was one of the longest reigning popes, and he it was who really systematised the whole process of canonization and restricted its operation entirely to the Holy See. So with Alexander III in office it was fairly clear that the canonization of Charlemagne would not have been recognised by Alexander and his successors, hence Charlemagne is very seldom referred to as a saint.

A Glimpse Of Glory

THE NORTH NAVE CLERESTORY WINDOWS (FROM EAST TO WEST)

The clerestory windows follow the arrangement in the south clerestory: four lancets.

Bay 1 In each early 15th century lancet in this bay the lower three panels are filled with geometric designs; the next four panels contain a figure beneath a canopy, and the top two have what appears to be a chariot or anvil. The easternmost lancet depicts the coronation of the Virgin Mary, the next is a crowned saint with his right hand raised and an orb in his left, than a lady at prayer with her hands together, and finally a bishop saint with mitre and chasuble and holding a crozier. This window also had temporary glass in 2013.

Bay 2 has, in the eastern lancet, St Paul, while the middle lancets have each a kneeling donor facing east, and the fourth is full of geometric designs. This is a 14th century window.

Bay 3 has an early 15th century window with Rayonnant tracery. The top four panels in each lancet are taken up with canopies, under which is a figure in the outer lancets and only a head in the middle two. The remainder of the lancets are filled with geometric designs. The eastern lancet has as the figure an image of the Trinity: God with a cross bearing the crucified Christ against his chest. The next

The Nave Vault

has the head of Our Lady and the Child, then a priest holding a cross, and in the western lancet the deacon St Stephen wearing a dalmatic presents the donor and her daughters who kneel before him.

Bay 4 has three quatrefoils in the tracery, the two top panels and the bottom three of geometric designs and the remainder made up of fragments of a depiction of Jesus risen from the tomb, St Louis and Mary Magdalene. The window is dated 1524.

Bay 5 has three quatrefoils at the top and then the usual four lancets with four figures: a deacon saint, St Cosmas & St Damian, St Cyrus and St Peter, across the top half and the bottom half full of early C16th fragments and geometric designs. This bay has the same arrangement as the south side, with its arch lower than the remainder. So the two westernmost arches are the same height, then the four eastern ones are taller, rising to the pierced parapet. The nave has the symmetry north and south that is the essence of Gothic appeal.

THE SOUTH AISLE (FROM WEST TO EAST)

On the south wall of the western bay are four blind arches. Above these arches are two paintings, one of which is of the Crucifixion. The blind arcading of the western bay continues along the lower wall of the second bay, and is repeated with four blind lancets and tracery on its upper wall.

The First Chapel There is a door which leads to the Oratory, which is a large room reserved for private prayer. The window has four low lancets of modern geometric designs with tracery above. Although the chapel is now just a passageway, there is in the south wall what was once a double piscine with an arch over it, but in ancient vandalism half of it has been walled up. Remnants of fresco paintings can be seen on the east wall.

The Chapel of St Germain. He was a high-ranking Roman official who was converted to Christianity by Bishop Amator and later succeeded him as bishop in 414. With St Loup, he rid Britain of the Pelagian heresy. He died in Ravenna and his body was brought back to Auxerre for burial in his villa, where stands now the abbey bearing his name. Henceforth, he became the patron saint of the Diocese of Auxerre, before the see was suppressed after the Revolution.

The window, executed at the end of the 19th century, has four lancets, each with a scene from the life of the saint in it, with quatrefoils and trefoils in the tracery. The lancets on the left depict St Germain and St Geneviève and to the right the death of the saint at Ravenna. The chapel has a marble altar and to the north of it, against the east wall, is a wooden statue of the saint by the sculptor Francois Brochet of

A Glimpse Of Glory

Auxerre (1956–1958). Writing in 1905, Francis Bumpus reports an effigy above the altar of St Germain holding in his hand a bunch of grapes.

The Chapel of St Anne has a marble altar and a 17th century statue of St Anne with her daughter, the young Virgin Mary, learning her letters. Above it is a painting of the Assumption of the Virgin (1745) by Jean Restout. The largely 19th century lancets feature four Old Testament Prophets. In a niche on the west wall there is a lovely relief sculpture of St Martin dividing his cloak with a beggar at Amiens. Below it is a bas-relief depicting Christ appearing in a dream to St Martin; it is a story from "The Golden Legend". There is a large painting above the sculptures which could be another of the Assumption of Mary into Heaven.

The Chapel of St George is screened by four blind arches with trefoil tracery. The doorway leads to the organ, for the entire bay is filled by the great organ, with the trumpet pipes projecting out above the aisle *en chamade*. The instrument was built by Dominique Oberthur from Saintonge in 1986.

THE SOUTH TRANSEPT

The cathedral does not have extensive transepts; they extend only as far as the building line of the aisle chapels.

A Chapel in the east wall has a marble altar with a statue of a monk, in a brown habit, holding an infant standing on it. On the wall above is a painting of a figure wearing a helmet and holding a spear, with which he is about to kill someone lying naked on the floor; another person leans over to protect him, but the winged messenger—possibly the Archangel Michael—is not going to be stopped. Above the painting, beneath a pediment borne by a marble pilaster either side of the altar, is a gilded sculpture of a sunburst, with angels around a triangle containing an inscription of the Tetragrammaton. Above are four lancets with flamboyant tracery depicting figures, but the pediment partly obscures them.

In the south bay of the east wall, the triforium has two blind lancets, while the clerestory also has two lancets (early 14th century), where the subject is the Annunciation, depicting on the left the Angel Gabriel and to the right the Blessed Virgin. In the north bay of the east wall the triforium has a passage with four arches, but with no balustrade protecting it. The clerestory above has two large lancets, depicting St John the Baptist (left), and St John the Evangelist, with one large multifoil of the Virgin and Infant in the tracery. These, too, date from the early 14th century.

On the south wall, either side of the south door, are two blind arches in two registers with trefoil tracery; the upper with trefoils and quatrefoils going into a crocketted canopy with a pinnacle either side. In the lower register there are 14th century tempera wall-paintings, a bishop, allegedly St Peter, in chasuble and mitre to the west and to the east John the Baptist holding a lamb in his left hand. There are no such frescos on the west side of the door. In the upper arches either side there are two superbly carved column bases depicting four of the deadly sins: Wrath and Envy to the east and Sloth and Lust to the west.

The great 16th century renaissance rose window, also given by François II de Dinteville, Bishop of Auxerre, is dated 1550 and restored in 1575, 1840 and 1895, and is mounted above eight lancets, the outer two with quatrefoils above. They depict eight events in the life of Moses, from the burning bush to the revolt against him by Dathan and Abiram, each event depicted in two lancets. The rose itself has God the Father at the centre and surrounded by circles of angels and cherubim. The lancets were made in 1575 by the glazier Guillaume Cornuaille.

On the west wall of the south transept there are four blind arches, the southern pierced by a door leading to the organ, because above the arches is the gallery of the instrument and an arch filled with latticework forming the organ console. Above it, at triforium level, there are three arches with a passage behind it and in the clerestory there are three blind lancets with tracery above. To the north, the three arches protecting the passage continue over the south aisle arch and in the clerestory above are three lancets filled with grisaille glass in geometric designs and with a quatrefoil and two trefoils in the tracery.

THE CROSSING

In the centre of the crossing is a large platform on which stands a nave altar, and in the northeast corner the seats for the sacred ministers, and at the southeast corner a bishop's throne. The columns of the crossing soar up from very small plinths at ground level without interruption and bear the spring of the arches which form the vault of the crossing. Five slender engaged columns on each face of the columns go right up through the capitals, which appear as mere decoration, before springing across the vault to the other side of the transept and choir and up into the central boss of the crossing. Together with tiercerons, ridge ribs and a fine central boss, the vault is elegantly beautiful.

THE CHOIR

In 1217 the two Romanesque towers flanking the old choir collapsed, requiring a rebuilding of the sanctuary and choir. Work had, in any case, begun on a Gothic reconstruction of the sanctuary a few years earlier, but now a major work was initiated. The unknown architect produced an original design on a smaller scale

A Glimpse Of Glory

than the great examples of Bourges, Reims or Amiens, which were being constructed at the same time. But the tall arcade arches around the choir, surmounted by a high triforium and a light clerestory combine to give a vertical elegance that is impressive. Added to this is the good fortune of having nearby the excellent limestone quarries of Tonnerre. This enabled the masons to cut the columns along the grain of the stone all in one length, thus bringing to the site slender columns of unusual strength but which gave the appearance of a fragile beauty.

The architecture of the choir continues the three-stage arrangement of the nave. Each bay has a stilted arch springing from foliated capitals, and above the string-course a triforium of simple lancet arcades of four arches on slender detached shafts in front of a passage which continues around the apse. Above the triforium is a lofty clerestory, one large plate-traceried window of two lancets crowned with a rose in each bay, which fills the entire wall up to the vault, reminiscent of Chartres. Further east, around the sanctuary, the pillars become more slender, the arches become narrower giving an enhanced sense of the vertical, and the triforium reduces to three arches to similar effect.

The subjects of the high clerestory windows in the choir, which date from the mid-13th century, are: (starting nearest the south transept) Christ enthroned on a rainbow with a martyr holding a palm (1190); Ezekiel and St John; unidentified apostle and prophet; Amos and an apostle; Aaron; Isaiah and an apostle; St Lawrence and St Amator. The central bay of the apse depicts Christ on the Cross between the Virgin and St John (south), and Christ in Majesty between St Matthew and St John (north). The Paschal Lamb is in the centre of the rose above. There follows on the north side: St Germain and St Stephen; an apostle and Daniel; an apostle and Moses with the tablets; St Paul and Obadiah; St Peter and Malachi; St James and Habakkuk; finally, near the north transept, Christ holding the Cross of the resurrection between the Virgin and St John, and St Camille (1190).

The choir and sanctuary are enclosed by a high wrought iron screen in black with gilt decoration, which is in need of refreshment. Originally, the choir was separated from the nave by a rood screen and enclosed by a wall, until, in 1746, railings were made in Paris by Dhumier, but all that remains of them is the great gate at the entrance to the choir from the nave, and the railings around the sanctuary. The remainder were placed here in 1794 following the Revolutionary devotion to the goddess Reason. The only break in them is in the second bay on the north side where the choir organ console is surmounted by three ranks of pipes. The choir has two rows of ancient chapter stalls either side. They are of shoulder height with no canopies. The first stalls were by Laurent Adam, the woodworker who later made the pulpit at the Cathedral of Notre Dame, Rouen, but the Huguenots destroyed them in 1567. The present stalls were made in 1574, and some have fine, carved misericords. The centre area of the choir is filled with chairs facing east for use in worship.

Auxerre

THE SANCTUARY AND HIGH ALTAR

The High Altar is shaped like a huge marble bath on two stubby columns and with a marble retable behind it bearing a crucifix and six large candles. Either side of the retable is a life-size statue of an angel in white marble. To the west of the altar is another, free-standing marble altar, and known as the 'Ferial Altar' for ordinary use. It seems that the Pontifical High Altar is reserved for the Bishop's use. A large cross stands to the south side of the High Altar platform, but the area behind the High Altar is sadly used for storage; an old organ was dumped there on one of my visits. There is no evidence of a bishop's throne or a pulpit in this area.

THE ROMANESQUE CRYPT

The entrance to the crypt is through a door in the south ambulatory. Turning east, descend a flight of steps through a gate into an undercroft with a quadripartite vault, and then down six more steps into an ante-chamber with a cross barrel vault, then east again through another door. Descend more steps into the crypt itself, which has the timeless fragrance of old stone. It was constructed in 1023–35 to serve as a foundation for the Romanesque choir above, and has been the site of five successive cathedrals since the 5th century. The crypt is all that remains of the fourth building here.

The roof has barrel vaulting and covers a wide central nave surrounded by an ambulatory with a central eastern chapel called the Trinity Chapel. The square pillars of the nave are flanked each side by an

The Crypt, The Trinity Chapel

A Glimpse Of Glory

The Crypt Vault Fresco

engaged half-column and topped with solid imposts, which bear the thrust of the groins and arches of the vault. At the east end of the nave there are two narrow arches with a central column, behind which you can see the east window of the Trinity chapel. The window is a surprise, but is explained by the eastern slope of the ground down to the river Yonne. Two blocked openings in the west wall used to allow access from the former Romanesque cathedral.

Two columns with superimposed capitals flank the sanctuary of the Trinity Chapel and support the rib which springs across the vault forming a frame for the 13th century fresco of Christ Pantocrator (the All-powerful), surrounded by the symbols of the four evangelists, though only Matthew (winged figure) and John (eagle) can be discerned clearly. The ceiling of the chapel is covered in a remarkable late 11th century fresco painting of a huge cross on which is superimposed the figures of Christ riding a white horse in the centre, surrounded in the four quarters of the cross by four angels on horseback. The image can be found in the Bible—Revelation, chapter 19, verses 11–14.

THE SOUTH AMBULATORY

Three steps descend into the south ambulatory, which has a quadripartite vault. The coloured glass in the windows of the ambulatory date from near the end of the

Troyes, Crucifixion of Christ, eastern window of the clerestory

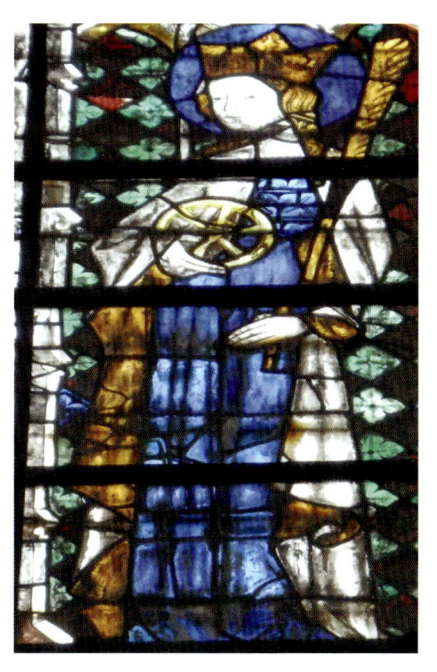

Troyes, St Catherine, north transept

Troyes, central four Prophets, triforium beneath south rose

Troyes, Crucifixion of St Andrew, Chapel of St Joseph    *Troyes, St Peter converts the Centurion Cornelius, Chapel of St Loup*

Troyes, the South Rose

Troyes, the Nativity

Auxerre, South Transept Window

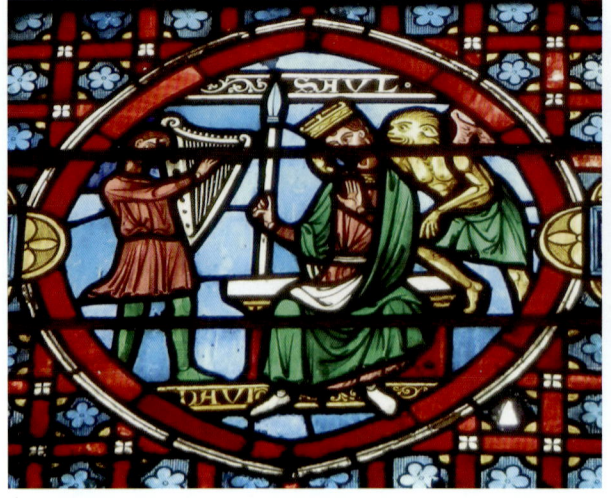

Auxerre, David plays the lyre before Saul—detail from the David window

Auxerre, St Mary of Egypt buys bread—detail from the Bishop's Chapel window

Auxerre, Joseph (right) receives his brothers as they beg for food, North Transept lancets

Auxerre, the West Rose

Auxerre, Theophilus befriends the devil, detail from the Axial Chapel window

Reims, centre of the south rose

Reims, the West Façade

Reims, the West Rose

Reims, the West Rose lancets

Amiens, The central portal illuminated, west façade

Auxerre

episcopate of Bishop Henri de Villeneuve (1220–1234), as do the windows in the choir clerestory.

Bay 1 has three arches in the south wall, each containing a wooden door. There is a passage, as in the Reims pattern, beneath the window, which has two lancets with clear diamond quarry glass, the original glass having been destroyed by the Huguenots in 1567 during the Wars of Religion (1562–1598); this is the case with the first three bays.

Bay 2 is decorated with a row of four arches supported by a slender column at either side, while the remainder end in a corbel, finely carved with foliage, and on top of which is carved a fine head. The western head in this bay resembles the 'Green Man' of English folklore. Above the arches is a passage beneath two lancet windows as before. This decoration of three heads per bay beneath two lancets and a passage continues around the ambulatories, together with carved panels depicting the Stations of the Cross.

The Chapel of the Sacred Heart is now a bookshop so the central corbel ends in a pendant while the other two corbels rest on a column rising from a plinth on the floor. The lancets are filled with diamond quarry glass.

The Chapel of St Catherine is also screened by a doorway which gives access to the Treasury. Half of the two lancets above are bricked up, but the upper registers are coloured: they depict St Catherine of Alexandria to the west, and St Vincent and the discovery of the relics of St Bris to the east.

The Bishop's Chapel bay is pierced beneath the corbels by a double doorway and to the west of it there are remains of a wall-painting, which continues across the top of the doorway, between the arches. The painting on the east side has been lost. The spandrels above the arches are also full of ancient colour. The central carved head has a wide, impish grin. During my visit in 2013 the chapel was laid out as a meeting room with a throne facing a table around which chairs had been arranged.

Here, too, the lower registers of the lancets are filled in, but above is beautiful blue 13th century glass depict two Marys: to the west St Mary Magdalene, and to the east St Mary of Egypt, with panels from windows on the Ascension and Pentecost. In the latter window, the middle panel at the bottom depicts an apostle receiving the Holy Spirit at Pentecost, and above it is a fine panel depicting the resurrection of Christ.

The ambulatory begins to curve at this point and the vaulting is cleverly adapted to accommodate the turn.

A Glimpse Of Glory

Bay 6 The wall is subdivided into three bays with a corbel and head in each, as in the previous bays, but the heads each have a little hat carved above them, with the exception of the easternmost of the three heads, which has the hat firmly on the head. The columns separating the bays have finely decorated capitals. The two bays to the west are blind and a wooden doorway pierces the third.

Above are three lancets; the western two have beautiful 13th century blue glass depicting St James the Great and the discovery of St Stephen's relics in the centre; in the lower central panel is depicted the discovery of the tomb of St Stephen, and in the panel above it the saint's body is transported to Constantinople (an episode mentioned in "The Golden Legend"). The lancet to the west depicts St Eligius and the miracles of St Nicholas; but the eastern lancet has a crucifix, with the seated figure of St James the Great beneath it, in the centre of otherwise clear glass.

Bay 7 is the bay before the axial chapel. Three blind arches again subdivided by pendants, each carved with a head. In the western arch stands a statue of Christ indicating his sacred heart. Above are three 13th century lancets: to the west, a window depicting the Prodigal Son, with panels of the three lower registers depicting scenes from the Apocalypse of St John; in the centre, St Germain and St Nicholas; to the east, St Martin and St Eustace, worked about 1250.

The Axial Chapel of Our Lady of Virtues at the east of the cathedral is a square chapel with no apse. Two splendid, slender shafts, each cut in one piece, form the most elegant entrance which gives the chapel a pre-eminence and dignity and displays the innovative confidence of its mediaeval architect. The altar is freestanding in marble and decorated at the front with a bas relief of five blind arches. Standing on a plinth behind the altar is a statue of Our Lady with her right hand raised and a book in her left hand. This statue came from the old chapel of Notre Dame des Vertus, the remnant of which can be seen on the south side of the west façade. It was considered to be miraculous and has therefore been venerated since the 14th century. The corbels with a head above continue around the walls of the chapel, as does the passage above. Eleven of the carved heads were destroyed to make room for woodwork displaced from the choir in 1774. Modern copies replaced them during the refurbishment of 1866.

The windows of the chapel are 13th century, but those in the east wall above the altar were largely restored in the 19th century. The exception is the centre lancet, with scenes from the life of the Virgin, which was made in 1879 to replace one destroyed by a Prussian shell in 1870. The lancet on the right of it depicts the legend of Theophilus (who sold his soul to the Devil), and in the right hand panel at the bottom we see the intimate friendship. In the lancet to the left is the Tree of Jesse. The two bays of the south wall have each a lancet, St Germain to the west and a grisaille glass to the east.

Auxerre

There is a large aperture (5ft by 6ft) in the wall in the southeastern bay and a very low sedilia in the south western bay. The pendants of the corbel table are neatly in line with the columns of the sedilia. There is a similar, but smaller, rectangular space in the north wall, containing a free-standing aumbry in the eastern part of it. The western bay of the north wall has an icon of Our Lady in the centre of the two heads. The chapel is closed by a tall wrought-iron screen with candle spikes, which can also to be seen on Laon cathedral choir screen.

On leaving the chapel you are facing the back of the high altar, where there is an open case lined with red velvet with a gold reliquary containing relics of St Germain.

THE NORTH AMBULATORY

The carved heads continue as before, and the windows have the same beautiful 13th century glass as we have seen in the south ambulatory and the axial chapel.

Bay 1 has three lights: two full length lancets and the left hand one with the bottom register filled with masonry. The eastern (right) lancet depicts the lives of St Peter and St Paul. Reading from left to right and bottom to top: panel 1—St Peter the Galilean fisherman; 2—Simon the magician (Acts 8, 18), 3—miraculous fishing, 4—Christ with an angel, 5—St Peter before Christ, 6—St Paul lies blind in Damascus, 7—Ananias and Sapphira before St Peter (Acts 5, 1-10), 8—the resurrection of Dorcas (Acts 9, 40), 9—an angel frees Peter from prison (Acts 12, 7), 10—Simon the magician kills himself trying to fly, 11—Emperor Nero and a servant, 12—Paul held up by two men, 13—Peter's vision of impure animals (Acts 11, 5), 14—Peter meets Christ near Rome and is asked 'Quo vadis?', 15 & 16—Agrippa the Roman Prefect assists at Peter's crucifixion, 17 & 18—angels with thuribles.

The western (left) lancet depicts the life of St Lawrence and a fragment from a window of Pentecost and of St Peter and St Paul; Samson and fragments of Genesis and Exodus. There is a statue of St Thérèse in a rectangular niche in the lower part of the western part of the bay. She is holding a book on the front of which is the image of the head of Christ.

Bay 2 the three lancets have the lowest two registers filled with masonry. The right hand lancet depicts the life of St Andrew; the central lancet tells of the life of St Margaret of Antioch in the round medallions flanked by semi-circular medallions. From left to right reading up from the bottom – her judgement by Olibrius; her flagellation in prison; the Devil (a dragon) appears to her in prison; she tramples him underfoot; she is condemned to deat; she is at the stake; she witnesses observe her; two scenes of the massacre of new converts; Olibrius beheading her, three witnesses; her soul carried by angels.

A Glimpse Of Glory

The left hand lancet depicts the life of St Joseph.

The ambulatory turns west again here with the same clever adjustment in the vault.

Bay 3 the bottom three registers of the two lancets in this bay are filled with masonry. The right hand lancet depicts Noah, Abraham and Lot, while the left tells of creation and original sin, but is completed with three panels (St John, the horseman of the Apocalypse, and Moses with the bronze serpent) from other windows.

In Bays 4 and 5 the passage beneath the windows is raised up a few steps, but the vault is at the same level so the windows are shorter in these two bays.

Bay 4 has two splendid lancet windows with medallions. That on the right depicts the life of St Mammès. The saint was born to his Christian parents in a prison in Caesarea. Legend relates that, when he was fifteen and already orphaned, Mammès was tortured by the governor of Caesarea for his Christian faith, and again later by the Roman Emperor Aurelian, who cast him on a mountain to be attacked by wild beasts. Mammès tamed the lions and other animals, and rode on the back of a lion to Duke Alexander, who condemned him to death by stabbing him with a trident. The scenes begin at the bottom left panel with the saint's birth, and are followed by his schooling. As you read upwards the stories of torture become apparent.

The Scourging of St Mammès

Auxerre

Painting of the Stoning of Stephen

The window to the left of it depicts the life of King David. It begins in the bottom left panel with the anointing of David as king of Israel (1 Samuel 16); 2—David plays the lyre before Saul; 3—David kills a lion; 4—he puts on Saul's armour (1 Sam. 17, 38); 5—David fighting Goliath (1 Sam. 17, 48-51); 6—David decapitates Goliath; 7 & 8—David is given a triumphant banquet; 9—Saul tries to murder David (1 Sam. 19, 10); 10—the murderers find a statue of an idol in David's bed; 11—David escapes through a window; 12—Ahimelech gives Goliath's sword to David (1 Sam. 21, 9); 13—David cuts a piece of cloth from Saul's cloak (1 Sam. 24, 4-7); 14—Saul is defeated at Mount Gilboa; 15—Saul falls on his sword (1 Sam. 31, 4); 16—Uzzah dies beneath the Ark of the Covenant (2 Sam. 6, 6-7); 17—David plays the lyre; 18—Joab kills Absolom (2 Sam. 14, 18); 19—David enthroned. Panels 1 to 9, and 11 to 13 were heavily restored in 1874.

Bay 5 the two lancets have had clear diamond quarry glass since the mediaeval glass was destroyed in 1567. Below the corbel heads is an oil painting on wood of the 'Stoning of Stephen' dated 1550 and executed during the episcopate of François II de Dinteville by a local artist who remains unknown. The Bishop of Auxerre is depicted in the figure of the High Priest, who is looking straight out of the painting and pointing at Stephen. On his robe are verses from the Ten Commandments, which Stephen accused the Jews of ignoring. This painting is classed as an historical monument.

Bay 6 has a staircase descending to the crypt. The two lancets are glazed in clear diamond quarry glass with the lower third filled with masonry.

Bay 7 also has the lower part of the two lancets bricked up and the rest glazed in clear diamond glass. The passage beneath the windows ends in a doorway at this point.

A Glimpse Of Glory

The Chapel of the Chastellux Family Between the two eastern corbel heads in bay 7 there is a central column which allows access to this small funerary chapel of the Counts of Chastellux. The mausoleum was destroyed by the revolutionaries and this chapel replaced it in 1822. Claude de Beauvoir, at the head of the Anglo-Burgundian armies, was victorious in a battle against the army of the Dauphin in 1423. He captured John Stewart, Earl of Buchan in Scotland and returned the town of Cravant to its owner, the Chapter of Auxerre. His reward was to be made an Honorary Canon of the Cathedral, and appeared in Chapter dressed in a surplice over his uniform, a sword at his waist and a falcon on his arm. The chapel has a stone altar on three little columns with finely carved capitals supporting it. The altar stone itself is missing, so it is not now used for worship. There is a mutilated bas relief carving above the altar with a marble inscription. On the north wall is a bas relief sculpture of two figures lying side by side. The chapel has a quadripartite vault with the ribs springing from corbels in the four corners of the chapel. The two western corbels have sculpted heads and the two eastern corbels have foliage. Between the third head and the western end of the bay is a doorway not open to the public, but from which comes the slow ticking of a clock escapement.

The North Ambulatory

Three steps raise us to the North Transept, where immediately there is a statue of Joan of Arc in an attitude of prayer facing south with her back to the little altar.

THE NORTH TRANSEPT

The north wall has the same arrangement as in the south transept: two blind arches either side of the doorway at two levels but the tracery in the north transept is flamboyant in design. The centre arch, an ogee rising to a finial at the top, is higher than that in the south transept. The eight lancets above have scenes from the life of Joseph in two registers beneath flamboyant tracery. We can see the story of his sale into slavery, Jacob with his blood-soaked coat, Joseph with Potiphar's wife, with Pharaoh, and then the reconciliation with his brothers. The lancets support the great north rose, dating from 1528 and from the workshop of Master Germain Michel of Auxerre. Its subject is the Litany of the Virgin. At the top is the Trinity, Mary is in the centre surrounded by angels and symbols of her Litany.

The west wall has four blind arches at lower level and above is a recessed arch containing two blind arches with trefoil tracery. Above that is a string course beneath the pierced parapet in the triforium, which is divided into two arches in this northern bay, and each arch has two lancets with a quatrefoil above. The parapet protects a passage, which continues across the north aisle arch, as does the string course and parapet and two arches, each containing two lancets. At clerestory level, the northern bay has four tall lancets filled with clear diamond quarry glass and with flamboyant tracery above and the southern of the two bays has again four tall lancets but they depict one scene of the Tree of Jesse. At the very top of the tracery is the Virgin and Child.

The Chapel of St John the Baptist stands in the east wall. The large marble altar, with the same decoration of pilasters and pediment as in the south transept, was created in the 19th century with marble from an old 18th century altar. The large painting above the altar has as its subject the baptism of Christ by John the Baptist (1774) by the artist Jean-Jacques Lagrénée. A statue of Our Lady in a white gown stands on the altar. To the north of the altar is a free-standing marble font, which is now in use as a holy water stoup.

There are four lancets with tracery recessed above the reredos. They all have clear glass, although little flowers can be seen in the centre of each register. The passage above continues from the ambulatory with four blind arches in the triforium over the north ambulatory arch, and the clerestory has two lancets, each with a figure, and a rosette above them. The passage then comes to an abrupt end. The northern bay of this east wall has two blind arches decorating the wall and above are two narrow lancets with a figure in each.

THE NORTH AISLE (FROM EAST TO WEST)

The Chapel of St Sebastian is almost an apse, as the north wall is angled from the centre. It has a wooden altar on which is a tabernacle with a cross above it. On the wall behind it is a large painting of the martyrdom of Sebastian. In the northwest angle of the wall is a window with two lancets with a quatrefoil in the tracery. Four scenes decorate the 16th century glass depicting original sin: Adam and Eve either

A Glimpse Of Glory

side of a serpent with a woman's face are at the bottom left, then Cain and Abel, two of the Trinity and two angels with instruments. The west wall has fine 16th century wooden panelling which enclosed the choir until the 18th century. Above the altar there are remains of a renaissance wall painting, which continues around to the northeast wall. Painted during the time of François II de Dinteville, it depicts sainted bishops of Auxerre.

North Side of the Nave

The Chapel of St Peregrinus has four late 19th century lancets with two levels of scenes in each, which depict the life of St Peregrinus. The lower half of the wall is decorated with three blind arches, each cusped at the top.

There is an altar on the east wall with, above it, a statue of a mitred St Peregrinus holding a palm in his right hand and a cross in his left. A large wall painting hangs above the altar and another adorns the west wall. One has as its subject St Germain before the Empress Gallia Placidia in Ravenna (17th century French), the other, dated 1745, is of 'Saint Peregrinus Overthrowing the Idols' by Jean Restout. The saint wears a voluminous red cloak and carries a shepherd's crook in his left hand.

The Chapel of St Joseph has three blind arches on the north wall, with the badly damaged remnant of a 17th century wall painting depicting St Claude, St Joseph and a saint-bishop. The four lancets above have two levels of scenes from the life of St Joseph in late 19th century glass. There is a lovely family scene on the bottom register, second from the left, of St Joseph putting a ring on Mary's finger, and a bishop blessing them in the background. An altar against the east wall has a statue of St Joseph holding the infant Christ, and above it is a large wall painting of the heavens opened to reveal a crown of thorns.

The Chapel of Joan of Arc has a large niche in the north wall, under a very old archway and pediment, with a monument in the lower half of it. The memorial tablet below the statue records that the monument marks the resting place of

Auxerre

Monsignor Ernest Deschamps, the archpriest of Auxerre, who died aged 81 on the 1st December 1949. He founded AJA, a local youth club that, in turn, grew into a famous French soccer club. The three large lancets above have quatrefoils in the tracery and depict, in one large scene, Joan of Arc delivering Orleans from siege. It was made in 1914 by the master glazier Edouard Socard of Paris, and is the only example in the cathedral of 20th century glass. On the east wall there is an altar dedicated to Our Lady without the Walls, a parish church of Auxerre now destroyed. Above the altar is faded wooden panel work with a central frame (minus its painting), and above that a large painting. On the west wall there is on the floor an old sarcophagus with no inscription. This chapel has an Interesting quadripartite vault with liernes.

The Fifth Bay is simply a wall with the top of four arches with pendants, but no heads here, merely carved foliage on the corbels. The column on the eastern side is missing. Above this decoration are four blind arches with deep tracery at the top.

The Sixth Bay has some fine arches and a sexpartite vault, but it is closed to public access by a wall rising halfway up the arch and pierced by two wooden doors of the same height. There are four slim lancets with a central mullion, all in diamond clear glass. Either side of the lancets are two blind lancets. On the east and west walls there are again blind arches with tracery.

This completes our visit to the delightful St Stephen's Cathedral Church, Auxerre.

My last visit was on Sunday 23rd June 2013, when I attended the Sung Mass. The city had been packed for a 'Fête de la Musique' the evening before. As I joined the throng the smell of barbecues and the sound of laughter filled the evening air. Before the west door of the cathedral a large crowd was enjoying an exhibition of dance styles; in Place des Cordeliers the theme was disco music; around the corner near the post office a band 'L'Yonne en scéne' was performing 'Beatles' music to an enthusiastic teenage audience, while in the Rue de Paris a man in his sixties was belting out traditional French songs, sometimes accompanied by a female singer, to an appreciative mature audience sitting at the café tables about him. The mediaeval narrow and winding streets made it possible for all these different music groups to perform simultaneously without the sound spilling from one to another. Auxerrois of all ages jostled and jived in the streets of their city with great joy.

The following morning, the nave was quite full of men, women and children as the Mass started promptly at 11.00 am. A large procession of young children wearing red scarves about their shoulders were followed up the central aisle by the crucifer and two young acolytes, who were followed in turn by three men altar

A Glimpse Of Glory

servers and the parish priest. As the celebrant of the Mass he was dressed rather like an Anglican priest in a cassock-alb with the cowl outside a flowing 'Gothic' chasuble.

The children in the procession were seated in the south transept where they formed the choir, and were conducted by the Chanteuse, who led the singing from the lectern. The priest preached a lengthy but enthusiastic sermon on the Gospel of the day, and the communion of the people was in one kind from three 'stations' at the head of the nave. It was preceded by the Peace, which did not take the form of a social occasion, unlike the growing trend in the Anglican Church. After the Mass, as I prepared to leave, there was, however, a great deal of meeting and greeting and conversation, which is appropriate to any community life. And as I walked back to my hotel I noted that the streets were spotlessly clean after the noisy party of the night before.

DO NOT MISS
1. The bas-relief panels on the bases of the west portals.
2. The nave clerestory windows (binoculars useful).
3. The 13th century glass in the ambulatories.
4. The mediaeval statue of the Virgin Mary behind the altar in the Axial Chapel of Our Lady of Virtues.
5. The painting of the Stoning of Stephen
6. The Crypt.

CHAPTER 8

REIMS

Reims is built on the site of Durocortorum, the capital of the Remi, an ancient people of Gaul. Now alongside the A4 Autoroute, it is a major trade centre for textiles and the marketing of champagne. It is also involved in the manufacture of processed food and aerospace equipment.

The city centre is dominated by the 13th century Cathedral of Notre Dame, but try to include a visit to the Church of Saint Rémi, begun in the 11th century and dedicated to St. Remigius, Bishop of Reims 459–533, and the Palais du Tau, which was the residence of the Kings of France as they prepared for their coronation in Notre-Dame de Reims, and has housed the Musée de l'Œuvre since 1972, displaying statuary and tapestries from the cathedral, together with reliquaries and other objects associated with the coronation of the French kings.

Other places worth visiting include the Porte Mars, a Roman triumphal arch dating from the 3rd century AD; and, of course, a champagne cellar. I stay at the Mercure Reims Cathédrale hotel, which is an easy three-minute drive from Autoroute 4, exit 24, and has a private car park. It is a ten minute stroll to the cathedral.

THE CATHEDRAL CHURCH OF NOTRE DAME

The first cathedral at Reims was consecrated in 401 and dedicated to 'The Virgin Mary Theotikos' (The Virgin Mary Mother of God) by Bishop Nicasius. Together with his sister, Eutropius, he was decapitated by the Vandals on the cathedral steps in 407; a sculpture on the northwest tower of Laon Cathedral depicts the scene. The crypt beneath the high altar is all that remains of this cathedral. Clovis, King of France, was baptized here by St Remigius (St Remi), the 15th Bishop of Reims, in 496, together with 3000 of his soldiers.

A Glimpse Of Glory

REIMS—KEY

1 The Central West Portal
2 Portal of the Crucifixion
3 Portal of the Last Judgement
4 The South Transept Façade
5 The North Transept Façade
6 The West End of the Nave
7 The Nave
8 The site of the Labyrinth
9 The Pulpit
10 The Chancel Stalls
11 The South Aisle
12 The Crossing
13 The High Altar
14 The Nave Altar
15 The Choir
16 The former High Altar
17 The South Transept
18 South Door & 'Champagne Window'
19 The South Ambulatory
20 Chapel of the Rosary
21 Chapel of St Thérèse
22 Chapel of St Joseph
23 Axial Chapel & Marc Chagall Windows
24 Chapel of the Sacred Heart
25 Chapel of St Joan
26 Chapel of the Holy Sacrament
27 The North Ambulatory
28 The North Transept
29 The 15th century Clock
30 The North Aisle

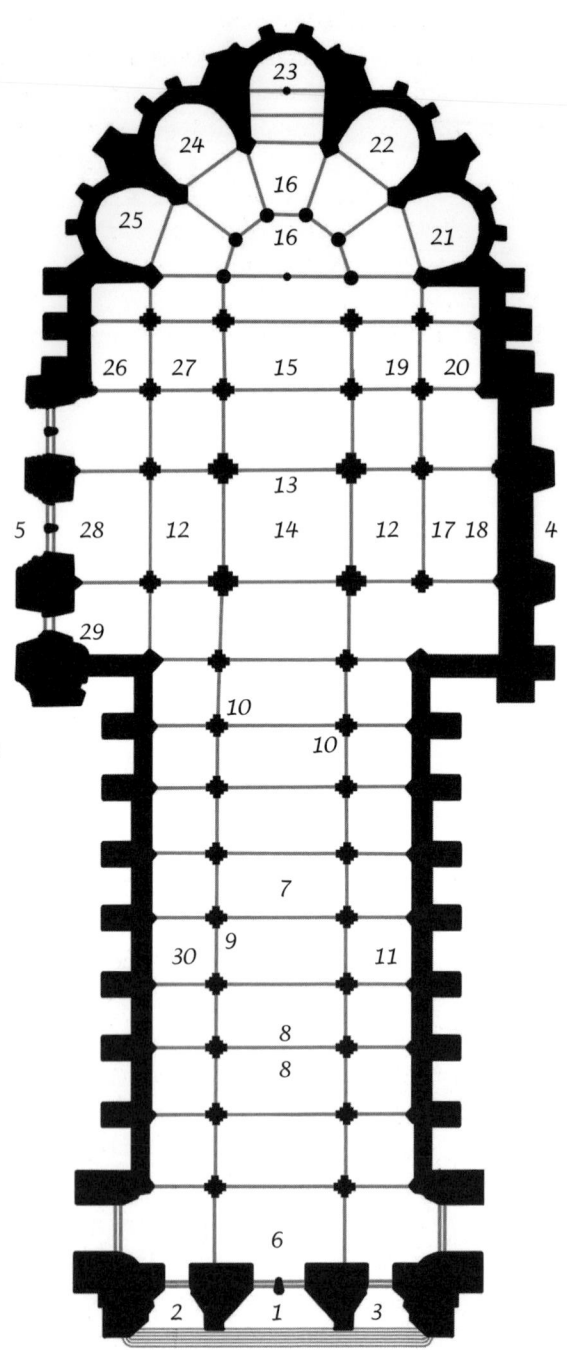

Reims

The second cathedral was consecrated in 852 by Archbishop Hincmar (845–882). The small Romanesque doorway in the north transept façade and a window in the south transept belong to this cathedral. In 1210 a fire swept through the city destroying most of it including the second cathedral. Plans for the present building were drawn up by Jean d'Orbais and the foundation stone was laid in 1211. The building was largely complete by 1290. On 24th July 1481 a careless fire broke out in the rafters and destroyed a large area of the cathedral; reconstruction continued until 1512. Straw palliases for wounded German soldiers caught fire in the nave on 19th September 1914 and caused great heat damage, which was furthered by the shelling in 1918. Post-war restoration was completed in 1938.

THE EXTERIOR

THE WEST FAÇADE

In a photograph of the west front of the cathedral taken before the First World War, the foreground shows a narrow cobbled street of houses, which partly obscure the south portal. A tramline runs down the middle of the cobbles and turns to the left before the central portal. This scene has long vanished, and the cathedral has been separated from the city by an open square. From across this parvis, the West Façade of Notre Dame de Reims presents as magnificent a sight as the façade of Amiens, Chartres, Paris or even Strasbourg. Indeed, on close inspection one has

The West Portals

A Glimpse Of Glory

to admit that Reims is sublime. Its levels of delicate decoration with crockets and finials are hard to match anywhere in the Gothic world, but it is the statuary which takes your breath away, and explains why this cathedral has been compared with the Parthenon in Athens, for with only a few exceptions Reims has preserved the superb original 13th century sculptures of its western portals. During a visit in 2010 some of the most damaged statues were being removed for remoulding and restoration, but in 2013 the work appears to be complete, and the scaffolding has been removed.

The lowest level of the façade is taken up with the three enormous, deeply recessed portals. The fact that above each door the tympanum is devoted to large decorative windows, instead of the usual sculpted scenes, adds a surprising beauty to the façade.

The North (left) Portal

This is known as 'The Crucifixion Portal' because of the sculpture in the gable which surmounts the porch.

The sculpted scene beneath a decorated gable on the front of the buttress to the left of the portal depicts the discovery of the true Cross. Two statues, thought to represent St Stephen (or St Thierry) and St Remi, adorn the inner face of this buttress, while in the left splay of the door, the famous statue of the Smiling Angel of Reims stands nearest the door and is followed by St Nicasius, an angel and St Clotilde (Clovis' Queen). Facing them in the right splay of the door stands St Florent nearest the door, followed by St Jocond, St Eutropia and St John. The statues on the buttress separating this door from the central portal represent St Rigobert, the Queen of Sheba and Isaiah. The head of the Smiling Angel (Le sourire de Reims) was shot away in November 1914, but has been restored very well.

The orders of the archivolt contain scenes of the Passion of Christ to the left, and his resurrection on the right.

The Smiling Angel, Northwest Portal, West Façade

Reims

THE CENTRAL PORTAL

This doorway is divided by a trumeau bearing the statue of Our Lady of Reims, for this portal is dedicated to her, and on the gable above the archivolt is a sculptured group of the heavenly coronation of the Virgin by the enthroned Christ.

In the left splay, Anna the Prophetess (nearest the door) looks at Simeon holding a cloth to receive the child Christ, who in turn looks at Mary holding her infant, and beyond her is Joseph carrying the offering of a turtledove: it depicts the Presentation of the infant Christ in the Temple. In the splay of the door to the right, the

Virgin and Child, West Façade, Central Trumeau

Archangel Gabriel (nearest the door) announces to Mary the forthcoming birth of a son, followed by the Visitation of Mary to her cousin Elizabeth. The statues on the buttress to the right represent Elizabeth's husband Zachariah or David, Solomon and St Remi.

The archivolt has no fewer than five orders, each separated by a foliated moulding. Eighty-one prophets, saints, martyrs and angels, all exquisitely carved, fill the vault as a foretaste of heaven.

THE SOUTH (RIGHT) PORTAL

The sculpture of the Last Judgement on the gable over the archivolt gives its name to this portal.

The statues in the left splay represent two apostles, Pope St Calixtus or St Peter, then another apostle, while facing them are Simeon holding the child Christ (nearest the door), followed by St John the Baptist holding a medallion bearing the symbol of the lamb of God, Isaiah, and Moses with the tablets of the ten commandments and holding a staff

The Presentation of Christ in the Temple, West Façade

A Glimpse Of Glory

with a serpent.. The statues on the buttress to the right are Abraham with his son Isaac, then Samuel.

The little statues in the archivolt represent images from the Revelation of St John, the final book in the New Testament.

At the next level of the west façade, the four statues in the pinnacles either side of the great rose window and the adjacent lancets, are (from the left) St Thomas, St John, Christ dressed as a pilgrim, St Mary Magdalene, St Peter and St Paul. On the inside of the two central pinnacles and facing each other across the width of the rose are two disciples on the road to Emmaus (St Luke 24, verses 13–35).

The great west rose was the work of Bernard de Soissons, and occupies the whole width of the central section of the façade. Above the rose is a bas relief carving of the combat between David and Goliath while in the arch below are scenes from the lives of David and Solomon, kings from the Old Testament period. David can be seen being consecrated by Samuel, and Solomon anointed by Nathan. The scenes which followed were destined to suggest that if God raises kings above all men he expects them to be courageous, so David kills Goliath, and to be just, Solomon restores the child to his rightful mother; to be pious, Solomon builds the Temple. The theme of kingship is never far from view at Reims, but time has taken its toll on this sculpture.

Above the scene of combat, a gallery of fifty-six kings runs around the base of the towers. It is a reminder that when Clovis was crowned here at Reims, France became Christian. Therefore, in the very centre of the gallery is Clovis standing in a baptismal font. To the right of him stands St Remi, who baptized him here in 496 and to the left is

The Upper West Façade

his wife Clotilde, who converted him to her faith. These giant 14th century statues each weigh about four tons and depict the kings of Judah, who were ancestors of the Virgin, in the guise of the kings of France. Placed in their canopied niches, they are not all upon the same plane, for they follow the surface, raised at intervals by the intrusion of a buttress, and they turn the corners, making a tour of the towers. Over twice the height of a tall man, these kingly figures suffered greatly in the bombardments of the Great War. Two that stood in the yard of the cathedral, having been taken down for restoration, were completely blown to pieces by a shell. If you look carefully, it is plain which are old and which new by the colour of the stone: the old stone is warm and soft, the new hard and grey. Some of the figures have been refaced, while others have been replaced by modern copies.

Above the gallery of the kings, two great west towers rise in splendour either side. The spurs to support the spires are evident at the corners of each tower, but the spires were never built.

THE SOUTH ELEVATION OF THE NAVE

Substantial buttresses flank the lancets and tracery of the south aisle windows, dividing the bays and rising to launch the double flying buttresses over the aisle roof to receive the thrust from the clerestory wall. At that height each buttress has a statue of an angel with wings outspread under a decorated canopy. These canopies, which continue from the west façade, are each supported by two slender columns, which appear to me to resemble a row of open sentry boxes in which stand the angels guarding the cathedral. Each buttress is crowned above the angel canopy by a decorative pinnacle which terminates in a finial high above the line of the roof. Behind the line of pinnacles, lining the foot of the roof is a continuous band of slender arches each of which has a trefoil in its gable. As if to remove all doubt about this church's royal foundation, the ridge of the roof is crowned by a delicate line of fleurs-de-lys. The gilt originals were destroyed by the Revolutionaries.

THE SOUTH TRANSEPT FAÇADE

Both the south and north façades are framed by twin towers, which are capped with pyramids below the height of the parapet. The three transept lancet windows with the three small roses above them fill the central section of the façade below the great rose.

Above the rose, which dates from the 1230s, high in the south transept gable end, above a gallery of statues of seven prophets, angels are bearing the Virgin Mary aloft in a glorious Assumption scene, her crown carried above her by other angels. A figure of Sagittarius, the Archer, crowns the gable. His target was a bronze Stag

A Glimpse Of Glory

The South Trancept Upper Façade

The Archer, South Trancept Façade

situated in the palace courtyard. In the 12th century this stag appeared on the seal of the Archbishop's ecclesiastical court, and came to symbolise his power. The independence and authority of the Archbishop provoked the canons of the cathedral next door to such a level of jealousy, that they erected the Archer on the gable overlooking the courtyard. The stag was melted down in the late 17th century. To discover the former location of the stag, follow the direction of the arrow.

The quickest way to the north side of the cathedral is to retrace our steps across the west front. The interesting route is to walk past the west front into Rue de Tresor and turn right into the main thoroughfare of Rue Carnot. After about a hundred yards you will see on your right the old entrance to the canon's cloister. Above an open arch, twin turrets rise two storeys under conical caps. Walk through the arch into Place du Chapitre, possibly the site of the canon's accommodation, straight on into Rue du Preau, and ahead is the north façade. An interesting approach, but give it a miss in the rain.

THE NORTH TRANSEPT FAÇADE

The base is broken by three asymmetric doors, which were probably designed by Jean d'Orbais, and seem to have been constructed for another location, perhaps the west front.

The West (right) portal is Romanesque and is a relic of the embellishment by Archbishop Samson de Mauvoisin (1140–1161). This door used to be the usual access to the cathedral from the Canon's cloister, which was demolished in the Revolution. In the tympanum there is a polychrome carving of the Virgin and Child crowned and seated in majesty, under an exquisitely carved canopy of arches and towers. Over the tympanum a funerary arch of eight angels is crowned with two angels receiving the soul of a dead person. Their compassion is almost tangible.

The central portal is known as the Portal of the Saints and concerns the saints of the church in Reims. On the trumeau is the martyr St Calixtus (Pope Sixtus ll), not

The North Transept Portals

to be confused with the first Bishop of Reims, whose relics were preserved here. He is depicted wearing the papal tiara, the rationale and pallium. Dated 1230 the portal was originally intended for the west façade. When it was part of the canon's cloister, ceremonial processions would have passed through its doors.

The tympanum is superb. The lintel depicts the martyrdom of St Nicasius (left) and the baptism of Clovis (right). Above that, to the left, is the healing of the blind hermit by St Remi, then the scene as he casts out demons from a young girl, and to the right he casts out demons from Reims after they had set fire to the city. The third level depicts episodes from the life of Job, but more miracles of St Remi occur above it: the resuscitation of the young girl on the left, and the miracle of an empty barrel being

Tympanum, Portal of the Saints, North Façade

A Glimpse Of Glory

filled with wine on the right. At the top of the tympanum sits Christ flanked by kneeling angels.

The statues dated c.1220 are, to the left of the trumeau: an angel, St Nicasius holding his decapitated head in his hands, and his sister St Eutropia (near the door); to the right of the trumeau are: Clovis in his baptismal robe (his crown removed at the Revolution), St Remi who baptised him, and an angel who has lost its wings. The archivolt is decorated with bishops on the inner rib, then patriarchs, and popes on the outer rib.

The left portal is dedicated to the Last Judgement. The trumeau bears the statue known as the Beau Dieu. His head was destroyed by a shell in 1918, and we see a modern restoration. This statue is older than the Beau Dieu of Amiens, which resembles it.

The bottom level of the tympanum has the damned to the right and the redeemed to the left. While the latter are handed to Abraham who holds them safe in his bosom, the damned are being led off to the right, chained together, to the cauldron. On the second level, the redeemed are the virtues and to the right the vices above the damned. The third and fourth levels show what one guide book calls "the gymnastics of the dead" as they climb out of their coffins at the resurrection. At the top of the tympanum sits Christ in judgement between two angels with St John and the Virgin before him.

Tympanum, Judgement Portal, north façade

St Bartholomew, St Andrew, St Peter, left splay, Judgement door

The inner rib of the archivolt has little sculptures of the wise virgins to the left of the arch and the foolish virgins on the right, reminding us of the words of Jesus that we do not know the time of our judgement so we must always be ready, like the wise virgins. There are deacons around the centre rib and angels around the outer rib of the archivolt.

The statues facing each other across the portal are, to the left of the trumeau: St Bartholomew, St Andrew, St Peter (near the door); and to the right, St Paul (near the door), St James and a clean-shaven St John the Evangelist.

Writing in 1928, in her book, "Cathedrals of France, published by Methuen, 1929, Helen Henderson described this portal in these words, "The expression of Saint Paul's face as he stands steadfast beside his headless Saviour . . . is lifted with a divine look of unalterable faith and noble endurance. Saint Andrew has a lettered nimbus: it is almost intact. Beside him, opposite Saint Paul, is a fine, vigorous Saint Peter, with the crisply curled hair and beard of the tradition. He holds fast to the keys. Saint John stands on the outer line of the doorway, opposite a saint whose head is gone. All six faces look at Christ, upon the central pier. I should say five, but that the attitude of the headless sixth is towards Christ and one knows that he looked at the Master. The Christ has cruelly suffered. His head is gone, one hand, which was raised in benediction, is missing; the fingers of the other, holding the globe, are nicked at the knuckles; the garments are badly battered, while behind him the wall is scarred where shots went wide." We are fortunate to see such skillful restoration before us today.

A Glimpse Of Glory

The rose of the north transept, which has the theme of creation in the glass, has (to the left) Adam and King Philippe Auguste and (to the right) Eve and the King, St Louis, all in niches beneath crocketted gables either side on the façade. Above the rose is another gallery of seven statues of prophets, while the gable end is decorated with a scene of the Annunciation dating to c.1497.

THE INTERIOR

THE WEST END

There are three portals: that in the centre of the nave can be called the great west door with a west door to the north and south aisles.

The central portal has two fine huge wooden doors with a central column which rises above the lintel, bearing a figure of St Nicasius the founder bishop, who was killed by the Vandals on the steps of his cathedral in the year 407. Either side are seven rows of recesses, separated by panels of carved foliage, holding in all fifty-two figures, three up the sides of the door then enlarging to four as the arch begins to close and then five and a half at the top. The bottom level on the left has John the Baptist, Isaiah and David; the bottom right has a Knight receiving Holy Communion, but is thought to be Melchizedek in 13th century dress offering the sacrament to Abraham on his return from war (Genesis 14.18). The lowest level on north and south has a carved curtain. The great west doors themselves have a lintel on the inside again with openwork sculpture across it, with figures alternating with foliage. The sculpture

Nave, North Side of West Door

continues into the return of the door, north and south. It has immediately above it a lovely rose window, with a crowned virgin and child in the centre.

The small rose below it, occupying the tympanum of the central portal, has as its theme the Litanies of Mary with Mary and Jesus in the centre.

Above the portal is an arcade of nine arches over a walkway, beyond which each arch has a lancet with one figure in it, except for the centre lancet which has the fleurs-de-lys motif. There is a balustrade above the arcade, protecting another walkway and above that the great rose window. Five very slender engaged columns spring up either side of the doorway, and rise uninterrupted, apart from the string courses which encircle them on their way, until they reach a third of the way up the rose, where the vaulting then springs out into a quadripartite vault over the first bay.

The great west rose is a masterpiece and was the chef d'oeuvre of Bernard de Soissons. Twelve and a half metres in diameter and dating from the 13th century, it rises up into the vaulting and occupies all the width of the nave. The fire of the 19 September 1914 ruined it, as the flames destroyed that great series of portraits of kings and bishops (in the clerestory windows of the nave). The rose which you see is a restoration, made so far as was possible of pieces of ancient glass. Helen Henderson recounts how, in a conversation with an elderly sacristan who was one of the few of the faithful who stuck it out during the whole of the First World War, she discovered that he and his colleague used to go about with baskets gathering up the fragments which had fallen and carrying them to a place of comparative safety.

Twelve petals radiate from the centre depicting the Dormition (falling asleep) and the Assumption of the Virgin Mary. She is surrounded by the twelve apostles; around them are arranged twenty-four musical angels; then the outer ring has two angels bearing crowns at the top, with the prophets Jeremiah and Ezekiel to the left and Isaiah and Daniel to the right. The remainder of the outer ring has six kings of Israel. At the bottom corners are two censing angels.

The west doors to the north and south aisles suffered somewhat in the fire of 1914 and later war damage, but in the thirty-four recesses around the southwest door the lower figures represent sixteen prophets, while above are scenes from the Apocalypse, including a dragon devouring a woman who holds a baby. The sculpture on the lintel of the door depicts the stoning of Stephen. Above the door a high pointed arch frames a most beautiful window, which must not be missed, especially if you are carrying your binoculars. A large quatrefoil is full of birds building nests, squirrels storing nuts and fishes swimming about. Above, in a trefoil, is a splendid Noah's ark. It is by a Reims artist and is dated 1959.

A Glimpse Of Glory

THE NAVE

The vessel itself is breathtaking at first sight. The very elegant height, with a vault 38 metres (126 feet) above the floor, is matched by the simplicity and uniformity of the nave, as it recedes into the semi-darkness of the east end due to the coloured glass windows in the clerestory. Soaring pillars and ribs rise from the abaci of the columns, with the eye drawn to the colonnade running behind the high altar and the glorious east lancets 138 metres (353 feet) away. The entire nave has quadripartite vaulting with delicate bosses on the crossed ribs.

Sit for a moment at the west end of the nave, and consider that in the aftermath of the First World War there was only a tiny portion which had been restored, and visitors were allowed to enter by the west doors and stand before a barricade which shut off the whole of the nave. As they stood here at the west end they saw before them the terrible desolation of the roofless ruin, its floor still piled with the debris of its shattered glory; a pulverized mass of stone pounded to dust by the repeated blows of over 287 recorded shells, besides all those which struck the building during the bombardments of 1917 and 1918. These had destroyed the vaulting, broken the windows, and burned the pulpit and stalls; only the great pillars of the nave stood firm.

Rodin said that if there was anything more beautiful than a beautiful thing it was the ruin of a beautiful thing. He could not have seen the ruin of Reims. Now look ahead of you and see what a great restoration has taken place.

In the nave, the western bay has massive pillars which support the towers above. They have engaged columns either side which rise to the level of the roof vaulting, with a string course at each level. Above the western arch of the arcade there are six arches with the central column thicker than the rest because it supports the mullion dividing the two clerestory lights above. The remaining bays are similar,

The Nave

but have only four arches at triforium level, and the pillars are all of equal thickness. Above each bay the clerestory has two lights in diamond quarry glass with a multifoil at the top.

The columns, which stand on mighty bases, really are massive: 1.55m in diameter (which is about 4.6m in circumference), much larger than in many other cathedrals, with four substantial semi-circular engaged columns. Two additional columns soar up each side from the abacus of the engaged column which faces across the nave, to support an arch over the clerestory window and a rib of the vault.

North Side of the Nave

The capitals, from which spring the arches of the arcade, are highly decorated with foliage; the sixth capital on the south side has a wine-harvest scene.

Against the fifth column on the north side is a large wooden pulpit. At the seventh column to north and south are two steps up to a platform for the chancel stalls which occupy the next two bays. They are really a part of the nave because the crossing is to the east of them. The reason for this is that since the coronation of Louis Vlll in 1223, this cathedral has been the coronation church of France, and this arrangement gives more room for ceremonial near the high altar. On the south side of this space between the stalls is a small freestanding organ, with the console facing north. This royal connection also means that in the 7th, 8th, 9th and 10th bays, while there is the same configuration of two lights and rosette, the clerestory windows are filled with coloured glass on the north and south sides. The other six bays of the nave have a simple clear design in the glass. The small roses over the eight restored windows of the nave are original. It was observed in 1918 that some of the glass in the upper parts of the windows of the nave were still intact, and during a lull in the bombardment, a small volunteer group of firemen from Paris, assisted by two stained-glass workers, were assembled from amongst the soldiers and these, under cover of fog and before daylight, climbed up into the iron armatures of the windows and at vertiginous heights salvaged the fragments with remarkable skill and courage.

A Glimpse Of Glory

Donatian and Viventius, South Nave Cerestory, Bay 7

The nave windows were once so different. The clerestory windows depicted the kings of France, each accompanied by the archbishop who crowned him, to recall the belief that royalty is a divine essence. Thanks to the bravery of those who saved the fragments of glass under bombardment, restoration work has enabled us to glimpse something of the mediaeval grandeur of the nave windows. In their book, "Gothic Stained Glass: 1200–1300", published by Thames and Hudson (1985), Grodecki and Brisac wrote, *"The glass saved from the bombardments in 1914 has been regrouped and reset in the four east windows of the nave clerestory. There are four figures of French kings, only one of whom is identified by an inscription: Karolus, (Charlemagne?). Each king is set above an image of an archbishop of Reims. In three double windows on the south side, the archbishops are identified by inscriptions: Donatian, Viventius, Barucius, etc.—the first prelates of Reims."*

The nave is beautiful architecturally, and the blank lower walls focus the attention on the columns themselves. The slender columns which support the ribs of the vault rise from the capitals of the core column, with its four engaged pillars. So the lower third of the nave appears relatively unadorned. Looking along the nave from the crossing it resembles a tidal basin after a surge: below the bank—the foliage of the capitals—the stone of the pillars is clean and looks washed. Then, from the capital upwards there is this great forest of rising pillars in stone, taking the eye up and up and up into the very simple vaulting. One thing is certain, your eyes are focussed about a half way up the walls and that draws you into the east end at the level of the coloured clerestory glass, and then your eyes drop to the Marc Chagall windows behind the high altar in the centre of the columns running around the apse, and you are content.

THE SOUTH AISLE

As all the windows have two wide lancets with a multifoil in the tracery, all in light geometric patterned glass, the aisle is light and lofty, under a series of quadripartite vault cells. A passage runs the length of the aisle under the window.

The wall below the passage is devoid of ornament. It has not always been so. A guide book I bought in 1986 describes how, between Easter and All Saints, the walls of the side aisles are adorned with early 16th century tapestries depicting the life of the Virgin Mary, which were once hung in the chancel. They are now exhibited in the Tau Museum, and the walls of the nave aisles were adorned in 2013 with old wooden shutters covered in grim paintings in garish colours.

Beginning in the west, bays one, two and six each have a doorway. In bay eight the north wall is screened with the back of the choir organ, and the next bay and a half is screened with the back of the two rows of chancel stalls.

THE CROSSING.

The centre of the crossing is covered by a large quadripartite vault without a lantern. The roof level continues from the nave through the crossing and into the chancel. Below, on a platform raised by five steps, is the marble floor of the choir and sanctuary, with the high altar to the east.

THE SOUTH TRANSEPT

The transept extends south for just one bay, but in width it also has a bay formed by the south aisle. So there is a large column (one of the nave columns) at the junction of the south aisle and the south transept, where the south aisle turns and becomes the west aisle of the south transept. The transept has two quadripartite vaults, one over the south aisle and south ambulatory entrances, and the other over the south transept itself.

A Glimpse Of Glory

In this western aisle to the transept, the bay to the south has in its west wall a similar window pattern to the nave aisles: two lancets and a multifoil above, here they are all in modern Reims glass. The decoration in the glass looks like straw being blown in the wind and is most attractive. (I shall describe this decoration in the remainder of the text as simply 'modern Reims glass' as I have seen it nowhere else.) Below it is a memorial to "the dead of the British Empire, 1914–1918." There is a door in the south west corner. In the centre of this bay is a freestanding marble font enclosed by a wrought iron grille. The south, or end wall of this aisle has two lancets and a multifoil above, again glazed with this modern design. Beneath the window a large wooden door stands on top of two high steps which extend along the length of the wall. This west side of the transept has very detailed foliage carved in the capitals of the columns from which rise the two arches supporting the clerestory above. The northern of the two arches has above it an arcade of four blind arches and two lights with a multifoil tracery.

Modern Reims Glass

The southern bay has an arcade of six blind arches, the central column being thicker than the others, because this bay is wider than the northern one, which merely spans the south aisle. Nevertheless, it has only the same two lights and multifoil above the arcade of six arches, but each of the two lancets has coloured glass in the central three registers depicting on the left St John the Baptist and Archbishop Henri de Braisne (1227–1240), and on the right a seated and crowned Virgin and Child above the Church of Reims. The glass has been recovered from elsewhere and enlarged for use in these two lancets that it has probably occupied since the 13th century. There is speculation that the window might have been made for the eastern window in the clerestory.

The east side of the south transept has precisely the same arrangement, (also reflected in the aisles), two lancets bearing a multifoil, but no coloured glass; all four lancets have grisaille glazing.

240

The south façade itself has a deeply-recessed door with plaques either side and above there are three lancets all with coloured glass with scenes and medallions; a beautiful window. It is known as "the Champagne Window." Worked by Jacques Simon in 1954, it is an appropriate patronage in the cathedral church of the champagne region! It illustrates the stages in the production of champagne: the tending of the vines (left), the harvest (centre) and the chemical processes of the cellar (right). Dom Perignon can be seen working away if you look carefully. The glass and cork industries are also represented, while around the border are depicted the churches of the champagne villages. Above it is a string course at triforium level and in the triforium are three multifoils all in coloured glass, Above is another string course and then the great south rose reaching up into the ceiling vault. The fillet of glass inserted above the rose to reconcile the circle of the rose with the arch of the vault is an innovation first seen here in Reims. Constructed in the 1230s it was reglazed in 1581 by Nicholas Dérodé, following a hurricane the previous year, and again in 1937 by Jacques Simon. It represents Christ in a red cloak surrounded by angels and apostles, who are helpfully named.

To the left of the south door there is a double door with a carving in the tympanum of the Virgin and Child, with a model of Reims cathedral being offered to the right, and to the left a censing angel. It leads to the Tau Palace. A simple carved arch rises over it and above that two lancets with a multifoil, all in the modern Reims glass seen on the west side, and a quadripartite vault above. On the southeast side of the transept there is a chapel occupying the first two bays of the south ambulatory. This chapel, enclosed by a wrought iron screen, is the Chapel of the Rosary (*see under the South Ambulatory*).

THE CHANCEL AND APSE

To the east of the chancel stalls there are five marble steps leading up to the platform which has on it a smaller dais on which stands the bronze nave altar directly under the crossing. In the first bay of the sanctuary, in line with the eastern pillars of the crossing, is a beautiful marble High Altar. It is long, and deep enough for the crucifix and six candles to stand in a row along the middle of it, so that the altar can be used from either side, except that the crucifix faces the west. The Archbishop's throne stands on the north side and on the south side there is a cedilia on a free-standing platform.

The sanctuary, which has now become a kind of retro-choir as it is behind the active altar, is enclosed by a tall wrought-iron screen and extends east into the apse. The original High Altar stands neglected now at the extremity of the apse, but still bearing a crucifix and six tall candles facing the backs of rows of chairs. A wooden pulpit stands against the third column on the south side of this choir.

A Glimpse Of Glory

The decoration on the capitals here in the choir is quite superb. The first bay has a quadripartite vault. The columns and the arcade reflect the nave. So does the triforium for there are five arches then a string course above which are two lancets with a multifoil above. It is in these high windows of the choir and apse that we see the oldest group of glass (about 1235).

Grodecki and Brisac describe the process, "The building was begun in 1212 or even earlier. Work progressed rapidly over twenty years in both the transept and the precincts of the choir. Problems beginning in 1232–1234 were followed by a complete stoppage. When work began again, about 1236–1238, the initial project for the overall elevation was modified, and the upper windows were lengthened by raising the vault of the upper choir. The choir must have been completed in 1241; the nave and façade, planned and started at the beginning of the century, did not acquire their final shape until after 1245."

In the centre of each lancet in the western bay are two figures, a king in the upper registers and a bishop below, in coloured glass surrounded by grisaille work. But in the next bay to the east we begin the sequence of apostles and bishops all in coloured glass. The third bay in the clerestory is shorter and so it has a stilted arch and only two, slightly larger blind arches in the triforium and then the two lancets are also narrower. The next bay is identical as we turn into the apse. The bay to the north of the eastern end of the apse is the same, as is the axial arch itself, and so on around the south side.

The east window depicts the Virgin and Child above the Church of Reims in the left lancet and the Crucified Christ between the Virgin and St John above the Archbishop of Reims in the right lancet.

To the north there is James the Great and Paul above the church and Bishop of Laon, then Philip and Thomas above the church and Bishop of Chalons, then Matthew and Judas above the church of Amiens and the Bishop of Senlis, then Barnabas and Mark above the church of Arras and the Bishop of Therouanne, and finally on the north side, two apostles above two bishops on a grisaille background. This latter window has grisaille in the multifoil above.

To the south of the east window there is Peter and Andrew above the Bishop and church of Soissons, then John and James the Less above the Bishop and church of Beauvais, then Bartholomew and Simon above the church and Bishop of Noyon, then Matthias and Luke above the Bishop of Cambrai and the church of Tournai, and finally two apostles above two bishops on a grisailles background. The apostles are positioned in the order in which they occur in the canon of the mass and the bishops of the Province of Reims are probably in the order they occupied in the Chapter based on the age of their diocese.

THE SOUTH AMBULATORY

The ambulatory continues in the width of the south aisle, and also has quadripartite vaulting. Two wide, low wrought iron gates give access from the transept.

The Chapel of the Rosary. The first bay forms the north side of the chapel in the south transept. It has a fine reredos carved in stone in two levels over a marble altar: the lower level has in the centre a beautiful pietà in a carved group, which is framed by two sets of double marble columns. Between each set, in a niche, is a carved figure looking inward to the group. These eight columns bear a marble pediment which supports the upper level. The inner pair of double columns is echoed above as they in turn bear a gabled pediment, but behind them is a smaller pediment borne on smaller columns which frame carved figures. In the centre, below the gabled pediment is a round arch framing a classical sculpture. Above all this is a crucifix which rises to two blind arches on the wall. On the south side of this bay are two lancets with a multifoil above in modern Reims glass.

The bay to the west of it has a fine mosaic floor measuring about ten feet by eight. There is a double lancet window in the south wall of this bay, the western one is blind and the eastern has modern Reims glass. There is a niche in the south wall. Each bay has a quadripartite vault. The chapel is enclosed by a low wrought iron screen.

The Chapel of St Thérèse. A blind arcade with painted decoration, somewhat faded, fills the lower level of the seven bays of this radiating chapel. Above it, the first two western bays are blind, but the next three bays have

Reredos, the Chapel of the Rosary

A Glimpse Of Glory

Joseph's Dream

each windows of two lights and a multifoil, all with 19th century coloured glass with medallions and scenes in them: the tree of Jesse on the left, the life of the Virgin from the Annunciation to the mystery of the Rosary in the centre window, and some miracles of the Virgin on the right side. The two remaining windows have blind double lancets rising up to the vault above. Under an openwork baldachino above the altar, in the form of a corona and supported by four marble columns, there is a statue of St Thérèse holding a crucifix.

The Chapel of St Joseph. This chapel has only five bays, the first bay on each side is blind and the three central lancets with multifoil have clear diamond quarry glass. At the lower level is the usual blind arcading with the remains of geometric fresco painting. The floor tiles contain scenes from the life of the Old Testament Joseph. The scene depicting the sheaves of corn bowing to Joseph's sheaf (Gen: 37, 7) is very nicely done. The marble altar has a retable with two medallions and a tabernacle in the centre. There is a double piscina in the south wall.

THE AXIAL CHAPEL

Observe the fine ceiling to this chapel: the western bay has a narrow quadripartite vault while the remainder is covered by an apsidal vault. Again, there is blind arcading around the lower level. The stone altar rests on stone columns either side of a central pillar, and the retable has four panels, each with two carved figures: on the left we see an angel announcing to Mary that she will bear a son; then we see Mary with her cousin Elizabeth; on the right we see the three Wise Men bringing gifts to the infant Christ, the beam of the guiding star pointing to him in Mary's arms. There are two niches in the wall on the southeast side, the eastern one is a piscina.

The three outer bays are blind each with two lancets in bas relief, but the middle three windows each have two lancets with a multifoil above, all in beautiful blue glass by Marc Chagall. The subject matter is (left to right of all six lancets, starting at the bottom and reading up):

left window – lt. Saul the rejected King, David playing a harp, imploring people; rt. out of the side of Jesse springs a tree bearing the Kings of Judah, Solomon delivering justice, the Virgin Mary carrying the infant Christ; in the rosette, the prophet announcing the birth of Christ; at the top, the Menorah, a candelabra with seven branches which is an ancient symbol of Judaism.

centre window – lt. Jacob's dream, Isaac blesses Jacob, the sacrifice of Isaac, the descent from the Cross, Christ arising from the tomb; rt. Abraham's dream of the covenant, Abraham receives the three angels at Mamre, Abraham and Melchizidek, Christ crucified; in the multifoil, the radiance of the Holy Spirit; at the top, the hand of God the Creator;

south window – lt. the coronation of the young Saint Louis, St Louis delivering justice, across two registers at the top, left, the Good Samaritan, right, the Kingdom of Heaven, above, proposal to the earthly kings, rt. the baptism of Clovis by St Remi, the two registers above, the coronation of Charles VII in the presence of Joan of Arc.

Marc Chagall (1887–1985) was a French painter born in a small village in Belarus in a community of oriental Jews. Charles Marq and his wife Brigitte Simon, whose glass workshop in Reims is said to be one of the oldest in France, helped Chagall to make these windows in 1971.

THE NORTH AMBULATORY (moving east to west)

The Chapel of the Sacred Heart. This chapel, again, has five bays, the outer two blind with carved lancets with multifoil tracery rising to the vault and blind arcading at lower level. The three northeastern windows are all glazed with clear diamond quarry glass. The altar is borne on six columns against the northeast wall with a retable above containing carved panels and a carved statue of Christ above that. In 2013 the chapel was dominated by a model of the cathedral.

The Chapel of St Joan. Above the altar there is an extravagant open-work baldachino, similar to that in the south ambulatory and also supported on four marble columns, under which stands a statue of Joan of Arc, wearing armour and a tunic decorated with the fleurs-de-lys and holding a sword point down in front of her. The Oriflamme stands behind her. There is blind arcading at lower level with fresco painting decorated with squares and flowers. The two outer bays are blind with the usual two blind lancets. The three northeastern windows have two lights each and a multifoil at the top, all in clear diamond quarry glass.

The Chapel of the Holy Sacrament. This chapel has exactly the same arrangement as on the south side: two bays form a chapel which opens off the north transept and in the north ambulatory is enclosed by a low wrought-iron screen. Both bays have a quadripartite vault and the east wall has two blind lancets and a multifoil above, but most of the wall is covered by the reredos of the altar. It's supported by two marble columns with decorated capitals and a semi-circular arch above. In the archivolt there are decorated ribs and on the central plinth stands a large statue of Our Lady holding the Child beneath a shell vault and standing on a globe decorated with stars. On the retable below is a tabernacle and six candles. The window of the eastern bay has a double lancet and multifoil above, all glazed in modern Reims glass, while the western bay has only the eastern lancet glazed in the same glass; the western lancet is blind. Below this window, on a plinth, is a carved statue of St Jean-Baptiste de la Salle and to the east of it is a recess for a double piscina. In the recess is a plaque commemorating the fact that Pope John Paul II prayed in this chapel on Sunday 22nd September 1996.

The south wall of the ambulatory at this point has the staircase descending to a crypt.

THE NORTH TRANSEPT

The north transept has only one bay protruding north, but is made larger by a bay which links the north ambulatory with the north aisle, just as in the south transept.

The eastern wall, therefore, has a bay formed by the arch, which matches those in the nave arcade, over the north ambulatory as it joins the transept. Above this arch the triforium level has four blind arches over the walkway with two lancets and a multifoil above, all in grisaille. Above the wider arch to the transept proper there are six blind arches protecting the walkway and above that two lancets and a multifoil with grisaille glass.

In the north wall of this bay there is a large area of panelling with two doors in it, under a large semi-circular arch, which encloses a vestry. Above the arch can be seen the top of the two blind lancets with a blind multifoil above. To the west of the panelling is a large sculpture of an enthroned St Peter, a copy of that in St Peter's Rome. A copy can also be seen in Beauvais Cathedral.

A large northeastern arch, again matching those in the nave, gives access to the Holy Sacrament chapel and supports a quadripartite vault above. The arches spring from finely decorated capitals on the centre column, which is enormous, and like all the columns in this church it has four semi-circular engaged pillars.

The west wall of this transept is a mirror image of the east wall, including the grisaille glazing. Here the north aisle turns to form a western aisle to the transept under two quadripartite vaults. There are two doors in the east wall under a central arch and above the doors the arch is deeply recessed but blind. Above that is a wrought-iron grille, behind which are top portions of two lancets with a multifoil above, all in clear glass decorated with a lattice work design. The west wall of this bay has two lancets with a multifoil above, all in the clear decoration of the nave aisle

The Clock in the North Transept

windows and is a kind of lattice-work in outline. In the northwest corner of this bay is a ground level staircase of four steps leading to a doorway and above it is a lovely 15th century clock in wood sprouting out of the corner, with little figures on it and with wooden tracery above the clock face rising to a gable with pinnacles either side. It tells the phases of the moon and every hour two little processions emerge: the Adoration of the Magi and the Flight into Egypt. It is very attractive and keeps accurate time.

The centre part of the north wall of the transept itself has a large double doorway, and above is the organ loft and casing bearing the pipework of the great organ, which has 6,742 pipes and 87 stops. The tops of coloured lancets peep above the organ and they, in turn, support the great north rose, which fills the upper north wall of the transept under a quadripartite vault. This great rose window is a glorious sight. Its date is c.1240, slightly later than the clerestory windows of the apse, and its theme is creation, with God the Creator in the centre surrounded by scenes from Genesis of Adam and Eve and Cain and Abel. The outer medallions contain scenes from the natural world. In the fillet above the rose, Mary suckles the infant Jesus, although through powerful binoculars

A Glimpse Of Glory

mounted on my tripod the child rather resembled a grumpy crusader. But Grodecki sounds a note of caution: *"The windows in the cathedral of Reims ... are, unfortunately, little more than wreckage carefully put back together after the First World War. ... The rose in the north transept now contains an incomplete series of Genesis panels in disarray."*

Like many other windows in the cathedral, the rose was heavily restored in the 17th century, but if it's wreckage, it's glorious wreckage.

THE NORTH AISLE

The vaulting is quadripartite along the length of the aisle. Each window has a double lancet with a multifoil in the tracery above, all glazed in an outline lattice pattern. There are steps, which look like benches, in the lower north wall; running along the top of these unadorned walls there is a walkway, which is called the "passage champenois". It seems to have no purpose other than to lighten the mass of the wall. A similar passage in Lincoln cathedral is called "Reimois".

Bay 7 has a large niche in the north wall below the windows in which stands a statue of St Anthony with his hands together in prayer. He is looking up at a child who is standing on his left upper arm.

Bay 8 has a slightly lower window glazed in lattice outline glass, except for the top two registers, which are coloured with pieces of old glass. The rosette above is certainly coloured; it has little scenes around a central scene. Below this window is the bookshop.

We have returned to the west end and concluded our tour of this magnificent cathedral.

IN CONCLUSION

I have said that the history of this Cathedral Church of Our Lady of Reims is steeped in coronations and royalty; the statuary alone will not let you forget it. Even today, in the modern French Republic, you cannot escape it, for it is in the veins of the people who live here. On Sunday, 27th June, 2004, I attended the early Gregorian Mass in this cathedral. After

The Chapter Doorway

Reims

the Mass had ended there was the sound of a marching band outside in the Parvis. I had observed several people in mediaeval dress strolling in the streets the evening before, and here they were again. It was the Fêtes Johanniques.

Soldiers formed a Guard of Honour outside the west doors,

Archivolt, Romanesque Portal, North Transept Façade

and to thunderous organ music a large and colourful procession of folk dressed as monks, and Ladies of the Court in mediaeval dress, together with men dressed as Crusaders, made its way through the great west doors and up the aisle to the high altar, where they were ushered into the semi-darkness of the north transept. Then, during the introit hymn (sung to a tune we know as "Old Hundredth"), a procession of banners carried by men and women in uniform, much like our British Legion parades, followed by the army generals, senior civil servants and the Mayor of Reims, entered the cathedral.

Bringing up the rear was "Joan of Arc", an attractive young lady wearing a long flowing green gown, her dark hair about her shoulders, and carrying the Oriflamme (the long banner which in the 11th century replaced St Martin's cope as a rallying point on the battlefield), which draped down to the ground behind her. She was attended by a lady in waiting, and on her right was a solemn young man dressed as the Dauphin, Charles VII, arriving for his coronation. He looked very regal in a long, dark blue cloak, dotted with gold fleurs-de-lys, and with a deep ermine collar, and who was attended by a page in a colourful tabard. As this handsome couple approached the crossing, the clergy procession slipped in front of them. Mgr de Monléon, the Bishop of Meaux, who was preaching, and the Archbishop of Reims, Mgr Jordan, who was presiding, both looked distinctly underdressed in their purple cassocks and with a metre of lace on their cottas.

As "Joan" took her throne at the north side of the sanctuary and the "Dauphin" went to a throne on the south side, facing each other, press photographers spoiled the moment as they wandered about in front of the high altar, most of them photographing the young lady with the Oriflamme.

I have no doubt that Reims could be ready for a coronation within a week if a monarchy was ever restored to France.

A Glimpse Of Glory

DO NOT MISS

1. Time to study the sculpted statues and portals on the west façade.
2. Note especially the Smiling Angel of Reims in the north (left) doorway.
3. The 'Archer' crowning the gable of the South Transept.
4. The funerary arch in the tympanum of the west doorway in the north façade.
5. The sculptures around the interior of the west doors.
6. The beautiful window above the west door of the south aisle.
7. The 'Champagne Window' in the South Transept.
8. A carved Pietà in the Chapel of the Rosary in the South Transept.
9. The story of Joseph in the floor tiles of The Joseph Chapel in the South Ambulatory.
10. The Chagall windows in the Axial Chapel.
11. A 15th century clock in the North Transept.
12. The Palais du Tau on the south side of the cathedral facing the South Transept.

CHAPTER 9

AMIENS

The name of the city comes from the Ambiani Gauls, who were in this area in antiquity. In 481 Clovis was crowned here. Amiens was a major fortress for many centuries, protecting Paris from a northern attack. The old fortifications are now boulevards. It is the central city of the Department of the Somme and has been involved in the textile industry since the 16th century. The University of Picardy is based here.

With the travelling time by car from Calais being within two hours, it is possible to pay a day visit to Amiens, but this would be unfortunate. This attractive city on the banks of the Somme has much to offer the overnight visitor. I find the Ibis Hotel in the town centre a cheerful and inexpensive place to stay, and it has a secure underground car park. The cathedral is a five-minute stroll away and a few minutes beyond it are the colourful riverside restaurants.

THE CATHEDRAL CHURCH OF NOTRE DAME

The Cathedral of Our Lady (Notre Dame) is one of the largest Gothic cathedrals in France. It was built between 1220 and 1270. It is 143 metres (470 feet) long and its nave is 43 metres (140 feet) high. Approaching the cathedral past the Tourism Office in rue Dusevel, one suffers an affront to the senses on observing the appalling modern buildings jutting out on the right and which obscure a view of the west façade of the cathedral until you actually arrive at the Place Notre Dame. Nevertheless, the sight which awaits you as the cathedral comes into view banishes from the mind this vandalism.

The sculptor, Rodin, wrote of Amiens in his book, "Cathedrals of France", published by Hamlyn in 1965: *"This Cathedral is an adorable woman, a Virgin. What joy, what solace for the artist in finding her as beautiful as ever! Each time more beautiful! Between the Cathedral and the artist what intimate accord! No vain*

A Glimpse Of Glory

AMIENS—KEY

1 The Central West Portal
2 Portal of St Firmin
3 Portal of Our Lady
4 Statue of St Christopher
5 The South Façade
6 The North Façade
7 The Nave
8 The Tombs
9 The Labyrinth
10 The Pulpit
11 The South Aisle
12 Entrance to the Towers
13 Chapel of St Christopher
14 Chapel of the Annunciation
15 Chapel of St Nicholas
16 Chapel of St Stephen
17 Chapel of St Margaret
18 The South Transept
19 Chapel of N D de Pilier Rouge
20 Chapel of l'Aurore
21 "Vierge Dorée"
22 The Crossing
23 The Choir
24 The Sanctuary
25 The South Ambulatory
26 The St Firmin Panels
27 Chapel of St Joseph
28 Chapel of St Eloi
28a Entrance to the Treasury
29 Chapel of St Francis of Assisi
30 Chapel of St James the Great
31 Axial Chapel of Our Lady
32 The "Weeping Angel"
33 The North Ambulatory
34 Chapel of St St Augustine
35 Chapel of St John the Baptist
36 Chapel of St Quentin
36a Entrance to Chapel d'Hiver
37 Chapel of N Dame de la Pitié
38 Relic of John the Baptist
39 The John the Baptist Panels
40 Chapel of the Pilier Vert
41 The North Transept
42 Chapel of St Peter
43 The North Aisle
44 Chapel of St Agnes
45 Chapel of St Louis
46 Chapel of St Honoré
47 Chapel of St Michel
48 Chapel of St John Evangelist
49 Chapel of St John the Baptist

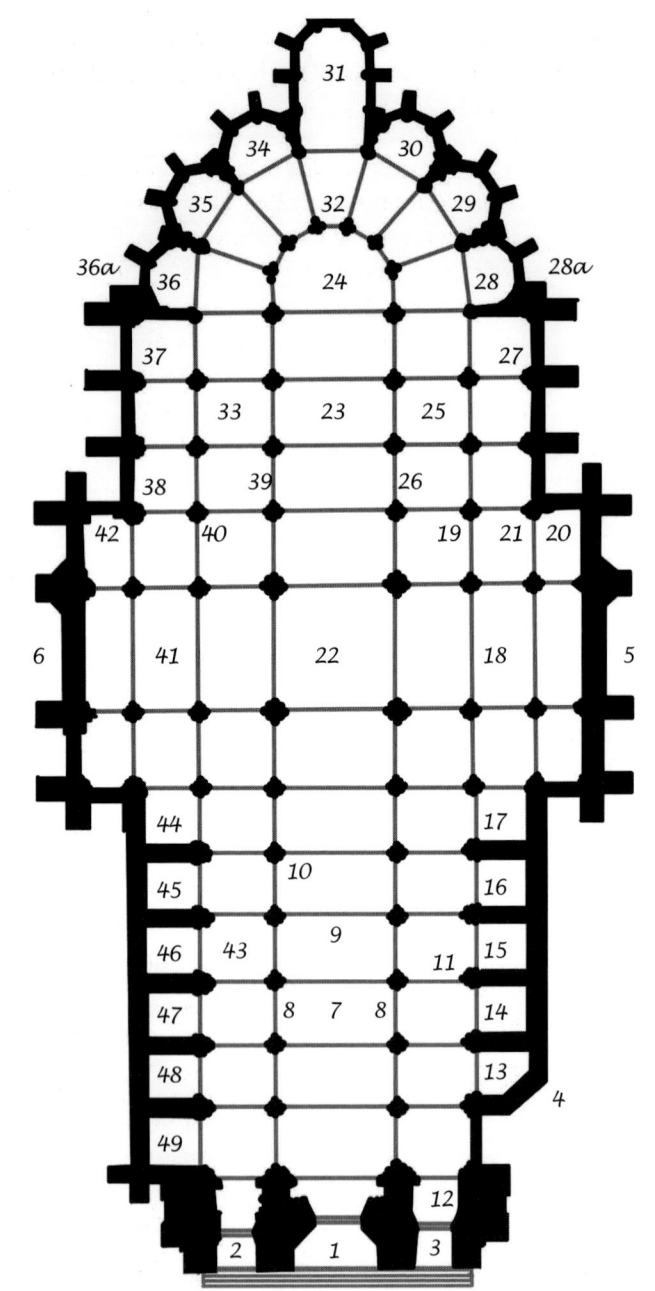

Amiens

confusion here, no exaggeration nor inflation. This is an empire of supreme elegance. This Virgin rose here during an epoch of sincerity, to fire and perpetuate the love of beauty in men's hearts."

Yet, there was a contest going on even during the construction of the building. The architect at Amiens in 1220 had seen Reims (1210) and, supremely, Chartres (1194), so he tried to take the style further. The windows at Amiens were so wide and high that they fell out in quantities in the 16th century and were not replaced in kind. The surface of glass was four times that in Chartres. Helen Henderson, in her book, "Cathedrals of France", published by Methuen in 1929, wrote: "Of what [glass] was left, the best up to the time of the War were in the chapels of the choir. These were dismounted during the War, packed in straw and put in what was thought to be a place of security, where, however, much later they were accidentally destroyed by fire."

We begin our tour of the cathedral, which M. Viollet le Duc called 'The Parthenon of Gothic Architecture', in the square facing the west front.

THE EXTERIOR

THE WEST FAÇADE

The Place Notre Dame affords a fine opportunity to stand back and admire the entrancing west façade built c.1220, and now that it has been cleaned it is striking. The eye is at first drawn to the deeply recessed portals, and then up to the gallery of arches corresponding to the triforium inside. Above that is the gallery of twenty-two Old Testament Kings, each of which is 3.7m high, and which tourists often believe, mistakenly, to be the Kings of France. Above them is the exquisite flamboyant tracery of the great rose window. Finally, the façade is crowned with the two 14th century towers, which are

The West Rose

253

A Glimpse Of Glory

separated by a screen of five arches beneath seventeen narrow arches reminding one of a piece of lace.

The crocketted gables over the portals are quite steep and are separated by pinnacles rising to the level of the gallery of the kings and decorated with blind arches. These conceal the fact that the façade is actually supported by four substantial buttresses. Each pair of doors is divided in the middle by a stone column called a trumeau, on which stands a statue of the saint to whom the portal is dedicated.

The north (left) portal of a Gothic cathedral is often dedicated to a local saint. At Amiens it is dedicated to the martyr St Firmin, who brought Christianity here and was the first Bishop of Amiens. He appears on the trumeau in the episcopal dress of a bishop. John Ruskin, in his book, "The Bible of Amiens", compares him unfavourably with the kind and gentle St Martin: "St Firmin, the impatient missionary, riots and rants about Amiens' streets, insults, exhorts, persuades, baptizes, turns everything, as aforesaid, upside down for forty days: then gets his head cut off, and is never more named, out of Amiens." The tympanum depicts the discovery of his body and its solemn recovery to within the city walls. There are three orders of carved figures in the archivolt, together with three decorated mouldings. The statues either side are of saints from Picardy and the Noye valley, whose bodies used to lie in the cathedral. Two of them on the left (north) side, Ache and Acheul, were beheaded for their Christian faith and carry their heads in their martyrdom. The quatrefoils depict the signs of the Zodiac and the labours of the seasons.

The centre portal is dedicated to Christ. His statue on the trumeau is known as the Beau Dieu, the beautiful God, and it is the most celebrated work of art in Amiens. It has a timeless severity which commands attention from all who approach this door. It is Christ the teacher saying to all who approach: "I am the Way, the Truth and the Life." Christ is accompanied on either side of the doors by the twelve apostles: Peter holding the keys of the kingdom, Andrew with his cross, James the Great with a basket of pilgrim shells, John holding a chalice from which a viper escapes, Simon a palm and Bartholomew a hatchet – all these are to the right. To the left are St Paul, James the Less, Thomas, Matthew, Philip

Beau Dieu, Central Portal Trumeau

Amiens

holding a stone, Jude a palm. Either side there are two prophets: Isaiah and Jeremiah to the left and Ezekiel and Daniel to the right. Daniel is pointing to a cross as a potential reference to his role as the Son of Man, a title claimed by Jesus. Below the apostles appear quatrefoils of the virtues and vices. The tympanum above the door represents the Last Judgement, a popular subject of the period. In the centre of the bottom register St Michael the Archangel weighs the souls while a demon and an angel try to outweigh each other. Either side are scenes of the resurrection. Above is the separation of the sheep and goats, and at the top is the Lord in judgement. There are eight orders of carved figures in the archivolt.

Simon and Bartholomew, Right Splay, West Central Portal

The south (right) portal is dedicated to Our Lady (Notre Dame), the Mother of God, and the Patron Saint of the cathedral. Her other-worldly gaze is Byzantine. She stands on the trumeau, holding the infant Christ without looking at him. Lower down, the trumeau is carved with four scenes from the story of Adam and Eve in the Garden of Eden. At the upper left they are at peace in the garden; to

Tympanum, Central West Portal

A Glimpse Of Glory

the right they are tempted by an anthropomorphic serpent; on the lower right they are banished from the garden by an angel and to the left they are wearing animal skin skirts and Adam has to dig and delve! Either side are scenes from the life of the Virgin: to the right (south) are statues representing the Annunciation, the Visitation to Elizabeth and the Presentation of Christ in the Temple. To the left (north) are the Wise Men (or Magi) and Herod questioning them, and to the extreme left a virgin holds a crown. Above, in the tympanum, we see the childhood of Christ, the death of Mary, her Assumption, and her coronation in Heaven. The quatrefoils depict scenes from the Old Testament, such as the burning bush in Exodus.

Not everyone delights in the west front of Amiens. In his book, "The Gothic Cathedral", published by Thames & Hudson in 1990, Christopher Wilson writes: "*Among these 13th century French architects was Robert de Luzarches. Unfortunately his west front at Amiens is as unsatisfactory as his nave is superb. The extremely tall proportioning of the main vessel resulted in a huge gap between the rose and the central portal, which Robert filled with a gallery of kings and a 'triforium'. Skied above this plethora of arches the rose looks insignificant. No less unhappy is the squatness of the aisle windows and the way they lurk behind the huge side portals. The portals owe much to Laon, but their arches have become disproportionately tall compared to the jambs, and the pinnacles between the gables appear ludicrously big in relation to the gable and to the buttresses of which they form part.*"

When stated so robustly who can disagree? Well, I do; for when the late afternoon sun brings out the warmth of the newly cleaned stone and the statues seem to stride out of the stone towards the visitor, and the spirit is lifted at the confidence of the craftsmen, Dr Wilson's strictures can be set aside for another day.

THE SOUTH SIDE

St Christopher

Do not miss the lively statue of St Christopher with the infant Jesus on his shoulder as you walk along the south side of the church from the west front. It was a popular belief in the middle ages that St Christopher saved from sudden death those who looked upon his image. That is why he often appears carved on the entrances to churches of that period.

The South Transept Façade

The modern copy of the 14th century Virgin with the Infant on the trumeau of the south transept portal (the original is in the south transept) is so different from the

Amiens

The South Façade Portal

majesty 13th century sculpture on the trumeau of the west front. Compare the two of them. The 'Golden Virgin' of the south door is undoubtedly human. Mary smiles at her Son. The smile, which seems to include the visitor, and the informal stance as she supports the child slightly on her hip, make us feel comfortably at home in her presence. Three little angels hold a fluted nimbus behind her head. The remainder of the sculpture is older and of the period of the west front. The tympanum has in its lower register a group of the twelve apostles conversing in pairs. Helen Henderson describes it thus:

"They contribute to the gaiety of the doorway by their animated attitudes, their easy movements, and their smiling faces which reflect nothing of divinity and in which their martyrdom is for once forgotten. Like the young care-free Virgin, they are perhaps a trifle colloquial, but after the immense solemnity of the great portal, is it not permissible to think that even the Virgin and the apostles had moments of relaxation and were not always strung to the high pitch of their destiny?"

The four upper levels of the tympanum depict scenes from the life of St Honoré, a Bishop of Amiens. The large 13th century statues in the splay of the door portray an angel nearest the door followed by three saints either side.

Scenes from the Old Testament form the subjects of the four orders of the archivolt: Noah building the Ark, Isaac blessing Jacob, the Judgment of Solomon, Judith with the head of Holophernes, Jonah and the Whale, Daniel, Suzannah and

A Glimpse Of Glory

the Elders, and the like, are all delicately wrought and often charmingly picturesque.

We return via the west front to see the north elevation of the church.

THE NORTH SIDE

The piers which separate the chapels of the north aisle bear sculptures of persons contemporary with the building. On the pier separating the last two chapels and on the two faces of the double buttress which supports the north tower is a series of nine statues in three vertical rows. These are of the greatest artistic merit. Portraits, admirably truthful, they count among the most important works of sculpture of the reign of Charles V.

On the west-facing corner of the first bay there are three statues on brackets and under canopies. At the top are the Madonna and Child; beneath is Charles V with his shield of fleurs-de-lys beside him; beneath him is Cardinal de la Grange with his shield. He was the Bishop of Amiens from 1373 to 1375. The cardinal has special point here as he built these last two chapels on the north side of the nave.

Northwest Corner Statues

On the north-facing corner there are three more statues. At the top is John the Baptist dressed in camel-skin coat and holding in his left hand a nest of wild bees. Beneath him is the Dauphin Charles, later Charles VI holding a fleurs-de-lys. At the bottom is Bureau de la Riviere, a counsellor of the court.

The upper figure of the next pier, holding his head in his hands, is Saint Firmin the Martyr and under him, the infamous Louis d'Orleans, second son of Charles V, and an unidentified personage at the bottom. Of particular note is the statue on the second pier west (right) of the transept; it is one of the oldest known portraits of the Saint-King Louis. With him is Guillaume de Macon, the bishop who, in 1302, built the fifth chapel on the north side in honour of the King.

The North Transept Façade

The north door is dedicated to St Honoré and is altogether a much plainer façade than the south door. Three engaged columns each side of the north door support an archivolt of three unadorned ribs rising from small foliated capitals. The tympanum is largely filled by an arch enclosing a window of flamboyant tracery. A central trumeau, bearing a weathered statue of St Honoré under a canopy, separates the two wooden doors. The whole is framed by a crocketted gable which rests on a very slender column each side. Above the portal five arches, each with three lancets, are squeezed into the space between the buttresses which rise either side of the Rose window. From the exterior it is strange to note that the rose is fronted with three pointed arches.

The northeast buttress is against the north face of an octagonal staircase tower. The northwest buttress is only crowned with an octagon, as if the staircase was demolished for the buttress. Either side of the buttresses can be seen the north face of the east and west bays of the transept, each of which has a window with a double lancet with a multifoil rosette in the tracery. At the eastern and western ends of the façade the buttresses rise only to the height of the triforium, whence a pinnacle supports a bridge type flying buttress to support the clerestory of the transept.

THE INTERIOR

THE NAVE

With the exception of Reims, Gothic cathedrals usually had a plain interior west wall as if not wishing to detain the worshipper from leaving the building after prayer. The west door here at Amiens is framed on the inside by a totally plain archway. It has two wooden doors with a central stone column, totally without ornament. To the side, between the corner of the west wall and the first pillar, which has a cluster of engaged columns, there are three blind arches with trefoil tops, two on the west wall and one on the north wall, forming a corner. The arrangement is exactly the same on the south side.

High above the west door, almost up to the level of the rose window, is the wooden casing of the organ console. The engaged columns on the pillars go straight up to the foot of the rose window from which springs the ribs

The Nave

A Glimpse Of Glory

of the round vault of the west end; not an arch but a rounded barrel vault, with blind arches to north and south at both triforium and at clerestory level. The rose window fills the arch above the organ casing and is supported by an arcade of delicate columns. This 15th century organ gallery, paid for by a tax collector and his wife, is rather beautiful with delicate carving and ogee arches in the north and south, and the pipework in the centre. The statues represent a bishop, St John the Baptist, the Virgin Mary, St Firmin and a deacon.

Standing beneath this great organ, facing east, the view is compelling. The nave arcade of seven bays each side is very lofty, bearing a small triforium, above which is a tall clerestory. The aisles are wide and also high, and beyond them the chapel vaults are the same height as the aisle. There is, therefore, a great horizontal expanse rising to quite a height, which gives enormous support to the downward thrust of the roof.

The nave pillars stride away along the length of the nave; six of them each side before coming to the crossing. Each pillar has four engaged columns. There are six narrow pointed arches supporting a blind triforium, each bay of which is divided into two arches with a central cluster of columns. In each subdivision, two single columns form three arches. Above that are four lancets under two arches with a trefoil in the top of each of the two arches and, at the vault, a multifoil oculus. A quadripartite vault spans the roof of the nave.

It is a fine nave. The capitals of the pillars are quite high up, decorated with foliage, bearing an abacus from which the arches spring across to the next pillar. The engaged column which faces the nave gathers the two small, enclosed columns, and continues from the abacus; the larger column, up to the triforium level and then on through the triforium string course to the clerestory, where there is a stringcourse, and then on, half way up the clerestory windows, from whence the ribs spring from an abacus above a foliated capital. It is at that point we can see the new architectural technique of

The North Side of the Nave

Amiens

'tas de charge' in its early form. To increase stability in the high vault, a series of radially constructed rib blocks are placed on top of each other on the abacus, so that the point where multiple ribs come together is now far stronger in the area where the lateral thrusts of the vault are to be found, and thus permits a thinner wall in the clerestory.

Below the triforium there is an abundance of carved foliage decorated all along the length of the string course from the west end to the crossing. Such is the architecture of the north side of the nave; the south side is identical.

Between the pillars of the third bay, enclosed by wrought-iron railings, there are two monuments of extreme rarity, one on the north and the other on the south side. These are the bronze tombs of the Bishops Evrard de Fouilloy, who died in 1222, (south side) and Geoffroy d'Eu, his successor (north side). The former was the bishop who laid the foundation stone and was a prelate of noble birth. His effigy is cast in one piece and is richly decorated. Six lion cubs support both effigies.

In the centre of the floor of the nave is 'a labyrinth'. They were popular with pilgrims, who called them 'The Jerusalem Way', and examples can be seen at Chartres, Reims and Sens. It was first laid in 1288 but was mutilated during the Revolution and the original stone has been removed to the Museum of Picardy in Amiens. The present labyrinth was laid in 1894 and is a faithful copy of the original, including the names of the king, the founding bishop and the three successive architects at the centre of the 234 metre-long path. Henderson has a story that in the Middle Ages, on Easter Day after Vespers, both here and at Reims, the Canons would gather for a game of tennis on the labyrinth while the choir sang the anthem 'Paschal Victim'.

On the pillar before the crossing on the south side there is a large carved crucifix facing the corresponding pillar on the north side, where there is a wooden pulpit, painted to resemble marble and decorated in gold in the style of Louis XVI. The sounding board above it bears an angel holding

The Pulpit

A Glimpse Of Glory

books, which carry a legend which can be translated as: "Do this and you shall live." Three statues of Faith, Hope and Charity support the pulpit, made in 1773 by local craftsmen. The figure on the left, apart from supporting the pulpit, is breastfeeding an infant. At the back, cherubs are holding a golden curtain behind the preacher.

The nave is quite light because most of the glass is clear. The only exceptions in the clerestory are the third, fourth and fifth bays from the west on north side, which have geometric coloured glass. The windows on the south side are filled with clear diamond quarry glass.

THE AISLES

The chapels have quadripartite vaults like the nave; except that the two westernmost chapels either side have more developed vaulting using liernes. They are all closed with high, ornate, wrought-iron screens. The lower walls in all the chapels of the south aisle are panelled in wood, although some are painted to resemble marble.

We begin our tour of the interior at the west end of the south aisle (to the right when facing the altar) and continue in an anti-clockwise direction around the church.

THE SOUTH AISLE

There are two doors divided by a central column under a blind, pointed arch and above that a cusped rose window, with mouchettes in geometric designs. At ground level inside the southwest doorway there are on the north side two blind arches with trefoil tops and on the south side there is a plain wooden doorway under a single arch. It gives access to the staircase ascending to the south tower. It is a stiff climb, but for €2.5 (in 2004) it is worth the effort. One climbs to the level of the rose and can cross below the great window to climb the north tower to the top.

Monument to Canon Bury

Amiens

On the pillar at the west end of the south aisle is a wonderful funerary monument to Pierre Bury, a Canon who died in 1504, and it is supported by two slender octagonal columns, with a scroll borne by two angels beneath the pediment, which bears the statue of Christ bound (Ecce Homo), with the canon and his patron saint praying before him. Beneath the scroll there are two skulls peeping out to say 'Hello!' as you study the monument. Facing it, on the first pillar of the south aisle is a similar monument to Canon Antoine Niguet (d.1652) by Nicolas Blasset.

The First Bay. There are two wooden doors forming the southwest door. They are flanked by two columns and there is a blind arch either side.

South Aisle Looking East

Set back beyond the doors can be seen six blind arches rising on the south wall below six lancet windows with quatrefoil tracery and a fine ceiling boss.

The Chapel of St Christopher. It was dedicated in 1358 and decorated in 1762 by the sculptor Jean-Baptiste Dupius. The retable has a statue of St Christopher with the infant Christ on his shoulder. It is interesting to remember that there is a colossal statue of the saint on the exterior wall of the cathedral about this point. The four lancet windows in the south wall have quatrefoil tracery above each pair of lancets, with more tracery in the top of the window where there are trefoils and mouchettes, all in clear diamond quarry glass but with coloured borders. Then the wall angles from the south towards the northwest and there are four lancets in the upper level but the lower level is blind with the remains of painted blind arcading. The west wall is plain. The chapel has an interesting vault; the liernes seem to go all over the place because of the angle of the south west wall. There is an altar against the south wall. Like all the chapels of the nave, it is enclosed by a high wrought-iron screen.

A Glimpse Of Glory

The Chapel of the Annunciation is dated 1383, but in 1878 it was named Notre Dame de Foy. There is a window of six lancets with trefoil tracery half way up the window, before the lancets continue up again to quatrefoil tracery at the top. The vault has ribs forming a cross and diagonal, with liernes supporting the cross ribs. Behind the altar there is a bas-relief sculpture of the Annunciation by Nicolas Blasset for Antoine Pièce Maitre in 1655. A fine little reliquary of Notre Dame de Foy, made in 1879, stands on a pedestal to the west of the altar.

The Chapel of St Nicholas is dated 1427, but called the Chapel of the Incarnation or the Assumption in 1892. It was erected by "the Woaders." Woad is a blue dye produced from the leaves of a flowering plant of the brassica family, and then, as now, Amiens was a noted centre of the textile dyeing industry. The windows are the same as the previous chapel, except that the tracery at the top of the lancets is far more flamboyant and has coloured triangles in the trefoils. The chapel has a plain quadripartite vault. There is a stone altar against the south wall with a statue of the Assumption in black and white marble made by Nicolas Blasset in 1637.

The Chapel of St Stephen dating to 1292–1300, is also called the Chapel of St Lawrence. The decoration was executed in 1768. There are six lancets again divided in the middle, the lower lancets are clear diamond quarry glass as in all the other chapels, but the upper levels of the six have coloured glass with six medallions in each of the lancets, and above there are quatrefoils with little square pieces of coloured glass with scenes in the middle. The medallions also have scenes but it is too dark to make them out. Above the altar there is a sunburst with a cherubim looking down from on high. The retable has a painting of the "Pâmoison de la Vierge" (Mary and Divine Love) by Laurent de La Hyre in 1628 and the two statues of St Stephen and St Nicholas are attributed to Nicolas Blasset about 1637. St Stephen is on the left of the altar and St Nicholas wearing his mitre is to the right. There is a memorial to St Stephen on the east wall and one to St Augustine, partially hidden by a confessional, on the west wall. The painting "Communion of St Bonaventure" hangs above the panelling on the east wall (missing in 2012).

The Chapel of St Margaret c.1292. This chapel is the final chapel before the crossing. The decoration was executed between 1768–1770. The panelling either side of the altar has medallions in bas-relief of St Peter and St Joseph. On the reredos is a plaster statue of St Margaret by Jaques-Firmin Vimeux in the 18th century. The windows have just four lancets with two quatrefoils above and then a big trefoil with a kind of 'bulls-eye target' in coloured glass in the centre. The rest is clear diamond quarry glass, except that the lower lancets have instead irregular geometric shapes – like cubes coming up/down. The eastern half of the window is a *trompe l'oeil* of four lancets, painted rather poorly. An altar stands against the south wall and on the east wall is a freestanding statue of the Virgin and Infant,

17th century by Michel Martin. On the lower west wall is a painting of Christ in the tomb by Désiré Letellier.

THE SOUTH TRANSEPT

The transept is very wide and spacious because it spans the eastern bay of the nave: the south aisle turns after the sixth bay to become the west aisle of the transept. In the west wall of this bay is a fine polychrome carving, in four panels, under four little ogee arches going up into pinnacles with a pierced screen in between each arch above the sculpture. They depict scenes from the life of St James the Great (he wears the pilgrim's shell motif as a badge in his hat), including his conversion of the magician Hermogene, and date from 1511. Above the panels are two open arches and a circular stone decoration. Below are black marble tablets dating to 1648, which list the Masters of the Confrérie who worked in the cathedral from 1389 to 1729, and who on their election gave a work of art, known as 'a Puy', to the cathedral. There is a doorway opening to the west in the south west corner with two wide lancets above in clear quarry glass, and a multifoil window above that. In the south wall of this bay there is a similar window above wooden panelling at ground level. There is a quadripartite vault above each of these three western bays.

St James the Great (extreme right), south transept

The transept itself has on the south wall a double doorway in the centre with a pointed arch above it and three trefoils. The central trefoil is inverted to accommodate an angel with outspread wings. At the lower level there are three blind arches on either side, with blind arches rising almost to the base of the triforium; eight blind arches in pairs with blind tracery at the top. The doorway arch pierces all of them. Below the triforium there is the foliated stringcourse, which continues all around the transept. The triforium has five open arches, each revealing a small lancet, which are beautifully coloured with figures, behind a passage. Above the canopies of these arches is another level of figures under little arches, above which is the beautiful South Rose, which has only fragments of the 15th and 16th century glass. Yet, it is glorious under a rounded arch with a narrow rounded vault. The rest of the south transept vault is quadripartite.

Above the three big arches of the west wall, on each of the two columns are three enclosed columns, two of which bear the spring across the bay, but the middle one continues half way up the clerestory and carries the spring of the vaulting—exactly as it does in the nave. Each bay has at triforium level, again as in the nave, two arches, each subdivided into three arches, with a trefoil above, and this arrangement

A Glimpse Of Glory

is continued from the nave along the west side of the transept. Above, eight lancets all in clear quarry glass with rose windows above them and trefoils in the top of the tracery below the rose windows. On the pillar marking the junction of the south aisle with the south transept there is a fine memorial to Canon Claude Pierre, who died in 1650. On the other side of the pillar is a memorial to the soldiers of the New Zealand Division who fell in the battle of the Somme and those who liberated Amiens. A similar memorial to the Australian soldiers is fixed to the south side of the pillar. The next pillar, nearest the south door, has a memorial to members of the Royal Canadian Dragoon Guards who died in 1915–18, and one to the war dead of Great Britain and Ireland.

The east wall is identical to the west side in its architecture. The windows all have clear quarry glass.

The Chapel of Notre Dame de Pilier Rouge (1334) or Notre Dame de Puy (1627). The pillar marks the junction of the transept with the south ambulatory. The chapel is enclosed with a marble balustrade. Above the altar there is a large painting of the Assumption by François Fancken le Jeune (1628). The statue of the Virgin and Child, with Mary pulling a child from a well, on top of the painting, is the statue of Notre Dame de Puy, and either side of the painting are 18th century statues of St Geneviève by Cressent (north) and Judith holding the head of D'Holopherne (south). A crowned David with his harp is to the north and a crowned Solomon with tablets in his hand to the south. It is a very fine ensemble. The statue of Geneviève represented "Liberty" in a Revolutionary fete in 1793!

In the southeast corner of the transept a few steps lead to the following chapel enclosed by a wrought iron screen and occupying the first bay of the south ambulatory.

The Chapel of L'Aurore (of St Paul in 1233, St Peter and St Paul in 1610). The chapel was refurbished in 1749. The painting of the Adoration of the Magi is by Joseph Parrocel (1704–1781) and the statues of Peter and Paul were sculpted by Jean-Baptiste Dupuis (1749). The small font, which dates from 1672, was placed here in 1792.

The Crossing

Do not miss the famous statue of the 'Vierge Dorée', the Golden Virgin, on the left pier of this chapel. It was removed from the trumeau of the South Door in 1980 and replaced by a replica. After restoration it was mounted here in 1995.

THE CROSSING

The sheer loftiness of the vault at the crossing is impressive. The vault is one of the oldest with liernes and tiercerons in any French Gothic cathedral. It was raised towards the end of the 13th century and inspired many English cathedral architects of that period. It is replicated in the western chapels of the nave.

THE CHOIR

Five steps lead up to a semi-circular wooden platform on which stand a nave altar, a lectern, ambo and liturgical chairs. Behind this platform are two fine wrought-iron gates, which give access to the choir. Designed by Slodtz (1705–1764) and made by Vivarais, they replace the stone Rood Screen destroyed in 1755. Either side of these gates is a stone screen with three blind arches decorated with small, sculpted, angels' heads. Two enormous stone statues stand against them, one each side: St Charles-Borromée sculpted by Jean-Baptiste Dupuis in 1755 (left), and a 19th century St Vincent de Paul by the Duthoit brothers (right).

It was Ruskin's advice to anybody pressed for time at Amiens to spend the whole of his visit in the cathedral choir. *"Aisles and porches"*, he said, *"lancet windows and roses you can see elsewhere as well as here, but such carpenter's work you cannot. It is late, fully developed flamboyant, just past the fifteenth century, and has some Flemish stolidity mixed with the playing French fire of it; but wood-carving was the Picard's joy from his youth up, and, so far as I know, there is nothing else so beautiful cut out of the goodly trees of the world."*

Either side of the choir are the 110 canons stalls in two rows, all beautifully constructed in oak and each canopied; with fine misericords and return stalls either side at the west end. This 16th century carving is full of wit and fun. Helen Henderson agrees with Ruskin:

"There is a unity in the choir of Amiens due partly to the fact that it was practically all done by two wood-carvers under the direction of a third and assisted by a fourth superior artist, known as a 'tailleur d'images'—a figure carver. We know their names : the master carpenters were Alexander Huet and Arnoult Boullon; the chief was Jean Turpin. These artists were above all faithful to the tradition of the Middle Ages and the subjects, whether they be drawn from the life of the Virgin or whether they depict 'Pharaoh's Dream' or the story of 'Joseph and his Brethren', are illustrated with utmost clarity and in the liveliest manner. The full date of the start of the work, '3

A Glimpse Of Glory

juillet 1508' may be read upon another elbow-rest. The choir was finished on Saint John's Day, 1522."

The centre area of this light and airy choir is filled with chairs ready for Sunday Worship, weddings and funerals. Sitting here during the Sunday morning Mass, with the choir full of people singing "Kyrie Eleison" in plainchant, I was struck with the agelessness of Christian worship in this place. It is so light because the windows on either side of the clerestory are clear diamond quarry glass. Above the light triforium level, the centre windows of the clerestory are coloured: four narrow lancets with two trefoils and a rose above. On the south side, the centre of each triforium window contains figures in coloured glass but the rest are all clear quarry diamond glass. On the north side the centre triforium in the first group (the centre western one of the first bay) is coloured, but the right one is not. In the next bay neither are coloured but the glass has been temporarily removed. In the third bay the centre one is coloured, the right hand group of three are all diamond quarry glass. In the next bay both sets of three have figures in the centre. Then in the last bay before the apse, there is only clear diamond quarry glass.

THE SANCTUARY

At the east end of the choir the eye is drawn to the seven narrow lancet-filled bays of the clerestory surrounding the high altar, which stands beneath on a marble platform. Behind the altar and rising almost to the triforium windows is an amazing bas-relief, which is a blaze of glory from on high. It is more work by Dupuis and was painted in the 18th century. The reliquary in the bottom of it contains the relics of St Firmin. Beneath the reliquary is a tabernacle containing the Blessed Sacrament.

The bishop's throne is on the north side of the sanctuary, with a rather nice bas-relief carving in a medallion behind it depicting a head with a cherub below, and two angels either side standing upright underneath a canopy of red velvet curtains edged in gold, drawn back either side, with the throne in the centre.

THE SOUTH AMBULATORY

Bay 1 The ambulatory extends in width into a double aisle, which is at first occupied with the side of the Chapel of L'Aurore which opens from the east side of the south transept. The chapel is enclosed by a wrought iron grille in black with gilt decoration. In the south wall there are three tall lancet windows with two and a half rosettes in the tracery above. All the windows are in diamond quarry glass.

Bay 2 has blind arcading above the bench at ground level and in the centre is a modern bas-relief sculpture of St Martin dividing his cloak with a beggar at the gate of Amiens, which was placed here on 11th November 1997. The two easternmost sections of blind arcading are obstructed by a doorway, which has above it two fine carved heads, one of a man and one of a wimpled maiden. Above are three lancets and a quarter of a lancet, the quarter is to the west of the window, and, again, three rose windows above all in clear quarry glass with coloured borders.

Bay 3 has four lancets; the outer lancets east and west are of clear quarry glass with coloured borders, but the centre two have circles and diamonds, also in quarry glass with borders, and three rosettes in the tracery. At ground level there is a large archway with two blind arches either side containing war memorial tablets. In the centre is another war memorial with sculpted weeping people either side and, in bas-relief, Our Lady with her arms outstretched. It is the work of Albert Roze and is dated 1923.

Bay 4 has again six little blind arches, with memorial tablets in the central and the two western arches; the eastern arch has a storage cupboard and a double piscina in the second arch from the east, and the eastern arch has burial tablets in it. It is a fine little arcade with four lancets above and rosettes in the tracery, all in diamond quarry glass.

Chapel of St Joseph (originally St Charles Borromée). The east wall to this southern aisle in the south ambulatory ends in this chapel, with its Baroque altar, and the barleytwist columns in marble with gold foliage in the curls, and a statue (1832) of St Joseph and the infant Jesus (who is standing on what appears to be a stem of a palm tree) in a niche above and behind the altar. The columns have Corinthian capitals, decorated in gold, and bearing a semi-circular pediment, above which there us a gold sculpture with a dove in the centre and statues either side; that on the right appears to be Moses. There is a gilded bas-relief beneath the statue of St Joseph which looks tempestuous; there are medieval tents in the background which can lead one to a false conclusion. The scene is, I believe, of the Israelites in the Sinai wilderness being told by Moses to gather the manna which can be seen falling on the left and looks like bunches of grapes on the floor.

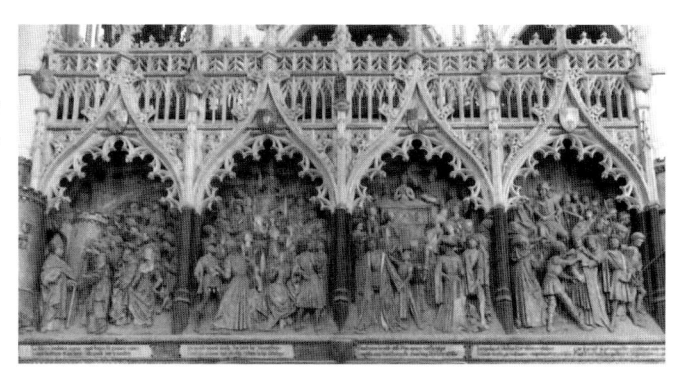

The Life of St. Firmin

A Glimpse Of Glory

In the inner ambulatory, on the north wall, forming a screen to the choir, there are fine polychrome carved panels, which in two bays depict the life and times of St Firmin the martyr and first Bishop of Amiens in the 13rd century. They were carved in 1495 and the figures are all in mediaeval dress, superbly carved and give a very good insight into the period. The subject matter in the first bay is the entry of St Firmin into Amiens, his preaching, the baptism of the people of Amiens and his arrest and beheading. This latter macabre scene is on the eastern side of the carved panel in this bay. Below the panels in this west bay, angels hold apart a painted curtain revealing the effigy of Bishop de Ferry de Beauvois, the Bishop of Amiens who died in 1472, lying in his tomb. Inside the curtains there is, at either side, a tonsured priest holding another curtain exposing the front of the sarcophagus, on which are the symbols of the four evangelists: an eagle (John, upper left), a winged lion (Mark, upper right), a winged ox (Luke, lower left), a human angel (Matthew, lower right), and the Agnus Dei (Lamb of God) in the centre of a white cross.

The next bay has again four arches and here the carved panels were done in 1530 and have as the subject the preaching of St Sauve, the revelation of the sepulchre of St Firmin, the exhumation of St Firmin and the translation of the relics. Below it is another effigy, similar to the previous bay, but in this bay it is Adrien de Hénencourt, the Dean of the cathedral ('doyen de chapitre'), dating from the 16th century, and surrounded by quatrefoil medallions of the bishop's life.

The entrance to the choir and the high altar occupies the next bay. First we have on the left three little blind arches and then a larger column with a triumphant capital above, but only bearing a stone urn. Then there is a fine wrought-iron gate in the screen which encloses the sanctuary. This screen is also wrought iron in black, the decoration picked out in gold; rather a lovely screen. In his delightful book, "Cathedrals of France", 1914, Auguste Rodin delighted in this screen: *"The grillwork of Amiens makes perfect harmony with this Gothic monument. Just as all beautiful things are always in accord with each other! These Louis XIV grilles are superb in simple elegance and nobility. Sumptuously they rose at the foot of the columns."*

The Apse begins at this point; note the chevrons in the floor tiles.

Chapel of St Eloi. The final bay on the south side is not really a chapel but leads to a cusped doorway giving access to the Sacristy and the Treasury. This bay is behind the Chapel of St Joseph with its twisted columns. It has blind arcading on the two east and two west walls, both of the outer walls are angled towards the doorway in the south wall itself. The doorway is nicely framed by a square stone moulding with little colonnettes either side and tiny little capitals from which springs a depressed arch, and above it a pediment with little diamond shapes in it. It is all delicately done. Of the five walls only two have glass. Above the door are two lancets rising to the apsidal vault; they contain three and a half registers of clear diamond quarry glass with quatrefoil tracery and then three registers of coloured glass ending in three quatrefoils. The upper section has diamond quarry glass, with trefoils at the very top. The lowest three registers are blind.

To the east are two lancets reaching right up to the vault with little trefoils at the top. The east wall has two blind lancets rising to the vault and the west wall has a similar arrangement. The southwest angle also has blind lancets. At ground level the bench continues around the ambulatory and the plinths of the blind arches rest on the bench. There are wall murals of "Les Sybilles" dating to 1506 in the lower blind arches. The 19th century painting on the east wall is of the "Hermits Domice and Ulphe." An altar designed by Viollet le Duc stands against the east wall, with a single piscina to the right of it.

The Chapel of St Francis of Assisi since 1494, The Chapel of St Nicholas in 1340. The chapel has three lights, each of two lancets in coloured glass. The window on the left (east) has a fine 13th century Tree of Jesse in oval medallions in the centre of each lancet, and fragments of 13th century glass depicting the tree of Jesse, recomposed by Jeanette Wreiss-Gruber in 1991. The centre (south) window has medallions in each window with scenes in them; the right (southwest) window has two lancets with quatrefoil medallions. The bays nearest the aisle to left and right have each two blind lancets rising to the roof vault. The 18th century retable has 19th century wooden bas-relief sculptures, by François-Léon Bénouville, depicting scenes from the life of St Francis of Assisi. The painting is a 19th century work of the death of St Francis. The chapel is enclosed by a higher wrought-iron screen (1775–1779).

The Chapel of St James the Great (1337), or Sacré Coeur (1886). The Chapel was consecrated to the Sacré Coeur (Sacred Heart) following an epidemic of cholera in 1886. It was decorated by Viollet-le-Duc and he really has gone to town on it. At the lower level of the entire chapel there is a blind arcade of four arches in each bay. In the southeast bay there are two little piscina in the middle of the arcade. The three windows have two large lancets in each, with beautiful red coloured glass, which appears to be very modern. In the north and south windows there are two blind lancets to the vault and in the top of them are three trefoils in each of the three lights. The glass is magnificent and at the bottom of the right hand light in the centre window one can read the name of the glazier, "Gaudin, Paris" and the artist, "J. le Breton 1933."

The scenes in the window include Mary Magdalene washing Christ's feet; above that is the miracle of the loaves and fishes; and above that is Christ washing the disciples' feet. The brass altar by Poussielgue-Rusand, from a sketch by Viollet-le-Duc, is dated 1837. The retable has a tabernacle in the centre bearing the motif of the Lamb of God (Agnus Dei), a bas-relief carving of the Last Supper on the left

A Glimpse Of Glory

and another on the right of Jesus. There are four pillars on the front framing three little rows of medallions, all in bronze. The Newfoundland, the Australian and the New Zealand flags are laid up in this chapel to acknowledge the friendship shown to those countries during 1916–1918.

The Lady Chapel is The Chapel of Notre Dame de Drapière (1259) and the chapel where the Blessed Sacrament is reserved. It was constructed through the generosity of the Corporation of Drapers (Amiens is a textile town) and was decorated by Viollet-le-Duc in 1859. It is deeper than the other chapels, with three bays north (left) and south (right), and three bays in the east at an angle. The stone bench continues around the ground level of this chapel. There is a blind arcade of four arches in each bay at the lower level of the chapel, above the bench and below the windows. In the third bay on the south side the central two of the four blind arches contains an aumbry and a piscina in niches.

The first bay on either side has two blind lancets decorated with fleurs-de-lys rising above the blind arcade to the vault. The next two bays on either side each have two lancets, all with geometric designs in grisaille glass. The three eastern windows have three lights, each with two lancets, soaring up behind the altar.

The altar itself, designed by Viollet-le-Duc, is borne on four columns with decorated capitals and the retable has three bas-relief scenes in three crocketted arches rising to decorated finials above each side of the tabernacle. To north and south there is a column rising above the little pinnacles, each bearing an angel holding a candelabra. Above the tabernacle there are four pillars bearing a plinth with little turrets at each corner and a crocketted spire above the central niche. In this niche is a four-foot high bronze statue of the Virgin and Child, an angel with folded wings at each corner.

The Lady Chapel Tombs

In the north wall there are two arches, gabled and crocketted, over 14th century effigies of bishops. The front of each sarcophagus has a row of lovely little carved monks, known as 'weepers'.

Face west at this point and observe three fine memorials. The white stone dado is thought to be that of Bishop Arnoul de la Pierre (1236–47); the white marble effigy is of Cardinal Jean de la Grange, Bishop of Amiens (1402); but I am attracted to the marble memorial of Canon Lucas (1628), an orphan benefactor, who is depicted kneeling before the Virgin and Child. It is the work of Nicolas Blasset and is famous for the little angel leaning on the head of a dead man, with an hourglass by its side, and known as the 'Weeping Angel.' It would invoke more pathos if the angel was not so chubby! In addition, for many years there has been a cobweb descending from the Canon's nose which rather detracts from the solemnity of the monument.

Monument to Canon Lucas

THE NORTH AMBULATORY

The Chapel of St Augustine of Canterbury (13th century) or St Theudosie (1853). The blind arcading of four arches to each bay continues around the lower level of the chapel, but they are badly affected by rising damp. The outer bays north and south have blind lancets rising to the vault, and the other three windows have each two lancets with quatrefoils in the top. The northernmost of these three windows has in the three lowest registers a scene of the Empress Eugenie (on the left) and the Emperor Napoleon (right) in prayer with a register of fragments of grisaille glass above it and then a register of blue glass with medallions, and so it continues to the top of the window. The window is dated 1854 and is the work of Alfred Garente. It has an inscription: "Réalisée grâce aux dons de Napoléon III et de l'Empertrice Eugenie, venus en visite en 1853 et 1854." The Empress placed the relics of St Theudosie in this chapel, presumably in the reliquary on the altar. The centre window has only fragments of grisaille glass. The southernmost window has some 13th century scenes: the lower two registers depicting the textile workers of Amiens, then fragments, and, above, two more registers of scenes in medallions depicting the lives of St Firmin and St Honoré, then more fragments, and so on to the top of the window.

A Glimpse Of Glory

The Chapel of St John the Baptist (1388). The outermost bay on the south and north sides has two blind lancets rising to the vault. There are again three lights with two lancets in each, all in clear diamond quarry glass with trefoils in the tracery. At the lower level, instead of the blind arcading, there is wooden panelling around the walls with a marble altar in the centre. Behind the altar is a carved high-relief sculpture of St John the Baptist by Vimeux (1775), framed by two marble columns with carved capitals bearing a semi-circular pediment above. Freestanding in front of the altar is a shrine of the last saint from Picardy, St Antoine Daveluy. He left Amiens in 1818 and was martyred in Korea in 1866. He was canonized by Pope John Paul II in 1984. There is an 18th century painting of the Ascension on the west wall. This chapel is also enclosed by a higher wrought-iron screen.

The Chapel of St Quentin les Meurtris (1291) or St Thérèse and the Infant Jesus. The altar was designed by Viollet-le-Duc. The window has 18th century glass depicting the history of the Virgin and St Leonard. There is an 18th century painting on the east wall above the altar of the death of a Carmelite. On a plinth behind the altar there is a statue of St Thérèse holding a crucifix. In the northeast wall there is a double piscina with finely decorated canopies above them in the blind arcade. In the equivalent bay on the other side of the chapel there is a very narrow doorway. Above the altar, the wall has two blind lancets rising to the roof vault. Similarly, the west wall and the northwest wall also have two blind lancets. The north wall has two lancets; the lower three registers have clear quarry diamond glass, but above that are coloured scenes. The northeast wall has two lancets in clear quarry glass.

Chapel d'Hiver, Doorway

The doors are 14th century and used to give access to the cloister, but now they open to a short corridor leading to the Chapel d'Hiver.

The Chapel d'Hiver. The chapel has a 'modern' feel to it. It stands on the site of the Chapel of the Catechumens. It has a wooden barrel vault, with an altar at the east end under a simple pointed arch. The eastern window has three lancets, while each side of the nave has pairs of rectangular windows with a multifoil above each pair, all with clear diamond quarry glass. There is a pulpit half way along the north wall and a small organ standing at the west end on the wooden floor.

The Apse ends at this point and the North Ambulatory becomes double aisled.

The Chapel of Notre Dame de la Pitié. In the northern of the two aisles there is an altar similar to the St Joseph Chapel in the double aisled part of the south ambulatory: twisted columns with golden decoration and a semi-circular pediment borne on two Corinthian capitals. In the niche in the centre of the reredos above a marble altar there is a large 18th century marble statue of the Virgin Mary clasping her hands in anguish, the 'Vierge des Douleurs', by Jean-Baptiste Dupuis. The blind arcading continues along the north wall at the lowest level and above it there are four lancets in clear diamond quarry glass with three rosettes above it in the tracery.

The next bay has the usual blind arcading, except that the eastern two sections have been interrupted by a doorway under a round arch in a square stone frame. The windows are exactly the same. There is another fine carving of the bound Christ, "Ecce Homo" ("Behold, the Man"), on a column dividing the two aisles. (It was missing in 2012)

The third bay of this north aisle of the north ambulatory also has the blind arcading interrupted in the second section from the east by a wooden doorway with a red velvet veil above. In this doorway there is a reliquary with what is claimed to be the front part of the skull of John the Baptist. It was stolen by Walon de Sarton, a Canon of St Martin at Picquiny, from the ruins of an ancient palace during the pillage of Constantinople, called the Fourth Crusade, in 1204. It is known locally as 'The Pious Theft', for he brought it to Amiens in 1206 and gave it to the bishop. This relic became the focus of celebrated pilgrimage and a source of prosperity for the town.

The next couple of arches are interrupted by a tomb bearing the effigy of Bishop Gisant de Gérard de Conchy, Bishop of Amiens 1247–1257. He lies, with his right hand erect in blessing and his left holding the remnant of a crozier, under an arch surmounted by a crocketted gable with a trefoil and bas-relief foliage in the tympanum.

A Glimpse Of Glory

The final bay in the north ambulatory is in fact a black wrought-iron screen with gilt decoration, and enclosing the Chapel of St Peter, accessed from the north transept.

In the inner ambulatory, on the south wall, which screens the choir from the north ambulatory, there are fine polychrome carved panels in two bays, similar to the life of St Firmin in the south ambulatory. Here the subject is St John the Baptist. They were made in 1531 and we can see the vision in the Temple in which Zachariah learns that he is to father a son to be called John; the Visitation of Mary to Elizabeth, the mother of John; St John in the desert; John baptising Jesus; John before King Herod; John in prison; Salome asking for the head of John on a plate; his martyrdom; and the miracles at his grave. These panels are treasures by an unknown artist. Auguste Rodin adored them. In his book, "Cathedrals of France", published in 1914, he wrote:

"Saint John preaches in a little wood. Like Christ speaking to the people, what dramatic truth of gesture! Actors should come to study these models; they would find precious lessons. The Pharisees have on their breast wide bands of material covered with inscriptions; on the breast, not in the heart."

Like the choir stalls, these panels are of the Renaissance period but are wholly Gothic in spirit and execution, and are thus of a piece with the building and not ornaments to it.

The Chapel of St Sebastien (1339) or the Chapel of the Pilier Vert. This chapel stands against the pillar straight ahead. It balances the chapel of Notre Dame de Pilier Rouge on the south side of the crossing. An 18th century painting of the Crucifixion in a gilt frame is surmounted by a statue of St Sebastien martyred by many arrows, and flanked by statues of Justice (right) and Peace (left), with cherubs above holding palm leaves. The painting has a statue either side: on the right, in armour with a sword on the left and the right hand gathering a cloak is Saint Louis; on the left is a statue of St Roch with dogs at his feet. These latter statues are attributed to the Duthoit brothers in 1832. A black marble balustrade screens this chapel which is the work of Nicolas Blasset (1635).

THE NORTH TRANSEPT

The east aisle of the transept has an arcade of three bays supporting a triforium above of two arches in each bay, each subdivided into three arches, and above which are six lancets in two groups of three, with trefoils in the tracery and a rose in the very top of the tracery. This is repeated in each of the three bays—exactly the same as in the south transept.

Amiens, West Facade

Amiens, the Martyrdom of St Firmin

Amiens, the North Rose

Amiens, Lady Chapel Altar

Amiens, Chapel of Notre Dame du Pilier Rouge

Beauvais, Martyrdom of St Vincent, St Vincent Chapel

Beauvais, Marissel Reredos, Chapel of St Leonard

Beauvais, The Visitation, 13th century south centre lancet, Axial Chapel

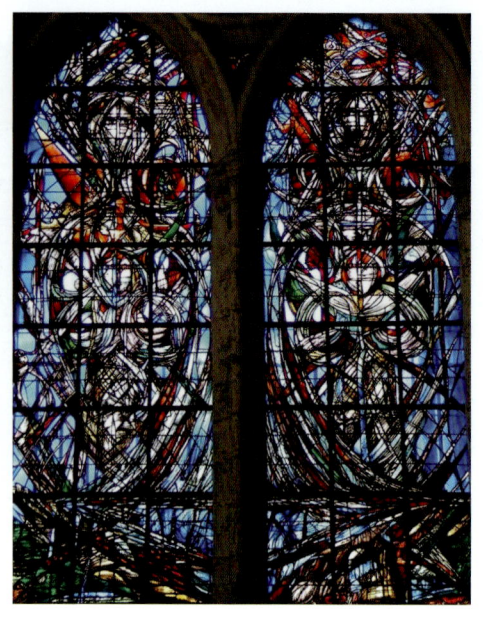

Beauvais, The Fountain of Life Window

Beauvais, The Crucifixion, Chapel of the Virgin

Albi Cathedral from the south-west

Albi, Last Judgement (detail)

Albi, Nave Vault Boss

Albi, Nave Vault (detail)

Albi, Rood Screen with St Cecilia

Albi, the Annunciation, south ambulatory

Albi, the decoration above the canons' stalls

Albi, the catafalque of St Cecilia, the Chapel of St Margaret

Amiens

The Chapel of St Peter (1291) or St John of the Vow (Du Vœu) (1668). Recalling a vow made during the last plague in 1668, the chapel opens westward from this east aisle of the transept. Until the Revolution John the Baptist was venerated here. It was redecorated in the 18th century. On the east wall there is a fine marble altar with plinths either side bearing to the north a statue of St Firmin the martyr and to the south St Francois de Sales, and in the centre a large marble bas-relief carving of Christ, an aureole behind his head, with his left arm around the cross and his right arm in blessing. Cherubs and the Virgin Mary, with St John kneeling, are all around. Above it is a classic pediment bearing a gilded bas-relief carving of angels and cherubs. It is quite an amazing piece of work. In the retable there is a reliquary with gilded cherubs either side of the grille. Behind the altarpiece are the tops of two blind lancets, above which is a small multifoil window glazed with clear diamond quarry glass but with little motifs in the cusps. In the north wall there are three lancets in clear rectangular quarry glass with little rosettes above in the tracery. Below there is a memorial to Monsignor Faure (1687).

The north wall of the transept has a central doorway with clear modern glass in the tympanum, and above that there is a large crucifix with statues either side. It could have come from the Rood screen. On either side of the doorway there are three blind arches at the lower level; on the west (left) side at ground level there is in the centre a carving of a priest holding a chalice while his feet rest on a grinning demon, and on the east (right) side there is a memorial to Petrus Sabatier, a Bishop of Amiens who died in 1733.

Above these blind arcades, two blind lancets with trefoil and quatrefoil tracery rise each side to just below the decorated foliage stringcourse, which runs right around the cathedral. At the level of the triforium there are five open arches in front of the passage which runs around the cathedral. Narrow lancets of coloured glass depicting figures can be seen in the east wall of the passage. A further ten lancets with coloured figures are above them in support of the rose. The North Rose is noted for its pentangle at the centre, from which radiates such intricate tracery. The Immaculate Virgin at the centre is the focus of the window, and she is surrounded by images such as the ivory Tower, the Ark of the Covenant, the Rose of Sharon, the lily and others from the Litany of Loreto, which was composed in the late 15th century. Each image is announced on banderoles. The Holy Trinity appears at the top, but the original glass can be seen in the lowest figures of St Peter and St Paul.

The west wall has two bays—the third is actually the north aisle—and the northern of these two has blind arcading at low level, interrupted by a wooden doorway, and above that two lancets with a rose above in clear diamond quarry glass. The next bay to the south has blind arcading at low level with some tablets on the wall between the columns. Above are four arches all with delicate canopies above with four polychrome scenes, similar to those we have seen in the south transept west

A Glimpse Of Glory

Basin, North Transept

wall. Here we see different parts of the Temple in Jerusalem: the Outer Court, the Tabernacle, and the Holy of Holies where the Ark of the Covenant was kept. The subject is Jesus driving out the moneychangers from the Temple.

Standing parallel with the north wall is a freestanding stone trough with a wooden cover. It is 12th century, and was possibly used for washing and laying out the dead. It stands on four decorated columns with a central column and a figure at each corner, all carved in marble.

The west aisle of the north transept is identical to the east wall except that in the clerestory, in the bay nearest the nave, there are fragments of coloured glass not making any pattern. The north wall of this west aisle has wooden panelling at ground level with two confessionals built into it, and above two wide lancets all with fragments of glass, some of which do make complete scenes.

THE NORTH AISLE

As in the south aisle, the chapels are all enclosed by 18th century wrought iron screens and give the impression of being largely neglected.

The Chapel of St Agnes and St Brigitte (1296) or St Firmin the Martyr (1871). At low level there is wooden panelling, which looks like marble, around a marble altar with a statue of St Firmin the martyr by Vimeux (1781) above it. It would be good if the statue was spotlighted. It is framed by two plain columns with scroll capitals and a pediment above that. On the east side there are two paintings (the first two Stations of the Cross) and, above the wooden panelling, blind arcading framing the back of the polychrome carved panels in the north transept. There is a painting of the Last Supper on the west wall (missing in 2012). The eastern half of the north window is blind and has painted lancets on it; the western half has four narrow lancets divided across the centre. The top three registers of the lower half has four figures in coloured glass and the rest is in clear diamond quarry glass, as are the four lancets above. Sadly, the chapel is dark and dreary.

Amiens

Adjoining the column which divides the chapel from the next is another work by Nicolas Blasset (1644), it is a single marble column on a marble plinth bearing a memorial, in the bottom of which is an alarming carving of a fractured skeleton – the allegorical figure of death – looking out as we pass by. It is a funerary monument of Jean de Sachy, the first échevin (Alderman) of Amiens who died in 1644 and his wife Marie de Revelois who died in 1662. The two are kneeling at the statue of the Vierge du Puy, which stands on the top of this column.

The Chapel of St Louis (1297–1302) or Notre Dame de la Paix 1767. Behind the altar in the north wall are six lancets divided across the middle, with trefoil tracery above, but all with diamond quarry glass. The statue behind the altar is of Our Lady of Peace (Notre Dame de la Paix) by Nicolas Blasset in 1654. Either side of the altar above the panelling are some bas-relief carvings of St Louis and St Francis Xavier and a painting which is the 3rd Station of the Cross. The chapel has the air of a forgotten Victorian parlour.

The Chapel of St Honoré (c.1300). This chapel was provided by the bakers of Amiens and has wooden panelling around the lower level. An altar stands before a central niche on the north wall containing a plaster statue of St Honoré by Vimeux (1780) and above that a sunburst. In the north wall there are six lancets with tracery above, divided horizontally midway, all in clear diamond quarry glass, which makes the chapel much brighter than its neighbours. The east and west walls are plain, except for a painting depicting the 4th Station of the Cross.

The Chapel of St Michel (1389), St Crépin dite St Sauve 1791. The altar statue has an immense

'Saint-Sauve'

279

A Glimpse Of Glory

12th century crucifix known as 'Saint-Sauve', the Christ with arms stretched out and wearing a simple robe tied in the middle and displaying the marks of the nails in feet and hands. Tradition has it that this figure of Christ bowed its head in the 13th century as the relic of St Honoré was carried past. Either side of the statue are little arches containing votives behind glass. A bas-relief either side represents St John the Evangelist (right) and St Nicholas (left). There used to be a painting of Christ appearing to Mary Magdalene dated 1849 on the east wall, but in 2004 it had been replaced by the 5th Station of the Cross depicting Simon of Cyrene carrying Christ's cross. The 6th Station depicting St Veronica is on the west wall. The windows are of the same arrangement as in the previous chapels, except that the top three registers of the bottom half of the lancets each have a scene in coloured glass. They are 14th century fragments depicting scenes from the life of St Luke. Candlelight abounds in this chapel.

The Chapel of St John the Evangelist (1375) Notre Dame de Bon-Secours in 1767. The bas-relief carving either side of the altar here depict St Peter and St John the Evangelist. The statue in the reredos is of a Virgin and Child dated 1632 standing on symbols of Hell (a serpent) and Death (a skeleton) expressing the conviction that neither will ever triumph over people of faith. It is by Nicolas Blasset. The windows are as in previous chapels: six lancets divided in the middle with trefoil tracery above, all in clear quarry diamond glass. There is a large painting on the east wall of the Baptism of Attile by St Firmin, by Lecurieux (1846). This chapel contains the 7th Station of the Cross. The woodwork is very tired and depressing.

The Chapel of St John the Baptist (1373) du Saveur ou de l'extreme onction 1769. The statue of our Saviour behind the altar is attributed to Nicholas Blasset 1654. The usual wooden panelling appears around the lower level, and there are two bas-relief carvings. The arrangement of the windows is exactly the same as before in clear diamond quarry glass; the only exception is that the tracery is rather more flamboyant than the previous chapels. It also contains the 8th Station of the Cross, and in 2012 a modern counselling chamber which deserves the scorn of the author.

AU REVOIR

On a visit in 2004 I was fortunate to join a congregation which filled the nave on a Sunday afternoon for the ordination of a priest. At the conclusion a procession made its way to the great west doors, which were opened wide for the occasion. The acolytes and thurifer led the way, with the fragrance of incense flooding the nave as they passed. They were followed by some children in white and a deacon bearing the Book of the Gospels. Behind him came a group of deacons and then a long file of priests. They went out into the sunlight, now full on the west front of

Amiens

Amiens from the Northwest Tower

the cathedral, and stood in a huge semicircle filling the parvis before the building, turning to face the west doors. The Bishop of Amiens and the new priest brought up the rear of the procession and came to a halt on the top step of the entrance facing the robed clergy below them. The applause was instantaneous. Then, as the young man moved to greet his friends, a young lady among them shook his hand before giving him a hug, and then she knelt before him and asked for his blessing; a traditional request to a new priest. But this priest placed his hands on the girl's head and then bowed his head until it was resting on his hands; so, although in the midst of a large crowd, this blessing was very private. I felt that the Beau Dieu would have smiled had it not been sculpted in stone.

As you leave the shelter of this fine, spacious building, reflect on the words of the sculptor Rodin, who clearly thought as I do:

"The artists of those days must have thought that in the passage of time, art would need to be brought back to truth. I do not intend to enumerate all these models, but only certain ones that have particularly held my attention. This angel lifting his head to show us the sky. These two personages in prayer. This bishop, so rich in colour, dusty, patined; with his admirable head! There is a little dog, surely the artist's dog. Nearby a man is praying within himself, without speaking; the gesture of prayer governs the beautiful folds of drapery, black only near the lower edge. The bishop lying on his

A Glimpse Of Glory

tomb still speaks, a very calm precept on his lips. This bas-relief is among the most beautiful things that exist; it has the wisdom of a Parthenon. A Virgin places her foot on a chameleon that has a human face, slimy: superb. The Angel appears to the Three Kings. Upon the large plane these figures naturally acquire an extreme majesty."

DO NOT MISS

1. Time to study the west façade.
2. The St Christopher statue on the south side.
3. The Golden Virgin (the 'Vierge Dorée') in the south transept.
4. The painted carved panels either side of the choir screen in the ambulatories.
5. The carving on the canon's stalls in the choir.
6. The polychrome carved panels in the transepts.
7. The labyrinth.
8. The free 'son et lumière' in front of the west façade each evening at dusk from mid-June to the end of September, and throughout December.

During the process of laser cleaning in the 1990s, it was discovered that the western façade of the cathedral was originally painted in rich colours. A technique was perfected to determine the exact colours as they were applied in the 13th century. Then, in conjunction with the laboratories of EDF (Electricity of France) and the expertise of the Society Skertzo, an ingenious process was carried out, consisting of a light projected through a translucent screen on which the original colours of the statues have been reproduced. Hence, these colours are projected directly on the façade with precision, recreating the polychromatic appearance of the 13th century. When projected on the statues around the portals, the result is a stunning display that brings the figures to life. It is worth staying overnight just to see this.

CHAPTER 10

BEAUVAIS

The Gallic capital of the Bellovaci, a Belgian tribe, Beauvais was destroyed by the Roman army when they built a fortified camp here. In the middle ages the city was rebuilt and defensive ramparts were constructed, which may be traced today by the boulevards which circle the city centre. In June 1940 Beauvais suffered badly from aerial bombardment, and the old mediaeval streets described by Helen Henderson in her book, 'Cathedrals of France', published by Methuen, 1929, have largely disappeared.

I usually stay in the Mercure Hotel, at 1 Avenue Montaigne, near junction 14 of Autoroute16 from Calais. It has secure car parking, and on the opposite side of the road to the hotel entrance is a bus stop served by a frequent service on Line 3 to the city centre (the Mairie) for less than €1.

THE CATHEDRAL CHURCH OF ST PETER (ST PIERRE)

Instead of the long nave of a great Gothic church, there is, at Beauvais, the remnant of the old Romanesque cathedral, known as the Cathedral of Notre Dame de la Basse Œuvre. It was here, in April 845, that the first Synod of Beauvais was held, when Abbot Hincmar of Compiegne was solemnly consecrated Archbishop of Reims. Building began on the present church of Notre Dame in the latter half of the 10th century and was completed at the beginning of the 11th century. The holy Saint Bernard preached here, and Pope Calixtus II visited the church in 1119, followed by Pope Innocent II in 1131.

In 1180, and again in 1225, the old cathedral was severely damaged by fire. Originally a much more substantial building, complete with a choir and apse, three bays were demolished in the 16th century to make room for the transepts of the new Gothic church, and a century later another section was demolished to allow the construction of a buttress to support the transept.

A Glimpse Of Glory

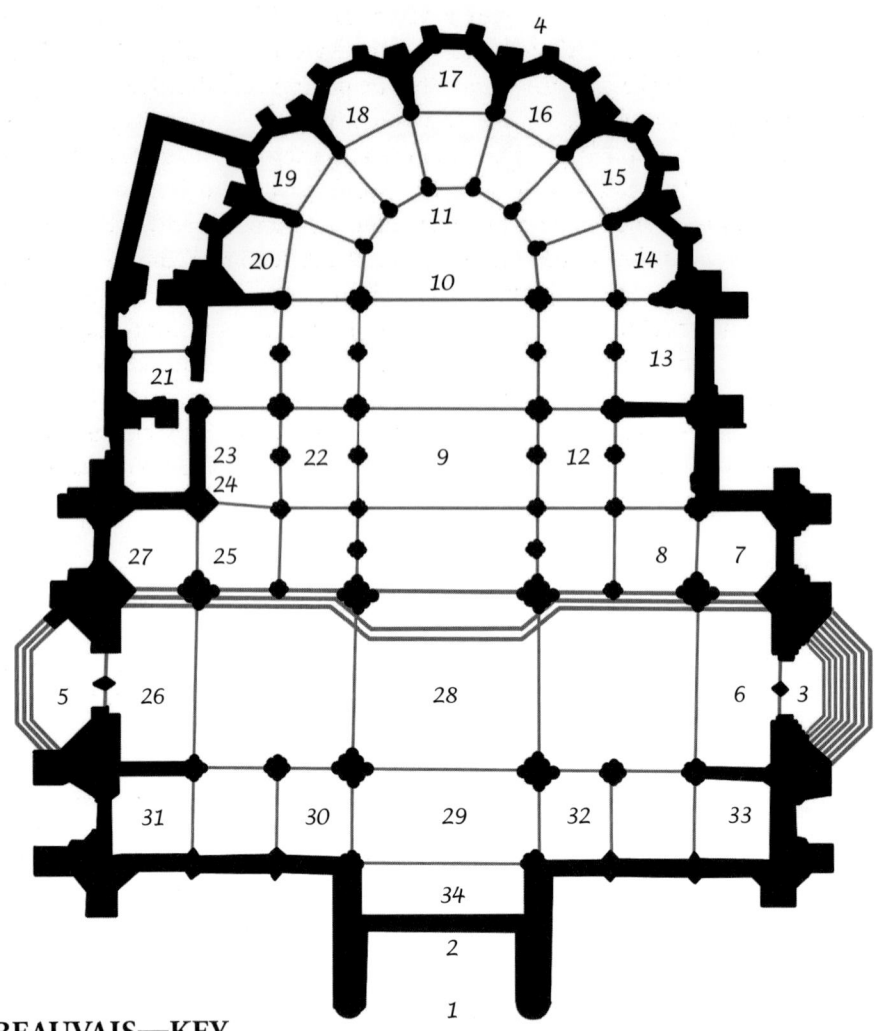

BEAUVAIS—KEY

1 The 'Basse Œuvre'
2 The West Façade
3 The South Façade
4 The Chevet
5 The North Façade
6 The South Transept
7 Chapel of St Cecilia
8 Chapel of St Angadrême
9 The Choir
10 The Sanctuary
11 The High Altar
12 The South Ambulatory
13 Chapel of St Leonard
14 Chapel of St Denis
15 Chapel of St Vincent
16 Chapel of St Joseph
17 Axial Chapel of Notre Dame
18 Chapel of St Anne
19 Chapel of Ss Lucien & Senastian
20 Chapel of St Joan of Arc
21 The Sacristy
22 The North Ambulatory
23 The 14th century Carillon Clock
24 'Ecce Homo' statue and Pietà
25 The Astronomical Clock
26 The North Transept
27 Chapel of the Holy Sepulchre
28 The Crossing
29 The Nave
30 The North Aisle
31 Chapel of the Sacred Heart
32 The South Aisle
33 Chapel of the Dead
34 The Great Organ

Beauvais

At the beginning of the 13th century the bishop, Milon de Nanteuil, was an ambitious man and was stirred by the great cathedrals being built at Reims, Laon, Paris, Bourges and Amiens, to the extent that he planned a building which would surpass these other cathedrals in size and scale. In 1225, Amiens was five years into its construction, and Helen Henderson relates the story that the architect of Amiens, Robert de Luzarches, drew up a plan for Beauvais which followed closely that of Amiens. But Beauvais was a much smaller city than Amiens, and its people were not wealthy, and the church did not possess a relic to rival the head of John the Baptist, which drew pilgrims from all over Europe to the shrine at Amiens. So the cathedral builders at Beauvais were always short of cash. Ambition and poverty constitute a recipe for disaster. While at Amiens the masons started to build the cathedral at the nave, at Beauvais they began with the choir. This enabled Luzarches to improve the choir at Amiens after the experiences suffered at Beauvais. In spite of the link with its near-neighbour, I see more of Bourges than Amiens in the cathedral at Beauvais.

Work began in 1238 with the choir aisles and the chevet, and after the appointment of Bishop William of Grez in 1249, the triforium and clerestory reflected the more delicate advance in Gothic design, and five metres extra height was added to the original plan. In addition, the architect was among the first to accept a glazed triforium. The entire choir was finished by 1272, when the first service was held.

Canonical joy was, however, short-lived, for in 1284 part of the vault above the choir bays collapsed, and the cathedral was abandoned while the bishop, architect and clergy planned the way forward, and money was collected to fund the work. By 1322 the repairs were completed under the master mason Guillaume de Roye, who constructed flying buttresses to transmit the stress of the high vault.

With only the choir completed at the end of the 14th century, the Hundred Years War and epidemics put paid to any further work, until, in 1499, the decision was made to build the transepts and nave, and Martin Chambiges of Sens, who was at that time working in Paris, was engaged to undertake the new work. The foundation stone for the south transept was laid in 1500 followed by that in the north transept ten years later. In 1537 the stained glass windows were fitted in the north transept and the entire transept was completed by 1540 thanks largely to the generosity of King François I when other charity had cooled; it was another ten years before the south transept was finished. Chambiges was in great demand and the canons of Troyes were desperate for him to finish his work there, but Beauvais refused to release him from the tight contract they had forced on him. They also refused to allow his son, Pierre, to assist him, but when his deputy, Jean Vast, died in 1524, and was interred in the chapel of St Peter and St Paul (now called The Chapel of the Dead) in the first bay of the nave, he was permitted to employ his son Jean to assist him.

A Glimpse Of Glory

The cathedral authorities then embarked on an exercise in hope over experience, for instead of proceeding with the planned nave, the new architect, Michel Lalye, persuaded them to build first a stone tower over the crossing and to surmount it with a fleche (spire) of oak. When it was completed in 1569 it reached 492 feet above the paving of the cathedral, which made the Cathedral Church of St Peter, Beauvais, the tallest church in Christendom, even higher than St Peter's in Rome, where Michelangelo was completing the enormous dome over the basilica.

But pride comes before a fall, and on 30th April, Ascension Day, 1573, the great tower collapsed, crashing through the transept vaults. There had been an early celebration of the Mass, and the clergy and congregation had just left by the south door preparing for a procession along Rue St Pierre, when the two western columns gave way without warning; a third tottered, leaving all the weight on the fourth, which simply crumpled as the fleche crashed down into the church, destroying the vaults as it fell. These were repaired and the crossing was given a wooden roof to reduce the weight, but the tower was not rebuilt. It was 1604 before the vault was in place over the first bay of the nave, but the following year the west end of the cathedral was closed with a provisional palisade of brick and slate, which became permanent.

During the Revolution the church lost its cathedral status together with its treasures, relics and gold and silver ornaments, and it was only in 1822, following the Concordat between church and state, that it became once again the Cathedral Church of St Peter.

THE EXTERIOR

THE WEST FAÇADE

Arriving in the Rue St Pierre it is difficult not to stop at once at the exquisite south façade, but to make sense of this building one must walk directly to view the west end. It might have struck you as odd as you walked towards the cathedral that there was no sign of any western tower, the hallmark of a Gothic cathedral, rising above the skyline. When standing near the twin towers of the old Bishop's Palace and looking at the west end of the cathedral the reason for that becomes clear: there is no nave.

Although I knew that the cathedral lacked a nave, it is still shocking to see the west end resembling a shored-up London tenement after the war. But exercise the imagination: if the designer/mason Martin Chambiges had been given the opportunity to construct a western façade in harmony with his transept façades we would be viewing a monument of fabulous grandeur. As it is, we can only marvel

Beauvais

The West Façade

at the folly of the bygone age which declined to build a nave in order to spend the money instead on a tower with a spire. Yet despite its imperfection, a visit to this cathedral is always a thrilling experience.

THE SOUTH FAÇADE

Having grasped the enormity of the failure to complete the cathedral as planned, let us enjoy and exult in what we have before us today, and retrace our steps to the south façade.

Fourteen steps ascend to the south portal containing two huge wooden doors divided by an empty trumeau. These doors are the original 16th century work

St. Peter Healing a Lame Man (South Door)

A Glimpse Of Glory

The conversion of St. Paul (South Door)

of woodcarver Jean Le Pot, and the panels on the left door depict St Peter healing a lame man at the temple gate in Jerusalem (Acts of the Apostles, chapter 3, verses 1 – 10), and on the right hand door the conversion of St Paul near Damascus (Acts of the Apostles chapter 9). They have endured mutilation over the years, but a salamander, the emblem of King François I, can still be seen.

Above the doors is a high, pointed tympanum, with carved brackets and canopies, but empty of statues. The same is true of the four orders in the archivolt and in the splays of the portal. A delicate crocketted gable rises above the arch of the portal. In the centre are three exquisite niches with a common base and three canopies above, the middle of which rises to the top of the gable and has another small niche either side. Either side is another small niche. This grand gable terminates in a finial at the gallery below the rose. This gallery has five Flamboyant arches, each subdivided into two to present ten small arches which mirror the lancet windows behind them. Along the top of the gallery is a row of stone decoration which resembles flames. Then there is the marvellous rose window, full of stone mouchettes, while the centre looks very much like a crown of thorns. Between the top of the rose and the pointed arch there is an arc of yet more mouchettes. The spandrels formed between this arch and the stringcourse above it, are filled with blind lancets. The upper gable has a decorative balustrade along the base, above which are more blind lancets decorated with finely carved canopies for long-lost statues.

This central section of the façade is supported on each side by a buttress disguised as a turret, for they each contain a staircase. These, too, are decorated with brackets and canopies which once contained statues. As they rise higher they diminish in circumference, culminating at the level of the summit of the roof in highly decorative little covered galleries, but every piece of stone plays a significant part in the downward thrust of the buttress.

To the east of the central section is a part of the original 1225 construction; the south window of the St Cecilia Chapel is surmounted by an open arcade with a pierced parapet along its top, behind which is a passage, and above that a wheel-rose. This wall is capped with a decorative frieze at a lower level to the corresponding bay to the west of the portal. The western bay has a window of two lancets with tracery at the lower level, above which a gable rises from a decorative arch to pierce a frieze of fleurs-de-lys at triforium level. The blank wall above is topped with a decorated wall at the same height as the gallery beneath the great rose window in the central bay.

Finally, at each end of the façade a substantial buttress rises to the height of the roof; that on the east side bearing the thrust of four flying buttresses, and that on the west two such buttresses.

Continue along the exterior to the east and view the chevet as it turns around the choir and ambulatory chapels.

THE CHEVET

The first two bays east of the south façade along the south side of the choir are supported by buttresses which resemble enormous walls of stone, decorated with tall blind lancets. There is the whiff of panic at the enormous size of them. The eastern of the two bays has four such lancets at its lower levels, and a small turret. This contains a stairway which provides access, via a bridge, to the exterior passage which circles the chevet at the level of the triforium behind a pierced balustrade over a decorated corbel table. Above the little bridge, three flying buttresses support the thrust at various levels of the high choir wall.

The remaining bays of the chevet each have the support of flying buttresses which spring from intermediate, freestanding buttresses. These, in turn, pass the outward thrust through shorter flying buttresses to the sturdy stone mass of the outer buttresses. These extend above the roof of the edifice and are decorated with three blind lancets; the extra height, the gargoyles, crockets and elegant gables at the top from which rise finials all serve to increase the downward thrust to the foundations. Another pierced balustrade encircles the chevet roof. At ground level, the radiating chapels have in addition two extra buttresses in each bay, which terminate at the decorated roofline of the chapels. It is

The Chevet

A Glimpse Of Glory

North Façade

a feast of Gothic architecture, yet the overall effect is of a forest of stone, which almost obscures the delicate nature of the building within.

THE NORTH FAÇADE

The north façade is very similar to the south façade with a high, pointed tympanum, a delicate crocketted gable rising above the arch of the portal to terminate in a finial at the gallery below the rose.

During a visit in 2012, an Hungarian architect who had spent most of his professional life in London engaged me in conversation in the north transept. We talked about the glass in the radiating chapels, and as it was time for the cathedral to close for the night we left through the north door. When he looked up at the north façade he was totally enraptured by the carved tree in the tympanum; he enthused about its unique beauty. He told his wife that they must stay overnight in Beauvais, for he wanted more time to study this façade.

The genealogical tree in the tympanum reminds us that the north transept was completed only with King François I's generous donations of money from the sale of salt from his reserves in Languedoc and Normandy. The branches of the tree are entwined around the emblems of this Prince and the House of Valois: the initial 'F', the salamander (his device), the fleurs-de-lys under the crown of France, together with dolphins and ermines.

It is time we explored the interior of this building, and I prefer to walk around the west end to enter through the south door, but you might prefer to enter via the north door and cross the transepts to the south side.

Tympanum, North Portal

THE INTERIOR

One enters the cathedral by the South Transept door and at once is confronted by the exquisite North Transept. In a glance one takes in the beauty of the vista and the enormous wooden buttresses keeping the edifice intact, before the eye is drawn irresistibly to the breathtaking loftiness of the Choir.

THE SOUTH TRANSEPT

The East Wall of the Transept. The high arches of two southern bays give access to the two chapels, while the northern arch covers the entrance to the south ambulatory. The south bay has a blind wall above the arch, but the other two bays each have a blind arcade in the triforium, above which is a clerestory of four narrow lancets, each of which is divided in the middle by ogee arches.

The Chapel of St Cecilia occupies the southeast corner of the transept.

Internal Buttress

A Glimpse Of Glory

Chapel of St. Cecilia

A free-standing marble font stands before the altar. Against the east wall of the chapel is a marble altar decorated on the front with a Maltese cross, and on the wall behind it there are some lovely fresco paintings. These three gothic frescoes are vibrant 16th century work. The four lancets above are filled with modern geometric designs, and with little trefoils and quatrefoils in the tracery. Above that is a triforium of five columns protecting a passage, above which a rose fills the vault. In the south wall of the chapel there are two lancets with modern glass with a multifoil and mouchettes in the tracery. It represents the Fountain of Life and is by Claude Courageux, dated 1981. The triforium returns along the south wall with five pillars protecting the passage, and above it a rose, following the pattern of the east wall.

The Chapel of St Angadrême (also called St Nicholas), occupies the central bay of the east wall of the transept (under restoration in 2012).

A statue of St Angadrême is on the second pillar of the south ambulatory, facing the chapel. There she stands, a 16th Century Abbess, painted in polychrome. She is reading a book held in her left hand with a crozier in her right hand. The window in the south wall has three lancets with three trefoils above, and a rose above that with tiny trefoils. It is filled with fine modern glass.

The West Wall of the Transept. The wall of the south bay is blind from floor to the vault, the only relief being a painting of the Annunciation on the lower wall. The windows in the other two bays of this wall each have four lancets in the triforium, and the clerestory also has four lancets at two levels; they appear to be continuous long lancets, as there is no passage and they are divided only by a string course decorated with carvings of small animals.

The South Wall of the Transept. At the lower level, in the centre of the south wall there is a portal containing two modern doors in a wooden frame which has gothic arches glazed in diamond quarry glass. On either side are three very slender blind arches with a doorway in the western one beneath a canopy decorated with a crocketted ogee arch and finials. The east side of the south wall of the transept is similar to the west side except that the door under the ogee arch is reached by five steps.

The South Rose is high under the vault. The theme is creation, and in the centre is the figure of God the Father, while the mouchettes which surround him are teeming with all manner of living creatures. Immediately above the centre can be seen the Sun, the Moon and the stars. Lower down can be seen images from the history of the Jewish people: the Tower of Babel and Noah's Ark. In his book, 'The Rose Window', published by Thames and Hudson in 2005, Painton Cowen suggests [page 148] that it can be considered as the masterpiece of the designer mason Martin Chambiges. He was born in Paris around 1460 and was soon the most famous mason of his day in France for his Flamboyant façades, commanding fees well in excess of other masons. The canons at Troyes referred to Chambiges as the 'Supremus Artifex', and in addition to the cathedral at Troyes, his work can also be seen in Sens and Senlis. His earliest rose was the south rose at Sens in 1494. He hardly ever varied his designs, and in the north rose at Sens the figures to the right mirror those to the left. This was of great benefit to the glaziers, who were often overwhelmed by the scale of Chambiges' designs, as it reduced the number of cartoons which had to be drawn. Yet, for all his popularity, his style did not survive his death in Beauvais in 1532.

Ten Prophets, South Transept Window

A Glimpse Of Glory

Doctors and Evangelists (detail), South Transept Window

The rose is supported by ten lancets depicting Jewish prophets; from the left are David, Isaiah, Jeremiah, Ezekiel, Daniel, Hosea, Micah, Zechariah and Amos, who holds the scroll bearing the date of the window—1551. The glass is by the glazier Nicolas le Prince. Below the prophets, there is another gallery of ten figures depicting four doctors of the church and the four evangelists, flanked by St Peter and St Paul, each in a little lancet with tracery above.

Crossing Vault

In the middle of the transept, on a large plinth near the doors, is a copy of an enthroned St Peter; the original can be found in St Peter's Basilica in Rome.

Stand under the wooden vault of the crossing, and look up at the high vault. Near the boss in the centre of the sexpartite vault over the first bay of the choir the date "1575" is inscribed; near the boss in the south transept vault is the date "1577" near the north transept boss is the date "1578". These dates relate to the rebuilding of the vaults following the disastrous collapse of the central tower in 1573.

THE CHOIR AND SANCTUARY

An arcade of narrow bays forms the choir and the sanctuary. Each pier has clustered columns which rise to the decorated capitals. It was not always so. Following the collapse of the high vault in 1284, the master mason, Guillaume de Roye, raised the alternate piers in the choir, doubling the number bearing the weight, all of which detracted from the original concept of great height on slender support. These additional piers are those where the outermost column rises without a capital or any decoration right up to the top of the clerestory to support the additional webs of sexpartite vaulting of the roof, restoring an impression of verticality which emphasises the extreme height of this choir; at 48.5 metres it is said to be the highest in the world. There is clear evidence that the bays either side of the choir were subdivided: examine the top of the arches and notice traces in the stonework of the wider arch which once embraced a pair of the present bays.

South Side of the Choir

In each bay the triforium is divided into two arches, each of which is subdivided by little collonettes, protecting the circulating passage. Behind the passage are four small coloured lancets. As you gaze up, consider the fact that on Christmas Day in mediaeval Beauvais choir boys sang the "Gloria in excelsis" from this lofty triforium.

The clerestory has in each bay three very tall, narrow lancets, with a multifoil and quatrefoils in the tracery above. The central registers of each of the clerestory windows are glazed in coloured canopied figures, forming a kind of coloured frieze around the entire clerestory. The registers above and below have clear geometric patterns in them, although on the south side some bays have coloured glass in the lower registers.

A Glimpse Of Glory

Choir, Southeast Clerestory Window (detail)

There are two rows of canons' stalls on either side. They were brought here from the Abbey of St Paul (now the Préfecture) in 1801 to replace the ancient stalls which had long disappeared. On the north side of the choir in the third bay from the west, is the choir organ.

The choir is surrounded by a wrought iron screen; on the gateway and around the sanctuary it is beautifully gilded. The sanctuary has a polychrome marble altar (1758) decorated with gilded bronzes, and above and behind it, between the pillars, there is a towering Rococo sculpture in plaster by Nicolas Sebastien Adam (1705–1778) of the seated Virgin holding the infant Christ, who is standing on a globe while stabbing a serpent with a lance in the shape of a cross. All around stand these massive columns supporting the lofty clerestory.

Choir Vault

THE SOUTH AMBULATORY

The lustre of the view from the west end of the cathedral is partly due to the coloured triforium windows of the ambulatory. The height of the inner ambulatory permits the provision of another passage behind an arcade of six open arches in the triforium, above which are two arches supporting a multifoil with mouchettes, the whole in glorious coloured modern glass looking out over the roofs of the outer choir aisles and chapels, but there appears to be a tribune chamber beyond the passage, which could give access to the void above the chapel vaults.

Beauvais

The piers of the ambulatory are massive with a cluster of engaged columns rising to support the high vault of the ambulatory. The arches are narrow and sharply pointed at the top.

The first two western bays of the south ambulatory are in fact the north side of the transept chapel and are covered by a quadripartite vault. The remaining vaults are sexpartite, each covering two bays. There are four bays before the apse, in the fifth bay are highly decorated and gilded black wrought iron gates giving access to the choir and sanctuary. All the chapels are enclosed by low wrought-iron screens.

The Chapel of St Leonard (also called St Vincent de Paul). The carved reredos over the altar against the east wall was made in the 16th century for the Marissel church and was brought here in 1966. It illustrates in two registers scenes of the Passion and the Resurrection of Christ: from the left the arrest of Christ, the trial, the deposition, the entombment and the resurrection. In the centre above is the crucifixion. On the base of the reredos, Jesus can be seen with his twelve Apostles at the last supper. There were two side panels depicting scenes of the Passion and the life of the Virgin, which have been lost.

The Chapel of St. Leonard

The south wall has a window of four lancets, quite beautifully done, with the tracery of each group of two lancets having a quatrefoil at the top supporting a large multifoil. The two figures in the window represent the two canons who donated it. It is contemporary glass but contains fragments of 14th Century glass and it is by Jeanette Weiss Gruber.

A Glimpse Of Glory

Apart from two paintings, the west wall is quite blank. The chapel floor is covered with decorative tiles, but the steps up to the chapel are constructed of old tomb stones.

The Chapel of St Denis. This is the first of the radial chapels in the polygonal apse. The chapel has five bays, with two lancets with multifoils above, glazed in modern glass, in the southern and the southeastern bays, while the two bays to the right and the outermost bay on the left are decorated with blind lancets and a rose. In the southwest wall is a double piscina with a cupboard to the side of it. All the radiating chapels of this ambulatory have an altar against the south wall. In this chapel the altar has a statue above it of St Vincent de Paul holding the hand of a child and offering a loaf. The consecration stone has been removed from the altar.

The Chapel of St Vincent (also called Notre Dame de Lourdes) is very light and airy. There is a similar arrangement of five bays in this chapel: the three centre windows have two lancets in each, with multifoils above. The outermost bays are decorated with blind lancets and a blind multifoil above; at lower level the walls are painted, as are the blind lancets.

The left hand window has 14th century glass depicting the Martyrdom of St Vincent: on the left St Vincent is martyred on a gridiron, while on the right his body is thrown to the savage beast, but a miracle happens and he isn't killed.

The centre window, from the beginning of the 14th Century depicts on the left St John the Theologian on the island of Patmos writing to the churches of Asia Minor. On the right is the crucifixion; the rose at the top depicts the coronation of the Virgin, with the symbols of the four Evangelists.

The window on the right is 13th century. The lancet on the right depicts the Crucifixion of St Peter, and on the left St Peter walks on the water. The bishop who donated this window, Raoul de Senlis, is represented at the bottom left. In each lateral multifoil is an angel swinging a censer. The painted murals and oil paintings are 19th century.

The steps at the entrance to the Chapel are once more made of old tomb stones, including that of Bishop Raoul.

The Chapel of St Joseph (also called St Stephen) has the same arrangement: five bays, that in the centre with three windows, each containing two lancets with very fine modern coloured glass medallions by Louis Barillet, depicting the childhood of Christ, with a multifoil above. The outer bays have two blind lancets with rose above. The walls are painted in decorative designs. The altar itself has six little colonnettes framing five arches. The retable has four quatrefoils, two either side of the tabernacle, above which is a statue of St Joseph with the infant Christ in his arms.

The inner wall of the ambulatory is screened with a high stone wall. There is a painting of the martyred St Sebastian facing the Chapel of St Joseph.

The Axial Chapel of Notre Dame has 13th century glass in three windows, each with two lancets.

In the centre window, the right hand lancet has much yellow glass, depicting scenes from the Nativity of Christ: the annunciation by the angel can be seen in the bottom diamond, rising through the Visitation and Birth of Christ to the three Wise Men and the Flight into Egypt at the top. The left lancet depicts the Tree of Jesse, the Ascension, and the Crucifixion in the rose window above the lancets.

The two lancets in the northeast window each contain seven medallions superimposed on scenes from the life of a Saint-Bishop, thought to be St Martin.

The southeast window has four cartouches in each of the lights, with a rose above, all depicting the Miracle of Theophilus. This popular mediaeval legend was told by one Fulbert of Chartres, and concerns a deacon in Sicily in the year 537 AD who was dismissed unfairly by the bishop from his office of Diocesan Administrator. In despair he sold his soul to the Devil; in a pact signed in his own blood he repudiated Christ and his Mother, and the Devil arranged for him to be reinstated. In time the man came to his senses and implored the holy Virgin to help him. She appeared to him and made him renounce the Devil and confess his faith in Christ, and in token of his forgiveness, she appeared to him again and returned to him the scroll he had given to the Devil as a sign that he was now a free man. The modern glass in the rose above depicts the Virgin fighting with the Devil for the poor man's soul.

The outermost bays are blind, decorated with two blind lancets and a multifoil above. Claudius Lavergne, a pupil of Ingres, restored the chapel between 1856 and 1858 and included the neo-Gothic altar. I find the altar is rather dark and dreary with four clustered columns supporting it, though the four little scenes of the life of the Virgin (the Annunciation, the Nativity, Deposition from the Cross, and Our Lord blessing his mother) painted on the wood of the retable at the back of the altar are rather fine. There is a reliquary containing some bones on the northeast wall. A little double piscina, filled with flowers during my last visit in 2012, occupies a space in the southeast wall, with a reliquary above it.

The chapel windows on either side of the axial chapel have modern glass, but they do reflect very closely the mediaeval glass in the axial chapel itself and attempt to maintain the pattern of colours as faithfully as possible.

A Glimpse Of Glory

THE NORTH AMBULATORY

The Chapel of St Anne (also called St John the Evangelist) has the same arrangement of bays and windows as the chapels in the south ambulatory. The lower level is painted, and traces of mural paintings from the 14th and 15th centuries can be seen. The neo-gothic stone altar stands on four little collonettes with three rosettes in between the arches thus formed. The retable has a bas-relief and tabernacle in the centre, with St Anne with her infant daughter Mary. There is a double piscina on the southeast wall and three windows, each containing two lancets. The windows contain contemporary glass by Jacques le Chevallier depicting the life of St Anne, with a multifoil above. Again, as in the other chapels, the two outermost walls have two blind lancets with tracery at the top. The floor of the chapel his very fine modern tiles, probably 19th century.

The Chapel of St Lucien and St Sebastian has the same general arrangement of three lights of modern glass, each of two lancets and a multifoil above; the eastern and western windows each have two lancets and a blind multifoil. The windows are by Louis Barillet, and depict scenes from the life of St Lucien (or Lucian), who was martyred during the Christian persecution in c 290 AD. At Beauvais, he had acquired fame for his mortifications and penances. He preached against the Roman gods and lived in a house that is considered to be the place now occupied by the collegiate church of Saint-Nicolas. Denis and Rieul visited him here. According to Rolandus, the author of the Acta Sancti Luciani, he retired to a mountain near the city, living as a hermit on grass and water. The legend relates that the assassins Latinus, Jarius and Antor were sent by the Roman Emperor to kill him. They killed his disciples first and then beat Lucian with rods, and finally beheaded him. The legend states that after Lucian was decapitated, he picked up his own head and walked towards Beauvais. Having crossed the river Thérain, Lucian stopped at the entrance to Beauvais, and died there, thus indicating that he wanted to be buried on that very spot. He is certainly regarded as the founder of the diocese.

The stone altar is supported on four colonnettes and has three quatrefoils carved on the front. The statue, dated 1884, is of St Lucien, the first Bishop of Beauvais, wearing his mitre; his left hand once grasped a crozier, which is now missing. His right hand is raised in the act of blessing. There is a double piscina in the northeast wall and the walls of the blind arcades are painted with geometric shapes, but they are in a very poor condition. On the northeast wall is a painting (1782) by the famed artist Mauperin depicting the Supper at Emmaus (St Luke, chapter 24).

The Chapel of St Joan of Arc (also called the Chapel of St Mary Magdalene), like the other chapels, is constructed of five bays; the two western bays and the eastern bay have two blind lancets with tracery above. The north window, and the northeastern window are glazed and they each have two lancets, divided by a central mullion, with a multifoil above, all in modern coloured glass. Below the northern window is a bas relief sculpture and standing before it is St Joan of Arc looking down at a kneeling priest. She is depicted holding the Oriflamme, the battle standard of the King of France.

At this point the ambulatory doubles in width to the north of bays 1, 2 & 3, under a quadripartite vault at the same height as the vaults of the radiating chapels. On the north wall of these two bays there are two blind windows in one arch, but the tracery has coloured glass.

Bay 3. On the west side of the bay is the Sacristy door, and on the east wall there are four blind lancets with tracery. On a plinth is a statue of St Thérèse of Lisieux. Behind her is a double niche containing a double piscina, but it is obscured by the plinth.

14th Century Carillon Clock

Bays 1 & 2 continue west along the north ambulatory, but the two tall arches dividing the northern bays from the ambulatory are completely filled with wooden bracing. On the north wall, next to a little doorway, is a small tower with a decorated canopy above, which looks like the top of a gothic tower, on top of which is the 14th century Carillon Clock, said to be the oldest of its kind in working order in the world. The little tower contains the weights of the mechanism, which is accessed by way of the doorway which leads to the staircase going up to the clock. The dial displays the lunar cycle. The clock was the gift of Canon Etienne Musique who died in 1323. On the top is a little wooden bell-tower holding the oldest clock bell in France.

It is an interesting little corner. A fascinating, lovely little wall with the label-stops of the arches which decorate the tower, and the corbels, carved with wooden imps or little children, with a grizzly old man to the west, and to the east a little imp hanging on for dear life. The pinkish stone shows remains of mediaeval paint.

A Glimpse Of Glory

Beneath the staircase to the clock, there is the marble monument of Cardinal Toussaint de Forbin-Janson, Bishop of Beauvais, who died in 1713. He is holding a cardinal's biretta in his right hand. The monument originally stood in the choir, but was thrown out of the cathedral during the Revolution and has stood here since 1804.

Beneath the clock tower, under a wooden canopy, stands a polychrome figure of Ecce Homo (1880). On a pillar dividing these last two bays is a small wooden Pietà. Above are the instruments of the Passion.

Pietà and Ecce Homo

The huge Astronomical Clock fills the final bay of the north ambulatory. The clock, which is an imitation of the cathedral clock in Strasbourg, was finished in 1868 by a Beauvais clockmaker, Auguste-Lucien Vérité, and installed here in 1876. It presents fifty figures and displays the movement of the planets and the lunar cycles, in addition to the hours.

THE NORTH TRANSEPT

The east wall of the transept has three bays, each with three tall open arches rising to the triforium. Above this arch, the north bay is blind to the vault. The other two bays have a blind triforium containing two arches divided by a mullion, each subdivided into two smaller arches which are cusped. The clerestory in each bay has four lancets divided by a crossover arch in the centre with tracery at the top.

The east aisle has two southern bays which give access to the North Ambulatory. The triforium returns north in the central bay, the open arcade of narrow lancets bearing two open arches with a multifoil above, providing evidence of a tribune chamber beyond it.

The Chapel of the Holy Sepulchre in the northern bay of this east aisle now houses the mechanism of the large astronomical clock. This bay is enclosed by a wooden screen.

Beauvais

The North Rose and the Wise and Foolish Virgins (detail)

The east wall of this chapel appears to have one blind arch with a rose at the top under a quadripartite vault. The window in the north wall of the aisle has a double lancet with a multifoil, all in clear quarry glass. Above them, the triforium arcading returns along the north wall of the aisle and above it is a rose window with coloured glass.

The north wall of the transept is similar to the south wall of the south transept. At ground level there are three blind arches on the left, one with an eccentric doorway, and canopies above, and these arches are repeated to the east of the north portal. There is a large painting above the portal depicting Christ Healing the Sick, which some attribute to the artist Jean Jouvenet.

The Rose, which was installed in 1538, depicts scenes of the Last Judgement, and is supported by two galleries of ten lancets, as in the south transept. The lower gallery depicts the Wise and Foolish Virgins in five groups of two, while the higher gallery, which supports the rose, depicts ten Sybils. While the Sybil gallery escaped damage, the painter-glazier Max Ingrand remade parts of the great rose and the figures in the Virgins' gallery in 1958, following the destruction caused in the Second World War.

The west wall of the transept has a blind northern bay from floor to vault without any decoration. The remaining two bays each have four lancets in the triforium, and in the clerestory

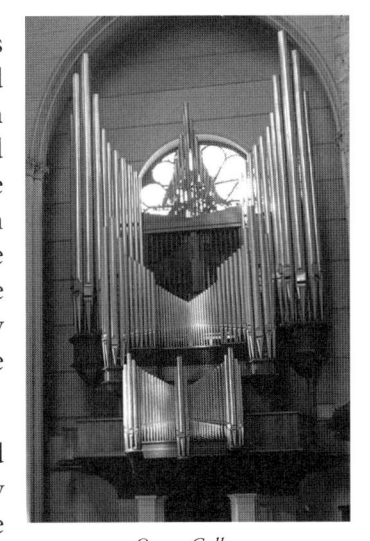

Organ Gallery

303

four tall lancets, each divided in the middle by a crossover arch. All the glass has geometric designs.

THE NAVE

The Nave has only one bay, which is covered by a quadripartite vault, with chapels to north and south. The pulpit stands on the northwest pier of the crossing.

The great organ occupies a recess in the west wall and the pipes rise in ranks, partly obstructing the window. It is one of the ten largest in France. During the bombardment of 6th, 7th and 8th June 1940 that devastated Beauvais, a few bombs fell on the cathedral and one of them completely destroyed the great organ. The inauguration of the new organ took place Sunday, May 20th 1979, with the international concert organist Pierre Cochereau, and two hundred singers in the presence of a crowd of six thousand enthusiastic people, after almost forty years of silence. Above the organ arch the west wall is blind to the vault, with the exception of a small eight-light window divided into two levels of four.

Both the north and south walls of the nave have a much lower arch than those found in the choir, and mirror the west wall of the transept in that above the arch is a triforium of four cusped lancets. The clerestory has four very tall lancets, each one divided in the middle. Here, too, the glass has geometric designs in it.

THE NORTH AISLE

There is a double aisle forming a continuation of the north ambulatory, each aisle under a quadripartite vault, and open to the two southern bays of the north transept. The west wall, which terminates the nave and its aisles, has a modern door in each aisle and a modern window above in diamond quarry glass.

The Chapel of the Sacred Heart (also called the Chapel of St Barbara) extends to the north of this aisle and is enclosed by a low screen. There is a window of two lancets in coloured glass, each having a canopy in the tracery forming a rather 'twee' heart at the top.

Chapel of the Sacred Heart

Beneath these two lancets is an altar with a tabernacle. The painting in the reredos is framed by fluted Ionic columns supporting a Baroque niche containing a statue of Christ revealing his sacred heart. Either side of the columns is a panel bearing a classical emblem. The entire 18th century structure is in painted and gilded wood, and was bought from the church of St Laurent in 1803.

The west wall of the chapel is painted at the lower level in a marble effect, and above is a window containing three lancets with tracery. The glass in the lancets is by Engrand le Prince, and dates drom1522. The scene depicts the two donors with their patron saints—Louis de Roncherolles with St Louis at the bottom left, and Françoise d'Halluin with St Francis of Assisi at the bottom right. They frame a Pietà, and at the top left is St Hubert with the stag, and to the right is St Christopher, framing a scene of a Crucifixion.

The east wall of the chapel has a painted marble effect at the lower level, above which are painted three lancets with tracery.

The chapel is covered with a delightful lierne vault.

THE SOUTH AISLE

This aisle mirrors the north aisle with its continuity of the double aisles of the south ambulatory, and its two quadripartite vaults. The west wall of the inner aisle has a modern window of four lights in clear diamond quarry glass above a huge memorial, which fills the lower wall of this aisle, dedicated to the dead of the First World War. The west wall of the outer aisle also has a modern window of four lights in clear diamond quarry glass. Below the window is a painting above a memorial plaque to the million dead of the British Empire in the First World War, "of whom the greater part rest in France".

The Chapel of the Dead (formerly called the Chapel of St Peter and St Paul) is enclosed by a low stone balustrade. The lower walls are painted black, and an altar dated c.1830 in black marble, stands against the south wall. The reredos has a painting of the 'Descent from the Cross' which is mentioned in a description of the cathedral

Chapel of the Dead

A Glimpse Of Glory

in 1685. It was painted by Charles de la Fosse (1636–1716), and it is framed by two black marble fluted Ionic columns each side, and a classical pediment above. These columns and the painting came from the rood screen erected in 1680 to replace the rood of 1571, but which was destroyed in 1793 during the Revolution. With the present day vista of the choir in all its glory, it is hard to imagine it obscured behind a high marble screen.

The east wall of the chapel is decorated by four painted lancets divided in the centre by a crossover arch.

The west wall has four tall lancet windows each divided in the centre by a crossover arch. They are filled with temporary glass, as are the two lancet windows in the south wall above the altar.

IN CONCLUSION

The name of the rare genius master mason who designed the plan of St Peter's Beauvais is lost in history, but he inspired the architects of at least two other great cathedrals: Amiens, where the choir was started a quarter of a century after Beauvais, and Cologne only twenty-three years later. Both are clearly built to a plan similar to that of Beauvais. His calculations were correct and his conception admirable.

Viollet-le-Duc wrote that the architect/mason had profound knowledge of the laws of equilibrium, *"Part of this edifice fell less than a century after the construction of the choir; yet it was so planned that it should have remained standing for centuries."* He considered that the stone was the reason for the collapse, for it was the custom to use local stone or stone from a donated quarry, irrespective of the quality. *"If the mason had possessed the quarries of Burgundy, or certain hard strata from the valleys of the Oise or the Aisne, the work would have stood."*

All that apart, I still believe that the nave should have taken precedence over the tower.

DO NOT MISS

1. The mediaeval wall paintings on the east wall of the Chapel of St Cecilia.
2. The reredos in the Chapel of St Leonard.
3. The floor tiles in the Chapel of St Anne.
4. The 14th century Carillon Clock and tower in the north ambulatory.
5. The carved Ecce Homo beneath the clock tower, and the Pietà beside it.
6. The carved panels on the south doors.
7. The genealogical tree in the tympanum of the north doorway.

CHAPTER 11

ALBI

Approaching Albi from the north, along the N88 from Rodez, the mighty Cathedral of St Cecilia can be seen from miles away, appearing at first to be a giant grain silo on the horizon. There is a Mercure hotel near the river bridge, but I usually stay at the Hotel Cantepau because it is quiet with a friendly staff and has a private car park. It is only a five minute stroll from the cathedral.

In mediaeval times the area was the centre of the production of dyer's woad, and is today a major agricultural centre. An open market often swirls about the east end of the cathedral, giving the forbidding exterior of the cathedral a festive, pastoral contrast. On such days you have to make your way past squawking poultry and masses of fresh vegetables to reach the entrance to the former Bishop's Palace at the northeast corner of the cathedral. The Palace now houses the Toulouse-Lautrec Museum, and should not be missed. The collection is particularly poignant because it was presented by the artist's mother. In the square facing the east end of the cathedral and the museum are some lively bistros and restaurants; there are more in the town at Place du Vigan.

THE CATHEDRAL CHURCH OF SAINT CECILIA

Leaving the inexpensive Hotel Cantepau, I cross the high bridge over the River Tarn to admire the old bridge dating from the year 1030 AD skimming the water is a few hundred metres downstream, and the Cathedral standing foursquare above the town, with little 'minarets' sprouting on the roof. From this distance, the tower seems to resemble the great Lantern of Ely Cathedral. In the foreground, with its terraces forming the bank of the river, is the great bulk of the former Episcopal Palace. Having crossed the high bridge, bear right into Rue Emile Grand and walk to the end of it, and then go past the south side of the cathedral to the south west of the building and the foot of the west tower.

A Glimpse Of Glory

ALBI—KEY

1 The West Tower
2 The Gatehouse
3 The South Façade
4 The Nave
5 The Last Judgement
6 Chapel of St Claire
7 Chapel of the 3 Marys
8 Chapel of Holy Innocents
9 Chapel of St Ursula
10 The Pulpit
11 Chapel of St Bartholomew
12 Chapel of All Saints
13 The South Door
14 The Rood Screen
15 The Great Choir
16 The Sanctuary
17 The South Ambulatory
18 Chapel of St Radegonde
19 Chapel of St Michael
20 Chapel of St Anne
21 Chapel of St Stephen
22 Chapel of St Lawrence
23 Chapel of St Magadelene
24 Chapel of St James
25 Chapel of Ss Peter & Paul
26 The Lady Chapel
27 Chapel of the 2 St Johns
28 Chapel of St Michael
29 Chapel of the Holy Cross
30 Chapel of Holy Sepulchre
31 Chapel of St Lazarus
32 The North Ambulatory
33 Chapel of St Christopher
34 Chapel of St George
35 1st Bay of Nave (north)
36 Chapel of St Margaret
37 Chapel of St Amans
38 Chapel of St Cosme
39 Chapel of the Holy Crucifix
40 Western Bay (north)

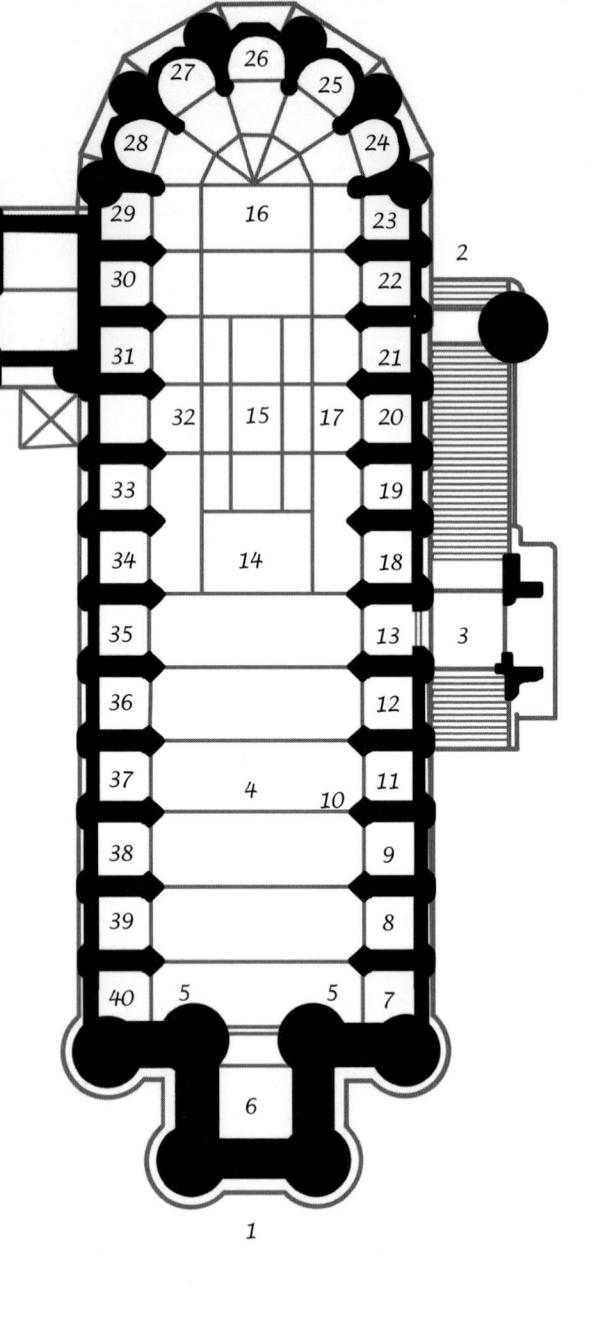

Nothing in writing can prepare you for the shock of seeing the building close up. It looks like the wall of a water-dam rising above you. Built in brick, it is more a feudal fortress than a church. Helen Henderson, in her book, "Cathedrals of France", published by Methuen, 1929, makes a good point when she writes, "*If there is a character in the Golden Legend which stands out above all others as a symbol of gentleness and grace, it is Saint Cecilia, the patron of musicians, who by her tender eloquence 'changed to the gentlest of lambs the spouse whom she had accepted as an untameable lion'. And if, by contrast, one were asked to name, among the cathedrals of France, the one which appears most war-like, least in harmony with the disposition of the saint, who would not immediately think of Albi? Surely the blessed lady, when she paused for a moment in her celestial concert, must have deplored the bellicose aspect of the cathedral dedicated to her.*"

No northern influences have touched this building. Christopher Wilson in his work, "The Gothic Cathedral", published by Thames and Hudson, 1990, believes that this cathedral is a mid-13th century Toulouse Friars' Church writ large: "*The bishop was a Dominican, preoccupied with the suppression of heresy, whose cool relations with the French crown may well have encouraged him to reject the Rayonnant style. Since the endemic anti-clericalism of the southerners deprived great church building of much popular support, the cheapness of Albi proved to be better suited to local needs.*"

It might be Gothic in execution, but it is completely Roman in plan and structure. Its Gothic style is the application of a foreign convention. To understand it's gaunt, austere architecture it is helpful to know something of the terrible history of the Albigeois, of which Albi was the capital. From the twelfth century on its bishops began to encroach upon the authority of the local lords. The predecessor of the present edifice showed conclusively that there was nothing like strong walls for insuring respect for the house of God. Arnaud Catalan, one of the inquisitors of this epoch, had been obliged to take refuge there in 1234 against the fury of the crowd, and was thus able to excommunicate the whole city with some sense of security.

In 1264, the chief temporal power in the city was granted to the bishop. In order to maintain this position, when Bernard de Castanet was enthroned as Bishop in 1277, he began to build this new cathedral to replace that "undermined by the wars and the heretics", and which would afford him perfect safety; for it was not by gentleness that Bernard de Castanet intended to lead his flock. This holy inquisitor hung, immured, and tortured rich citizens whose fortunes he confiscated. The rise of Catharism in the 12th century was suppressed as the Albigensian heresy, in the cruel massacre of its adherents, men, women and children. Only about fifty survived in the whole of Languedoc. Yet, still not a week went by without someone being arrested, tortured and thrown into prison. When he was asked by his executioners

A Glimpse Of Glory

how they could tell the difference between the heretics and the faithful, his reply was '"slay them all; God will know his own." (This quotation has also been attributed to the Abbot of Citeaux at the sack of Beziers.) The present cathedral reflects the bishop's fear of the hatred voiced against him, even by his own Canons.

Bernard de Castanet was far adrift from the teaching of Christ and his apostles. But Castanet's day came to an end, and when Pope Clement was induced to inquire finally into the proceedings at Albi, his prelates liberated many unfortunates whom they found chained in the narrow cells of the Episcopal Prison, without air, without light, having awaited their trials for five years and more. It was a dark and fearsome period in history, from which every Christian soul shrinks in horror. After the Albigensian war the estates of the viscounts passed to Simon de Montfort, and then to the crown of France.

THE EXTERIOR

THE WEST FRONT

From the car park to the southwest the cathedral rears above you. The bases of the great west tower come out like great bastions as if supporting an entire city. There is no great west door, in fact, no entrance at all, but a medieval donjon, reinforced at the corners by circular buttresses built to withstand a siege. It was built between 1282 and 1390 facing the castle of the Montforts, who were outside the jurisdiction of the Bishop and therefore a threat.

Base of the southwest corner

Albi

THE SOUTH PORTAL

As the cathedral is built on the summit, the hill had to be levelled and the slopes embanked. It was therefore impossible to have an entrance at the West End of the nave and so the grand entrance was built on the south side. To reach it a steep ramp was made and this contributes to the Cathedral's originality. At the foot of the ramp there is a gatehouse, protected by battlements, built by Bishop Dominique de Florence (1392–1410). In the tympanum of the arch are sculptures dating from the restoration of 1865–1870. St Cecilia is flanked by Mary Magdalene and Bishop de Florence, who is presented by his Patron Saint. The tower, which was formerly used as a prison, is the only remnant of an earlier gateway. A stone stairway of fifty steps mounts towards the baldachino, a porch carried on columns before the church.

Entrance to the south door

The South Portal

Built of white stone and standing out against the pink brick of the cathedral, it is a most imposing entrance, and Violet le Duc regarded it as one of the most beautiful entrances of its time. The canopy is supported by two robust pillars, which are sumptuously decorated with spiral columns, flamboyant ribs and lace-like pinnacles. It is a riot of late Gothic excellence.

Originally this entrance was a simple brick construction, which was easily walled up and is mirrored by a similar door on the north side, long since filled in. It was enlarged and graced by the present structure between 1519 and 1535. The elaborate carving on this canopy is the only preparation for the magnificence of the interior of the building.

A Glimpse Of Glory

THE WINDOWS

The windows were inserted twenty metres from the bottom and are long narrow slits. The lower windows, which spoil the elegance of the exterior, were cut in the 15th century to admit more light.

THE INTERIOR

THE NAVE

The cathedral resembles a basilica: one big nave without columns, aisles or transepts. It is 98 ft high by 61 ft wide, and is bisected by a splendid Rood Screen. There are chapels either side of the nave, which were inserted between buttresses 5 ft thick and 20 ft deep. The original plan was to have the vaults of the chapels at the same height as the main vault. Many scholars consider that the alteration to this scheme was unfortunate, for each chapel now has another above it in a tribune gallery. This unhappy arrangement deprived the choir of light, a problem which was solved by opening small windows in the brickwork of the apse, thus spoiling the aspect of the east end. Slender shafts rise against the buttresses each side, and from the smallest of capitals the ribs spring across to support the quadripartite vault.

Louis of Amboise became Bishop of Albi in 1473. He was a confidant of King Louis the Xll, a great patron of the arts. However, the private life of the Bishop was so scandalous that he was obliged to resign his see in 1502. He arranged for his nephew, also named Louis, to succeed him. Between them, these two bishops were responsible for the upper stages of the west tower, the porch, the enclosure of the choir, and the mural decoration. But they were also responsible for the decision to divide the chapels with a tribune gallery. The whole of the inner surface of the cathedral is decorated with painting and fresco work. Bishop Louis ll's episcopate (1502–1511) saw the team of Italian artists arrive from Bologna and in six years' they covered the walls and vaults with the best-preserved Renaissance frescoes to have survived in France. Wim Swaan, in his book, "The Gothic Cathedral", published by Elek in 1969, describes them as *"the swansong of Gothic art."*

THE VAULT

The paintings of the high vault were done between 1509 and 1512 and have never been restored. They form a catalogue of biblical figures and events on a blue and gold background.

In the apse at the east end Christ can be seen in Judgment at the end of time, surrounded by his apostles. On the left, the sequence begins with Matthias, followed by Thaddeus, Bartholomew and Thomas, Philip and Andrew, and, in the easternmost segment of the apse, Mary on the left, John on the right, followed by Peter and Paul, James the Great and James the Less, Simon, and finally Matthew. Close to Matthew is Eve, and Adam is on the north side of the vault, next to Matthias. Between them, and close to Christ, are St Jerome and St Augustine to the left and St Gregory and St Ambrose to the right.

The next bay contains symbols of the Virtues together with Old Testament prophets and patriarchs. Then there is the Coronation of the Virgin Mary and the wise and foolish virgins. Much further down the building, above the Rood Screen, can be seen the Annunciation by an Angel to Mary, flanked by St Catherine on the north side and St Mary Magdalene on the south. In the centre of the western part of the nave can be seen the Transfiguration of Christ (Matthew, chapter 17, verses 1–9).

The Vault Looking East

THE LAST JUDGMENT

The west end of the nave commands your attention as soon as you enter the church through the south door. This is the parish end of the church, as at Rodez, and a large nave altar made out of pieces of marble and decorated with Lapis Lazuli has been set up on a platform reached by two steps. From behind the altar the priest faces the Rood Screen, or Jubé, a glorious sight, but the congregation facing west have an even more stunning prospect, for behind the altar is the enormous painting of the Last Judgment.

Its surface area was originally 65ft by 48ft, and consisted of the two inner gigantic towers, which support the great central belfry and the wall between them. Only the two extremities remain today. It is a superb example of French art and pre-dates the Italian frescoes, which surround it, for it is thought by some scholars to date

A Glimpse Of Glory

Last Judgement on West End of Nave

from the episcopate of Louis l of Amboise (1473–1502). Painted with powder, egg yolk, fats and glue, it bears no signature; the Master remains a mystery.

Whereas the Rood Screen deals with creation, the west wall is concerned with man's destiny. Immediately under the organ gallery, which was installed in 1736 for the Great Organ built by Christophe Moucherel, can be seen the angels in the heavens and on the south side (left) are the 12 apostles dressed in white and seated on a red-backed bench. In the crowd gathered before them can be seen a cardinal, a pope and a bishop among the townspeople. Beneath them are the redeemed, each with the book of life, recording their good and bad deeds, hung around the neck. Rising up below them yet more men and women, their hands in an attitude of prayer, come to their glory. On the north side, however, are the damned receiving the accusation of the archangel. The lower level on both sides

The Horrors of Hell (detal)

314

depicts hell. On the left is the punishment of the arrogant, the envious and part of the wrathful. Then come avarice, gluttony and extravagance. The cruelty of the torments and the expressions of the damned are extremely realistic, and make one sit up and take note during the confession in the Mass.

'Sloth' has disappeared, together with the most important section of any depiction of the Last Judgment, which is Christ flanked by Mary and St John and assisted by the Archangel Michael with his scales. These would have occupied the central portion of the west wall, but they were destroyed in the late 17th century when the revered Bishop Le Goux de la Berchère removed the wall between the towers to connect the nave with the Chapel of St Claire under the tower. It was vandalism on a grand scale.

The Chapel of St Claire. This Chapel behind the parish altar, in the base of the tower, contains the Blessed Sacrament. There is a tiny slit window in the west end, and a huge Altar lamp hanging from the quadripartite vault. It was originally the Chapter House for meetings of canons, and was closed until the wall was removed between the towers. The whole chapel is beautifully painted and has a window to the north and south. The theme of the paintings is the Eucharist. On the vault are painted four Doctors of the Church, two from the Greek Church and two from the Latin Church. In Genesis chapter 14, verse 18, Melchizadek offered Abraham bread and wine. This sacrifice of Melchizedek is depicted on the side wall to the left, together with the wedding ceremony at Cana. To the right can be seen the Jewish Passover, the disciples of Jesus on the road to Emmaus, and four local saints. The west wall depicts the creation of the universe by God, while above the eastern arch are the twenty-four elders of the Apocalypse.

There are six bays in the nave from the west wall to the Rood Screen. The westernmost bay has a pierced parapet halfway up on the north side, which pushes the arch higher into the vault, permitting two lancets, with the result that it is slightly higher than in the other five bays, which all have open chapels with a single barrel vault in each. They also have a chapel in the tribune gallery as well as a clerestory. Each bay is quite separate, being set between the walls of the buttresses.

THE SOUTH SIDE OF THE NAVE

The Chapel of the three Marys (The western bay). A doorway in the wall, which rises halfway up the arch, gives access to the Sacristy. There is a stone pierced parapet along the top, as on the north side.

The Chapel of the Holy Innocents. The bay contains a large marble freestanding font and a large painting on the south wall.

A Glimpse Of Glory

Nave Chapels

The Chapel of St Ursula. This Chapel is also known as the Chapel of Penitence. The vaulted ceiling decoration depicts a woman scourging herself, thus personifying the virtues of penitence. On the east wall, to the left, a painting of St Paul, a convert, symbolises the call to repentance for our sins. On the south wall is a tall crucifix and beneath it is a representation of the city of Jerusalem. Surrounded by foliage, the half figures of four prophets announce the pardon which Christ bought for us with his life and by his own sacrifice. The west wall depicts St Ursula and her companions, for the chapel is also the seat of the Fraternity of St Ursula.

The Pulpit. Between this bay and the next there is an enormous pulpit reaching right up to the top of the arcade, with an angel leaning out from the top and a vicious eagle on the front, with cherubs all round. The pulpit itself is a great marble edifice supported by two huge bronze carvings of muscular men with scrolls for the lower half of their torsos. It was built in 1776 in the baroque style by Mazetti and Maderni. The staircase to the pulpit extends along the west wall of the next chapel, terminating just to the west of the altar.

The Chapel of St Bartholomew and Our Lady of Good Counsel. The vault contains a detail of noteworthy interest: in a central medallion the artist wished to give a visual representation of the mystery of the Holy Family. Although clumsily executed, the image is, nonetheless, profoundly Christian. The face of the figure is seen from three sides; the front and both profile angles. With the right hand the figure is bestowing a blessing, in his left he holds a globe surmounted by a cross and his halo appears to be triangular. The heavenly choir surrounds the medallion itself. Opposite stands a reproduction of the miraculous icon worshipped in Genezano in Italy.

The Chapel of All Saints. There is a marble altar and tabernacle with a great altarpiece. Above is a bishop, possibly St Loup, in gold leaf and holding a crozier in his right hand and a book in his left, and with a shell in gold behind his head. Two Corinthian columns on plinths either side of it support a pediment with a cross on top of it. On the pediment is written, "Saint Loup, ora pro nobis" (*St Loup, pray for us*). The statue holding the infant is that of St Anthony of Padua. There are four medallions in the vault of this Chapel.

The South Door occupies the eastern bay of the nave.

THE CHOIR

It is a great joy when entering the church to see that the Rood Screen, or Jubé, is in place. And what a splendid Rood Screen it is, with a fine carved pendant between the double arches over the doorway bearing a statue of St Cecilia holding a martyr's palm branch in her right hand and a portable organ in her left. On her head is a crown of flowers. Look up as you enter the Rood Screen and note the twelve small star-vaults which cover the inside of the Rood Screen in two rows of six. They are supported on the outer sides, but where they meet along the centre line, between the two rows, they hang freely, giving the effect of a fan vault.

In the choir there are return stalls at the west end and all around there are two rows of canons' stalls each with a gable rising to a pinnacle. Dividing the stalls,

The Vault of the Rood Screen

A Glimpse Of Glory

The Choir Facing West

way above head height, are angels with gold wings, each with its own personality, its gesture and musical instrument, in niches with carved canopies, all beautifully painted in polychrome. Cardinal Richelieu, on a visit in 1629 when he was Chief Minister and *de facto* ruler of France, was convinced that the delicate carving of the angels was stucco, until he mounted a ladder and tapped the stone of the canopies.

Lincoln has its 'Angels Choir', so does Albi. Alternating with them and reaching down to the wooden back of each stall, is red and green brocade. In his book "Gothic Architecture", published by Yale in 2000, Paul Frankl describes the Rood Screen and choir as *"one of the late and most magnificent blossoms produced in a spiritual hothouse."* The walls of the choir and the chapels above the tribune arches are decorated with fresco painting.

In the north clerestory of the choir, above the first bay from the west, the central registers of

The Choir, the screen above the canons' stalls

both lancets each have a figure in the glass. The first and third lancets have clear diamond quarry glass. The left-hand lancet is of a saint in a red cloak holding a chalice and with a hand pointing to heaven. The right hand side features St Paul bound to a pillar about to be scourged; an incident from his time in Paphos, Malta. Both have blue backgrounds and a cathedral tower above which is not unlike St Gatien cathedral in Tours. The rest of the clerestory windows, with the exception of the extreme eastern bay north and south, all have clear diamond quarry glass.

Emerging from the Choir after one of many visits over the years, I fell into conversation with one of the cathedral clergy. When he discovered I was also a priest, he tried to refund the entrance fee I had paid to go in. I refused to accept it, so he was equally adamant that he would not accept any payment for the three postcards I held in my hand. After this kind encounter we conversed at length, and the following day I heard him preach a fine sermon during the Mass.

The Sanctuary

To the east of the canons' stalls on the south side, just before the gateway into the south ambulatory, there is a statue of St Jude, and to the east of that gateway a statue of St Philip. There is an equivalent gateway on the north side. These statues of the apostles continue around the apse of the sanctuary. They stand between the wonderful stone mullions and tracery of the blind arcade around the high altar. After St Philip is St Matthew, St James the Great, St James the Less, St Peter, John the Baptist, then the crowned Virgin Mary with the infant Christ in the centre, then St Paul, St Andrew, St John, St Thomas, St Bartholomew, St Simon and then the gateway into the north ambulatory, and finally St Matthias.

St. Matthias

THE AMBULATORIES

The stone screen enclosing the choir is magnificent. It is pierced around the Sanctuary, but solid with blind tracery behind the choir stalls, above which there are six lancets with Rayonnant tracery in each of the bays. Each bay is separated by the decorated column which bears the nearly full-size statue of a prophet under an ornate canopy, with arches above the blind windows going right up to the top of the screen and ending in a finial, all decorated and crocketted. Take time to study Esther, the 4th from the west on the north side, and Judith, the 5th from the west on the south, for they are particularly well executed and enigmatic images. This screen is the most beautiful example of the stonemason's art.

Judith

A Glimpse Of Glory

THE SOUTH AMBULATORY

The door at the west end of the south ambulatory is similarly decorated. On the eastern side of the doorway the tracery contains a statue of the Virgin Mary, and on a pillar to the right an angel looks up at her: it is the scene of the Annunciation. The angel is telling her that she is to bear a son. The western bay is pierced with flamboyant tracery because it overlooks the inside of Rood Screen where there is a small bookstall. Reflecting the doorway into the choir, here too, one can see pendants suspended from the vault of the Rood Screen.

The bay opposite has a wall filling the arch to a height of about 15 ft, above which the rounded arch is decorated with foliage against a blue background. This, in turn, is surmounted by a balustrade, above which are the clerestory lights, which rise to a quadripartite vault. This arrangement is repeated in each bay of the south ambulatory.

The Chapel of St Radegonde. This is the first chapel near the Annunciation door and dates from 1343. St Radegonde was a sixth century Frankish princess who founded the Monastery of the Holy Cross at Poitiers. She is a patron saint of Jesus College, Cambridge. There is a delightful Romanesque church dedicated to her near the east end of Poitiers Cathedral.

The Chapel of St Michael and St Thérèse of Lisieux. In the vault of the chapel, St Michael is depicted as a young warrior. The walls are covered with the signs of the Zodiac and the hand of the four winds, no doubt signifying the universal power of St Michael. The painting on the right represents St Francis of Assisi. The 20th century stained glass in the window depicts St Thérèse, as does the 20th century statue on the altar. The window is signed, Maume-Jean, Paris Mendaye. There is a niche in the south wall.

The Chapel of St Anne. In the centre of the vault is the Paschal Lamb with symbols of the four evangelists in the four corners of the vault. Since 1925 the chapel has been dedicated to the citizens of Albi who gave their life in the Great War. There is a bust of Canon Birot, a former priest of the cathedral who was responsible for making this chapel a War Memorial.

The Chapel of St Stephen and Our Lady of Pity. The centre medallion, or boss, of the vault represents God, his triple halo signifying the Holy Trinity. He is depicted in the act of benediction. St Stephen figures in a painting on the south wall and overhead is depicted the vision of the saint at the moment of his martyrdom. On the right wall is St Mammès and on the left wall is the Virgin Mother. The altar carries an impressive portrayal of Christ being mocked by his accusers. This 15th century 'Ecce Homo' was saved from the Revolution. Five bishops are buried beneath this chapel.

At this point there is a low wrought iron screen across the ambulatory and gates permit access to the axial chapels. The screen links up with the southeast gate to the Great Choir.

The Chapel of St Laurence, St Blaise, and St Foy. In the centre of the vault, the boss bears the arms of Louis II of Amboise. On the south wall, between the two alcoves, stand St Cecilia and St Valerian. On the west wall is St Blaise holding the instrument of his martyrdom (a vicious garden rake), while on the east wall St Laurence is depicted holding a gridiron, which symbolises his martyrdom. The 20th century glass in the window in the south wall depicts a scene from the life of St Benoit and his sister St Scholastica.

Ecce Homo

The Chapel of St Magdalene, St Catharine and St Bartholomew. The fresco on the west wall depicts the three Marys mourning at Christ's tomb. The painting in the centre of the reredos on the east wall depicts the Martyrdom of St Bartholomew. At the west of the south wall stand statues of St Catharine, and to the east St Martial. Overhead, to east and west, are St Mary Magdalene (in the east) and St Salomé (west). The 20th century glass in the window represents St Vincent de Paul.

The Chapel of St James and St Diocletian. This is a pilgrimage chapel for those on the route to Santiago Compostela in Spain. The left wall depicts St James' standing; the other walls depict three other Apostles—St James the Less, St Philip, and St Simon (west). On the left, above the altar, is a painting by Léon Soulié, which is a portrait of St Diogenien, Bishop of Albi. The window is particularly good; the 20th century glass depicts the crucifixion of a muscular Christ together with the repentant Thief and the Samaritaness at the well.

The Chapel of St Peter and St Paul. The scene on the left wall depicts the conversion of Saul on the road to Damascus, related in Acts of the Apostles, chapter 9, verses 1–9. On the same wall to the right, can be seen the struggle of Peter and John with Simon the sorcerer (Acts 8, 18–24). The two paintings on the right wall represent Christ calling St Peter and his reply. The 20th century glass depicts the

A Glimpse Of Glory

shackles of St Peter being loosed by an angel (Acts 12, 7). The vault represents the conflict between church and synagogue. The synagogue is personified by the sacrifices of the old covenant, destined to disappear, while the Eucharistic Sacrifice personifies the Church.

The Axial Chapel of St Maria Maggiore and St Cecilia. The baroque style of the decoration in this Chapel is derived from the restoration of 1778, and is the work of the sculptors Mazetti and Maderni. The statue of the Virgin Mary is particularly graceful. The four paintings by Fauré, dated 1777, sent from Rome by Cardinal de Bernis, represent (from right to left) the Annunciation, St Cecilia and music, of which Cecilia is the patron saint, the assumption of Mary and the death of Cecilia. The glass in the window represents four angels sounding trumpets.

THE NORTH AMBULATORY

The Chapel of the two St Johns. The Gothic lettering suggests a date for the decoration in the second half of the 15th century. The keystone of the 16th century vault depicts the Paschal Lamb. On the left are four scenes from the life of John the Baptist. Overhead one can see the announcement of the birth of John the Baptist, and that saint preaching repentance. Underneath are paintings portraying the baptism of Christ by John, and the beheading of John ordered by King Herod Antipas. On the right are scenes from the life of John the evangelist, including his martyrdom, and his presence at the death of the Blessed Virgin Mary. These scenes are partly obscured by a black marble tablet, with the epitaph of Archbishop Quiqueran de Beaujeu, 1737. The glass in the window depicts St Louis, King of France, as he sets sail from Aigues-Mortes on the 8th Crusade.

The Chapel of St Michael and St Martial. A mass for the dead was once celebrated every day in this chapel. Four angels can be seen sounding the trumpet, when the dead shall be gathered on Judgement Day. The four angels appear a second time in the vault; in one web St Michael can be seen holding the scales of judgment in his left hand and a sword in his right. In another, the Archangel Raphael is seen leading the young Tobias (the book Tobit in the Apocrypha). The

King David (detail)

glass in the window, by Burgstahel, portrays the appearance of the Archangel Michael to Joan of Arc.

The Chapel of the Holy Cross. There is a gold reliquary on the altar of this chapel. Originally the chapel was the shrine for the relic of the True Cross, but this was destroyed in the French Revolution. The reliquary was reported as being in the shape of a Carolingian or a Merovingian cross, made of silver gilt and with stud nails and pendants. On the walls are painted nine scenes based on the discovery of the True Cross. At the top the main character is Constantine the Great. The north wall depicts his victory in battle near Rome in 312 against Maxentius, Roman Emperor in Italy and Africa, which Constantine believed he won because he had mounted the Cross on his standards. The four other walls depict scenes of St Helena, Constantine's mother, and her son, now the senior Roman Emperor, seeking the cross in Palestine. From right to left at the bottom of the north wall Cardinal Jean Jouffroy, with his protector St Jerome and his nephews Helion and John, are seen kneeling with their protectors St Cecilia and St John. The cardinal and his nephews are buried in this chapel. In the west wall recess of the tomb a 16th century statue of St Sebastian has replaced Cardinal Jouffroy.

The Chapel of the Holy Sepulchre. Frescoes on walls depict scenes from the passion and resurrection of Christ. The left upper section shows the betrayal by Judas; in the centre Jesus is carrying his cross while receiving a kick to help him along, and on the right is the Crucifixion. The work by the sculptors has been destroyed, along with a Pietà and a portrayal of the entombment which stood beneath it. There remains a painting of three angels holding chalices to collect the blood which flowed from Christ's wounds. The angels are partly obscured by an aborescent cross installed in 1830. An aborescent cross is one which appears to be made of living wood having shoots of new growth. To the right of the chapel, on the north wall above the dado, is a remarkable Renaissance altarpiece with a copy by Marc Gaida of Hans Holbein's harrowing painting, *"Christ in the Tomb"* (1521). The lower section contains two paintings depicting the resurrection, the one on the north side shows Christ leaving the tomb, and on the west side, his appearance to Mary Magdalene. The vault depicts the Ascension of Christ surrounded by a 'gloriole' of twelve seraphs with ten angels carrying the instruments of his passion. At the springing of the vault arches are six other adoring angels.

The Chapel of St Lazarus and St Martha. There is a gate from the ambulatory into the nave, and in the next bay can be found the pay desk to enter the choir.

The Chapel of St Christopher. Between the altar and the confessional there is an armchair, which I presume is for the priest. There is a single deeply recessed window containing one panel of stained glass.

A Glimpse Of Glory

The North Aisle of the Nave

The Chapel of St George. This chapel has an altarpiece but also a table with three armchairs around it. Again there is a single window depicting St Roch with the dog.

THE NORTH SIDE OF THE NAVE (FROM EAST TO WEST)

The First Bay. Against the north wall a large crucified Christ is flanked by two columns which bear a pediment that rises to the vault. Below the tympanum of the pediment is written, "Pro omnibus mortuus est Christus." (Christ died for all). This bay is much taller than the remainder, and might have once accommodated the north door.

The Chapel of St Margaret. There is here a delicate, serene and lifelike sculpture of St Cecilia lying peacefully on her side on a catafalque. The altar behind the statue has her reliquary where the tabernacle would normally be found. By her side are four sculpted angels bearing electric lights, and on the wall above there is a saint with a halo, holding a flower in the right hand. "Tu eris super domum meam" is inscribed below the tympanum, high up on the wall. It can be translated as, "Thou art (watching) over my house."

The Chapel of St Amans and St Claire. Inscribed on the wall below the tympanum are the words, "Et quid volo" ("And it is what I will"—i.e. 'the Lord agrees with it'). There is a round medallion of Christ painted on the north wall, his right hand raised in benediction and his left indicating his Sacred Heart.

The Chapel of St Cosme and St Damia. There is a statue in gold leaf of Our Lady with the Infant above the altar, and behind it is a cross the inscription, "Regina sacre semper", which might mean, in 'dog Latin' "(She is) For ever the Holy Queen".

The Chapel of the Holy Crucifix. This bay is filled with an organ, the console of which faces the parish altar.

The westernmost bay. The wall reaches halfway up the arch with a pierced parapet running along the top, which is a mirror image of the south wall.

IN CONCLUSION

The soft clay from the alluvium of the Tarn has provided the building material for most of the old city of Albi, and the warm tones which result from firing this clay over a wood fire, the ancient method of making bricks, enables the rather massive elevations of the cathedral to be charmingly grand rather than formidably awesome. In fact, Albi is a charming little city, and one to which I return always with anticipation and pleasure. It has been said that this cathedral influenced Sir Basil Spence when he was designing the new cathedral for Coventry in 1950.

Returning from supper in La Tartine, a restaurant near the cathedral, one evening in late April 2002, I was crossing the high bridge when I noticed three

A Remnant of the 12th Century Romanesque Cloisters Reconstructed to the Southwest of the Cathedral

A Glimpse Of Glory

planets very close together in the night sky: Venus, Mars and Saturn were bright and low in the west. This close grouping was a rare experience. It was certainly a spectacular conclusion to a lovely day.

DO NOT MISS

1. The view from the high bridge over the river.
2. The view from the car-park area to the west.
3. Time to sit in the nave and admire the vault.
4. A close-up study of the Last Judgement.
5. A close-up study of the Rood Screen and the statue of St Cecilia.
6. The angels in the choir.
7. The statue of Judith in the south ambulatory, and Esther in the north.
8. The sculpture of St Cecilia lying on her side in the St Margaret Chapel in the north aisle.
9. The Toulouse-Lautrec Museum in the old Bishop's Palace next door.

A GLOSSARY

OF ARCHITECTURAL AND ECCLESIASTICAL TERMS

A

Abacus	The flat slab on top of a capital.
Abutment	A solid structure which resists the thrust of an arch or vault.
Acanthus	An ornament based on the broad scalloped leaf of the acanthus plant.
Aisle	The lateral division of a church, parallel with the nave.
Altar	The elevated table at which the Holy Eucharist is celebrated. See also: High Altar
Ambulatory	The aisle extended around the east end of the church behind the altar.
Annulet	A small flat band, or ring around a column.
Annunciation	An angel tells Mary that she is to bear Jesus, the son of God.
Antependium	A painted or carved panel on the front of an altar.
Apse	The semicircular end of a church.
Arcade	A series of arches supported on piers or columns.
Arch	A curved structure of wedge-shaped bricks or stones (Vousoirs), held together by mutual pressure and supported only at the sides.
Architrave	The moulded frame surrounding a door or window.
Archivolt	The under curve of an arch, or the moulded band of this curve.
Ashlar	Squared hewn stone laid in regular courses.
Aumbry	A recess in the (usually north) wall of a church, containing a safe for the reservation of the Blessed Sacrament.
Aureole	A pointed oval shape. When framing the image of Christ it is sometimes called a Mandoria.

B

Baldachino	A canopy over an altar or tomb, usually supported on columns.
Baluster	A small pillar or column supporting a rail or coping.
Balustrade	A series of balusters.
Baroque	The style of architecture, painting and sculpture current in Italy in the 17th century.
Basilica	A church with a nave higher than the aisles.
Bas-Relief	Sculpture in low relief used in decoration.
Bay	A division of a building marked not by walls, but by two columns, buttresses, units of vaulting, or other repeated constructional feature.
Blind Arcade	A succession of arches, attached to and used to decorate a wall.
Blind Tracery	An imitation of window tracery on a flat solid surface.
Bracket	A projection designed as a support for a statue or other object.

A Glimpse Of Glory

Buttress	A mass of masonry or brickwork built against a wall to give it stability or to counteract the outward thrust of an arch or vault.

C

Came	H-shaped lead rod used to assemble the pieces of glass in a panel.
Canopy	A suspended or projecting cover to protect an altar, statue, throne or other object.
Capital	The uppermost part of a column or pilaster.
Chancel	The eastern section of a church where the high altar is placed.
Chapter	The term for a group of senior clergy who administer the cathedral.
Choir	The area where the choir sings the liturgy, and where the chapter has its stalls.
Choir Screen	A stone, wrought-iron or wooden screen which separates the choir from the nave.
Clerestory	The upper storey of the nave, above the aisle roofs, pierced with windows to light the church. Also called Clearstorey.
Cloister	A covered and often vaulted walk around an open space.
Clustered column	A group of several slender shafts joined to form a single column or support.
Colonnette	A diminutive column.
Column	A vertical supporting member consisting of base, shaft and capital.
Corbel	A supporting projection on the face of a wall, often carved or moulded.
Crocket	Curved projection usually of stylised leaf form, decorating the edges of pinnacles, gables, etc.
Crossing	The space formed by the intersection of nave, chancel and transepts in a cruciform church.
Crypt	A subterranean chamber, usually beneath the east end of churches.
Curvilinear	A 14th century form of tracery consisting of sinuous lines.
Cusp	A point formed by the intersection of two arcs in a Gothic arch or tracery.

D

Dado	The lower part of a wall which is clearly delineated.
Diaper	All over pattern of carved or painted motifs usually of small square shapes.

E

Easter Sepulchre	A recess bearing a representation of the burial of Christ, usually placed on the north wall of the chancel.
Elevation	The external front of any building.
Extrados	The outer curve of an arch.

Glossary

F

Façade	The face or front of a building, especially the principal front.
Fillet	A narrow flat band used to separate two mouldings.
Fillet	It can also mean a narrow band of glass placed between two lead cames to ensure that two elements of a window lead smoothly into one another.
Finial	An ornament crowning a pinnacle, spire, gable or roof.
Flèche	A slender spire rising from a roof, sometimes covered with lead.
Flying Buttress	An arch used to carry the thrust of a vault or roof from the walls of a building to an outer pier or buttress.
Fresco	Painting done on fresh plaster while it is still wet.
Frieze	A decorative band or feature.

G

Gable	The triangular portion of a wall at the end of a ridge roof.
Gargoyle	A spout in the form of a carved grotesque head, projecting from the top of a wall to throw out rain water.

H

Hall Church	A church with nave and aisles of the same height.
High Altar	The principal altar in a church, usually in the eastern end of the apse or sanctuary.
Hood Mould	A projecting moulding over an opening to throw off rainwater; also known as a drip stone.

I

Impost	A flat, projecting stone on which the ends of an arch rest.

J

Jamb	The vertical side of a doorway, window or arch.

L

Label Stop	An ornamental boss terminating a hood mould.
Lady Chapel	A chapel dedicated to the Blessed Virgin, usually placed at the east end of a church.
Lancet	A tall, narrow pointed window.
Lantern	A central tower raised over the crossing containing windows to admit light.
Light	The glazed part of a window divided by mullions; usually forming a lancet shape' in Gothic windows. A window divided by two mullions would be a 'three-light window'.

A Glimpse Of Glory

Lierne Ribs	Secondary vault ribs which are employed as decorative links between the main ribs.
Lorraine, Cross	The vertical arm of the cross has two horizontal bars, the upper being shorter.
Lucarne	A small window, usually projecting from a roof or spire.

M

Mandoria	see Aureole.
Medallion	A round or oval section of a stained glass window, depicting a figure or event.
Misericord	A bracket on the underside of a hinged choir stall seat, which when the seat is turned up gives support during long periods of standing; often carved with animal and allegorical figures.
Monstrance	A vessel used for the public display of relics or, today, the Eucharistic Host.
Mouchette	A curved dagger motif found in curvilinear tracery.
Moulding	A projecting or recessed band used to ornament an arch, wall or surface.
Mullion	A vertical member dividing a window into lights.
Multifoil	A panel of a window formed into five or more leaves by cusping.

N

Narthex	A vestibule stretching across the west end of the nave, or main entrance of a church.
Nave	The main body or central aisle of a church extending from the entrance to the choir or chancel; sometimes called the vessel.
Niche	A recess in a wall, pier, etc., usually semi-circular and arched, to receive a statue or other object.

O

Oculus	Any small round or oval window.
Ogee Arch	A pointed arch formed of two convex arcs above and two concave arcs below.
Oriel Window	A bay window projecting from an upper storey.

P

Parvis	An open area before the main entrance of a cathedral, which may once have been enclosed.
Pediment	A low-pitched rectangular gable.
Pendant	An elongated boss projecting downwards from a vault.
Pier	A large column to sustain the thrust of an arch.

Glossary

Pilaster	A rectangular column projecting slightly from a wall.
Pillar	A detached upright support.
Pinnacle	A pyramid or conical ornament used to terminate a gable or buttress.
Piscina	A shallow basin with a drain in which Mass vessels are washed, usually placed in a niche south of the altar.
Portal	Any imposing entrance.

Q

Quarry	A square or diamond shaped piece of glass.
Quadripartite	A ribbed vault in which each bay is divided into four compartments by two diagonal ribs.
Quatrefoil	A panel of a window formed into four leaves by cusping.

R

Radiating chapels	The chapels radiating from the apse or ambulatory of a church.
Register	A horizontal section of a tympanum or window.
Relieving arch	A plain arch built into a wall above a true arch or lintel to relieve it of some of the load and thrust.
Reredos	The ornamental structure or screen covering the wall behind and above the altar.
Respond	A half pillar or similar shaft engaged in a wall to support an arch, usually at the end of an arcade.
Retable	An altar-piece or picture behind, but attached to an altar.
Romanesque	An 11th and 12th century style of architecture, preceding the Gothic.
Rood Screen	a screen at the west end of the chancel separating nave and choir and built below the loft (rood-loft) upon which the Rood, or Crucifix, was placed. With the disappearance of the rood and loft it has become synonymous with choir or chancel screen.
Rose Window	A circular window with concentric or radiating tracery patterns.

S

Sacristy	A room where the sacred vessels are kept.
Sanctuary	The holiest part of the church around the high altar.
Sedilia	A series of three seats on the south side of the sanctuary or chancel for use by the clergy, often recessed into the wall and crowned with canopies.
Sexpartite	A ribbed vault in which each bay is divided into six compartments by two diagonal ribs and one transverse rib.
Shaft	The body of a column between the base and the capital.
Spandrel	The triangular areas either side of the apex of an arch, or the surface between two adjacent arches and the horizontal moulding above them.

A Glimpse Of Glory

Splay	The diagonal surface formed by the cutting away of a wall, especially the jamb of a portal.
Stiff-leaf	A lobe-shaped sculptured foliage found on capitals.
Stilted arch	An arch sprung from a point above the impost; vertical masonry between the impost and the springing line resembling stilts.
Stringcourse	A moulding or projecting band, running horizontally across a façade.

T

Tabernacle	An ornamental niche or receptacle in the retable of an altar, which contains the Blessed Sacrament.
Tas de charge	The masonry which contains the downward thrust of ribs in the spandrel of two arches.
Tierceron rib	An intermediate rib inserted between the transverse and diagonal ribs to give additional support.
Tracery	The ornamental work formed by the branching of mullions in the upper part of a Gothic window.
Transom	The horizontal member dividing a window.
Transept	The transverse arm of a cruciform church.
Trefoil	A three-lobed panel of a window.
Tribune	An upper storey above the aisle of a Romanesque or early Gothic church.
Triforium	A wall passage with arches or blank arcading open to the nave below the clerestory.
Trumeau	A vertical column dividing the principal doorway of a portal and usually bearing a statue on a bracket.
Tympanum	The space between the lintel of a doorway and the arch above it.

V

Vault	An arched roof or ceiling; an underground chamber for burial.
Vesica Piscis	A pointed oval shape; when framing the figure of Christ it is called an aureole.
Vestry	A room where vestments are kept and the clergy robe.
Voussoir	One of a series of wedge-shaped stones or bricks used to form an arch.

For many of the definitions above I am indebted to Bernard Kaukas, Architect, and to his gifts of T.D. Atkinson's "A Glossary of English Architecture" published by Methuen in 1928, and Harris and Lever's "Illustrated Glossary of Architecture 850–1830", published by Faber in 1966.

A BIBLIOGRAPHY

Blum, Pamela Z: Early Gothic Saint-Denis, Restorations and Survivals.
    Pub. University of California Press, 1992.
Brisac, Catherine: A Thousand Years of Stained Glass.
    Pub. Chartwell Books,2001.
Bumpus, T. Francis: The Glories of Northern France.
    Pub. Dennis and Sons Ltd. London, 1905.
Bumpus, T. Francis: The Cathedrals of Southern France.
    Pub. T Werner Laurie Ltd, London.
Cottle, Basil: All the Cathedrals of France.
    Pub. Unicorn Press, London, 1992.
Cowen, Painton: The Rose Window.
    Pub. Thames and Hudson Ltd, London, 2005.
Cowen, Painton: English Stained Glass.
    Pub. Thames and Hudson, London, 2008
Frankl, Paul: Gothic Architecture. Revised edition, Paul Crossley.
    Pub. Revised edition, Yale University Press, 2000.
Gaborit, Jean René: Great Gothic Sculpture.
    Pub. Reynal and Company, Inc, 1978.
Grenacre, Roger: The Catholic Church in France, an Introduction.
    Pub. Church of England Council for Christian Unity, reprinted 1998.
Grodecki, Louis and Brisac, Catherine: Gothic Stained Glass,1200–1300.
    Pub.Thames and Hudson, 1985.
Harvey, John: English Mediaeval Architects, a biographical dictionary down to 1550.
    Pub. B T Batsford Ltd.,London, 1954.
Henderson, Helen: The Cathedrals of France.
    Pub. Methuen, 1929.
Hurlimann & Bony: French Cathedrals
    Pub. Thames & Hudson, 1961.
Lillich, Meredith P.: The Armor of Light, Stained Glass in W. France, 1250–1325.
    Pub. University of California Press, 1994.
Martindale, Andrew: Gothic Art.
    Pub. Thames and Hudson Ltd, London, 1967. Reprinted 1996.

A Glimpse Of Glory

Perkins, Jocelyn: The Cathedrals of Normandy.
    Pub. Methuen, 1935.

Radding, Charles M. & Clark, William W: Medieval Architecture, Medieval Learning.
    Pub. Yale University Press, 1992.

Raguin, Virginia C.: The History of Stained Glass.
    Pub. Thames and Hudson, 2003.

Rodin, Auguste: Cathedrals of France.
    Pub. Hamlyn, 1965.

Rose, Elise Whtlock: Cathedrals and Cloisters of the Isle de France (Volume 2)
    Pub. G P Putnam's Sons, 1910

Toman, Rolf (Ed): Romanesque, Architecture, Sculpture, Painting.
    Pub. Könemann. Koln, 1997.

Voragine, Jacobus de: The Golden Legend. Trans. W G Ryan. Volumes 1 and 2.
    Pub. Princeton University press, 1993.

Wilson , Christopher: The Gothic Cathedral, The Architecture of the Great Church 1130 –1530.
    Pub. Thames & Hudson Ltd, London. 1990. Reprinted, with revisions, 2000.

ABOUT THE AUTHOR

Brian Lucas was born and brought up in the steel town of Port Talbot, South Wales. Educated at St David's College, Lampeter, and St Stephen's House, Oxford, he was ordained at Llandaff in 1964 and was appointed to the cathedral staff.

Three years later he moved to build a new church in the parish of Neath. Following the consecration of that church he was commissioned as a chaplain in the RAF. He served on bases both at home and overseas, including a staff appointment in the Ministry of Defence. In 1989 he was appointed an Honorary Chaplain to Her Majesty The Queen. In 1991 he became the Chaplain-in-Chief and Archdeacon of the Royal Air Force. In November that year he was also installed as a Prebendal Canon of Lincoln Cathedral. In 1993 he was appointed as a Companion of the Most Honourable order of the Bath.

Archdeacon Lucas retired from the RAF in 1995, and in 1996 he became Rector of the Benefice of Caythorpe in rural Lincolnshire. He retired from full-time ministry in 2003 and has since travelled extensively in France researching and photographing the many great cathedrals as well as tasting some fine wine.

For ten years he was also the Honorary Secretary of the Savage Club in Westminster, London, and continues to enjoy his membership of that august gentleman's club.

In 2011 Adastral Books published Archdeacon Lucas' memoirs under the title, "Reflections in a Chalice".

INDEX

Abraham 7, 17, 29, 40, 111, 132, 144, 163-164, 166, 191, 216, 228, 232, 234, 245, 315
Acts of the Apostles .. 99, 129, 144, 154-155, 162, 190, 201, 288, 321
Albigensian Crusade 309-310
Ambrose, St 128, 169, 185, 313
Anselm 35
Ark of the Covenant 217, 277-278
Astronomical Clock 284, 302
Bathsheba 113, 200
Bec Abbey 93-94, 132
Becket, St Thomas .... vi, 10, 25, 27-29
Bede, The Venerable 165
Belshazzar's Feast 184, 336
Blum, Pamela 4, 333
Brisac, Catherine 124, 157, 160-161, 173, 238, 242, 333, 336
Bumpus, Francis 20, 22, 25-26, 107-108, 119, 145, 208, 333, 336
Bury St Edmunds 37
Canterbury Cathedral 11
Catherine Brisac 124
Chagall, Marc 224, 239, 245
Chambiges, Martin 15, 17, 177-178, 285-286, 293
Charlemagne 35, 132, 203, 205, 238, 336
Chartres Cathedral 3-4, 11, 27, 80, 94, 108, 124, 137, 139, 146, 197, 210, 225, 253, 261, 299
Clairvaux Abbey 183, 187
Clovis 2, 107, 134, 137, 223, 226, 228, 231-232, 245, 251
Cluny Abbey 2, 109, 111-112, 116, 127, 136, 139
Concordat of 1801 81
Conques 2
Constantine the Great 110, 323
Constantinople 165, 188, 214, 275
Cottle, Basil 59, 180, 333
Coutances 18, 65
Cowen, Painton 43-44, 192, 293, 333

Czestochowa, Black Madonna 31
David, King 113, 200, 217, 322
Dubost, Bishop Michel iv
Duruflé, Maurice 77
Ecce Homo . 30, 89, 191, 263, 275, 284, 302, 306, 320-321
Emmaus .... vi, 56, 127, 228, 300, 315
Flaubert, Gustave 95, 336
Frankl, Paul 9, 150, 160, 173, 318, 333
Gaborit, Jean René 178, 333
Gobelin 155
Golden Legend, The ... 8, 145, 165-166, 208, 214, 334
Greenacre, Canon Roger 2
Grodecki and Brisac 157, 160-161, 173, 238, 242
Hanford, Richard iv
Henderson, Helen 1, 35, 139, 233, 235, 253, 257, 267, 283, 285, 309, 333
Henry II, King of England 29, 94, 96
Henry V, King of England 94, 103, 175
Henry VI, King of England 105
Herod, King 13, 56, 68, 87, 133, 200, 256, 276, 322
Holbein, Hans 323
Hugo, Victor 108
Huguenots 98, 141-142, 200, 210, 213
Ingrand, Max 82, 89, 96, 303
Inviolata 83-84, 104
Isaac 29, 40, 164, 191, 228, 245, 257
John Paul II, Pope 246, 274
Jordan, River 200, 249
Kaukas, Bernard .... iv, 332
Labyrinth 224, 252
Lécuyer, Jean 158
Le Mans Cathedral 96, 141, 147
Liesse, Our Lady of 34, 54
Lillich, Meredith 333
Lincoln Cathedral .. 2, i, 46-47, 65, 248, 318, 335
Louis, St 11, 100, 103, 106, 116, 130-131, 205, 207, 234, 245, 252, 279, 305, 322

Mackervoy, Robin iv
Martindale, Andrew 47, 174, 333
Matilda, Empress 94
McAvoy, Brian iv
Meridian Gnomon, The 138, 151
Monreale Cathedral 67
Moses .. 16, 27, 130, 157, 191, 209-210, 216, 227, 269
Narbonne Cathedral 3, 337
Nebuchadnezzar 38
Nevers Cathedral ....iv, 5, 11
Noah 142, 144-145, 198-199, 216, 235, 257, 293
Noyon Cathedral 242
Oriflamme, The 245
Paphos 319
Perigeux Cathedral 1
Perkins, Canon Jocelyn 1, 69, 83
Pietà ... 97, 126, 135, 250, 284, 302, 305-306, 323
Poitiers Cathedral 1-2, 46, 55, 108, 167, 320
Radding and Clark 149
Richard Lionheart 64
Richelieu, Cardinal 318
Rodez Cathedral 1-2, 307, 313
Rodin, Auguste 270, 276, 334
Rose, Elise Whitlock 103
Rouillard, Huguette v
Ruskin, John 254

Salome 68-69, 104, 200, 205, 276, 337
Santiago Compostela 321
Sées Cathedral 2, 87
Senlis 3, 177, 242, 293, 298
Sheba, Queen of 113, 226
Soissons Cathedral 35, 53, 197, 228, 235, 242
Solomon, King 113
Southwell Cathedral 3
Strasbourg Cathedral 126-127, 225, 302
Suger, Abbot 4, 9, 36, 120
Swann, Wim 35
Synagogue 108
Theophilus 115, 214
Tobit 322
Toulouse-Lautrec 307, 326
Tours Cathedral ... 2, 83, 134, 141, 177, 192, 197, 319
Tree of Jesse ... 22, 67-68, 184, 191, 214, 219, 271, 299
V & A Museum 155
Viollet le Duc . 115, 120, 124, 126, 132, 178, 253, 271
Virtues 226, 325
William the Conqueror 65
Wilson, Christopher 139, 149, 175, 256, 309
Zarnecki, George 46
Zechariah 38, 294

A Glimpse of Glory

in the Gothic Cathedrals of France

by Brian Lucas

Foreword by Bishop Michel Dubost, Bishop of Évry, Paris.

To be published by Adastral Books in January 2014

A Guide Book to French Cathedrals

During the last fourteen years Archdeacon Brian Lucas has travelled through much of France tracing the development of the Gothic style of architecture, and recording in word and photograph the local interpretation of that idiom. This book is written as a series of monographs, each examining one cathedral. It is an attempt to explain to visitors in a cathedral what they are looking at, and, at the end of each chapter it highlights things you must not miss if you are on a brief visit. In many cases some hotel accommodation is suggested.

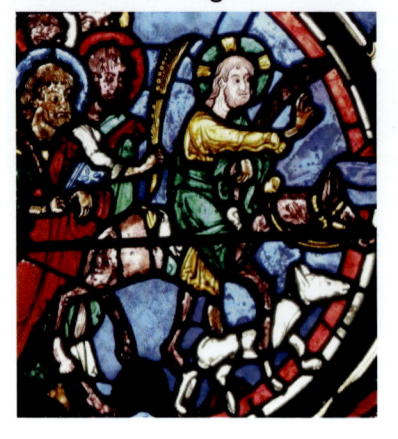

Christ enters Jerusalem on a donkey
Bourges Cathedral

The book is illustrated with 170 black and white photographs, and 32 pages of colour plates, covering the following cathedrals:

Sens, Laon, Rouen, Paris, Bourges, Troyes, Auxerre, Reims, Amiens, Beauvais and Albi.

ISBN 978-0-9567588-1-1

**This first edition is limited to 250 copies, and will be available for £19.95 (plus £2.50 p&p).
To secure a copy write now to:**

Brian H. Lucas CB
**Adastral Books, 6 Arnhem Drive, Caythorpe, Lincolnshire.
NG32 3DQ.**

or email: **brian.lucas@savageclub.com**

Cheques should be made payable to: B H Lucas.